THE FIRST SALUTE

THE FIRST SALUTE

THE FIRST SALUTE

Barbara W. Tuchman

Thorndike Press • Thorndike, Maine

Library of Congress Cataloging in Publication Data:

Tuchman, Barbara Wertheim.
  The first salute / Barbara W. Tuchman.
  p.   cm.
   Bibliography: p. 605
   ISBN 0-89621-904-6 (alk. paper : lg. print)
   ISBN 0-89621-944-5 (pbk. alk. paper : lg. print)
   1. United States--History--Revolution, 1775-1783--Naval
operations. 2. United States--History--Revolution, 1775-
1783--Campaigns. 3. Large type books. I. Title.
[E271.T83   1989]   89-31632
973.3'--dc20   CIP

Large Print edition available in North America by
arrangement with Alfred A. Knopf, Inc.

Large Print edition available in the British Commonwealth
by arrangement with Michael Joseph, Ltd.

**Cover illustration by Richard Hess.
Cover design adapted from the original
by Gun Larson.**

To my grandchildren,
Jennifer, Nell, Oliver and Jordan,
lights of the new generation.

Contents

Material has been deleted from this edition.
Please refer to the following page numbers
in the Alfred A. Knopf, Inc. edition for:

THE FIRST SALUTE

Illustrations

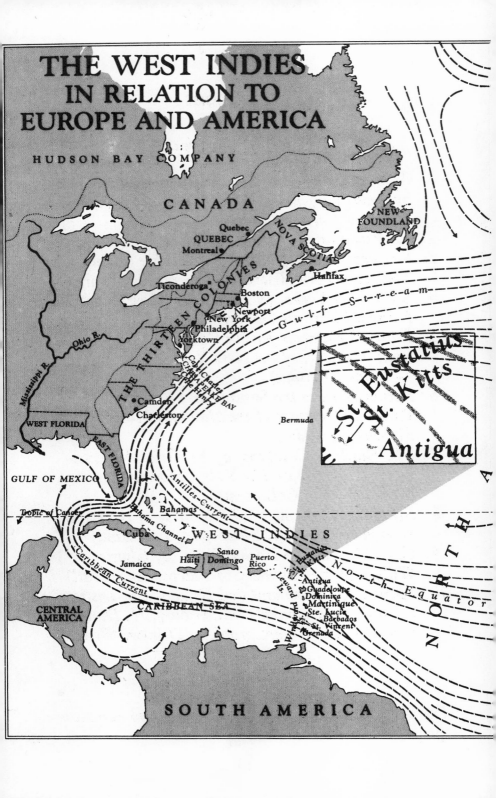

THE WEST INDIES
IN RELATION TO
EUROPE AND AMERICA

HUDSON BAY COMPANY

CANADA

NEW FOUNDLAND

Quebec
QUEBEC
Montreal
Halifax

NOVA SCOTIA

Ticonderoga
Boston
Newport
New York
Philadelphia
Yorktown

THE THIRTEEN COLONIES

Ohio R.
Mississippi R.

Camden
Charleston

WEST FLORIDA
EAST FLORIDA

GULF OF MEXICO

St. Eustatius
St. Kitts
Antigua

Bermuda

Gulf Stream

Antilles Current

Tropic of Cancer
Bahama Channel
Bahamas

Cuba

WEST INDIES

Haiti
Santo Domingo
Puerto Rico

Jamaica

Caribbean Current

CARIBBEAN SEA

CENTRAL AMERICA

St. Eustatius
St. Kitts
Antigua
Guadeloupe
Dominica
Martinique
Ste. Lucia
Barbados
St. Vincent
Grenada

Leeward Is.
Windward

North Equator

NORTH

SOUTH AMERICA

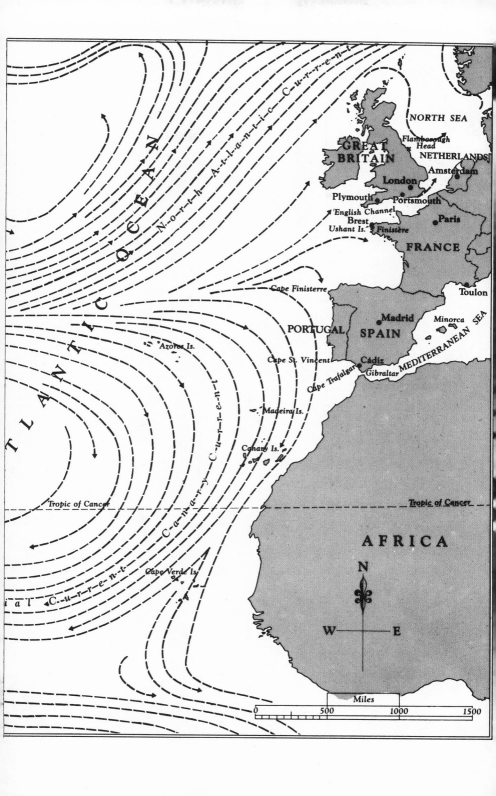

ATLANTIC OCEAN

North Atlantic Current

NORTH SEA

GREAT BRITAIN

Flamborough Head

NETHERLANDS

London

Amsterdam

Plymouth

Portsmouth

English Channel

Brest

Paris

Ushant Is.

Finistère

FRANCE

Cape Finisterre

Toulon

PORTUGAL

SPAIN

Madrid

Minorca

MEDITERRANEAN SEA

Azores Is.

Cape St. Vincent

Cádiz

Cape Trafalgar

Gibraltar

Canary Current

Madeira Is.

Canary Is.

Tropic of Cancer

Tropic of Cancer

AFRICA

Cape Verde Is.

Equatorial Current

N

W   E

Miles

0   500   1000   1500

Acknowledgments

I would like to acknowledge with thanks those persons and institutions who helped me to locate sources in an unfamiliar field and otherwise assisted in the production of this book.

First, to my husband, Lester Tuchman, whose dependable presence and aid in support of failing eyesight is the rock on which this house is built.

H. E. Richard H. Fein, Ambassador of the Netherlands to the United States, who gave the initial impetus by an invitation to address the Commemoration in 1985 of the fortieth anniversary of the liberation of the Netherlands.

Dr. Fred de Bruin of the Ministry for Foreign Affairs of the Netherlands.

Special thanks to my daughter Alma Tuchman for persistence in untangling confusions, detecting errors and setting things straight, and additional thanks to my granddaughter Jennifer Eisenberg for help in the preparation of the reference notes.

A. B. C. Whipple of Greenwich, Connecticut, author of *Fighting Sail,* for clarification in the language and understanding of naval matters.

Dawnita Bryson, my secretary and typist, for devoted work through a difficult maze.

Han Jordaan of The Hague for records of Johannes de Graaff in the Archive of the West India Company.

G. W. Van der Meiden, Keeper of the First Section, Netherlands Rijks Archive.

Colonel Trevor Dupuy for guidance in the military history of the American Revolution.

Professor Simon Schama of Harvard University on questions of Dutch history.

Professor Freeman Dyson of the Institute for Advanced Study, Princeton, New Jersey, for supplying the quotation from Hakluyt on naval education (page 232).

Galen Wilson, Manuscript Curator of the William L. Clements Library, University of Michigan, for records of Sir Henry Clinton.

Dr. Marie Devine, Joan Sussler, Catherine Justin and Anna Malicka, librarians of the Lewis Walpole Library, Yale University, whose acquaintance with and instant recall of the contents of their collection is stunning.

Mark Piel, Director of the New York Society Library, and his staff for their kind assistance in many ways.

Rodney Phillips, Elizabeth Diefendorf and

Joyce Djurdjevich of the New York Public Library for bibliographical help and guidance in the reference division. Bridie Race, secretary to the corporation, who pulls all wires with charm and efficiency.

Todd Ellison of Greenbelt, Maryland, for finding the Van Bibber correspondence in the Maryland Archives, and for his careful analysis of Clark's *Naval Documents*.

Dorothy Hughes, London, for research assistance at the Public Record Office.

Joan Kerr, Richard Snow and Arthur Nielsen of *American Heritage* for picture research.

Geraldine Ostrove and Charles Sens, Music Division of Library of Congress, for material on "The World Turned Upside Down."

The staff of the Historical Museum of St. Eustatius.

The staff of the Greenwich Library, in Connecticut, for answering many queries with unfailing courtesy and for efficient service in interlibrary loans.

The Historical Society of Pennsylvania for records of the flag of the Continental Congress made by Margaret Manny.

New London, Connecticut, Historical Society and The National Maritime Museum, London, for naval records.

The MacDowell Colony, which has understood and arranged the perfect conditions for a place for uninterrupted and consecutive work away from the distractions of home.

The Dana Palmer House, at Harvard University, for a working residence next door to a great library.

Mary Maguire and Nancy Clements of Alfred A. Knopf and Barbara DeWolfe for indispensable aid in the publishing process.

18

Notice

A number of difficulties and discrepancies exist in the narrative: the first is the peculiar peregrination of Windward and Leeward islands in the Caribbean whose location and designation find no agreement among various atlases and current sources on the West Indies. The cartographic division of the National Geographic Society explains one reason for the confusion, namely that there is a "slight overlap" of the islands at the midpoint of the West Indian chain. According to the National Geographic, Dominica and the chain extending north of Martinique belong to the Leeward group and those south of Dominica down to and including Barbados and Tobago belong to the Windward group. I leave this problem to the controversy that will inevitably ensue, knowing that the definitive is elusive.

A second problem is the continual elasticity in the given number of ships in a squadron or fleet. As explained in the footnote on page 471, the count suffers from uncertain visibility at sea and depends upon whether frigates and merchant ships are counted along with ships of the line and whether a certain number may have left the squadron or been added to it after the count was made.

Money, that is, the value of a foreign currency in the late 18th century, or its equivalent to a better-known currency or to our own in contemporary terms, is of course a perennial problem in all historical studies. I can do no better than quote what I wrote in the foreword to *A Distant Mirror,* a book on the 14th century, that because value and equivalency keep changing and are impossible to make definite at any one time, I advise the reader not to worry about the problem but simply to think of any given amount as so many pieces of money.

Finally, the problem of non-agreement among authorities: e.g., on the identity of the Dutch Admiral who, in a famous incident of the Anglo-Dutch wars of the 17th century, sailed up the Thames with a broom tied to his mast. The English historian Wingfield-Stratford says it was Tromp, while Professor Simon Schama, historian of the Netherlands, says the admiral was de Ruyter.

Or, the case of King George II as godfather to Admiral Rodney, so stated by Rodney's biographer, David Hannay, while a second biographer, David Spinney, says that claim "is a myth."

Or, the utter confusion surrounding the battle or battles of Finisterre in 1747. The naval historian Charles Lee Lewis deals bluntly with one aspect of the problem by saying other accounts "are all incorrect." (That's the spirit!) The confusion among historians arose in this case because there were several battles of Finisterre closely following each other, and there are two Finisterres, one in France and one, the true land's end of Europe, in Spain.

ONE

"Here the Sovereignty of the United States of America Was First Acknowledged"

White puffs of gun smoke over a turquoise sea followed by the boom of cannon rose from an unassuming fort on the diminutive Dutch island of St. Eustatius in the West Indies on November 16, 1776. The guns of Fort Orange on St. Eustatius were returning the ritual salute on entering a foreign port of an American vessel, the *Andrew Doria*, as she came up the roadstead, flying at her mast the red-and-white-striped flag of the Continental Congress. In its responding salute the small voice of St. Eustatius was the first officially to greet the largest event of the century — the entry into the society of nations of a new Atlantic state destined to change the direction of history.

The effect of the American Revolution on the nature of government in the society of Europe was felt and recognized from the moment it became a fact. After the American rebellion began, "an extraordinary alteration took place in the minds of a great part of the people of Holland," homeland of St. Eustatius, recalled Sir James Harris, Earl of Malmesbury, who was British Ambassador at The Hague in the years immediately following the triumph of the American Revolution. "Doubts arose," he wrote in his memoirs, "about the authority of the Stadtholder" (Sovereign of the Netherlands and Prince of Orange) . . . "indeed all authority came under attack when the English colonists in America succeeded in their rebellion." What the Ambassador was witnessing — in idea, if not yet in fact — was the transfer of power from its arbitrary exercise by nobles and monarchs to power stationed in a constitution and in representation of the people. The period of the transfer, coinciding with his own career, from 1767 to 1797, was, he believed, "the most eventful epoch of European history." The salute to the *Andrew Doria*, ordered on his own initiative by the Governor of St. Eustatius, Johannes de Graaff, was the first recognition following the rebel colonies' Declaration of Independence, of the American flag and American nationhood by an official of a foreign state. Dutch priority was not the most important aspect of the event, but as other claimants have disputed the case, let it be said that the guns of Fort Orange were confirmed as first by the President of the United States, in a plaque presented to St. Eustatius in 1939 over the engraved signature of the incumbent Franklin D. Roosevelt. The plaque reads, "In Commemoration of the salute of the flag of the United States fired in this fort November 16, 1776, by order of Johannes de Graaff, Governor of St. Eustatius, in reply to a national gun salute fired by the U.S. Brig-of-War *Andrew Doria*.... Here the sovereignty of the United States of America was first formally acknowledged to a national vessel by a foreign official." Thereby de Graaff found a place, though it may be the least known of any, in the permanent annals of the United States.

The *Andrew Doria,* vehicle and protagonist of this drama, was not just any ship but already the possessor of a historic distinction. She was one of the first four ships, all converted merchantmen, to be commissioned into the Continental Navy created by act of the Continental Congress on October 13, 1775, and she was shortly to take part in its first active combat. She was a brigantine, a small two-masted vessel, refitted for belligerent action in the newly created American

Navy. She had sailed from the New Jersey coast town of Gloucester near Philadelphia on October 23, under orders of the Continental Congress to proceed to St. Eustatius to take on military supplies and deliver a copy of the Declaration of Independence to Governor de Graaff. With only her limited sail area to catch the westerlies, her crossing in a little over three weeks to arrive by November 16 was a notable feat. Sailing times from North America to Europe and back varied widely depending on the type of ship, with the heavier warships taking longer than frigates and merchantmen, and depending on the wind, which might sometimes shift erratically from the prevailing westerlies blowing eastward to the reverse. At the time of the Revolution, the eastward passage to Europe, called "downhill," ordinarily took about three weeks to a month as opposed to the westward "uphill" voyage to America against the wind and the Gulf Stream, which took about three months.

Eustatius' salute was of no great importance except for what it led to. By intentionally encouraging, in defiance of his own government, the Dutch trade in military armament to the Colonies, the Governor assured the continuance of shipments from St. Eustatius, a critical factor in saving the American Revolution at its frail beginnings from starvation of firepower. In the first year, wrote George Washington, in the whole of the American camp there were not "more than nine cartridges to a man." In October, six months after the Colonies had put their rebellion to the test of arms, Washington confessed to his brother, "We are obliged to submit to an almost daily cannonade without returning a shot from our scarcity of powder which we are necessitated to keep for closer work than cannon distance whenever the redcoat gentry pleases to step out of their Intrenchments." In the tight fight for Bunker Hill in June, 1775, when American powder was nearly exhausted, the soldiers had to combat the British with the butt ends of their muskets. Long kept dependent on the mother country for military supplies because of a persistent suspicion in Britain of a rebellious American potential, the Colonies had developed no native production of weapons or gunpowder and lacked the raw material in saltpeter and the skills and facilities for its manufacture. Ammunition from Europe shipped via the West Indies was the only source of supply. As neutrals, the Dutch, for whom commerce was the blood in their veins and seafaring as ocean navigators their primary practice, became the essential providers, and St. Eustatius, the hinge of the clandestine traffic to the

Colonies, became a storehouse of the goods of all nations. The British tried every means to stop the shipments, even to pursuing vessels right into Eustatius' harbor, but the Dutch shippers, with the advantage of local knowledge of winds and tides, could outwit their pursuers, and stubbornly continued to sail. British protests that the "traitorous rebels" in the Colonies must receive no "aid and nourishment" from any friendly power grew in anger, conveyed in the arrogant language of the British minister, predecessor of Sir James Harris, the "high and mighty" Sir Joseph Yorke — as John Adams described him. Sir Joseph, son of the Lord Chancellor (Philip, first Earl Hardwicke), was an imposing personage in the diplomatic society of The Hague. He kept a "splendid and hospitable" table, according to Sir William Wraxall, an English visitor, with effect more overbearing than cordial, for his deportment was "formal and ceremonious" of a kind that evidently appealed to the Prince of Orange, the Stadtholder, who, says Wraxall, felt for him "a sort of filial regard." The ambassadorial manner had less effect on the merchant-shippers, who cared more for business than for diplomatic niceties.

Cadwallader Colden, British Lieutenant-Governor of New York, had warned London in November, 1774, that "contraband between this place and Holland prevails to an enormous degree. . . . Action must be taken against the smugglers but it would not be easy because the vessels from Holland or St. Eustatia do not come into this port, but in the numerous bays and creeks that our coast and rivers furnish, from whence the contraband goods are sent up in small boats."

How the system of contraband delivery worked was revealed in the reports of Yorke's network of agents. A particularly active shipper was shown to be a certain Isaac Van Dam, a Dutch resident of St. Eustatius serving as middleman for the Americans, who was sending quantities of goods and money to France for the purchase of gunpowder to be delivered to St. Eustatius for transshipment to America. For Britain's envoy to see the contraband go forth under his nose was particularly painful. "All our boasted empire of the sea is of no consequence," lamented Sir Joseph Yorke. "We may seize the shells but our neighbors will get the oysters."

Exasperated by the traffic, Britain in 1774 declared the export of "warlike stores" to the Colonies to be contraband and therefore subject to search and seizure under her rights as a belligerent. Threats to the Dutch government followed, demanding prohibition of the military shipments by Dutch subjects. These were no longer the days of a century before when, in the series of struggles between the Dutch and English for maritime supremacy, Holland's Admiral de Ruyter, according to legend, had sailed up the Thames to the very gates of the enemy capital with a broom nailed to his masthead in token of his intent to sweep the English from the Channel. Failing that happy result, he burned English ships and towed away the *Royal Charles*, one of the principal ships of the Royal Navy, an ill event that brought anguish to Samuel Pepys, a secretary of the Admiralty. "My mind is so sad," he recorded in his diary for June 12, 1667, "and head full of this ill news ... for the Dutch have broke the chain and burned our ships, particularly the *Royal Charles*, and the truth is I fear so much that the whole kingdom is undone." The blaze of the ships burning in the river was seen in London. The Anglo-Dutch wars, however, merely continued indecisively through the 17th century until both countries concluded that contest for supremacy was costing more than any profit supremacy could bring, and since both were strained in their resistance to the aggressions of Louis XIV, King of France, they found a joint interest in combining against him instead of fighting each other. In 1678,

England and Holland* had entered into defensive alliance pinned to several treaties requiring each to assist the other with the loan of troops or other aid in the event of aggression by a third power. After nearly a hundred years of this relationship, England took it very ill that Holland, instead of lending her 6,000 troops upon request under the terms of the old treaty, was instead saving the American enemy from empty arsenals and enabling the Revolution to continue.

Conscious of naval weakness relative to Britain, which now in the 1770s had 100 ships of the line (warships of over 60 guns), compared to eleven of the same size for the Netherlands, the government of the Netherlands felt compelled to comply with Britain's demand to cease supply of war material to the Colonies. In March, 1775, Dutch rulers announced to their subjects a six months' embargo of export to the Colonies of contraband (arms and ammunition) and naval stores (lumber for repairs, ropes for rigging and all materials needed to keep a ship afloat), even clothing, under penalty of confiscation of cargoes and heavy fines, and confiscation of ships

---

*Following the practice of the 18th century, Holland, as the chief of the United Provinces of the Netherlands, is the name used here for the whole of the country.

in case of non-payment. In August the prohibition was extended from six months to a year, and again prolonged for each of the next two years. As an unbearable restraint on a lucrative trade, the order aroused wrathful resentment in the merchant class and was routinely disobeyed. The natural result was a great increase in smuggling, to such an extent that Sir Joseph Yorke was instructed to inform the States General, governing body of the Netherlands, that English warships were ordered henceforth to show "more vigilance and less reserve" in their attentions to St. Eustatius. Their guard became so close as to make it difficult for mariners to bring in provisions. Indignation at this treatment provoked in Holland a proposal to blockade the ambassadorial residence of Sir Joseph Yorke in retaliation, though the records show no evidence that this undiplomatic enterprise was carried out. In January of 1776, King George III ordered the Admiralty to put more warships on duty because "every intelligence confirms that principally St. Eustatius, but also all the other islands are to furnish the Americans with gunpowder this winter." If Eustatian shippers had not been indefatigable in defying the embargo and evading their pursuers, continuance of the American rebellion at this stage might have been a close call. Militarily it was a hardpressed time. A crushing defeat in the Battle of Long Island in August, 1776, had left the British in control of access to New York and the New York coast. Washington had, at least, safely brought his forces out of Manhattan, where he could maintain the connection of New England to the South which it was the principal British strategic aim to disrupt. Soon the British had penetrated Pennsylvania and were threatening Philadelphia, the congressional capital. At Christmas time of 1776 the Continental Congress fled to Baltimore. In September, 1777, Sir William Howe with a large army and naval force sailed imposingly up Chesapeake Bay to the Delaware to enter and occupy Philadelphia, the largest city and busiest manufacturing and commercial center of the country. Occupation by the British meant the closing of America's two major ports by the enemy, cutting off the delivery of cargoes. The Dutch, however, not disposed to abandon a lucrative trade, slipped into smaller ports and estuaries and managed to maintain the supply of guns and powder that kept the patriot fight for independence alive.

The cause, however, suffered another blow in the loss of Fort Washington, on Harlem Heights, opposite Fort Lee in New Jersey, thereby losing control of the Hudson and opening New Jersey across the river to invasion by the British. The new defeat called for heavy campaigning to save the territory. The bedraggled army, without proper clothing and short of medicine and hospitals and care for the wounded, and especially of fresh recruits, was further weakened by the constant drain of short enlistments. Washington could muster perhaps 2,500 men at the most against Howe's 10,000. The imbalance was made up by his gift for miracle in a crisis. On the same Christmas when the Congressmen were running to save their skins, Washington with his worn-out force crossed back over the Delaware to inflict a smashing knockout on the Hessians at Trenton, gaining their surrender and 1,000 prisoners. For his own cause, the gift in energy and morale was incomparable.

A similar indomitable will had already carried the Dutch people through an eighty years' war of rebellion to overthrow Spanish sovereignty and brought them by their seafaring enterprise to overseas empire and to a role in the 17th century equal to that of the great powers. Though now slipping into decline, they were not disposed to acquiesce readily in British dictation of what their ships could or could not carry or to submit to search and seizure on command.

Mutual hostility between Dutch and English was to mount to a climax in the five years following the salute to the *Andrew Doria* with definitive effect on America's fortunes. In January, 1776, the hostility became overt. In strong language voiced by Abraham Heyliger, the temporary Governor, Eustatians vehemently protested that the British, in pursuing merchantmen into their harbor, committed "irregularities so flagrant that they must be considered as a total violation of the laws of all civilized nations." The protest was — with more caution than the original version — addressed not directly to the British, but to the West India Company in Amsterdam, which governed the trade with America. Admiral James Young, commanding the British Leeward station, shot back at once a denunciation of "the very pernicious traffic carried on between his Britannic majesty's rebellious subjects . . . and . . . St. Eustatias." King George's order to the Admiralty to show "more vigilance" followed in the same month.

Now become illicit under the embargo, the arms traffic to the Colonies could continue from St. Eustatius only with benevolent observation by the island authorities — in particular, the Governor. Ironically, Johannes de Graaff obtained that post as the result of another British protest, which had demanded replacement of his predecessor, Governor De Windt, as being too favorable to the American cause and too lax in preventing the smuggling of contraband. When De Windt conveniently died in 1775, Holland, without appearing to submit to a foreign demand, appointed de Graaff, secretary of the island administration for 24 years, to take his place.

Among the many applicants to the West India Company for the post of governor, de Graaff was seen as everyone's competitor. Some made a point of his strong qualifications, others of his disqualifications, including the complaint of a citizen that his wife was as "stingy as sin. She served us food that was three days old," and what was worse, "where do you think her tablecloths came from? From Osnabrück! Have you ever seen decent people use them? Let alone common folk like them?" Despite this mysterious local dereliction, de Graaff was appointed. Born in St. Eustatius to wealthy parents in 1729, in the same decade as Sam Adams, and educated in the Netherlands, he had returned to St. Eustatius, married the daughter of the then Governor, Abraham Heyliger, rose to be commander of neighboring St. Maarten and, after serving as secretary to the administration of his home island, succeeded to his father-in-law's former post as governor. He was sworn in on September 5, 1776, giving him nine weeks in office before he precipitated the *Andrew Doria* crisis. He was said to be the richest merchant and planter on the island, owning a quarter of the privately owned land with 300 slaves, and inhabiting a splendid home built as a showplace fifty years before by the wealthiest merchant of that time. De Graaff had furnished the spacious rooms with the same pewter and Delft porcelain and polished mahogany that adorned the homes of the rich Regents of Amsterdam. In addition, he was alleged to own sixteen vessels trading between Europe and St. Eustatius. From the second-story balcony of his house he could watch the crowded company of ships entering and leaving the harbor with the cargoes that earned him a rumored income of $30,000 a year. According to complaints from fellow-residents, he held many mortgages, being thus in a position to keep many people dependent on him, the more so as he put friends and relatives in administrative office so that he entirely controlled the five-man assembly or Council of St. Eustatius. Members of the Council were prosperous merchants and farmers of his own kind, as were most of the members of the church consistory; together they formed a body that managed the government and administration of justice in support of their own interests, in a manner not unknown elsewhere. Local complaints which charged the Governor with acting arbitrarily suggest an autocrat and make it quite clear that de Graaff was not a nominal or absentee governor, but fully aware and in control of all activities on his island.

If the British expected him to put guards on the port to suppress the smuggling trade, any such hope was disappointed. He proved to be even more of a partisan of the American cause than his predecessor. The port is "opened without reserve to all American vessels," protested Captain Colpoys, an English sea captain commanding the *Seaford* anchored off St. Kitts, the neighboring British island, while the American agent in St. Eustatius, Van Bibber of Maryland, wrote home, "I am on the best terms with H.E. the Governour. . . . Our Flag flys current every day in the road. . . . The Governour is daily expressing the greatest desire and intention to protect a trade with us here." The Dutch West India Company, which employed the Governor, could hardly have been ignorant of these sentiments, and, being eager to augment its revenues from the American trade, doubtless had appointed him because of them.

His domain — little St. Eustatius, or Statia, as it was familiarly called in the region — has a number of distinctive qualities, not the least of which is that the authorities seem not quite sure where it is. In histories and atlases and in 18th century usage it is always named one of the Leeward Islands, whereas a modern brochure published by the local official tourist bureau places it among the Windward Islands. To the average reader, likely to be a landlubber like the author, this odd contradiction may be a matter of indifference, but in the days of sail it lay at the heart of the matter. "Leeward," meaning the direction toward which the wind blows, hence generally toward the shore, and "windward," meaning the direction from which the wind comes to fill the sails, represent the absolute polarity and determinant of maritime activity, as distinct from each other as inside from outside. For a place that was once the wealthiest port of the Caribbean and played a crucial role in American history, this uncertainty about nomenclature seems a bit casual, not to say careless. Regardless of such confusions as may have slipped into print, St. Eustatius may confidently be stated, along with the Virgin Islands, to belong to the Leeward group of the Lesser Antilles.

The West Indies as a whole make up a curved chain connecting North and South America, from a point off Florida down to

Venezuela, which lies on the north coast of South America, the coast known in the days of piracy as the Spanish Main. Here pirates lay in wait in ports of the mainland to raid Spanish treasure ships heading home loaded with the silver of Peru and the goods and riches of the Spanish Colonies of the New World.

Separating the Atlantic from the Caribbean, the chain of the West Indies protrudes on its outer curve into the Atlantic and on its inner curve encloses the Caribbean as in a bowl. Tree-covered humps of land, each wearing around its base a white-fringed skirt of waves breaking on the shore, the islands of the West Indies lie comfortably in an unthreatening sea under a wide coverlet of quiet sky. Changing from slate blue when under cloud cover to turquoise in the sun, the sea twinkled with little white-caps while it bore flotillas of sail coming to unload produce or pick up cargoes at the island ports, or perhaps to disembark troops of a hostile invasion with intention to seize and occupy an island for attachment to the invader's own nation. This happened regularly, causing changes of sovereignty with hardly more excitement than when a man changes his clothes. Because of their wealth in the flow of international trade, lifeblood of the 18th century, and from the new crop of sugar sweetening the tongue of Europe and from the slave trade bringing labor to do the hot and heavy work on the sugar plantations, the islands were prizes for any nation greedy for the hard currency believed at that time to be the stuff of power. Apart from actual seizure, invaders could devastate the plantations, reduce product, cut revenue to the sovereign nation and thereby reduce its war-making capacity. St. Eustatius, the most lucrative island, boasted twenty-two changes of sovereignty in little more than a century and a half.

Within the Caribbean bowl, the islands lie in three groups, with the Bahamas at the top, followed at the center by a group of the largest islands, comprising Cuba, Jamaica, Puerto Rico and the divided island of Haiti-Santo Domingo. At the eastern edge is the thin vertical chain of the Leeward Islands where Statia was located, with British-owned St. Kitts as its nearest neighbor, eight miles distant. Further into the ocean, the Windward Islands, including Martinique, Barbados and Grenada, and Trinidad and Tobago, hold the windward position. Home base in Europe was far away, an average distance, depending on the port of destination, of about 4,000 miles, and an average sailing time from the West Indies to Europe with the push of the prevail-

41

ing westerly wind (blowing from west to east) of five or six weeks. The coast of North America lay much closer, some 1,400 miles across the Caribbean and South Atlantic. The typical voyage from the Indies to America took an average of three weeks. Enough geography.

De Graaff's salute of the rebels, and his countrymen's defiance of the embargo risking retaliation by a greater power, raises the question of motive. In all this affair the primary Dutch interest was a profitable commerce rather than liberty. De Graaff was not intending a mere routine ritual, as he later pretended when under investigation, but a deliberate one. In the subsequent furor, the Commander of Fort Orange, Abraham Ravené, testified that he had been reluctant to respond to the *Andrew Doria* but the Governor at his elbow ordered it. The applause of the island's inhabitants tells why. It confirmed to them that their new governor was not going to enforce the prohibition of trade in contraband or cut off the wealth that trade engendered.

Statia rejoiced. After the salute, as the Maryland agent reported, Captain Robinson of the *Andrew Doria* was "most graciously received by his Honour and all ranks of people . . . all American vessels here now wear the Congress coulours. Tories sneak and shrink before the Americans here." Because de Graaff's interests lay with the Company and the merchant class, the first salute was clearly intended to assure the unruly Eustatians of the benevolent eye they needed to pursue their profits. For added emphasis, de Graaff gave a party after the salute in honor of Captain Robinson, inviting all American agents and merchants to the entertainment, as Van Bibber happily reported to his principals in Maryland. Confirming the motive behind the salute, Van Bibber also wrote, "The Dutch understand quite well that enforcement of the laws, that is, the embargo, would mean the ruin of their trade."

With some glee, the entertainment for Captain Robinson was reported on December 26, 1776, in an American journal, *Purdie's Virginia Gazette*, based on an account in a St. Kitts newspaper, which would certainly have been forwarded to London. There was no glee in London on learning of Dutch recognition of the rebel flag, denounced by the King's Ministers as "a flagrant insult to His Majesty's colours." Indeed, wrath in London, when informed of the salute by observers in the roadstead, was tremendous, and exacerbated by a report that the *Andrew Doria* on departing had taken on arms and ammunition for the Americans.

Admiral James Young at Antigua, British

commander of the Leeward station, informed de Graaff in a letter of his pained "surprise and astonishment to hear it daily asserted in the most positive manner that the Port of St. Eustatius for some time past had been both openly and avowedly declared Protector of all Americans and their vessels whether in private trade or armed for offensive war" and that even "the colours and forts of the States General have been so far debased as to return the salute of these pirates and rebels and giving all manner of assistance of arms and ammunition and whatever else may enable them to annoy and disturb the trade of His Britannic Majesty's loyal and faithful subjects, and even the Governor of St. Eustatius daily suffers privateers to be manned and armed and fitted in their port." It needs only this letter to convey the throb of British indignation at the insolence of rebels who "annoy and disturb" the sacred trade of the British Empire, and, worse, that a friendly nation — a member of the club, as it were — should not only condone but assist them. Now it was the Dutch more than the Colonies who were raising British blood pressure. Because the Colonies were not a recognized state, they had in the British view no belligerent rights and thus their sea captains no valid commissions, which explains why the British were so free with the term "pirates."

De Graaff's salute to the Continental flag was by no means a mere complimentary bow to the anticipated victor in the war, for the Governor fired his guns almost a full year — eleven months, to be exact — before Burgoyne's surrender at Saratoga (October, 1777) supplied evidence that the raggle-taggle colonial forces might actually prevail. It was this victory at Saratoga that persuaded France in 1778 to enter into the open alliance with the Americans that was to change the balance of the war.

Statia and her Governor, prospering in the bold disobedience of their enterprise, were not intimidated by the rising wrath of Britain — too little, perhaps, for their own good, as coming events were about to demonstrate.

TWO

The Golden Rock

The teapot of this tempest, St. Eustatius, a rocky meager spot less than seven square miles in area, hardly more than a volcanic outcropping above the waves, was an unlikely place for a rendezvous with history. Nevertheless, by virtue of an unexampled devotion to trade on the part of a virtually landless nation, and location at the hub of the West Indies, where it was a natural meeting place for trade coming from North and South America and for ships coming to the West Indies from Europe and Africa, the little island had made itself the richest port of the Caribbean and the richest territory per acre in the region — if not, as some boasted, in the world. Holland's declared neutrality in the struggle between Britain and the American Colonies had assisted its enrichment.

Geography favored Statia with a splendid roadstead that could shelter 200 ships at a time and an invaluable position at the center of a multinational cluster of territories —

English (Jamaica, St. Kitts, Antigua and Barbados), French (Ste. Lucie, Martinique and Guadeloupe), Spanish (Cuba, Puerto Rico and Hispaniola, the last divided between Haiti and Santo Domingo), and Danish (Virgin Islands). Taking advantage of Statia's neutrality, these nations, as well as British merchants of the area who were actually sharing in the trade with the enemy, made Statia's shores the principal depot for transshipment of goods to and from America.

Called the Golden Rock for the flood of commerce that flowed through its free port, stuffing its warehouses with goods for trade and the coffers of its merchants with the proceeds, it "was different from all others," said Edmund Burke in a speech of 1781 when Eustatius in sudden fame leapt into public notice. "It had no produce, no fortifications for its defense, nor martial spirit nor military regulations. . . . Its utility was its defense. The universality of its use, the neutrality of its nature was its security and its safeguard. Its proprietors had, in the spirit of commerce, made it an emporium for all the world . . . Its wealth was prodigious, arising from its industry and the nature of its commerce."

Two factors besides geography accounted for the prodigy of the Golden Rock: Holland's enterprising neutrality amid the ceaseless and circular wars of her larger neighbors, and Statia's role as a free port without customs duties.

The pressure of the merchant class represented by the formidable Dutch West India Company, which held a monopoly over trade with America, induced the States General to declare neutrality in the war of the British Crown against its Colonies. Neutrality, as the Dutch knew from experience in the preceding Seven Years' War of Britain against France, was good business, although in the American war it went against the natural bent of the States General, which favored the British as fellow-rulers. Popular opinion, however, in a rare combination with business interests, added its pressure for neutrality. Out of inherited pride in their own revolution to overthrow the sovereignty of Spain, the mass of the Dutch people openly sympathizied with the American rebellion.

Neutrality on the high seas, always the most contentious element in international relations, balances on a tightrope of mutual contradictions. According to the much-disputed doctrine of "free ships, free goods," a neutral had the theoretical right to pursue a normal trade with either belligerent so long as its supplies did not cause a military disadvantage to the other side. At the same time, the theory allowed a belligerent to prevent the subjects of a neutral state from sending military supplies in aid of the enemy. Between these two assertions — the right of a neutral to trade and the right of the belligerent to interfere to stop the trade — there could be no reconciliation.

Determined to take advantage of this condition, Dutch merchants and mariners, alert to every opening for commerce, braved the physical and financial risks of seaborne commerce to make it pay richly. Wealth filled their warehouses. The American Colonies sent rich cargoes of their products — tobacco, indigo, timber, horses — to exchange for naval and military supplies and for molasses, sugar, slaves and furnishings from Europe. Their agents in Amsterdam arranged the purchases and the delivery to St. Eustatius for transshipment to the American coast. Vessels loaded with 1,000 to 4,000 pounds of gunpowder per ship, and in one case a total of 49,000 pounds, made their way to Philadelphia and Charleston (the nearest port). To the rebels with empty muskets, St. Eustatius made the difference.

As a free port, Eustatius had reaped the profits both as marketplace and as storehouse where goods waiting sale or transshipment could be safely housed against predatory foreign fleets in search of loot.

The measure of profit in the munitions traffic can be judged from the price of a pound of gunpowder, which cost 8.5 stivers of the local currency in Holland, and 46 stivers or almost five and a half times as much on Eustatius, because its proximity saved American customers time and the risks of a longer passage. Trade swelled to and from the Colonies. On a single day in March, 1777, four ships from the Colonies came via Statia into Amsterdam bringing 200 hogsheads of tobacco, 600 to 700 barrels of rice and a large shipment of indigo. An English customs officials in Boston recorded, "Daily arrivals from the West Indies but most from St. Eustatius, every one of which brings more or less of gunpowder."

The second factor in Statia's golden growth came from her avoidance of the restrictive cult of mercantilism that prevailed among other nations.

Mercantilism was born of the belief that national power depended on the accumulation of hard currency to pay for the era's increasing costs of government and of maintaining armies and navies for constant conflict. In pursuit of the favorable balance of trade necessary to earn revenue, the mercantilist policy laid strict limits on imports of foreign and colonial goods and on the carrying trade of other nations. The rule applied to a nation's own colonies, which were considered to exist to serve the prosperity of the mother country and were therefore prohibited from exporting manufactured articles that could compete with the mother country's industries. Except for loot in wars and simple seizures of property from disestablished monasteries or expropriated Jews or from Spanish treasure ships carrying silver and gold from the New World, the excess of exports over imports was the only source of external revenue. Hence the century's overriding and pervasive concern with trade.

Subject to infinite variables of winds and currents, of supply and demand, of crops and markets, trade has a way of carving its own paths not always obedient to the mercantilist faith. The faith was embodied in Britain's Navigation Act, enacted under Oliver Cromwell in 1651 in the interests of the rising middle class and the industrial towns and major trading ports — the so-called Cinque Ports, so long influential in British history. Aimed specifically at the Dutch to protect British trade against its most dangerous rival, the Act raised a wall of customs duties, and permitted transshipment of goods only in British bottoms calling at British ports. The natural result had been maritime war with Holland and bitter resentment of customs duties in the

Colonies, feeding the spirit of rebellion which led to the American war. For Britain, the expense of fighting the Dutch and trying to suppress the American revolt was more costly than anything that could be gained by the trade laws, causing higher taxes at home and their natural consequence, a rise in domestic disaffection. That was not the least of Britain's afflictions in her embattled time.

The instinct of the Dutch for commerce early persuaded them that profits were more likely to come from a free flow of trade than from restrictions. Did something grow within the narrow limits of St. Eustatius that bred a greater need for open doors and looser rules? Whatever the reason, Statia became a free port in 1756 when she abolished customs duties in order to compete with St. Thomas, which had become her only trade rival in the Caribbean. From then on her prosperity flourished extravagantly. As the neighboring islands could not trade with each other in wartime when their principals were entangled in the various belligerencies of Europe, as they were most of the time, they brought their goods to buy and sell in St. Eustatius and to purchase edibles from foreign sources, for no one of the West Indies, concentrating on sugar and slaves, was self-sufficient in food.

In the next twenty-five years, Eustatius enjoyed its golden era. Population, which had numbered only a few thousand before the American war, rose to 8,000 by 1780, owing to the explosion of trade and storage service. Residences crowded up against each other along the shore of the Lower Town and were doubled by a row of stone warehouses occupying every space. Mercantile adventurers from all over flocked to St. Eustatius to store their goods, which otherwise might be lost on their own islands through the constant seizures of territory by naval predators in search of booty and land. Warehouses of the Lower Town overflowed with goods awaiting transshipment. The traders often took the precaution to become Dutch citizens while using the island as their depot. British blockade of the American coast and French entry into the war rendered American and French ports subject to attack, further encouraging the use of St. Eustatius for storage.

The Lower Town ended at Gallows Bay, where there was a sloping beach suitable for the bizarre business of cleaning ships' bottoms. Barnacles and marine growths had to be scraped off and the bottom repainted every few months in an excessively awkward process called "careening." It required hauling the vessel up on the beach and turning it over from one side to the other while masts, ballasts, guns and other equipment were removed or lashed in place. The fighting machine itself was out of action for the duration of its humiliation. Provided it had not bogged down in mud or been damaged by a squall while it lay helpless, it might then be relaunched. Rarely did human ingenuity fall so short of requirements as in this preposterous, almost farcical procedure. The only alternative, for navies which could afford it, was to sheathe their warships' bottoms in copper.

Through the 1770s and '80s, Dutch merchants continued to defy their government's embargo on contraband, and the Americans to ignore as before the Navigation Acts, to which as British Colonies they were subject. So tempting was the opportunity to get rich quickly, complained Sir Joseph Yorke, that munitions were loaded in Dutch harbors as publicly as if no embargo had been declared. He tried to insist to the States General that they must enforce their orders, but he could get nothing done. Writing to a colleague, he came to the sore point that galled the British the most: ". . . the Americans would have had to abandon their revolution if they had not been aided by Dutch greed." He did not see greed in the British merchants who were selling supplies to the enemy, for greed, like better qualities, often lies in the eye of the beholder.

THREE

Beggars of the Sea — The Dutch Ascendancy

At the time of de Graaff's salute, his fellow-countrymen had already registered and passed the peak of dynamic accomplishment in almost every realm of endeavor — in hydraulic engineering to make their own land habitable, in the longest successful revolt for political independence sustained against the greatest imperial power of the age, in flourishing commerce, business and banking, in maritime enterprise covering the oceans, in the supreme art of the Golden Age of Rembrandt, in everything but government, where they contented themselves with a paralytic system that would not have been tolerated by a primitive island of the Pacific. For all these qualities — positive and negative — the Dutch were the most interesting people in Europe, although few contemporaries would have said so. Except perhaps an American, specifically John Adams, our first envoy to the Netherlands, who wrote to his wife in 1780, shortly after his arrival in Holland, "The country where I am is the greatest curiosity in the world. . . . I have been here three or four weeks and . . . I am very much pleased with Holland. It is a singular country. It is like no other. It is all the Effect of Industry, and the Work of Art. . . . This Nation is not known any where, not even by its Neighbors. The Dutch Language is spoken by none but themselves. Therefore They converse with nobody and nobody converses with them. The English are a great nation, and they despize the Dutch because they are smaller. The French are a greater Nation still, and therefore they despize the Dutch because they are still smaller in comparison to them. But I doubt much whether there is any Nation of Europe more estimable than the Dutch, in Proportion." Jealousy of the extraordinary Dutch ascendancy in commerce clouded the European view from a similar appreciation.

As the primary ship-builders of Europe, the Dutch had added one more element of mastery in their lifelong contest with water. In prehistoric times when Europe was settled by Germanic tribes advancing from the East, one tribe called the Batavi, whom the Dutch in later centuries came to consider their ancestors, had pushed onward, seeking a secure area of their own, and kept going until they met the sea and could go no further. Here on the wave-flooded, water-soaked edge of Europe, having no other choice, they settled where the ground was too wet and life too difficult for any other group to wish to dispute the territory. By building mounds for the foundation of homes above water level and ramps to let their livestock enter and dikes to hold back the sea, by learning through practice and experiment to put windmills to work as pumps to drain the water eternally seeping from springs and streams and marshes, they put dry ground under their feet. Soon they were able to lift land from the bottom of lakes and swamps to create areas called "polders" for agriculture and habitation. By directing the drained water into ditches, they made canals for transportation. Maintenance of the drainage system required constant attendance and renewal; the work never stopped and was never finished. In a stupendous feat of labor and engineering, a nation succeeded in creating land for itself to live on, doing by the hand of man what only God had done before. If they could match the work of Genesis, they need fear no man nor element of nature and were infused by a sense of accomplishment. A people few in numbers on an insecure footing was enabled to launch a revolt against the rulership of Spain, the greatest empire of the day, and to persevere in a successful war of resistance lasting eighty years, from 1568 to 1648, against an enemy not as far removed as Britain was from the American Colonies, 3,000 miles and an ocean away, but on the same continent, an overland distance from Barcelona to Antwerp of about 900 miles. Eventually winning independence, the Dutch within one generation of autonomy had transformed themselves into the greatest trading nation in the world, holding the commercial center and financial heartbeat of Europe and resting on a seaborne empire that stretched from the Indian Ocean to the Hudson River.

The amazing growth and expansion of Holland was a phenomenon that causes historians to stutter and even caused wonderment to Dutch scholars. Like the draining of the country and the overthrow of the Spanish colossus, it may be a mystery only in the sense that the extreme exertions possible to the human spirit can never be wholly elucidated. Nevertheless, in the Dutch phenomenon some causes are discernible. Partly their rise grew from necessity — the need of a people on the edge of nowhere to find the means of livelihood and survival — and partly it came from the will and energy of a figurative little Napoleon moved to outdo his larger brothers, and partly from the impulse stemming from what they had already achieved.

While the expansion was happening, it was no mystery to the Dutch themselves, who clearly explained what drove them in a petition addressed by the States of Holland in 1548 to their sovereign, Charles V, Holy Roman Emperor and King of Spain. The petitioners described the unending reclamation work needed to protect the land from the sea by dykes, sluices, millraces, windmills and polders, and the heavy yearly expenditure required. "Moreover," they wrote, "the said province of Holland contains many dunes, bogs and lakes as well as other barren districts unfit for crops or pasture. Wherefore the inhabitants of the said country in order to make a living for their wives, children and families must maintain themselves by handicrafts and trades, in such wise that they fetch raw materials from foreign lands and re-export the finished products, including diverse sorts of cloth and draperies to many places such as the kingdoms of Spain, Portugal, Germany, Scotland and especially to Denmark, the Baltic, Norway and other like regions whence they return with goods and merchandise from those parts, notably wheat and other grains. Consequently the main business of the country must needs be in shipping and related trades from which a great many people earn their living like merchants, skippers, masters, pilots, sailors, shipwrights and all those connected therewith. These men navigate, import and export all sorts of merchandise hither and yon, and those goods that they bring here, they sell and vend in the Netherlands as in Brabant, Flanders and other neighbouring places."

A tangible element of the expansion overseas was the ships themselves. Through their grain trade with the Baltic countries, the Dutch had better access than their rivals to the timber of the Baltic, giving them a steady supply of the material for making ships. They used a more efficient design, distinct from that of warships, for cargo ships which could be handled by fewer in crew and which, having no guns, could carry a larger cargo and, through the use of standardized parts, were built more cheaply and quickly and in larger numbers than those of other nations. When Peter the Great determined to achieve sea power for Russia, he came to Holland in 1697 to the dry dock at Zaandam between Zuyder Zee and the North Sea to learn about shipbuilding. At Zaandam a shallow-draft 250-ton cargo ship called a "flute" cost half as much to build as its counterpart in English shipyards. With simplified rigging, a 200-ton ship could be sailed by ten men, whereas in England a ship of the same size needed a crew of twenty or thirty.

In the 17th century, national energies opened into a period of spectacular enrichment of trade and commercial expansion in which Dutch talents and methods led them to excel and acquire the status of a major power. Cash profits from the flow of new products — spices of the East Indies, cotton of India, tea of China, sugar of the West Indies — enabled the Dutch to lend money to their neighbors. Because of their shipping and financial resources, their alliance became valuable.

The phenomenon of their rise, apart from its specifically Dutch elements, took its impulse from the spirit of the age beginning in the latter decades of the 1500s. The doors of the Middle Ages were opening out into new realms of every kind — freedom of thought, information through printing and, physically, to a wider world. Construction of larger ships allowed merchant-mariners to leave the confines of the Mediterranean and the trade of its familiar shores for the products and materials and unknown peoples in distant lands — cotton, sugar, pepper and spices, tea and coffee, silk and porcelains, all coming to Europe to enrich life and enlarge commerce and initiate industry. Europeans burst from their continent, crossed the Atlantic, entered the Pacific, rounded the Cape of Africa, found the East Indies. The Dutch were soon in the forefront. With their engineering skills adapted to ship-building and having no wide acres at home available for purchase to draw their money into landowning, they invested in maritime ventures, usually in partnership which spread the risk and provided greater capital to equip and man the ships and support the long voyages.

After a first exploratory venture in 1595, the second merchant voyage on the long and hazardous journey to the East Indies sailed in 1598 in an argosy of 22 ships, from which, owing to tempest, disease of the crews, hostile privateers and other dangers of the sea encountered en route, only 14 returned. Yet the cargoes of pepper and spices and Indian objects they brought home more than matched the losses, attracting other investors to enter the competition. In 1601, 65 ships — three times as many as took part in the second venture — set out for the same destination, involving so many competitors that the States General advised amalgamation, and thus was founded, in 1602, the Dutch East India Company, first of the great commercial institutions that were to promote the Netherlands' rise. With ample capital to underwrite the far-flung argosies, with state-authorized regional monopolies of the trade, the East India Company was followed twenty years later by the Dutch West India Company with an eye on the sugar of Brazil, the silver of Peru and Mexico and expectations of the American fur trade. It was chartered in 1621 with a monopoly of American trade after Henry Hudson, an exploring agent of the Dutch East India Company hired to find a Northeast passage to the Orient, had found instead in the Western Hemisphere a great river equal to the Rhine and had surveyed the American coast from Cape Cod to Virginia. In the same decade, the colony of New Amsterdam was established between the river and the sea, with frontage on both. Proceeds from the two trading companies brought home the riches to enlarge the tax base and provide the government with more money for building and manning more merchant fleets with enlarged scope for expansion. The process was watched resentfully by other nations who, to soothe their envy, endowed the Dutch with a reputation as moneygrubbers. Certainly, moneymaking was a primary national interest and, combined with a strong sense of freedom and independence grown in a long revolt, was the key to the extraordinary Dutch enterprise.

Superior seamanship and superior ships were the means that carried the Dutch to the crest of world trade, taking the lead from Spain, thought to be the greatest sea power of the time, and from England, the self-appointed rival of Dutch enterprise. England's captains were limited by the nature of their society, which assumed that a gentlemanly land-ownership, unspoiled by manual or commercial work, was the highest and purest ideal of social life. English sea captains were likely to be volunteers of the nobility with narrow practical experience, if any, while Dutch captains and admirals were more often the sons of salt-sea sailors who had grown up handling the ropes. Dutch Admiral de Ruyter, hero of the 17th century navy, astonished a French officer by taking up a broom to clean his cabin and afterward going out to feed his chickens.

"Enterprisers" of the period, beginning in business as merchants, provided the capital and organization for long-distance trade and for new industries from newly available products — paper for the printing presses, shipyards for larger vessels for the merchant fleets that traveled the ocean routes, manufacture of arms, uniforms, barracks and all the equipment of war. Besides making men rich, the industries justified the mercantile idea — by keeping the poor at work to produce articles for export to bring in a favorable balance of trade and hard money for more ships and more armies. Enterprisers found that the simplest use of profits, as the Dutch soon learned, was in making loans to other enterprisers at interest.

In 1609, a memorable year, the Hudson River was discovered and the Bank of Amsterdam, the heart that pumped the bloodstream of Dutch commerce, was founded. Introducing new methods of regulating the exchange of foreign currencies and of minting coins of fixed weight and value and of allowing checks to be drawn on the Bank to provide credit and loans and of assuring the reliability of deposit, the Bank soon attracted a flow of money from every country, while its florins became the most desired currency. The regular listing of prices on the stock market printed and distributed by the Bank was an innovation for which the world may — or may not — thank Amsterdam.

In 1648, when the Dutch gained independence from Spain, they had risen to riches and power despite the energies absorbed in the prolonged revolt and the damages suffered to war-torn countryside and cities and the impoverishment caused by expenditure on arms and armies and by the emigration of so many men of substance. Through extraordinary enterprise and force of necessity and confidence gained in their ordeal, they had expanded their commerce and shipping until they had more than half the trade of Europe in their hands, and had access to ports on every foreign shore from the East Indies to Africa, from Brazil to the Caribbean and to New Amsterdam in North America. In the Ottoman Empire they had a concession to trade throughout Turkish dominions given by the Turks as a slap at Spain, which had beaten them at the Battle of Lepanto. More than three-quarters of the world's carrying trade in timber and grain from the Baltic, salt from France, fabrics from their own cities, spices from the East and sugar from the West Indies was shipped in Dutch bottoms. By the time of independence in 1648, they were, according to historians' estimate, the greatest trading nation in the world. They were said to have 10,000 ships at sea, carrying an international traffic estimated at a thousand million francs a year, a figure doubtless exaggerated by foreign mariners to shame their own governments into stronger competition.

Around 1634, eight years after they bought the island of Manhattan from the Indians, the Dutch entered the Caribbean with the capture of St. Eustatius and St. Maarten and of Curaçao and Surinam on the Spanish Main.

Sugar was a treasure greater than the spices, attracting the eager predators of every nation. The sudden delight of sweetening on the tongue as a regular article of diet and sweetener of other foods raised high the real-estate value of the West Indies. Nations came rushing, each to seize the coveted prize of an island where the tall canes grew. Planters became rich. In later years, William Pitt, as Prime Minister, saw, when driving through Weymouth, a planter's carriage with horses and fittings handsomer than his own. "Sugar, eh? All *that* from sugar!" Pitt exclaimed on being told the owner was a West Indian planter.

The heavy canes had to be cut, carted to mills, subjected to double and treble sets of rollers — worked, of course, by hand — to extract the juice, which was transferred to boilers for reduction to crystals, refined through several boilings for whitening and packed in molds to shape the loaves, or left dark for the unrefined product, then finally shipped to waiting markets. Because the local Caribs of the region sickened and died in the labor of the plantations, sturdier black labor was brought from Africa, forming in itself the lucrative slave trade.

In the midst of their extraordinary maritime and business enterprise, the Dutch were engaged in an upheaval against the rule of Spain, causing, it might be thought, one or the other, either economic expansion or revolutionary energy, to have weakened the other. Instead, both developments moved ahead parallel with one another.

The Revolt of the Netherlands was not a movement of national sentiment, which hardly existed, nor of political ideology. Although the issue partook initially of the 16th century's general conflict of Protestant versus Catholic erupting out of the breakaway of the reformed church from Rome, the motivating sentiment in the Netherlands was hatred of Spanish tyranny. Forces and events in the eighty-year struggle were a turmoil of infighting among sects and parties, of deals and overtures to foreign states, of mounting oppression by the Spanish rulers that augmented popular hatred to a frenzy and, in a deeply fragmented state, linked the fragments together in a common will for independence.

Having been swept up by the Reformation, especially by Calvinism, its most fanatic sect, the Dutch of the northern provinces, as the years went on, adopted Protestant reform with an intensity of conviction as stern as that of the Scots under John Knox. The southern provinces bordering France and the Hapsburg Holy Roman Empire remained faithfully

Catholic, hardening the divisions in the country. The Protestants were as rigid and unbending in their absolute refusal to return to the Catholic rite as was their monarch Philip II of Spain in his determination to restore them to the Roman fold.

When edicts issued by Margaret of Parma, Philip's half-sister and Regent and acting Governor of the Netherlands, forbade Protestant ritual in the churches and the public speaking of self-appointed Protestant preachers, the prohibitions lit a fire of indignant protest and active resistance. A petition to the King to cancel the edicts only confirmed Philip in his determination to tear heresy out by the roots and erect in its place a pillar of authority based on a firm foundation of royal absolutism. But it takes two — one to impose and one to acquiesce — to make authority function. Philip's subjects in the Netherlands were not prepared for the second role. In 1566, when their petition to the King went unanswered, they went on a rampage of desecration in the churches, smashing images and relics seen as the symbols of a despised idolatry. Led by a League of Nobles, staunch Protestants, which with unusual solidarity included members from every province although they clung as ever to individual conflicting opinions and separate working classes, the movement ignited agitation in the towns and among the industrial masses raising signals of national rebellion. When a band of 400 nobles marched in a body to the Regent's palace in Brussels to demand a stop to the Inquisition employed against the resisters, they evoked the sneer of an unsympathetic Count Barlaimont as "a bunch of beggars," immediately adopted as a proud title. At the League's banquet, members wore beggars' gray with beggars' wooden cups hanging around their necks, and the name thereafter honored their fight for freedom from Spain and afforded seamen the opportunity of calling themselves Beggars of the Sea for the pleasure of rubbing the noses of Spanish and English opponents in the fact that they were anything but that.

More was needed to organize revolt. In 1568, an impetuous and reckless expedition launched by Louis of Nassau against the authorities of the northern city of Groningen thrust into the action a decisive figure. He was Louis' brother, William of Nassau, Prince of Orange, who was to emerge as one of history's heroes under the name of William the Silent. Orange was a small principality in the South of France to which the Counts of Nassau held title. William was Stadtholder and Commander-in-Chief of Holland, Zeeland and Utrecht by appointment of the late Emperor. When Louis' rebellious assault was easily broken and Louis himself later killed, William inherited the movement of revolt. He infused the will and the vigor that would keep the struggle against tyranny going until the goal of an independent Netherlands was won eighty years after Louis of Nassau had lighted the sparks. Before that could happen, both Spanish tyranny and Dutch revolt intensified.

In the first years, King Philip's answer to the outbreaks was to send the ruthless Duke of Alva with 10,000 men, to compel obedience by a reign of terror. Alva's method was massacre in the towns, persecution of Protestants for heresy and creation of a special court, called the Council of Blood, which in the course of its operations held 12,000 trials, convicted 9,000 offenders and executed or banished more than 1,000. Nobles who were leaders in the revolt were beheaded, eighteen in one day in the market square of Brussels. Estates were confiscated, scores fled the country and everywhere rose the dread of the Inquisition, as distinct from secular persecution, being established in the Netherlands. To make sure that he made everyone of all classes an insurgent, Alva imposed a tax of a tenth on the sale of every article and a hundredth part of every income. The hated "Tenth Penny" did more to spur the revolt than all the atrocities.

The ruler, Philip II — that "odious personage," as Motley, classic historian of the revolt, cannot refrain in his Protestant Victorian rectitude from calling him — was himself too narrow and rigid to recognize as rebellion the trouble he was stirring up for himself; Philip could think only in terms of being ordained by God to root out Protestantism, and he rejected any consideration that might suggest an obstacle in the way of this task. A small thrill of triumph inspirited the Dutch at the first success of the revolt when, in 1572, a piratical force of the Sea Beggars captured the fortified port of Den Briel, at the mouth of the Meuse, where it controlled the entry to navigation of the river.

Extreme Calvinist partisans, arising from the early persecution of Protestants, and forming wild and ferocious bands of expert seamen, the Sea Beggars served the revolt by harassing Spanish shipping, while their activities added to the internal feuds of regions and factions.

The inveterate separatism and mutual jealousies of the cities and provinces of the Low Countries, in which each feared the advantages and influence that might be gained by its neighbor, could have permanently frustrated any united resistance to Spain if the struggle had not found a dynamic leader in William of Orange. By perseverance in what seemed a hopeless struggle, by remaining unshaken under every adversity or disappointment, by overriding the incessant contention of the provinces, by maintaining the single aim of union, by organizing his compatriots with political sagacity, William, though sometimes shifting ground and not always straightforward in his maneuvers, and mainly by strength of character, came to focus and personify the revolt. If it had carried a banner, it would have borne his words "It is not necessary to hope in order to persevere."

In 1574, the year after Den Briel, the heroic defense of Leyden against a Spanish siege rallied every city and citizen around the standard of revolt. Surrounded by lakes and laced by streams and canals of the lower Rhine, Leyden was a beautiful and prosperous cloth-manufacturing city on the rich soil of the Rhine delta called the Garden of Holland.

The weapon against Leyden was starvation. Alva had gone, but his successor tightened the siege until not a stray chicken nor a leaf of lettuce could get in. For seven months the enfeebled inhabitants subsisted on boiled leaves and roots and dried fish skins and on chaff from old threshings of wheat. When an occasional dog was slaughtered to feed the watch, the carcass might be torn apart in bleeding pieces and devoured raw. Disease stalked as always in the footsteps of famine, adding to the sick and wounded. In their extremity the inhabitants faced annihilation or surrender.

It was then they turned water, their old antagonist, into their weapon and ally. William of Orange proposed opening the dikes of the Meuse and Yssel and the rivers crossing the area between them and Leyden to flush out the besiegers and lay a shallow lake that would allow flat-bottomed scows and barges to sail over the land with provisions for the beleaguered city. Because of the potential damage of a flood to crops, the consent of landholders and farmers had to be gained. Messengers were sent on the dangerous mission through the lines to reach and return with their agreement. Daily more gaunt and feeble, no one in Leyden called for surrender. Meeting in Rotterdam, the States General rejected Spanish terms and accepted the proposal of William of Orange to open the dikes. They ordered 200 flat-bottomed barges and scows to be collected at Rotterdam and at Delft and other river ports, and to be loaded with arms and provisions. The boats also carried what proved essential for the relief, "a small but terrific" band of 800 grim-faced Sea Beggars, hideously scarred by the livid wounds of old battles.

In August, 1574, the order for breaking the dikes was issued. It was not just a matter of poking holes in the walls. Openings wide enough for the barges to pass through had to be breached under the not very efficient fire of the surrounding Spanish garrisons. Their weapons were the primitive muzzle-loading muskets of the 16th century, which after every discharge had to be reloaded with powder carried in bags around the soldiers' necks. The Sea Beggars countered the attacks with their accustomed ferocity, and forced abandonment of the forts, driving the soldiers into the open where in growing alarm they watched the rising water creeping toward their feet. A northwest wind blowing for three days drove the waters in greater depth toward Leyden, providing an avenue for the barges. Slowly the relief force advanced overland, lake by lake, smashing dikes as they came until they had penetrated within five miles of the goal. The work took weeks while the people of Leyden starved and died. At that point, a contrary east wind rose to blow the water back, leaving the surface too shallow to be sailed. For their last advance, the boats had to be pushed and pulled over the mud flats while the city's emaciated people waited in agony of expectation.

Fearing that their retreat could be cut off, the Spaniards had abandoned their fortified posts and, under continued assault by the Sea Beggars, they could not prevent the rescuers' approach. Through mud the awkward amphibian procession crawled like a turtle out of water nearer to the beleaguered city. Aided this time by a fresh wind, the strange fleet was blown forward to within a few hundred yards of the walls. The crews, jumping out, carried the scows through the shallows over the final distance. A last Spanish garrison was overcome in a brisk fight. The boats were pushed triumphantly up to the quays, and dripping crews threw loaves of bread to the citizens on shore weeping with joy at their deliverance. Leyden, with 6,000 dead of starvation and disease and its population reduced by a third, was saved from surrender. Hollow-eyed survivors crowded into the Cathedral for a thanksgiving service. To honor the city's steadfastness, William of Orange offered it a choice of relief from taxes during the lucrative annual fair or the establishment of a university. The burghers in hardheaded calculation chose the university, on the ground that taxes could come or go depending on politics, but a university, once established, would permanently benefit their city. Since that day, one of Europe's greatest halls of learning stands as the gift of the scarred Sea Beggars and the flat-bottomed scows of Leyden.

Spanish pride, trampled at Leyden, was compensated by the fearful sack in 1576 of Antwerp, the bustling and prosperous port at the mouth of the Scheldt, which served the trade, in and out, of all northern Europe. The sack was precipitated by a mutiny of Spanish troops who had not received their promised pay for 22 months. Philip II, having transferred the cost of the war into a huge debt owed to the merchants and magnates of Spain, had declared his exchequer in bankruptcy in 1575 and had received a dispensation from the Pope permitting him to revoke all promises or commitments "lest he should be ruined by usury while combating the heretics." With his customary lack of sense, the richest monarch of his time applied the dispensation to non-payment of his army on the theory that, as he was God's instrument for crushing heresy, whatever he did, whether or not wise, was right. Like most of Philip's policy judgments, it turned against himself. The mutineers in their rage set fire to every street in the wealthiest quarter of Antwerp as they broke into the city, not forgetting to fall on their knees in a prayer to the Virgin to bless their enterprise. It is a peculiar habit of Christianity to conceive the most compassionate and forgiving divinities and use them to sponsor atrocity. In the conquest of Mexico, Spanish priests carrying banners of Christ blessed the conquistadors as they marched to the torture and murder of natives in the country. In Antwerp, the mutineers killed every citizen who crossed their path or stood in a doorway, indiscriminately striking down aged householders, young women with infants, fellow-Catholic priests and monks or foreign merchants. In an orgy of pillage lasting three days, they ransacked every warehouse, shop and residence, accumulating money, silver, jewels and fine furniture to untold value, horribly torturing anyone suspected of concealing his wealth, leaving thousands dead and an increased abhorrence of the Spaniards in the surrounding "obedient" provinces. The immediate result was the most damaging to Spain that could have occurred — a movement toward confederation of the provinces, not firm or permanent but enough to mark the beginning of the end for the governing power.

Constant bickering between French-speaking Walloons and Dutch-speaking Flemings, between Catholics and Protestants, between the maritime and inland provinces, between nobles and commoners, between Amsterdam in its hegemony and everyone else had so far prevented common action in the revolt. Netherlanders were now beginning to realize that they must join forces if they were ever to expel the Spaniards. Persuaded of the necessity, William of Orange had initiated a series of letters to the Councils of the provincial states proposing a general peace among them to achieve their mutual purpose. Negotiations were already under way at Ghent. Four days after the "Spanish Fury," as the sack of Antwerp came to be known, the deputies of nine states brought to birth a treaty or pact called the Pacification of Ghent, pledging them to maintain peace among themselves and devote their lives and goods to delivering their country from the Spaniards and foreign oppressors. As in the case of the assembly almost 200 years later of the thirteen American Colonies, hitherto always at odds, in their first intercolonial Congress, joint action by the Dutch rebels was the one thing that the rulers could not overcome, and had confidently believed would never take place. In America the British, too, by their own actions, were to commit the outrages, by the Boston Port Bill and the Coercive Acts, that brought the fractious Colonies together.

In the Netherlands, the pact of Ghent was embedded in a maze of contracts and conditions defining the rights and duties, geographical, commercial and especially religious, of each city and province and the terms which the new Spanish Governor, Don John of Austria, half-brother of Philip, should be required to accept before meeting the States General, for he was on his way with that intention. It is odd that so soon after pledging to expel the Spaniard, the Dutch should be dealing with him, but at a time when a powerful mystique of royalty endowed every monarchy with absolutism, the Dutch were not yet ready to make the outright challenge nor had they the military means to do so. They lapsed, in the period immediately following the Pacification of Ghent, into such a welter of sectional rivalries and struggles over the dominance of the old versus the reformed religion and of local and foreign combinations and defections as amounted almost to civil war — and made a scrap of paper out of the supposed Pacification. Out of this strife and confusion, a movement for a "closer union" than had been achieved at Ghent took form, spurred by the fear of a separatist union by the northern provinces.

Under these pressures, deputies met in 1579 at Utrecht, the central city from whose tall Domkerk tower fifty cities could be seen, and a view as far as Rotterdam, now the largest harbor in the world. Although the assembled body agreed that they would thereafter "be as one province," the Union of Utrecht that resulted did not tighten the pact of Ghent, but on the contrary, because of the intractable religious issue, established the conditions that were so sorrowfully to split the emerging nation. The northerners did indeed form a union of the seven provinces that make a ring around the Zuyder Zee, the great inland sea of the north. With four inland and three along the coast of the North Sea, these seven as the United Provinces were to become the Dutch State. In response, the Catholic provinces of South Holland with the cities of Brussels, Antwerp and Ghent formed a union of their own that virtually seceded and was eventually to become with some adjustment of boundaries the separate state of Belgium. The consequence, in precluding united nationhood for a people so capable, was grave. Had they not split, and had they retained a larger territorial base and a greater population, they might have become masters of Europe if they had had the will for conquest — which they did not — and if the strength of unity had not been lost through religious dispute, whose intramural fights are always the most passionate and venomous of any. If they lost the mastery of Europe, they gained at this hour the mastery at last of their own country.

Through all the machinations and labyrinths of agreements and disagreements by the Dutch cities and parties, the one great motivator of nationhood, a clear call for independence, was missing. The Calvinist party, with its strong emphasis on individual rights, pressed for an expression of purpose from the States General, the only remaining body of native government. Assembled at The Hague in 1581, it passed the momentous resolution called the Oath of Abjuration that was the Dutch Declaration of Independence. Stating that Philip II had violated the compact and duty of a ruler to deal justly with his subjects and give them good not bad government, and that he had therefore forfeited his rights of sovereignty, the delegates claimed the inherent right of subjects to withdraw their allegiance and to depose an oppressive and tyrannical sovereign, since no other means remained to them of preserving their liberties. This has a familiar ring: a bell sounding 200 years before Americans heard the same summons.

If Thomas Jefferson thought his authorship of the American Declaration of Independence was his proudest work, as the inscription on his tombstone indicates, he might have spared a thought to the Dutch proclamation of 1581, which anticipated his argument two centuries earlier in almost identical terms. This is not to suggest that Jefferson plagiarized America's most important document, but rather that men's instinct for liberty, and belief in the people's right to depose a ruler who has governed unjustly, travels in deep common channels.

To confirm the break with Spain, all magistrates and officials were required to abjure the oath of allegiance individually and personally, which caused much anguish to those nurtured in lifelong obedience to a crown. The forswearing so worked on the feelings of a councilor of Friesland that in taking the Oath of Abjuration he suffered a heart attack or stroke of some kind, fell to the floor and expired on the spot.

Continued obdurate Dutch resistance was draining Philip's resources and, even more, his patience. Thinking to collapse the revolt at one stroke, he put a price of 25,000 golden crowns or approximately 75,000 guilders, a large fortune, on the head of William of Orange, dead or alive, together with a set of other rewards and pardons — and found a taker. Entering by treachery, the assassin, Balthazar Gérard, in 1584 killed William with a pistol shot on the staircase of his house in Delft.

The Dutch record at this time, it must be acknowledged, seems politically foolish to a point that defies common sense. Because they believed they could never throw off Spanish sovereignty except under the aegis of some other potent European monarch, they went about offering their sovereignty to a variety of princely candidates, even including Elizabeth, Queen of England, whose autocratic nature was anything but a secret and would be likely to fulfill the worst Dutch expectations.

The obvious candidate for King, while he was alive, the Netherland's own Prince of Orange, did not possess the advantages of other sovereigns in military strength or in money. Elizabeth, herself embroiled in Catholic disaffection and intrigue and putative rebellion at home, was too clever to get caught in more of the same trouble abroad, and did not accept the offer.

The assassination of William failed to fulfill Philip's purpose, for William had imbued the revolt with a life of its own. When, however, Antwerp was taken by Philip's Governor of the Netherlands, the Duke of Parma, giving Spain a strategic opening to the Channel coast across from Britain, this stroke invited unexpected assistance. It awoke Britain to the thought that it might be more in her interest, instead of wasting strength in endless inconclusive war with the Dutch, to aid them against Spain, whose intention to invade Britain caused constant anxiety. This became acute when the Duke of Parma, Philip's designated successor to rule the Netherlands, recaptured Antwerp, giving him a major port and an excellent naval base across the Channel, directly opposite the mouth of the Thames.

Unlike most rulers who fear change because it is change, the Queen of England, bold and canny Elizabeth I, was willing to reverse the ancient enmity and offer alliance to the Netherland rebels. In 1585, she sent an expeditionary force of 8,000 under her favorite, the Earl of Leicester, to help the rebels withstand Parma's advance. Vainglorious, ambitious and bullheaded, Leicester was not a well-chosen agent. Given the position of Governor General of the Netherlands, which the Dutch in their undue respect for foreign aid accepted, the more deeply, as they thought, to engage Elizabeth, Leicester intervened in Dutch Councils and followed his own idea of strategy without regard for the client's concerns. When he issued an edict against trading with the enemy, a normal contemporary practice, he committed the unforgivable sin: interference with their trade was a thing the Dutch would not permit. The vaunted alliance fell apart in mutual blame and Leicester departed unlamented. His errors and failures have been overshadowed in history by the more romantic and memorable reputation of his lieutenant, the poet Sir Philip Sidney. Mortally wounded at the Battle of Zutphen, he handed a cup of water to a no less wounded comrade with the memorable last words, "Thy necessity is yet greater than mine." Other than an immortal line for literature, nothing much came of the English intervention except indirectly to precipitate one of the turning points of European history. By arousing the anger of Philip II, it planted in his one-track mind a design to break up the Anglo-Dutch alliance, destroy the English and strike the final blow against heresy.

The blow was to be delivered at sea by a huge naval armada followed by invasion, which Philip set about organizing with insistent ineptitude in every aspect of command, strategy and supply. He chose as commander an admiral, the Duke of Medina Sidonia, who had never commanded in war at sea before and who was to sail to seas unknown to him, with no prearranged port for refuge in case of need, and dependent for success upon a plan of junction with Parma's forces in the Netherlands with whom it was planned to invade England. Blockaded by the Dutch, Parma's troops were never able to meet the rendezvous. Philip's great galleons, battered by heavy storms and by the British Navy, were sunk and scattered off the Hebrides. With half their crews lost to winds and waves and enemy guns and lack of food, the crippled Armada, forced to take the long cold way around Scotland and the west of Ireland, slunk home on a miserable and disheveled voyage, trailing no clouds of glory or conquest, but only the long shadows of defeat. The resounding failure of Philip's naval enterprise marked the end of Spain's primacy in European power politics, never afterward to be retrieved.

Wrapped in his single-mindedness, Philip did not give up, but threw what means Spain had left into the suppression of the Dutch, whom he found newly strengthened by their empire of commerce. Philip himself proved mortal and died in 1598, ten weary years after the Armada, and after completing the Escorial for his mausoleum, the greatest royal tomb since the pyramids. His unrelenting crusade against Protestantism, which had kept him continuously engaged in the religious wars of 16th century Europe, drained what offensive strength Spain had left for action against the Dutch, now grown rich and prosperous in the halls of business and markets of trade. Philip's own demise took the heart out of Spain's effort to maintain her rule. With Philip's death on the brink of the 17th century, the great century of the Netherlands' Golden Age began. Significantly the mark of new greatness was made in America where history's winds, moving westward, were about to blow.

In 1609, an English navigator in the service of the Dutch East India Company discovered the Hudson River. In that same memorable year of the birth of the Bank of Amsterdam, Spain agreed to a twelve-year truce which acknowledged in practice the independence of the union of the seven United Provinces of the Netherlands. The spectacle of grand and imperial Spain being brought to a truce by a webfooted republic newly established among the monarchies impressed the older powers. They now began to reckon the former Beggars of the Sea as a factor in the European game with whom it was desirable to be allied. It impressed the Dutch themselves, who at last were ready to face the climax of their effort. After the truce expired, Spain fitfully continued the war without decisive results and finally let go. In 1648, at the Treaty of Westphalia, when the European powers brought to an end the general European conflict of the Thirty Years' War, the most extensive and destructive of any before 1914, the signatories, including Spain, formally recognized the long-embattled independence of the United Provinces of the Dutch Republic. The articles were signed at the preliminary treaty of Münster, with the Spanish delegates placing their hands on a crucifix and the Dutch delegates holding up two fingers pointed heavenward. Burghers of the city formed two lines of an honor guard as the Dutch delegates marched to the Council chamber while cannon boomed in the medieval streets to celebrate the hour. It was the mid-point of the 17th century, a year before the high noon of royal absolutism felt the shadow of the executioner's axe as it severed the head of King Charles I of England.

While they had been pursuing the expulsion of Spain, the Dutch conducted a cultural life of great fertility. Although their governors were a stiff and conservative company, not, one would suppose, liberal in their sympathies, the cultural atmosphere was liberal and tolerant, allowing freedom of practice to Jews and to a variety of Christian sects, and known for hospitality to refugees fleeing bigotry and persecution abroad. The most notable of the refugees were the English dissidents, seeking religious freedom, who at the turn of the century settled in Leyden and twenty years later embarked on the voyage, carrying its great burden of the future, that in 1620 ended at Plymouth Rock. Another fruitful group were the Jewish émigrés from Spain and Portugal bringing the parents of Spinoza, born in Amsterdam in 1632.

Attracted to the Netherlands by its luxuriant publishing activity, the most vigorous on the Continent, European writers and scholars, whose works were blocked by censorship at home, came to find in the Netherlands willing publishers and distribution in Latin to an international readership. So it was that the Dutch press had the honor to issue one of the world's most significant books, by a Frenchman who preferred to live in Holland for twenty years rather than at home under the reign of Louis XIII: Descartes' *Discours de la Méthode* was issued in Leyden in 1637. Others of the most significant figures in European culture pursued their careers in Holland, although sometimes arousing the antagonism of colleagues. Baruch Spinoza, philosopher of humane religion, was a native of Amsterdam and though expelled as a Jew from his own synagogue for heretical views, he remained to live and publish his *Tracatus Theologico-Politicus* in his native land. Antony van Leeuwenhoek, developer of the microscope, pursued his scientific work in his native Delft. Grotius of Delft, a Dutchman himself, formulated in

Mare Liberum for all time the principle of freedom of the seas and in his *De Jure Belli ac Pacis* produced one of the most influential works on public law ever written. It had to be published in Paris in 1625, when he suffered a jail term instigated by private enemies. The renowned scholar Pierre Bayle, exponent of a rational skepticism in religion, whose works propounded his view that popular religious beliefs were based on human credulity rather than on reason and reality, was not a philosopher agreeable to an authoritarian Catholic regime. Forced to leave France, he came to Holland where he was given a chair and stipend in Rotterdam at the *Ecole Illustre*, established by the city to provide working shelter for refugee scholars. His famous *Dictionnaire*, a one-man encyclopedia published in Rotterdam in 1697, illustrated his explanations of natural phenomena and, though banned in its first edition in France, became a source and inspiration for Diderot and the French Encyclopedists. In this welcome to Bayle, Rotterdam gave a home to a man who expressed a supreme statement of tolerance. Remarking the loyalty of religious minorities to the Dutch State, as long as they were allowed freedom of conscience, he suggested that "an ideal society would extend its protection to all religions, and that since most theological problems are incapable of proof, man should pray for those he cannot convince rather than oppress them."* In these words Bayle antedates our First Amendment. Dutch rulers were unusual in that while enjoying security of position and comfort, they fostered a society that harbored the unorthodox. American Puritans of New England, whom the experience of real hardship had taught nothing of gentleness toward their fellowman but the reverse, formed in contrast a bigoted and punishing ruling group.

Owing to the tolerance of Dutch society, no large body of emigrants felt driven to find new homes in New Amsterdam, except merchants rich enough to support settlements of at least fifty colonists, who received land grants from the West India Company, becoming the patroons of the region. In the absence of a large rooted Dutch settlement, Peter Stuyvesant could not find enough men willing to form an army for defense when the English were to come in 1664 to capture the area and name it New York.

Was it the nourishing freedom of Dutch

---

*His prescription, like other wise counsels, was to be mocked by his fate. Tolerance was no more agreeable to the French Huguenot refugees than to the Catholics. The influence of the refugees made it necessary for him to resign his chair, though he continued to live and to publish in Holland.

society that gave rise in the mid 17th century to the glory of the Golden Age of painting in the appearance of both Rembrandt, the master of humanity, and Vermeer, the exponent of serene perfection? At the same time flourished the vivid portraitists Frans Hals and Van Dyck, and the portrayers of domestic scenes, Jan Steen, Ter Borch and de Hooch, and the landscape enchanters of leafy forests and sailboats riding the canals, Ruysdael and Hobbema. If the world cannot explain the Golden Age, it can only be grateful.

In its events, the Golden Age was not peaceful but filled with the bloodshed and alarms of invasion and war. The army of Louis XIV stormed over the frontier in 1672 in a wave of brutality called the French Fury, reminiscent of the Spanish reign of terror. The French penetrated to Utrecht in the center of the country and this time, too, the Dutch fell back on the weapon of water, opening the sluices to flood the land. At the same time, England renewed naval war in an effort, promoted by her own merchants, to destroy Dutch naval and commercial competition by force. The last of three such wars ended in the Treaty of Westminster of 1674, which set rules for the conduct of neutral trade that were to be a serpent's nest of future trouble.

Troublesome as they were to be, they could

not obscure the great political initiator of the Golden Age, the winning of the Netherlands' sovereignty and independence in 1648. In that act at Münster, the Dutch vindicated the struggle for political liberty that was to pass in the next century to the Americans.

FOUR

"The Maddest Idea in the World" — An American Navy

The *Andrew Doria*, vehicle and protagonist of the drama of the first salute, was not just any ship but already the possessor of a historic distinction. She was one of four converted merchantmen of the "singularly small" body — as one of its officers, John Paul Jones, regretfully acknowledged it — that composed the first navy of the United States, created by Act of the Second Continental Congress on October 13, 1775, and she was shortly to take part in its first belligerent action.

Named for a famed figure in the cause of liberty, the valorous Admiral of Genoa (Andrea Doria in his own country), who led the fight for the freedom of his city against the French in 1528, she was about 75 feet long and 25 feet in the beam, with a mixed or "hermaphrodite" rigging of square sails on her mainmast and a fore-and-aft rig of triangular sails on her mizzenmast. For armament she had sixteen 6-pounders, meaning guns that could fire small 6-pound cannonballs as well as a number of swivel guns mounted on deck for a wider field of fire. She carried a crew of 130.

The importance of sea power as a strategic arm was accepted as understood in the 18th century, well before Admiral Alfred Thayer Mahan in 1890 formulated it as a fundamental principle, to the surprise of seagoing nations which had risen or fallen by its means through the centuries. Defeat of the Spanish Armada had determined the rise of Britain and the decline of Spain 300 years before Mahan's discovery, and Nelson's ships at the Battle of Trafalgar put an end to the threat of Napoleon and altered the balance between Britain and France ninety years before *The Influence of Sea Power upon History* was published. Nations, like people, are often more pragmatic than they know or can explain.

The American Colonies had no need to wait for a principle. Their need for resupply of arms and powder, and their need to disrupt the enemy's supply lines and to defend themselves against British naval attacks on and burning of their coastal towns, was imperative. They were fortunate in a Commander-in-Chief who had formed in his own mind the fixed belief that the colonial forces could never achieve victory without sea power to use against the enemy. In August-September, 1775, to interrupt the British supply lines when he was besieging Boston, Washington had chartered and armed several small fishing schooners which had been commissioned by Massachusetts, Rhode Island and Connecticut to protect their coasts against British raids. By October 6, schooners commissioned by the Congress were watching the entrance of Boston harbor to fall upon British transports, which, not expecting naval action by the Colonies, carried no naval armament. "Washington's Navy," as the schooners came to be known, collected prizes of muskets, ball and powder and one fat 13-inch mortar, badly needed to bombard the British in Boston.

In his dire need of gunpowder, Washington in August, 1775, barely four months after the first shots were fired at Lexington and Concord, asked the Council of Rhode Island to commission an armed ship to go to Bermuda, "where," he said, "there is a very considerable magazine of powder in a remote part of the island and the inhabitants well disposed not only to our Cause in general, but to assist in this enterprize in particular."

Rhode Island, with its great bays and long

vulnerable seacoast, understandably shared the Commander-in-Chief's urgency about sea power. Going further than Washington, the colony, together with the associated Providence Plantations, passed a startling resolution in August, 1775, that no less than "an American fleet" should be built, and in the same month presented the resolve formally to the Continental Congress. Washington followed it in October with a request to Massachusetts for two armed ships to intercept two brigs loaded with military stores on their way from England to Quebec. Out of the need to organize this kind of enterprise on a larger scale and to interrupt British supply lines during the siege of Boston, the United States Navy was born. Privateers and fishing schooners manned by merchant seamen and fishermen were regularly commissioned and fitted out by the separate colonies. From this faint start Congress was being asked to authorize a national force responsible to the Continental government.

Because of the 18th century's fixed method of fighting by ship against ship and gun against gun, numerical odds were always considered the decisive factor, and for our first navy they were not favorable. Its ships numbered less than one-third and its guns less than one-quarter of the enemy's in American waters. The British were deployed the length of the coast from Halifax to Florida. They had three ships of the line and six smaller warships, with a total of 300 guns, based on Boston and at New England ports further north, two sloops of war in Narragansett Bay off Rhode Island, one ship of the line and two sloops at New York, three sloops in Chesapeake Bay, another with 16 guns at Charleston and ten smaller vessels of 6–8 guns at various ports along the way. Against these odds it was small wonder that some of the Patriot party who were offered commissions as officers declined on the grounds that "they did not choose to be hanged." Soldiers of the army if captured were treated as prisoners, but sailors as pirates. Bolder gentlemen accepted the assignments, among them Captain Nicholas Biddle of Philadelphia, who took command of the *Andrew Doria*, and his successor, Captain Isaiah Robinson, the captain who was to take the ship into St. Eustatius.

"Was it proof of madness in the first corps of sea officers?" asked John Paul Jones, looking back after the Revolution had been won, "to have at so critical a period launched out on the ocean with only two armed merchant ships, two armed brigantines and one armed sloop" (a fifth ship, the *Providence*, had been added to the first four). So small a force "had no precedent in history to make war against such a power as Great Britain. . . ."

Feeling the force of Jones's argument, the delegates in Congress nervously debated the proposal for a national fleet. Samuel Chase of Maryland affirmed that to build an American fleet to oppose Britain was, indeed, "the maddest idea in the world," but a fellow-delegate from Virginia, George Wythe, argued what was to be Washington's thesis, that "no maritime power near the sea-coast can be safe without it. Had not Rome built a fleet for the Carthaginian war? Why should we not take counsel from the example?" Even more than the practical need or historical example, it was the aching desire for a weapon of retaliation against the British for the savagery of their attacks on the coastal towns that created the navy. "You have begun to burn our towns and murder our people," wrote Benjamin Franklin to an English M.P. "Look upon your hands! They are stained with the blood of your relations! You and I were long friends. You are now my enemy and I am yours."

Embracing the delusion of all invaders in every time that punitive brutality will cow defenders into giving up their resistance, the British burned houses, farms, barns and timber resources, slaughtered livestock and left a trail of ruin wherever the redcoats and Hessians reached, and their marines were doing no less. Desire to return the injuries in some way upon their tormentors fired the Colonies' naval enterprise.

Adopting Rhode Island's resolution, Congress decided to establish a national navy, and on October 13, 1775, appointed a Naval (later Marine) Committee to govern naval affairs, with authority to spend up to $500,000 to purchase and equip four armed ships and construct thirteen frigates, the class of warship carrying fewer than 44 guns, next below ship of the line. With some overconfidence, it was announced that they would be ready for sea in three months' time. The first four were purchased in November, marking the physical birth of the United States Navy, called at this time the Continental Navy. Because the United Colonies possessed no regular ships of war, merchant and fishing vessels had to be purchased, converted and armed. Hulls had to be reinforced, holes pierced to receive the guns for the broadside firing that was the basic and only tactic of naval warfare. Masts and rigging had to be strengthened for belligerent action and crews had to be recruited. Washington arranged for the small rough vessels newly transformed into warships to be chartered, armed and manned by soldiers recruited from New England regiments. Sailing crews had to be assembled by press-gang procedures because naval service in wet and squalid quarters and the smaller opportunity on national ships for prize money — of which the greater part went to the government, leaving much less to be divided among the owners and crews than on a privateer — offered few attractions to volunteer recruits. The greater danger on national ships than on privateers, which preyed largely on merchantmen, and the longer enlistments further discouraged volunteers. For the Continental Navy, press-gangs were a necessity.

Privateers were essentially ships with a license to rob issued to them by local or national governmental authority. The practice was a paradox in the development of law and order, which, as it progresses, is supposed to represent the advance of civilization. Privateers were fitted out for the express purpose of attack and seizure of commercial cargoes for the profit of owner and crews and of the authorizing power. In this business of maritime breaking and entering, the commission to a privateer authorized offensive action while letters of marque covered seizure of the cargo. Equivalent to a policeman giving his kind permission to a burglar, the theory was one of the happy hypocrisies that men fashion so ably when they want to combine law and greed.

The Marine Committee, afflicted by nepotism, did not give much promise of greatly strengthening the new navy. Esek Hopkins, commodore of the new fleet, was an elderly merchant skipper who had followed the sea for forty years. With the disdain of the practitioner for the administrator, he designated the committee "as a pack of damn fools" (although one of them was John Adams), ignorant as lawyers' clerks, who thought the navy could help pay for the war. Esek's brother Stephen Hopkins was chairman of the Marine Committee, and his son John was given command of the *Cabot*, one of the first four ships of the squadron.

A flag was as necessary as commodore or crew, for a national navy was nothing without it. If a flag for an army unit or a headquarters on land was a tradition to express a sense of pride and loyalty, for a ship on the trackless seas it was a necessity as a sign of identity so that it should not be taken for a pirate. Until now, ships commissioned by the separate colonies flew the colony's flag, like the pine tree of Massachusetts, or a personal standard, like the coiled serpent of George Washington with its device "Don't tread on me." For the Continental Navy, a flag was wanted to represent the hard-won confederation of colonies under one sovereignty, the great step that made feasible a war of revolution. This flag, made at the seat of Congress in Philadelphia, by a milliner, Margaret Manny, was to be the one to receive the first salute. Everyone knows about Betsy Ross, why do we know nothing about Margaret Manny? Probably for no better reason than that she had fewer articulate friends and relatives to build a story around her.

Rather than venture into the tangled web of flag origins where a dispute attaches to every point, let us simply accept the fact that a red-and-white-striped flag made its appearance aboard a ship of the new navy at its dock in Philadelphia in December, 1775. What is on record here is that Margaret Manny, milliner, received from James Wharton of Philadelphia, 49 yards of broad bunting and 52½ yards of the narrow width with which to prepare an ensign. The goods were charged to the account of the ship *Alfred*, flagship of the squadron and, with 30 guns, largest of the first four. The finished product, leaving aside the question of who designed it, displayed thirteen red and white stripes, representing the union of the thirteen colonies, together with the combined crosses of St. Andrew and St. George in the canton or upper left quadrant retained from the Union Jack. The crosses had appeared on the British flag since 1707, when the two kingdoms of England and Scotland formed a union under the Crown of Great Britain. Their appearance on the American flag indicated that the Colonies were not yet ready to detach themselves from the British Crown or declare themselves a new sovereign state. Richard Henry Lee's path-breaking resolution in Congress in June, 1776, "that these United Colonies are, and of right ought to be, free and independent States . . . and that all political connection between them and the State of Great Britain is, and ought to be, totally dissolved" was still under heavy dispute. What the Colonies wanted at this stage was more autonomy, the irreplaceable sense of freedom of a mature people with the right to tax themselves, free of the imposition of taxes and statutes by the British Parliament without their consent, and what they were fighting for was to force Great Britain to accept this position.

On a mid-winter day, December 3, 1775, the new flag was flown. "I hoisted with my own hands the flag of freedom," Jones recalled on the deck of his ship, the *Alfred*, at her dock in Philadelphia in the Delaware River, while the commodore and officers of the fleet and a cheering crowd of citizens hailed the event from shore. Washington, shortly afterward, on January 1, 1776, raised what is believed to be the same flag on Prospect Hill in Cambridge, Massachusetts, during his siege of Boston. Testimony as to whether this flag, called the Grand Union, was carried at Trenton and Brandywine and other land battles is elusive, though it was soon to fly visibly in active combat at sea. The Grand Union gave way to the Stars and Stripes, officially adopted by Congress in June, 1777, with thirteen white stars on a blue field replacing the British crosses. In 1795, two stars were added, representing the adherence to the union of Kentucky and Vermont.

Congress did not wait until adoption of the flag to assign the newborn navy a mission. Ordered to attack the enemy in the Chesapeake if feasible, Commodore Hopkins decided on his own responsibility to pursue another objective. It was to seize, by a surprise landing of marines, the ports of Nassau on the island of New Providence in the Bahamas for the capture of military stores known to be cached there. The Marine Corps for land operations in support of naval action had been established within a month after creation of the Continental Navy.

Breaking ice in the Delaware, the little squadron, with the Continental flag waving from the *Alfred*'s mast, sailed out into the stormy seas of February at a low moment in American fortunes after the loss of Long Island and New York in August, 1776, gave the British control of the New York coast. Later, Washington succeeded in withdrawing his troops from Manhattan and retreating to Harlem Heights and into New Jersey, saving his army from dissolution and keeping unbroken his tenuous land front from New England to the South.

On its excursion to the Bahamas, the navy met success in the mission to capture arms: loot of 88 cannon, 15 mortars and 24 barrels of gunpowder were taken in the surprise attack on New Providence, and on the way home two small British marauders which had been raiding the coast of Rhode Island were captured as prizes.

The first memorable maritime fight followed on April 6, 1776. Against the dark horizon off Block Island at about 1 a.m., the *Andrew Doria* sighted a strange sail and signaled a warning to her companions. The stranger proved to be a British ship of force, the *Glasgow*, bringing dispatches from the Admiralty to British garrisons in southern ports. Fortunately, she was alone, for the American squadron suffered from untried crews, many sick from an outbreak of smallpox, and others unfit for duty, "having got too much liquor out of the prizes," while the ships themselves were clumsy sailers, burdened by the weight of the captured cannon. A three-hour duel lasting until daybreak was a helter-skelter affair under no combined orders, with each captain left to do as he thought best. The *Andrew Doria*, firing at close range, acquitted herself well until her aim was distracted by near entanglement with the *Alfred*, which, with her rigging damaged, had become unmanageable. Shots by others in the squadron found their target, forcing the enemy to crowd on sail for a retreat toward Newport. "Away came poor *Glasgow*," reported an observer on shore, "under all the sails she could set, yelping from the mouths of her cannon like a broken-legged dog as a signal [to the British fleet at Newport] of her being sadly wounded." The Americans gave chase, but the *Glasgow*'s superior speed, in spite of damages, brought her so close to Newport that the chase was abandoned for fear of being caught under the British guns coming out of the harbor in answer to *Glasgow*'s bellows of alarm.

With its prize of war material intact, the Americans made for New London, bringing the first Continental naval action to a successful, if not heroic, end. Officers in *ex post facto* critique were not satisfied with their performance. In Captain Biddle's words, "a more imprudent ill-conducted affair never happened."

Other encounters followed off the Delaware Capes and Bermuda and Nova Scotia and Cape Breton Island, of no great concern to this story except insofar as they made the Continental flag known to its enemies and no doubt to neutrals.

After her fight with the *Glasgow*, the *Andrew Doria*, repaired and refitted at her home port in Gloucester, New Jersey, sailed on October 23, under a new captain, Isaiah Robinson, carrying sealed orders from the Marine Committee. Opened at sea, they gave him his destination as St. Eustatius and his mission to deliver a copy of the Declaration of Independence to Governor de Graaff and to buy cloth and a load of arms and ammunition for the Continental Army. With a new national navy under his feet and "conscious of conducting a diplomatic mission," Captain Robinson wanted to make a noticeable entry. Sailing into the harbor, he ran up his striped flag and moved forward to anchor right below Fort Orange. Following custom, he dipped his flag to the fort and when the fort's flag was dipped in return he fired his entering salute. Abraham Ravené, the fort's commander, as he later testified, surmising the identity of his visitor and realizing that recognition would cause trouble with the British, was uncertain what to do. Sending hastily for the Governor, who lived close by, he was instructed to reply with two guns less than a national salute. The volley and the white puffs of smoke followed. Three English sailors aboard a sloop in the roadstead saw the whole scene and hurried afterward to discuss it with the excited townspeople of St. Kitts who had watched from on shore.

The colonial authorities, obviously pleased by the response gained by the *Andrew Doria*, were inspired to invite a repetition. In February, 1777, orders were issued by the Marine Committee to Captain Nicholas Biddle of the Continental frigate *Randolf* instructing him that "As you command the first American frigate that has got out to sea it is expected that you contend warmly on all necessary occasions for the honor of the American flag. At every foreign port you enter, salute their forts. . . ." No further salutes, however, were recorded.

Whether it was madness or not to launch a fleet, Congress made the naval challenge explicit on November 25, when it formally declared British warships, though not yet merchantmen, open to capture in retaliation for British attacks on American coastal towns.

At the same time it issued naval regulations for action at sea by the United Colonies of North America.

FIVE

Buccaneer — The Baltimore Hero

Straining for action, a privateer named the *Baltimore Hero,* not part of the Continental Navy but bearing a commission from the Council of Safety of Maryland, had not waited for formal authorization. On November 21, 1776, with more audacity than armament (between 6 and 14 guns), she captured a British-owned cargo ship, the *May,* three miles off the coast of St. Eustatius. The *May,* sailing out of St. Kitts, was taken within sight of both that island and St. Eustatius. A prize crew was put on board with orders to take her back to the Delaware in America. The owner, a British resident of Dominica, southernmost of the Leeward Islands, protested loudly through the Governor of Dominica to the ranking Imperial official in the area, the President of St. Kitts, who bore, with appropriate aplomb, the name of Craister Greathead.

A storm of diplomatic missives descended

upon The Hague transmitting President Greathead's accusations that the inhabitants of St. Eustatius had "daily and openly" furnished supplies to the Americans, had "assisted them in their treason and had become the protectors of their buccaneering"; that the action by the *Baltimore Hero* had taken place within range of St. Eustatius' guns. That the American ship had been allowed to return afterward, so Greathead claimed, to the port of St. Eustatius, "apparently enjoying every protection," was attributable to the unneutral permissiveness if not active connivance of St. Eustatius' Governor de Graaff. Summoning de Graaff for an explanation, he demanded restitution to the owners of the *May* and insisted that the "abettors" be found, apprehended and suffer "condign punishment" as a "terror to others." Going back to the prior outrage of the *Andrew Doria*, Greathead claimed without offering any evidence that the identity of the rebel flag was known to de Graaff when he saluted it. On the issue of the salute, he was even more indignant, calling for "exemplary atonement for the indignity offered to His Majesty's colours by the honours paid by Fort Orange to His Rebel Subjects."

In a wordy polemic he went on at length to deplore the "flagrant violation" of the many compacts existing between "our two courts" and the infringement of the law of nations in "extending assistance and avowed countenance to proscribed Rebels of Great Britain. . . . In no other light can these deluded people be lawfully considered . . . and the law of Nations recognizes no such right as that of Lawful War waged by subjects against their sovereign state and consequently these captures under the authority of their usurped powers can be but piratical depredations. . . . To the scandal of all Publick Faith and national honour it has remained for a Dutch Settlement to be the avowed abettor of their treasons and promotors of their piracies and for their High Mightinesses [the title used in diplomacy for the States General] to be the first publick recognizers of a flag hitherto unknown in the catalogue of national ensigns." His magisterial rhythms and copious rhetoric flowed on. (It must always be an amazement how 18th century letter writers — even, and especially, officials — had the time and capacity to produce their sculptured sentences and perfection of grammar and *mots justes*, while 20th century successors can only envy the past and leave their readers painfully to pick their way through thickets of academic and the mud of bureaucratic jargon.)

The further accusation that the buccaneer

was in fact co-owned by Van Bibber, the Maryland agent, and that he had promised shares in its prizes to a relative on the island, was emphatically denied by Mr. Van Bibber and a Mr. Aull, the alleged sharer in his piracy.

In final bitter reproach, Craister Greathead added that when given a chance to explain himself to the Governor of St. Kitts, de Graaff had refused to talk to him. For added effect, Governor Greathead arranged that his letter be delivered by the "respectable conveyance" of a member of His Majesty's Council, no less than His Majesty's Solicitor General. De Graaff was unimpressed. In a haughty letter of reply, he refused to respond to the summons or discuss the matter with President Greathead or anyone else from St. Kitts.

In answer to increasingly menacing protests of His Majesty George III, the States General claimed that neutrality required treating the Colonies the same as the Crown, and on that ground kept the Netherlands' ports open to American ships. By implication this meant that the Netherlands recognized the American party in the struggle as an equal belligerent, not merely as rebels. Nevertheless, the Dutch Republic, divided between the pro-American party of Amsterdam, loyal to trade and its profits, and the pro-British party, loyal to the Prince of Orange, was unprepared to meet the threat of war, and ordered the recall of de Graaff for a hearing and the posting of its own cruisers off St. Eustatius to search Dutch ships for arms and ammunition and other contraband.

Pleading reasons of health and family responsibilities, and the burden of official duties and, strangely for a Dutch subject, a "fear and aversion for the sea," being subject "to sea-sickness to an amazing degree" so that the whole voyage he would not be able to hold his head up to eat or drink, de Graaff tried to avoid going home. He was not excused. Seasickness, as a contemporary observed, "is a disease which receives no pity, though it richly deserves it." Though managing to postpone the voyage for more than a year, he had to go. Surviving seasickness, he returned in 1778 to Amsterdam, where he was examined by a committee of the West India Company on three main charges: the smuggling of contraband, the permitted capture of an English ship and the salute of the rebels' flag. In response to the third charge, he maintained that the salute to the *Andrew Doria* was a regulation courtesy to passing vessels with no regard for nationality and that it did not imply recognition.

The central question — whether de Graaff

had known the identity of the flag he was saluting — was not cleared up. Greathead claimed, without specifics, that the flag "was already known as the flag of the American rebellion." He probably drew this conclusion from a deposition of a young sailor from the *Andrew Doria* named John Trottman, who, on being examined by the Council of St. Kitts, testified that the *Andrew Doria* on arriving at St. Eustatius saluted Fort Orange with 13 guns and, after an interval, that salute was returned by the said fort by 9 or 11 guns, he did not remember which, and the ship during this time "having the Congressional colours then flying." The testimony suggested that if seventeen-year-old Trottman knew the Congressional colors, so must others. In fact, Trottman had been shanghaied aboard the *Andrew Doria* at Philadelphia, the birthplace of the flag, where he might well have witnessed the raising; thus his knowledge of the identity proved nothing about de Graaff. The likelihood is that de Graaff did recognize the flag when he saluted it; otherwise why would he have insisted to the commandant of the fort on a salute to an unknown flag? De Graaff did not either affirm or deny having recognized it; he simply asked how his accusers could show that he had recognized it. Considering that it had been flying in combats on land and on sea for the previous ten months and could hardly have escaped the notice of a busy port like St. Eustatius, his reply was disingenuous.

On the whole, his document for the defense of 202 pages with 700 pages of appendices was not a resounding challenge but a careful — almost a lawyer's — defense. Citing repeated British interferences with Dutch shipping, de Graaff reminded the Company that though he had a right to repel British searches and seizures by force, he felt that he had to "be cautious owing to want of sufficient means." His realism picked out the central Dutch flaw — that with regard to the trade with American vessels, as he said, St. Eustatius depended on outside sources for all its supplies and he believed it was his duty to do nothing to disturb its commerce. Outgoing cargoes were examined as strictly as possible, but there were always men who would violate the rules. He denied the charge of equipping American vessels, except to let them take on provisions and water for a period of six weeks, and declared that to call the Dutch "avowed collaborators" of the Americans was "an insult of the most ungracious and shameful kind." If that was protesting rather too much, he hurried on to demand witnesses of alleged wrongdoing and asserted that it would violate his commission as Governor to prosecute anyone without a plaintiff or condemn without evidence. With regard to relative insults, he felt himself to be the person insulted by being addressed as "Mynheer," which in English, he claimed, was a way of ridiculing and deriding the Dutch nation. Proudly he insisted that "no one on earth but his superiors was entitled to call him into account for acts of his administration."

As for the *Baltimore Hero*, he stated that its action had taken place outside the range of his guns and he could no more have prevented it than if it had taken place off the coast of Africa. He did not mention how, in a similar action a few months earlier when Captain Colpoys of the *Seaford* had attempted to seize an American ship off the shores of St. Eustatius, the commander of Fort Orange, Abraham Ravené, was indeed able to prevent it.

Taking the offensive, de Graaff charged that the Netherlands had more to complain of in British conduct than the other way around, and reminded the committee that two Dutch merchant ships had been seized for alleged contraband and should be released with their cargoes and indemnity paid for costs and damages.

Obviously pleased by this approach, the examining committee reported de Graaff's defense to be perfectly satisfactory, and recommended to the States General that he be returned to St. Eustatius as Governor. With more courage than bureaucracies normally exhibit, the States General, refusing to bow to the British demands, accepted the Company's verdict and sent de Graaff back to resume the governorship. Self-respect for Dutch sovereignty was no doubt one motive, and the knowledge that de Graaff would keep open the gainful trade with the Colonies to the satisfaction of the merchant class was certainly another.

De Graaff resumed his post at Statia in 1779. After his return as Governor, the trade of his island with the Americans manifestly increased. The affairs of the *Andrew Doria* and the *Baltimore Hero* seemed to have emboldened the Eustatians rather than otherwise. In thirteen months of 1778–79, according to the careful records of the Dutch admiral in command of convoys for merchant vessels, 3,182 vessels sailed from the island, amounting to the astonishing figure of seven or eight a day. One vessel, stopped and searched by the British, was found to be carrying 1,750 barrels of gunpowder and 750 stands of arms, complete with bayonets and cartridge cases in egregious violation of contraband. Supplies like these sustained the almost empty American war cupboards. In the same year, the Americans shipped to St. Eustatius 12,000 hogsheads of tobacco and 1.5 million ounces of indigo in exchange for naval supplies.

The increased presence of British watchdogs outside the port and their aggressive searches and seizures unquestionably cut back the number of American ships that ventured to run the gauntlet to pick up supplies. A difference exists among historians as to whether trade between St. Eustatius and America actually increased or decreased after the rise in British threats and protests. John Adams seems to have been in no doubt. "From the success of several enterprises by the way of St. Eustatia it seems that the trade between the two countries [United Provinces and United States] is likely to increase," he wrote in August, 1779, to the President of the Congress.

The Governor who presided over all this activity is memorable for no act of heroism or heroic utterance, but rather for a steady unwavering purpose effectively pursued. The importance of what he did to promote and encourage the provisioning of the Revolution was recognized by contemporary Americans in the naming of two privateers, one for him and one, in happy ignorance of her shocking taste in table linen, for his wife, named the *Lady de Graaff*. In addition, a self-described "grateful American citizen" F. W. Cragin of New Hampshire, and resident of Surinam, commissioned de Graaff's portrait "in honor of the first salute." The portrait now hangs in the State House of New Hampshire, native state of the donor.

Still pursuing the affair of the flag, the British informed the States General in Sir Joseph Yorke's most peremptory terms that it must formally disavow the salute to the rebels, punish the culprit and recall and dismiss the Governor of St. Eustatius. Further, until satisfaction was received, he warned that "His Majesty will not delay one instant to take such measures as he will think due to the interests and dignity of his crown." In the long intimate and cranky relationship of Britain and Holland, this was overt hostility.

Yorke's démarche was one that might be expected from this haughty envoy whose father, having been in April, 1754, raised in the peerage to an earldom — that step in the life of the English that went to their heads like wine — his son could now look down from heights that disdained the conventional, even advisable, courtesies of an ambassador. Adams said Yorke addressed the States General in the same tone the British had used to Boston.

His veiled threat was angrily met by the Duke of Brunswick, chief adviser to the Prince and unofficial premier, as "the most insolent and improper piece that I have ever seen sent from one sovereign to another." When made public, it caused furious indignation, although another of the Prince's advisers pointed out that it was "not easy to swallow, but *vana sine viribus ira* [wrath without power is in vain], and so we'll be compelled to come down a peg or two." And the needed power, the adviser pointed out, the Netherlands did not have.

To the British, de Graaff's return to his post in St. Eustatius was seen as an insult rather than the satisfaction London had demanded, and they began to contemplate active reprisal. A warning hint appeared in murmurs about abrogating the century-old Anglo-Dutch treaty of 1674, which Britain had always disliked as affirming rights of neutrality on the basis of "free ships, free goods." Holland was too disjointed politically to pay attention to the hint.

This was the time when wrathful citizens suggested blocking the delivery of supplies to the British embassy. Serenely unaware of how close had been his discomfort, Sir Joseph acknowledged with some satisfaction to his Minister in London that his memorial had "raised a violent fermentation through the country" and alarmed and frightened the people. On his part, the Duke of Brunswick replied to William V that the threat expressed by the Ambassador of the King of England was an insult as well as an injustice to the United Provinces. Worse, in his opinion, was Yorke's oral statement that he would be recalled if satisfaction were not given within three weeks. Yorke well knew, as the Duke reminded him, that the necessity of obtaining agreement by all the consultative bodies in the Dutch system precluded any decision within three weeks. Honor and dignity required, Brunswick said, that satisfaction be denied until the accused could be heard. The States General were obliged to protect the country's commerce and her ports. The Duke was clearly put out. The excess of Yorke's language had only succeeded in antagonizing a strong partisan of Britain. Brunswick concluded that Yorke's threat was a scare tactic to justify the searching and seizing of Dutch ships.

In this affair Yorke had accomplished the exact opposite of an ambassador's function — maintenance of mutual amiability cloaking whatever displeasure might lie beneath. In this atmosphere, the deepest and most serious debate in Dutch politics and public opinion erupted, and turned against the British. At issue was a demand of the Amsterdam merchants to the States General for a vote in favor of unlimited convoy, meaning in effect resistance to search and seizure in full performance of the principle of "free ships, free goods." From the beginning, Britain, in her assumption as dominant sea power of her right to make the rules on the high seas, had bitterly rejected the idea of a *mare liberum* or "freedom of the seas," as the United States was later to call it. The Prince-Stadtholder, anxious to keep Britain's good will, which he saw as his protector against French invasion and more especially against revolutionary overthrow by the pro-French Patriot party, was strongly opposed to unlimited convoy, and the Orangist party of his supporters was no less so. The advocates of convoy, representing the shipping magnates of Amsterdam, the province that paid the bills and exercised the greatest influence in the country, were determined to protect not only their own but the country's seaborne trade, the stream of its livelihood and source of its prosperity. They foresaw its ruin in unchecked British interference. The debate split the country, although not in class division, for the middle class of farmers, artisans and shopkeepers supported the demand of the merchants, as did many of the proletariat, especially seamen, because they were dependent on seaborne trade and on import of raw materials for the manufacturers who gave them employment. Consequently, they shouted for convoy along with the rich.

The government did not want war for fear of its total interruption of trade. When, after a year's stormy debate, Amsterdam carried the vote for unlimited convoy, the States General refused to confirm the provincial vote. While the Dutch in the West Indies tried to appease the situation, all men of substance, Adams wrote, "seemed to shudder with fear," and while Yorke keeps up the commotion, "I shall certainly have no success at all in obtaining a loan." He found himself avoided "like a pestilence by every man in government."

SIX

The Dutch and the English: Another War

Soon after the old century had turned over into the 18th, the multinational war called the War of the Spanish Succession came to an end. Essentially a war to prevent France from dominating Europe by combining the thrones of Spain and France in one kingship, it flickered out at the Treaty of Utrecht in 1713 with the successful thwarting of Louis XIV's boast, *"Il n'y a plus de Pyrénées"* (There are no more Pyrenees).

For all their worldly success, the Dutch in 1780 were losing their hold through a malfunctioning system of government, conflicting domestic interests, disunited policies and obvious military weakness. Immensely competent in their formative period, brave and determined in the 16th century, enterprising, invincible and even glorious in the 17th, the Dutch had allowed the disunity of their component parts to paralyze effective policy in the

18th century. The fragmented political system could hardly have allowed anything else. The constitution was "so complicated and whimsical a thing," wrote Adams to the President of the Congress at home, and the structure of government so cumbersome and the antagonisms of the parties so various, as to make his post here "the most difficult embassy in Europe."

Every province of the Netherlands had its own stadtholder, the provincial office often being given by election to the Prince of Orange in addition to his chief position. William the Silent while Stadtholder had also held the stadtholderships of Holland, Zeeland and Utrecht. Every province also had its own Pensionary, an executive office equivalent to the Governor of an American state. Over all, a Grand Pensionary elected by his colleagues functioned as the virtual Prime Minister. The Grand Pensionary of Holland, Pieter Van Bleiswijk, though described by Adams as "a great scholar, linguist, natural philosopher, mathematician and even physician . . . with great experience in public affairs," had no force of personality animating these talents and apparently no decided political position one way or another.

Money and empire had not had charms enough to placate separatism in the Netherlands and lure the Dutch toward unity. Business interests, to be sure, had succeeded in amalgamating merchant adventurers in the great trading companies, but the management of naval affairs with the duty to oversee the maintenance of warships was divided among no less than five regional admiralties: at Rotterdam on the Meuse in South Holland, at Amsterdam, Zeeland, Friesland and the "North Quarter." Their rival interests, conditioned by geographical location, made impossible a national naval policy essential to support an adequate and healthy fleet. The five admiralties could occupy themselves in protection of coastal waters against privateers and other marauders and in the supervision of prize courts and of the rowdy element, in all the port cities, of sailing men, who reportedly numbered some 80,000. Any man who could stand the appalling physical conditions of shipboard life — with its floggings and filth and poor or inadequate nourishment, plus the storms and the crashing of shells and flying splinters from enemy fire — was likely to be a rough character and, when ashore, ready for any riot or disturbance if discontented with the division of prize money or any other cause, or just to let off steam after being confined on the ship. Though an orderly people with a reputation for propriety and probity, the Dutch, like other nations, had their roughnecks.

In contrast, the governing class, called the Regents, was exclusively patrician. The Regents were the body and soul of Dutch governorship. They filled the offices of town councilors and deputies to the provincial and national states. They held office under a system nominally elective, but no candidate could even be considered for office unless he belonged to a known and substantial family of property and recognized social position, based on fortune and connections. Regents married into each other's families, supported each other, appointed each other to the important offices of town government — burgomaster, sheriff, captains of militia, members of the town council, directors of financial corporations, including the sacred seventeen who were the East India Company's Board of Governors — and through town offices to seats as representatives in the provincial and general estates. They kept outsiders outside. The system was the same as — and in fact was derived from — the medieval system of filling the offices of local government. As it became entrenched, the whole of the Republic came to be dominated after the Abjuration of 1581 by an oligarchy of the upper middle class representing some 10,000 persons, one-eighth the

131

number of working sailors. Yet, whether sailor or Regent, every man called himself a Haarlemer or Leydener, or Amsterdammer, identifying with his city rather than with the nation — to its loss.

Complacent and conservative, the Regents shared the point of view toward the working class of any privileged class prior to the French Revolution, seeing them as the "little people" — the *popolo minuto,* as the Italians called them — and were not shy about expressing it. "While the burgher is small," said a Regent of Dordrecht, whose family had been Regents in his city for generations, "he should be kept small." It was a calm assertion of the social order established, as was firmly believed, by the Almighty.

The belief of the Regents — like that of the English governing class, who undertook the actual work of government, and unlike the French *gratin,* who did nothing for the state but fuss about protocol and precedence based on the relative antiquity of their respective titles — was that they were qualified for the task, whereas "unqualified and mean persons," in the words of Jan de Witt, called "the perfect Hollander," should have nothing to do with government or administration "which must be reserved for qualified people alone." As Grand Pensionary or Governor of the province of Holland and the most effective statesman his country had produced to date, Jan de Witt could justifiably call himself qualified, except perhaps in political tact. Too open in his contempt for the commoners, de Witt made himself hated, with the result that he and his brother Cornelis were torn to pieces by a lynch mob in 1672, when the commoners, suffering the fury of a French invasion, believed the de Witts were responsible for failing to prevent it. The murder was a strange paradox of extremism to erupt through the orderly surface of Dutch life.

The Regents of the Netherlands upholding a tradition of care for the poor, not always a feature of a comfortable ruling class, supported a system of public charity that impressed foreign visitors. In Amsterdam every house had a box hanging by a chain on which was written "Think of the Poor." Small change from every merchants' sale was deposited and the boxes kept locked until the deacons came on their rounds to retrieve the money. Twice a week they rang a bell at every house to ask what donation the resident might be expected to leave in the box. Amsterdam's almshouse for the aged and indigent was a handsome building with a charming garden, which is still selected as a tourist sight in guidebooks. Orphanages, hospitals for "lame and decrepit" soldiers, shelters for aged sailors and for care of the insane were part of the system whose acts of charity were thought by William Carr, a contemporary English visitor, to "surpass all other cities in the world."

Political voice was confined to the upper class. Because commoners without property qualification had no franchise, there could be no popular vote. Policy was decided by vote of the States General depending upon an authorizing vote in the provincial states, which were headed by burgomasters of the town councils and made up of two councilors, two burgomasters, two *schepens* or judges and the Pensionary of the province. Though an important person, the Pensionary was under the authority of the burgomasters.

The political system reached an extremity of nominal democracy. Decisions of policy by the States General had to be referred back to the provincial states for a positive or negative vote, and by them to the town councils and by them forwarded back to the States General, with the result that a decision might have to be discussed by some 2,000 people representing fifty cities. As has been said of the Polish Diet, "They created chaos and called it a constitution." The result in delay and subdivision of authority was another sacrifice of efficiency to fear of dictatorship — sometimes, in cases of crisis, with serious consequences. In a petty case the problem was epitomized when the Grand Pensionary in an interview with the French Ambassador on an urgent matter was asked for an early answer to report back to the King. He replied, in despair and almost in tears, "You know I cannot get an answer in three weeks."

Though a tight and narrow company representing only one economic and social section of the population, Dutch government was so restricted by its method of policymaking as to be as impotent as Gulliver tied down by the strings of the Lilliputians. The system, as Adams, disenchanted, soon found out when he had to work with it, was a "complicated and perplexed constitution." In the first place, where was sovereignty? For nationals no less than for foreigners it was hard to locate. Nominally it resided in the Prince-Stadtholder, but did the last word lie with him or with their High Mightinesses of the States General representing the union of the seven United Provinces? The presidency of the States General rotated weekly among the deputies, hardly an effective method of functioning, but the Dutch seemed so afraid of any ruler gaining dictatorial control that they preferred an almost ridiculous precaution to the dangers of efficiency. Americans, too, in designing their constitution dreaded any whiff of monarchy, but they managed simply to write it out of bounds rather than put the chief of their deliberative body in a condition of helpless desuetude. In general, the Americans, facing many of the same decisions of statehood as the Dutch, came to more sensible solutions, no doubt because they were fortunate in the sensible and sophisticated political thinkers to whom their constitution is owed.

The chief of state was the Stadtholder, formerly the representative or viceroy for the Emperor Charles V in his capacity as King of Spain, grandson of Ferdinand and Isabella, who had come into possession of the Low Countries or Netherlands by inheritance from Philip the Bold, Duke of Burgundy, son of the King of France, and from the Hapsburg Holy Roman Emperor Maximilian through a convoluted set of relationships and dynastic marriages which we may ignore. Possession passed, when Charles V abdicated in 1555, to his son Philip II.

In 1579, year of the Union of Utrecht, the office of Stadtholder, then held by William the Silent, was made hereditary, though not royal. At independence it was occupied by his grandson William II. A young man with the Orange family truculence, he opposed the terms of independence at the Treaty of Münster because he believed there should be no dealing with Spain but only war to the bitter end. More significantly, he married the eldest daughter of Charles I of England, starting the succession by the Oranges of marriages to princesses of England that forged the connection with the English royal family in spite of past wars and future quarrels. Their son, William III of Orange, made the most noticeable of these alliances when he married Mary, daughter of James II of England. When her father was ousted in the overthrow called the Glorious Revolution of 1688, his Dutch son-in-law was invited to succeed him. Fitting neatly into the English numerical line, William accepted the invitation and became King of England as William III, ruling jointly with his consort as William and Mary. As England's King and, in his Dutch capacity, as ally, William was the centerpiece and driving force of the European coalition to stem the advance of Louis XIV for the control of Europe. Louis, seeing him as his chief European enemy, hated him vengefully and set his mind to destroy him and regain the former French Netherlands along the frontier. In his insatiable lust for extending French territory, Louis XIV was the prime generator of the epidemic of wars that afflicted Europe during his mature reign (c. 1660–1715). His drive for supremacy, and the determination of his fellow-nations to contain him, was the source of ceaseless conflicts at every border, most famously represented by the Battle of Blenheim in 1704, and by its chief captain, the Duke of Marlborough. "But what they fought each other for, I could not well make out," says the old grandfather in answer to the child's question in Southey's poem. With a greater perspective, we can suggest the answer. What they fought for was that bodiless yet weighty matter called the balance of power — essentially, that France should not gain supremacy in Europe by absorbing the dominions of the Hapsburg or Spanish empires.

Monarch since the age of five, Louis XIV had fed so long on autocratic command that his appetite grew by what it fed on and needed to be satisfied by continual increase. The appetite for power is old and irrepressible in humankind, and in its action almost always destructive. When exercised for the seizure of territory or suppression of liberties, it cannot be said to add to the welfare or happiness or improve the quality of life of those it rules, nor bring content to the ruler. What is it good for? As an inveterate activity of our species, it is largely a waste of time. Between Genghis

Khan and Hitler, Louis XIV was its primary exponent, reflecting his era which, as Lord Acton, who had more than one thing to say about power, declared, was one of "abject idolatry of power, when laws both human and divine were made to yield to the intoxication of authority and the reign of will." As the wars spread to the world outside Europe, Macaulay finds a different candidate for blame in Frederick the Great and his endless quarrels with Maria Theresa of Austria for possession of Silesia. A place that few could identify or locate, Silesia was like a magic stone that if rubbed, would cause wars to spring up. Frederick's greed and deceit, wrote Macaulay, who teaches history through a gift for language, was "felt in lands where the name of Prussia was unknown," where "in order that he [Frederick] might rob a neighbour . . . black men fought on the coast of Coromandel [India] and red men scalped each other by the great lakes of North America."

William III died childless in 1702, in a fall when his horse stumbled over a molehill, an obstacle that seems as if it should have some philosophical significance but, as far as can be seen, does not. William was succeeded in England by his wife's sister Queen Anne, and in the Netherlands by a collateral cousin of the Nassau family designated William IV.

Not an adventurer, William IV dutifully followed the path of English marriage, taking as his wife, Anne, daughter of George II. A genuine Hanover — who were not an easygoing family — Anne or Anna was left a widow with a three-year-old son, William V, who was to be Stadtholder in the years that concern us. As Regent of the Netherlands during his minority, she is called the Governess Anna by English-speaking historians, an ill-chosen term meaning merely the female of governor.

Ruling with stern authority, the Governess Anna left as her legacy the choice as adviser for her son of yet another strong character, who was to dominate the Prince and take hold as the real governor of affairs during the period of this narrative. He was the Duke of Brunswick, Louis Ernest Wilhelm of Brunswick-Wolfenbüttel, to distinguish him from many other Brunswicks of his family. He was a brother of the more famous Karl Wilhelm, reigning Duke of the German principality adjoining Prussia, an admired warrior, considered to be the very pattern of "an enlightened despot." This ruler fell rather short of the attributes that might be expected of such a figure in the episode for which history remembers him — his proclamation of the notorious Brunswick Manifesto, which exemplifies in a single case the nature of the ruling princes of the old regime — and their fall. In time to come, in 1792, the Duke was to command the Austrian and Prussian armies in the allied campaign to crush the French Revolution. Marching on Paris, he announced as his forces approached the French frontier that the allies proposed to restore Louis XVI to the throne and that the French people who dared to oppose his armies "shall be punished" according to the most stringent laws of war, and that "their houses shall be burned. If any harm was done to the King and Queen, the allies would inflict an ever-to-be-remembered vengeance by delivering the city of Paris to military execution and complete destruction." This fire-eating pronouncement naturally convinced the French public that the King in whose behalf it was issued was a traitor to France, in league with the Prussians and Austrians. The Brunswick Manifesto, rather than accomplishing Louis XVI's rescue, paved his way to the guillotine, which could have been foreseen if Karl Wilhelm had given the matter any forethought, but thinking ahead is given to chess players, not to autocrats.

We must not allow Louis Ernest of Brunswick to suffer from folly by association with his brother, for he seems to have been a reasonable man. He was a nephew and favorite of Frederick the Great, King of Prussia, who called him "fat Louis" with reason — for the Duke was indeed obese — if not with politeness. Are Kings polite? Perhaps not at the Prussian court.

Formerly Field Marshal of the Austrian Army, Louis of Brunswick had been brought to the Netherlands by William IV of Orange, who made his acquaintance in the course of one of the European wars, and was impressed by the abilities of the large Duke. Not an Orange by blood, William IV had no great military talents but enough to recognize the ill condition of the Dutch Army. He invited the Duke home to manage the reform of the army with the promise of a salary of 60,000 guilders and retention of his title of Field Marshal and a territorial estate of his own. After declining three times, the Duke accepted and was named Commander-in-Chief. The Regent Anna also formed a high opinion of him and gave him charge of the six-year-old Prince, the future William V, whom the Duke persuaded to sign a Secret Act of Advisership conferring governing powers on a personal Cabinet consisting of Duke Louis, the Grand Pensionary, the veteran *greffier* Fagel and the aged secretary of the Cabinet, De Larrey.

"I have rarely seen," wrote the visiting English diarist, Sir William Wraxall, speaking of Brunswick, "a man of more enormous bodily dimensions . . . but this prodigious mass of flesh, which it was natural to suppose, would enervate or enfeeble the powers of his mind, seemed neither to have rendered him indolent or inactive." Attached as he was, of course, to the pro-British party of his patron, Brunswick not unnaturally received kindly notices from a British observer. "The strength of his character," continued Wraxall, "and the solidity of his talents, while they supplied in some measure the defects of the Prince of Orange, animated and impelled the vast machine that he inhabited. . . . On the parade, and in his military capacity," Wraxall added, "Brunswick displayed equal animation and professional knowledge. . . . He manifested no somnolency when in company; nor was he ever betrayed at table, into excesses injurious to his reputation." These were delicate allusions to the Prince-Stadtholder, who himself tended to fall asleep at table and in the Council chamber because of what Wraxall diagnosed as a "constitutional somnolency . . . too frequently accompanied by excesses of the table particularly of wine."

Under the governance of a Hanoverian mother and a Prussian tutor, the meager share of Orange vigor that might have slipped through collateral inheritance into William's blood did not flourish, even less so when after his marriage yet another strong-minded character entered the domestic circle. His wife was Frederika Sophia Wilhelmina, a niece of Frederick the Great. Described as "well-educated, intelligent, energetic and amiable," she was well equipped to join mother and tutor in doing the Prince's thinking for him, leaving her husband all too aware of her effect.

"He is so jealous, not of her virtue but of her sense and power," wrote Malmesbury, "that he would not even go to paradise by her influence; and she has so mean an opinion of his capacity and in general that kind of contempt a high-spirited woman feels for an inferior male being, that I see no hopes of bringing them into cohesion."

In physical appearance, with the same bulging eyes and thick lips and pudgy body, William V resembled his cousin of Hanover blood, George III of England, while he lacked George's emphatic temperament. "His understanding," reported Wraxall, "was cultivated, his conversation . . . entertaining and even instructive, abounding with historical information that displayed extensive acquaintance with polite letters."

Suffering from the same sense of inadequacy felt by many of his English contemporaries who gained important governing positions from rank, rather than from merit and experience, William felt convinced that he was unequipped for the responsibility he held, a feeling that disabled him from acting with firmness or conviction. He tried to make up for the lack by conscientious attention to duty, rising at six and often working till midnight, filling his day with court levees and military reviews interspersed with prayers and meals. But keeping busy failed to dispel his anxieties or his belief that all his military training had fitted him for no higher rank than corporal. In one hard moment he exclaimed that he wished his father had never become Stadtholder and added, in so many words, "I wish I were dead." This was the unhappy man who was Sovereign of the Netherlands.

In this situation, weak and irresolute government began at the top. The Prince's advisers provided no one of reliable strength and consistency on whom to lean. Duke Louis of Brunswick was strong but unpopular, because his efforts to stay friendly with every faction made him distrusted by all and because he was resented for his influence with the Prince. Princess Wilhelmina, who might have formed a useful partnership with him in support of the insecure sovereign, resented his sway over her husband. Influenced by the pro-French sympathies of her uncle Frederick II, she took the opposite side from Brunswick of the great divide between the pro-British and pro-French parties. Consequently, William's two closest associates could give him only divided counsel in place of firm guidance. Engelbert François Van Berckel, Pensionary of the city of Amsterdam, with its dominant influence as the major mercantile center and largest taxpayer, was too firmly attached to the commercial and therefore anti-British interests to give any but one-sided advice or to put into the balance of policy anything but the direct interests of his city. The jealous friction of geographical regions and major cities had become the curse of the Netherlands. In their old struggle against the King of Spain and the Duke of Alva, counties and duchies and bishoprics had fought each other for advantage, laying the foundations of the deep and habitual rivalries that cut rifts through the country.

Deepest and most dangerous to the state was the rift over the issue of whether rearmament should go to the army or the navy. Both were in poor, close to useless, condition and the question of which was to receive priority of the state's expenditure divided the country in bitter political dispute, between friends of England, who wanted improvement of the land forces against France, and the mercantile interests led by Amsterdam, who wanted improvement of the navy to resist British interference with their trade. The Stadtholder, being half-English himself, naturally favored the British position but in his hesitations could not give a strong lead or come to a firm decision on which military arm should have priority. With the provinces and the States General blocking each other from a deciding vote, the result was that no new funds for either arm were appropriated and neither army nor navy was strengthened.

The army's forces at this time had fallen to a worrisome level below 30,000, of which a majority were German mercenaries. Recruits were not coming in because, according to Sir Joseph Yorke, who was of course tireless in pointing out the army's deficiency, the service was too ill-paid and could not subsist at all without half the force being absent on furlough. Some deep illogic seems to lie in a war-oriented society that was so careless about paying its armed forces. Non-payment precipitated the fury of the troops, who had erupted in the terrible sack of Rome in 1527 and again, as we have seen, in the mutiny of the Spanish troops who sacked Antwerp. It was true too of the American Congress which early in the Revolution did not exert itself to find the funds to pay the farmers and citizens who enlisted from their homes to fight for the birthright of their country. If the object was worth a war, why was attention to the strength of the armed forces so lax? Why were soldiers, the instrument of every state's policy, so stingily treated as bound to be mutinous and dispirited? The reason was less in some mysterious illogic than in the simple absence of regular revenue for organized armies. Military service had once been a required feudal service owed to the state without recompense. When history moved slowly, as it did before 1900, rulers were slow in learning realities in the exercise of government, and some, like the Bourbons, never learned at all. It took a very long time before rulers came to realize that armed service would have to be paid for or that they needed to concern themselves with the wants of the lower orders from whom their armies were drawn. We have been living since under Henry Adams' law of the acceleration of changing times, which obscures for us the time lag that existed for our ancestors between the fact of change and the social and political understanding of what had happened.

The navy, so bold and hardy in the days of Tromp and de Ruyter, today lay neglected at its moorings with torn sails and rotting timber. Harbors and dockyards had silted up; even the Texel, the deepwater roadstead in the Zuyder Zee that was the gateway to Amsterdam, had lost draft for seagoing vessels. Because the wage scale for sailors had sunk too low for voluntary recruitment in competition with merchantmen in the contraband trade, enough crews could not be assembled to man the ships even had they been seaworthy. Fortification of harbors had been neglected, so that any petty pirate or English privateer could break and enter. Increasing the disrespect for the Stadtholder, the public in the ports and maritime cities was demanding that measures be taken to protect shipping from British insolence. When a plan was proposed to send a squadron of twenty ships to the Caribbean to protect Dutch Colonies of the West Indies and the shipping that provisioned them, the navy did not have 20 ships available nor the sailors to man them nor the money for competitive wages. In fact, in 1767 William V had urged the States General to implement previous resolutions for building and equipping a fleet of 25 ships, but the provinces had refused to bear the cost. Ten years later, the province of Holland, declaring that the navy was near to ruin unless something was done, proposed construction of 24 ships of the line, the largest class, at a cost of 4 million guilders. Endlessly discussed for seven years, the proposal was only adopted in

1778, when Holland threatened to disband its land forces to enable the admiralties to pay for the ships. By then the hour was already late.

Foreign visitors to the Netherlands at this time felt a noticeable decline from the extraordinary ascent of the United Provinces to major power. What was left of Holland's dynamic energy, said Sir Joseph Yorke, who, while certainly not objective, was not alone in his judgment, "was the passion of her people for money making. They were all literally merchants or money getters at present." Sir Joseph, like the English gentry as a whole, equated commerce with avarice without noticing that the same could be said of politics in England, where greed for office and its monetary potential was as intense as commerce in Holland. Continental and even American visitors to Holland, with the snobbery of people who adopt the values of those who look down on them, reflected the English scorn of Dutch commercial success and saw it as a sign of decadence. A German visitor, Johann Herder, in 1769 thought Holland "is sinking of its own weight . . . the Republic counts for less in the balance of Europe. . . . There will come a time when Holland will be nothing more than a dead warehouse which is emptying out its goods and is unable to replace them." John Adams, disgruntled by his frustration in failing to persuade the Dutch to risk investment in a loan to his country, and disenchanted after his first enthusiasm, wrote, "This country is indeed in a melancholy situation; sunk in ease, devoted to the pursuits of gain, incumbered with a complicated and perplexed constitution, divided among themselves in interest and sentiment, they seem afraid of every thing." While deteriorating in their economy and lack of national unity, as Adams now saw it, and with a deep gap between rich and poor, they remain "too complacent," with a faded pride in the "strong sense of independence and republican temper" that was once so vital a trait of the national character.

From the perspective of a century later, the 19th century Dutch historian Herman Colenbrander acknowledged the urge to make money as the national passion, but said that in the period of William V it was "no longer the necessity which in earlier days drove profit-seeking Dutchmen over the whole world. They did not have to go abroad any more to gain gold, it could be found at home in the heritage from the fathers and they wanted only to increase it by piling interest upon interest."

Even more than Dutch complacency, it was the growing competition and new enterprise of other nations in foreign trade that started the slide downhill. The British had chartered a competitive company to enter the herring fisheries of the North Sea, and were luring Dutch fishermen into their employ; the countless fishing boats of the Dutch herring fleet that had employed thousands were reduced to a scattered few. The British were also taking the trade and, in some cases, the territories of the East Indies; Horace Walpole waxed lyrical over the products from Ceylon when the British, with the aid of local Rajahs, opened trade with the Island in 1782. Ceylon "is called a terrestrial paradise," he wrote, "we expect to be up to the ears in rubies, elephants, cinnamon and pepper. It produces . . . long pepper, fine cotton, ivory, silk, tobacco, ebony, musk, crystal, saltpetre, sulphur, lead, iron, steel, copper, besides cinnamon, gold and silver, and all kinds of precious stones, except diamonds. . . . Its chief commodity is cinnamon, the best in all Asia," and, for another superlative, "the Ceylon elephant is preferred to all others, especially if spotted."

Prussia, Sweden and every nation that could command a sail scrambled for a share of the Indies trade. Sweden pre-empted the tea trade with China; the commerce of Spain and Portugal was drawn away by France, England, Sweden and the Hanseatic merchants. Markets and manufacturers once monopolized by the Dutch were cut into by foreign "enterprisers" from all sides. Industries lacking the former fresh supply of raw materials for cloth and other manufactures were losing markets and closing down. Unemployment rose, spreading from town to town and from one occupation to the next. Beggars and the homeless appeared in the streets. Formerly spotless walkways were now littered, once shining and polished windows were dust-stained, no longer reflecting the green of tall trees along the canal.

Spokesmen of liberal discontent, impatient of the conservative *status quo*, were active partisans of the American cause. Their spokesman was the radical Baron Johan Derck van der Capellen tot den Pol, representative in the States General of Zwolle, capital of the Province of Overyssel. Member of an old noble family who had absorbed in every fiber the 18th century's ideals of liberty, van der Capellen was the author of a pamphlet on the history of liberty from ancient Thebes to his own country's struggle against Spain. His critics called him "a Lafayette with an even lighter head."

Rising to his feet in Parliament in December, 1775, he caused a sensation by a speech denouncing the loan to England of the Scots Brigade, the key issue of the pro-English party, and proposing a loan to relieve the financial poverty of the American Colonies, where money for conducting war was almost as short as gunpowder. The Scots Brigade had come to Holland after independence to help against the Catholic power of Spain and had remained in Dutch service as a barrier against the French. By the terms of the Dutch Treaty of Alliance with England in 1678, it was supposed to be loaned back upon request as one of the mutual subsidies the treaty called for if either party were attacked by a third. Supposed to number 6,000, it had dwindled because of the expense to 1,800, hardly proportionate to the hubbub it was exciting.

If the troops were loaned, England offered to lend the Netherlands a Hanoverian regiment in exchange or pay the cost of equipping a Dutch regiment to fill the place of the Scots. Creating yet another divided counsel, the Duke of Brunswick as Commander-in-Chief opposed the Prince on the issue, believing that to let the brigade go would reduce the land forces still further and that the loss would probably not be made up. Political adversaries of lending the brigade suspected that Lord North, the British Prime Minister, had planned the request expecting it to be refused.

He could then use the refusal as justification for demanding from Parliament a vote for additional German mercenaries for the American war, whose use, because of the hatred they aroused in the Colonies, was strongly opposed by the Whigs of the Opposition.

Certain that discussion of the Scots Brigade would be prolonged in the United Provinces where it had become a divisive issue, the British, to make it no easier, asked for a reply in a month.

Van der Capellen, roughly trampling on the local tradition of moderate discourse, excoriated the loan of the Scots Brigade as a violation of neutrality and an act of injustice to the Americans who were fighting for a righteous cause. Partisanship over the issue was growing sharp and neutrality thin and ever harder to maintain because the principle of "free ships, free goods" offered such profitable opportunity for making money. Nevertheless, no one yet ventured to come out openly for the rebellious American cause. Van der Capellen was the first to do so, and he did not stint. He said that whatever the outcome in America, he would always regard it as a glory and honor to have upheld the cause which he regarded as that of all humankind. He scorned neutrality as being merely a position taken for the benefit of Dutch commerce and industry. It would be shameful for a people who themselves had been rebels to intervene against a brave nation which deserved the respect of all the world for defending the rights received from God, not from England. It would disgrace Holland, he cried, to send a Dutch unit to fight against them.

The furor grew when van der Capellen had his speech printed and distributed, to the outrage of the Stadtholder, who could feel strongly even if he could not make up his mind.

Whether by the influence of the Prince or the members' own unwillingness to adopt the American cause, van der Capellen was expelled from his seat in the States General, an act that, as in the similar case of John Wilkes in England, caused a profound parliamentary scandal. In the Netherlands, domestic political liberty was still on the nation's tongue, not yet in its bones.

In his outright embrace of the revolutionaries in America, van der Capellen shocked even his own province, causing him to be expelled as a deputy and even dismissed as a Regent. They were expressing their disapproval of encouraging the Americans, for in spite of the golden dreams of commerce, the Regents' dislike of the social "leveling" they sensed in the Revolution was stronger. Moreover, they feared that American independence might set an example to the Netherlands' own colonies.

The question whether to grant Britain's request for loan of the Scots Brigade added another hot coal to the ill-tempers rising between the Netherlands and Britain. The issue provoked turbulent debate in the States General, with the pro-American provinces, led by influential Holland, firmly opposed. Holland objected chiefly on the ground of the cost to the army of replacing the manpower of the brigade. Ironically, not in response to van der Capellen's passionate plea but owing to Amsterdam's adamant refusal to lay out money for the cost, the States General after a lengthy debate voted in April, 1776, to reject loan of the Scots Brigade, whatever the cost in British wrath. As an unfriendly act and considering that Britain had offered to pay the cost, the vote was ill-advised, the more so in that it was not matched by preparations to meet a predictable hostile consequence.

England did not immediately press her demand, but her impression grew that the Netherlands was not showing itself a true ally in terms of the "law of sociability." This charming concept, so characteristic of the 18th century's desire for polite manners in all forms of intercourse, was not of course enacted law but an ideal of international relations according to which a state was expected to treat an ally or friendly neighbor in a helpful and obliging manner, as for instance by not refusing transit to its nationals, by giving shelter to its ships in storms, and help for the wounded after battle, and further to offer the same facilities to either of two opponents. At a time when every state had its claws into every other with intent to "confound their politics, frustrate their knavish tricks," as the British National Anthem has it, the idea of "sociability" in international relations reminds us that this was the age of Lord Chesterfield.

British hostility had been steadily rising ever since de Graaff's salute of the rebel flag. The indignation that swelled in British hearts over the affair endowed the incident with more significance than it had. "I find," wrote Captain Colpoys of the *Seaford* to his superior, Admiral Young, "that the salutes of their [the American] armed vessels are returned at St. Croix as well as at Statia." This additional insult had occurred in Colpoys' imagination, as no such salute at St. Croix had taken place. Sir Joseph Yorke had no need to call on his imagination to keep informed on the continued Dutch smuggling of contraband. He had the most highly organized secret service in Europe, and it was supplying a stream of evidence on the shipments that were evading the

Dutch embargo, their amounts and the routes they took. Shippers were sending their cargoes via Portugal, where they would be sold and the goods transferred to American agents. The brig *Smack*, prevented from leaving Amsterdam for fear of being seized by British vessels waiting outside, was sold by an American agent in Amsterdam and presumed to have left port under new ownership, a new name, a fresh coat of paint and neutral papers. Another smuggler, the brig *Betsy* owned in Boston, was reported to have carried 200 barrels of gunpowder of 112 pounds each, 1,000 muskets and 500 pairs of pistols with other stores.

Britain's humiliating inability to suppress the rebellion, which she held against the Dutch for their steady supply of arms to the Colonies, evoked from Yorke the most self-revealing British remark of the war. Some military success was essential, he wrote in May, 1778, to Lord Suffolk, a minister in Lord North's government, "to restore the appearance which Britain had such a right to assume," assuring that her neighbors would again speak the "language of respect and friendship." Crucial for empire though it might be, Yorke voiced something deeper, the craving not merely for respect but to be acknowledged top dog as the British nation felt itself to be. Philosophers may talk all they like about why men go to war; there are many reasons, but they need seek no further than Joseph Yorke for one answer. What he said about the desire for respect exactly describes the Kaiser's Germany in 1914. Believing themselves the most industrious and civilized of contemporary peoples, chosen by Providence to occupy the supreme place in history, the Germans wanted desperately to be acknowledged as paramount by lesser nations. It galled the Kaiser that visitors always went to Paris as the goal of civilized culture and not to his capital. In that sense, war, as Joseph Yorke's words suggest, can often arise from injured ego as much as from more serious cause.

The crosscurrents of Dutch politics in the conflict between rearming the army or navy determined the positions taken toward the American Revolution. The Stadtholder, followed by his party, was of course opposed to the American rebels not merely because he was by heritage in the British camp but because his domestic opponents who sympathized with the American cause expressed revolutionary republican views threatening his status as a hereditary sovereign. This group called themselves by the French word *patriotes,* and their strength grew in proportion as the Prince's place in public respect sank. The Duke of Brunswick as a British partisan, and believed by the public to have kept the Prince ignorant of the true state of affairs, was a prime object of the *Patriotes'* dislike.

The most important influence with regard to the Americans was the mercantile interest dominated by Amsterdam, whose leaders were convinced that the great unknown continent of America, once independent and freed from the grip of British mercantalism, offered a flowing fountain of trade for the export of Haarlem cloth and Schiedam gin and the import of rice, indigo, sugar, cotton, coffee and rum, and the financing of loans to American merchants that in their hands would break British supremacy of the Atlantic. As reported by a French envoy at The Hague, the opportunities were expected to "multiply like sand" and the Dutch would not want any other nation to get ahead of them in their relationship to a new nation of such "vast possibilities."

Yet, even in Amsterdam, Adams found few men of influence who took the Colonies' battle seriously, as anything but "a desultory rage of a few enthusiasts without order, discipline, law or government." Scarcely anyone had direct knowledge of America and its growing

161

population and trade. In their golden dreams, what did the Dutch really know of America? Its immensity left a feeling of awe which bred some very odd notions fostered by pseudo-scientists and scholarly pretenders to universal knowledge, such as the omniscient Abbé Raynal in his *Philosophical and Political History of the Settlements and Trade of the Europeans in the Two Indies*. As a late creation, America was pronounced to be still incomplete and unfit for human life, much less civilization. Its natural physical conditions, which the famed naturalist Buffon, in one of the wilder leaps of European fiction, managed somehow to describe as a "niggardly sky and unprolific land," prevented healthy development of flora and fauna and even of the human race, who were believed weak in virility. Buffon, of course, never crossed the Atlantic to see America in person. According to similarly qualified scientists, fully grown adults from other climates who settled there "lost their powers," and Buffon was able to satisfy himself in another of his peculiar findings that the native Indians "have small organs of generation" and "little sexual capacity." Climate in the New World, according to a best-selling French treatise translated into Dutch in 1775, made men listless and indolent; they might become happy but never stalwart. America, affirmed this scholar, "was formed for happiness, but not for empire." If this was intended to be reassuring, it hints at an underlying fear in Europeans of some huge primitive force in the New World that could rise to overwhelm them.

Fantasies about America produced two strongly contradictory conclusions that in the end came to the same point of injecting some caution into the golden dreams. According to one school, America was too big, too divided, ever to become a single country, its communications too distended for the country ever to be united. Were it to gain independence, it would fall apart in civil war, nor could its long coastline be defended against a foe unless it acquired decisive sea power. The other school maintained that America's immensity and large resources destined her for great power that must inevitably clash with the Dutch and threaten their trade, especially in the Colonies. Expectation of lucrative commerce, pessimists warned, must be held within this framework. Both arguments, that America was too weak and contrariwise too strong, were taken up by British propagandists in the effort to dampen enthusiasm within the Amsterdam group for closer ties with the American Colonies.

Combat at sea in 1779 over the tangled issue

of neutral rights brought matters to increased tension. The reason neutrality was a subject so rife in nuisance value was because in a climate of incessant wars the belligerents were in everlasting need of supplies, for which they were dependent on neutral shipping. Neutrality law, supposedly established upon the simple principle of "free ships, free goods," had been formulated by the great Dutch jurist Hugo Grotius in 1625; essentially it provided that anything carried in neutral bottoms except actual munitions of war was "free" to be delivered to a belligerent, while anything in a belligerent ship was *ipso facto* a prize of war. Subsidiary questions of what materials were "free" and what were contraband, what were a belligerent's rights of search and seizure and a shipper's right of convoy to protect against such action, had become so overregulated by treaties and protocols as to constitute a maze from which Theseus himself could not have found his way out. The purity of Grotius' principle had been modified with disorderly effect to exempt naval "stores," meaning materials, mainly timber, for ship construction, from the category of contraband. Limiting Britain's freedom of action, the naval stores' exemption and the principle of "free ships, free goods" were hated by the British, yet had been accepted in their Treaty of Westminster with the Dutch in 1674 in order to end the expensive and endless Dutch wars.

Naval stores brought the French vigorously into the picture. While individuals in France were fired by the ideals of liberty in the revolt of the Colonies, French official policy was not concerned with liberty but with aiding the rebels as a means of avenging herself on Britain for the loss of Canada and other defeats in the Seven Years' War. To this end France needed to build up her decayed fleet, for which she counted on Baltic timber delivered in neutral Dutch bottoms. Therefore adequate Dutch convoy, which was meager because of lack of ships, was an urgent French interest. To reduce and strictly limit convoy was of equal interest to the British.

Debate in the provincial states over the need and the cost of more ships was strenuous, plunging the provinces into more than their normal antagonism to each other, with Holland and Friesland, as the most dependent on foreign commerce and ship-building, ranged against Utrecht, Overyssel and Gelderland, which wanted reinforcement of land forces. Focus of the debate was the fiercely disputed issue of "unlimited convoy," meaning escort for all merchantmen that sailed from the Netherlands with any or all goods not specifically listed as contraband. As this raised the issue of naval stores and would have protected delivery of timber to the French, the British could not allow it, while the French insisted on it. For Britian the issue was wider than just ship-building material for France. Convoy implied resistance to search, disputing England's claim to sovereignty of the seas between her coast and the continent of Europe, as laid down, to the unbounded satisfaction of the nation, by the erudite historian of law John Selden in *Mare Clausum*, his answer to Grotius. In asserting Britain's exclusive rights over the seas surrounding her islands, Selden affirmed the supremacy that Yorke believed Britain had "the right to assume." Unlimited convoy would become another test of ego as a *casus belli*. Believing that England would fight rather than give up her right of search, there were many in Holland who advised against making the test.

Crossing provincial lines, the debate drew parties and groups into a turmoil of conflicts. The Stadtholder, counting on England as his supporter against the revolutionary ideas of the *Patriotes*, knew his mind well enough in the matter to be sturdily opposed. Artisans of the middle class and proletarians, seeing unlimited convoy as a means of increasing trade and reviving manufacture, were as strongly advocates. Had the Dutch been united, they could have taken a firm stand one way or the other, but there was no person or body having the force or authority to impose a decision.

The French Ambassador, the Duc de la Vauguyon, a suave and softspoken diplomat schooled in the tactful manners of the French court, where his father had been tutor to Louis XVI, was soothingly recommending to the Dutch to follow a policy of ease and quiet without expense, saying that they had nothing to fear from France but that, for their own sake, their national dignity required a strong navy. Yorke, growing more harsh and over-bearing the more he despaired of stopping the Dutch contraband trade, resorted to dire warnings, raising the prospect of England abrogating the Treaty of Westminster, leaving all Dutch trade open to seizure.

The States General failed to see in this a sign that Britain was approaching active reprisal, perhaps because Sir Joseph, the Thunderer, was too prolific in threats, and more because they could not believe that Britain, now engaged against both France and Spain as well as in America, would be so reckless as to take on another war. Events proved otherwise. In June, 1779, Spain had just entered the war on the side of the Colonies against Britain. As the most rockbound of monarchies, she had no interest in the success of the American rebellion, rather the contrary, and made no treaty of alliance with the Americans but only with France, in furtherance of their existing alliance known as the Bourbon Family Compact. Renewal of the compact was intended to bring the partners to that long-awaited day of which so many of her enemies have dreamed, the invasion of Britain. In joining the war, Spain planned the occasion for 1779, one hundred and ninety-one years since the drowned hopes of Philip's Armada. Her more modest war aim was the recovery of Gibraltar and Minorca, lost to Britain in 1704 in the War of the Spanish Succession. With Britain now pressed by both major continental powers at once, Spain believed her moment had come.

Dutch vessels carrying supplies to France were every week being stopped at sea by the British, deepening the anxiety of Dutch naval officers about their inferiority in a possible war. Advocates of the navy had urged the addition of more ships as convoys to protect the trade, but the reluctance of the inland provinces to vote for the cost and the ensuing prolonged debate had brought no additional naval guardians. At the same time, Admiral Bylandt, a commander of convoys, reported on the lack of island defenses in the West Indies, mentioning especially St. Eustatius, which he warned must have added arms and installations to enable her to resist attack and protect her flourishing commerce. No adequate response was made to his demand. Eight ships, not 24, were put under Bylandt's command for convoy duty when the building program produced its results.

Ease and quiet for the Dutch were not to be had in the new decade. As a means of bringing pressure for additional convoy, France was threatening to cancel import privileges granted to individual cities and provinces, doing injury to the Dutch pocketbook. On second thought, recognizing that a gift is always more persuasive than a threat, France instead granted exemption from import duties to Amsterdam and Haarlem and reaped a reward in the form of Holland's vote in March, 1779, in favor of unlimited convoy. But the controversy was kept alive when the States General, anxious about the British reaction, failed to confirm the provincial vote.

Ignoring this negative, which amounted to a prohibition, a convoy that had been waiting for permission to escort merchantmen with naval stores from the Baltic set sail anyway, under Admiral Bylandt, with four men-of-war. On December 31, 1779, the last day of the year and of the troubled decade, Bylandt met, off the Isle of Wight, a British squadron of six ships commanded by Commodore Fielding, who was under orders to examine all ships, convoyed or not. When his intention was signaled, Bylandt refused to permit the search, declaring on oath that none of the merchantmen under his escort carried contraband or timber. Asserting that iron and hemp could also be considered contraband, Commodore Fielding dispatched a sloop to conduct the search. As a warning to stop, Admiral Bylandt fired two shots and was instantly attacked by a heavy broadside from Fielding's squadron. Whether fearing to be overpowered by superior strength or to risk being the cause of war, Bylandt signaled to his captains to yield and, refusing to abandon his charges, was taken with them by the enemy to a port in England. In the Netherlands, disbelief was followed by furious indignation at England as the tyrant and scourge of the seas, and talk began of maintaining neutral rights, if necessary by force of arms. Still hoping to enjoy the profits of neutrality, the Dutch did not want war, but Britain's interference with her trade and maritime rights, and apprehension that Britain meant to destroy her life as a trading nation, made her reckless. When combined with indignation in the Fielding affair, this recklessness led the States General as a whole to vote defiantly in April, 1780, for unlimited convoy.

To the British, the vote was a hostile act, as injurious as Fielding's fire was to the Dutch. Both sides now had cause for wrath, and more was to follow when Britain suffered a blow to reputation and self-esteem that heated her growing war fever. The blow came not from the United Provinces but from the rebel colonies, dealt single-handed by the most intrepid fighter to burst from American ranks.

John Paul Jones, apprenticed as a sailor from the age of thirteen, had served as midshipman and mate aboard trading ships to the West Indies. When on one voyage the captain and mate both died on board, he took over command of the ship. Commissioned as a lieutenant in the Continental Navy, which, under the difficulties of recruiting, was described by one member of Congress as a collection of "tinkers, shoe-makers and horse jockeys," he was given preliminary command of the *Alfred* and took part in the fight with the *Glasgow* on the return from the raid on New Providence in the Bahamas. Though known as contentious, with commanding ambitions and eccentricities that could be "seen in his eyes," and though under accusation of killing a mutineer on his ship off Tobago, he was advanced to Captain in the navy in 1776. Sensing an enterprising captain, the Marine

Committee let itself go in a rash of visionary schemes they planned for him to accomplish as if he were a fairy prince of the sea: to capture storeships bound to Quebec, destroy the British fishery at Newfoundland, show the flag in French islands of the St. Lawrence, release American prisoners being forced to work in the coal mines at Cape Breton and capture the British collier fleet supplying General Howe's army in New York. In the course of rather more restricted operations, he showed his mettle in the capture of eight prizes and the destruction of several British schooners and brigs of superior size.

In 1777, happy to bear the news of Burgoyne's surrender at Saratoga, Jones, in command of the 18-gun *Ranger*, sailed for France, where he expected to be given command of the strong new warship *L'Indien*, under construction in Amsterdam. Charging that this was a violation of neutrality, Britain exerted pressure through her partisans in Holland to prevent the transfer; instead, Jones was given an ancient French merchantman, which he caused to be rebuilt and altered to fighting condition and renamed the *Bonhomme Richard*, in honor of Benjamin Franklin. Before the refitting and diplomatic arrangements could be accomplished, he received orders to conduct a free-lance cruise for "distressing the Enemies of the United States," a mission perfectly suited to his temperament. He headed from France in the *Ranger* straight into enemy waters, where he sailed right around England making raids on coastal towns, firing ships in the harbors, capturing merchantmen and capping his venture by seizure of the 20-gun frigate *Drake*. When he took this prize and the others into France, he was greeted as a hero and his European reputation began to build.

Seeking greater glory, and now in command of the *Bonhomme Richard*, he learned of a British convoy bringing home a large number of merchantmen, and scouted the seas for a sight of them. He caught up with them at sunset on September 23, 1779, off Flamborough Head on the Yorkshire coast. Ahead of him he saw a huge quarry of 41 ships escorted by the powerful new British two-decker *Serapis*. Her armament was 50 guns, including twenty 18-pounders, superior to Jones's 40 guns with six 18-pounders. As the two warships approached each other, both opened fire. For the next three hours, as the scene darkened between sunset and moonlight, onlookers watched the melodrama of a battle unforgettable in naval history. When the ships closed to a distance within pistol shot, a hit by the *Serapis* exploded powder charges on the

Richard's gundeck, killing many of the gunners and putting Jones's heaviest guns out of action. Having the advantage of the wind in his sails, an unquenchable spirit and a mastery of seamanship, he furled his mainsail to slow the *Richard* and bring her across the *Serapis'* stern in position for greater broadside or raking fire. Calculating his only chance, he closed for boarding and in a smart maneuver brought his ship alongside the enemy. Calling for grappling hooks, he fastened the *Richard* onto the *Serapis* while his sharpshooters fired at every British head, knocking men off the yardarms and strewing the deck with dead. Grenades lobbed onto the *Serapis'* deck blew up a pile of powder cartridges, wrecking half her cannon. Under the darkening sky, both ships at close range poured on fire. For the onlookers, flashes of flame lit the silhouettes of the two ships locked in their death grip like two fighting elk. The *Richard*'s decks were on fire and her hull taking in water. With his ship faced with the danger of sinking, the *Richard*'s chief gunner screamed to the *Serapis*, "Quarter! quarter! for God's sake!" Jones hurled a pistol at the man, felling him. But the cry had been heard by Pearson, the *Serapis'* commander, who called, "Do you ask for quarter?" Through the clash of battle, gunshot and crackle of fire the famous reply came faintly back to him: "I have not yet begun to fight!" Making good his boast, Jones sprang to a 9-pounder whose gun crew were killed or wounded, loaded and fired it himself, aiming at the *Serapis'* mainmast, then loaded and fired again. As the mast toppled, Pearson, surrounded by dead, with rigging on fire, hauled down his red ensign in token of surrender. Escorted to *Richard's* quarterdeck, he handed over his sword to Jones just as the *Serapis'* mainmast crashed over the side and its sail, nevermore to carry the wind, collapsed in a dying billow into the sea. *Bonhomme Richard,* the shattered victor, too damaged to repair, sank the next day. On board the *Serapis* as his prize, Jones headed east for Holland and, after a ten days' crippled sail, limped into the Texel on October 3. His destination, requiring shelter in a neutral harbor for his captive ship and the provisioning and care of the wounded and guard of his prisoners, was certain to make trouble for Holland with the British, and it did, exacerbating the British resentment that already existed.

That this was the deliberate purpose of Jones in going to Holland instead of to France, as he might have done, was believed to have been ordered as part of his mission by the Committee of Secret Correspondence of the Continental Congress, the department in charge of foreign affairs, and conveyed to Jones by Charles Dumas, the Committee's semiofficial agent and general busybody. Dumas was a collaborator of Ben Franklin, who was then in Paris conducting America's relations with France and was said to have acted as intermediary. Supposedly, the maneuver to use Jones as a cat's-paw to put Holland at war with Britain was a French idea of which the British were made aware through Sir Joseph Yorke's network of channels. He had access to Dumas' correspondence with Vergennes, the French Minister for Foreign Affairs, which was intercepted and copied for him by a person especially assigned to the task and who, over time, learned the cipher. In the 18th century, embassies were penetrated without benefit of electronic devices or seducible marines. It was the general practice of nations to open and copy correspondence of a foreign minister. Jones was happy to oblige the French idea. His greatest satisfaction, he wrote to Edward Bancroft, a correspondent of the American Commissioners and in fact a secret agent in the service of British espionage who has been called the "supreme spy of his century," "is in having used his position here to strain relations between Holland and England to a point past mending. Nothing now keeps Holland neutral except the influence of the ship owners who are doing almost the entire commerce of Europe at enormous rates." The Dutch people are for us, Jones reported, and Adams relayed his words in a letter to Congress. "Every day the blessed women come to the ships in great numbers, mothers, daughters, even little girls, bringing with them for our wounded all the numberless little comforts of Dutch homes, a tribute that came from the hearts of the people, and therefore far overlaid in effect all statecraft and all diplomacy against us."

Popular songs were composed in Jones's honor, and ballads celebrating his presence in Amsterdam were sold in the streets. His presence — and even more that of the shorn *Serapis*, which had nothing left abovedeck and lay rocking meekly in the harbor in sad solitude like a lost dog — was a daily unpleasantness for the British Ambassador, who began at once to assert his usual demands for retribution and his insistence that Jones be expelled. As a subject of the King, he informed the States General, Jones could only be considered a rebel and a "pirate" and, together with his ship and crew, should be surrendered to His Majesty's government. He told the Prince that he believed Jones's entrance into the Texel was "a plan formed to embroil the States with Great Britain," an outcome he professed to welcome, for it was better, he said, to have an outright enemy than one masquerading as a neutral, although the popular enthusiasm displayed for Jones was a constant distress.

"A thought struck me yesterday," Yorke wrote to the Admiralty on October 8, 1779, that "we could arrest him . . . " when he left his ship to come into the city. Sir Joseph was not a man to worry about the propriety of an ambassador arresting the guest of a neutral country. "I despatched a friend on purpose to attempt it," he continued matter-of-factly, but found himself thwarted by the High Bailiff, who said that "without proofs and affidavits of robberies and demands of moneys all of which we had not at hand," it was not in his power, as the affair would immediately become a political one, "I was obliged to give up that scent to my great regret." There is something irresistible about the straightforward methods of this ornament of the British foreign service.

If he could not effect a physical arrest, he tried next for a court order to force Jones's eviction, but that too was refused, because of the strong sentiment of the Amsterdam and other merchants. Jones's efforts to obtain care for the wounded — including the wounded English prisoners — became highly complex, because the problem of guarding English prisoners by American soldiers on neutral Dutch soil defied a solution. Finally, Jones was allowed to land a number of wounded prisoners on the Texel island and "to guard them by our American soldiers on the fort of that island with the drawbridges hauled up or let down at our discretion." Food and water and repairs of the ship, without which she could not sail, absorbed further discussion and were finally obtained with the help of Jean de Neufville, chief of a prominent merchants' firm of Amsterdam, who was deeply engaged in another American matter of greater moment.

While Jones was waiting for a wind that would let him leave the channel and escape the British who were lying in wait outside, de Neufville was negotiating a project that would break through the morass that clogged Dutch affairs and precipitate decisive action. The year before, France had signed a treaty of amity and commerce with America to take effect when the Colonies should become independent, and Franklin, Silas Deane and Arthur Lee, the American Commissioners in Paris, had sent a copy to the Grand Pensionary, Van Bleiswijk, suggesting that Holland do the same. The matter was also submitted to the more dynamic Pensionary of the city of Amsterdam, Engelbert François Van Berckel, a lawyer of combative character. As a leader of his city and of its dreams of America as a trading partner, he was eager to conclude a business contract with the Americans before they might succumb to British peace offers and fall back under the dominion of Britain.

With the Carlisle Peace Commission presently in the Colonies making overtures to Congress, the prospect of America yielding and never becoming an independent trading partner was now feared, even by those who did not relish a victory of the Revolution. For some past indignity, Van Berckel nourished a hatred of Britain, and for personal reasons would be delighted to see the de Neufville treaty puncture their pride. Although de Neufville's proposed treaty as an alliance with England's enemies was supposed to be kept secret, the Grand Pensionary, Van Bleiswijk, quite properly consulted his sovereign, William V, who flew into a passion, declaring the treaty was equal to recognizing the Americans as an independent state. He would lay down the Stadtholdership and quit the country with his entire family, he informed the Duke of Brunswick, rather than accept anything of the kind. The Duke was able to calm him and persuade him to approve the secret discussion of the proposal. Meanwhile, Van Berckel advised the Amsterdam Council not to communicate the proposed treaty officially to the States General but to pave the way by informing the other town councils. As a result, the secret was soon known to several hundred people, and before the end of the year the Republic buzzed with rumors, and leaks appeared in the English papers. Van Berckel also authorized de Neufville to negotiate a draft treaty with the Americans intended to be kept secret until England had recognized American independence. For Yorke, the rumors were the culmination of a series of affronts extending from de Graaff's salute to the adulation of John Paul Jones, and behind it all the constant nagging inability of the British to suppress the American rebellion. And now here was talk of a major power actually proposing to treat with the rebels.

He could see no answer but war. As an extension of policy, it was not in that era fearful to contemplate, but considered feasible and possibly advantageous. If prosecuted with proper energy and a sufficiency of arms and men, it offered British planners the opportunity to regain lost, or gain new, colonies to compensate public opinion for the failure in America up to now. The disadvantages — that Britain already had difficulty in making up a sufficiency of soldiers in America and, even more, that twenty additional enemy ships of the line would be added against Britain's ships already too few for her needs — were, like most contraindications to a happy plan, thrust under a mental rug. Yorke, unworried, held a reproachful interview with the Prince of Orange, expressing his distress that William had not discussed the proposed treaty first with his English ally. On his dignity, the Prince, who did not possess the status of royalty in the Dutch Republic, a deficiency that greatly annoyed his royal kinsmen in England, replied that since it was a document of state, he was not obliged to discuss it with anyone whatsoever. Not hesitating to rebuke the sovereign, Yorke stated that a project of "three wretches," meaning the American Commissioners in Paris, rebels against their King, could not be a state secret. As no action or further information was at hand, Yorke could not press his usual hot demands for "condign punishment" of the perpetrators; for the moment the matter was not pursued.

While the secret treaty smoldered quietly like a lighted fuse, a more importunate flame burned in the open. This was an international League of Armed Neutrality designed for common resistance to British assaults at sea and personally conceived and sponsored by a newcomer on the scene, Catherine II, Empress of Russia, an adventuress in power whom Voltaire named the Semiramis of the North and the world would come to know as Catherine the Great. With a territorial appetite like that of Louis XIV, she wanted to expand her borders over Austria and Poland, from which she had already taken a piece and was to take two more in the three partitions of that country. Another of her aims was to overthrow the Ottoman regime in order to revive the Byzantine Empire under Russian patronage. Most of all she wanted a warm-water base in the Mediterranean. When Malmesbury was Ambassador in St. Petersburg before he came to The Hague, he actually succeeded in persuading his government to offer Catherine England's precious Minorca if Russia would enter an offensive and defensive alliance and would succeed in mediating a just and honorable peace among Britain, France and Spain. Although it would have given her the prize she so long coveted, Catherine resisted the temptation because she suspected a trick in which too much would be asked of her in return, or, as she put it in a phrase that became a byword in diplomacy, *"La mariée est trop belle. On veut me tromper."* (The bride is too beautiful. They want to deceive me.)

Holland was not alone in resentment of British interference with trade. "Every nation in Europe," wrote Benjamin Franklin to the Committee of Secret Correspondence, "wishes to see Britain humbled, having all in their time been offended by her insolence." Catherine wanted a league to voice this sentiment not only because joint force would obviously be stronger than single, but because she did not wish to stand out herself as too anti-British. She wanted to be accepted as mediator in what had swollen from a mere colonial to a general war: Catherine saw her mediation as enhancing her prestige, of which, like all Russian rulers, she was a little uncertain. Besides, like everyone else, she wanted a head start in American trade, which, also like everyone else, she expected to be a bountiful cascade as soon as the Americans were free of the British. She wanted, too, to increase exports to take advantage of the increased demand by the belligerents for Russian goods, mainly naval stores which were being shipped to France and Spain by the Dutch. Two fuses — armed neutrality and the still-hidden treaty of commerce — were creeping toward each other. When they met, as soon they would, their junction was to light the spark of war.

When two Russian ships were seized by Spain off Gibraltar while penetrating a declared but not substantiated Spanish blockade, the Empress determined that she was the woman to bring order out of the maritime anarchy. She proclaimed her purpose on February 29, 1780, laying down five principles of neutrality which subscribers to the League would be expected to defend. Three of these specified that naval stores were to be exempted from contraband as before; that a declared blockade of a given port or ports would only be recognized if the blockading power assigned sufficient force to make it physically effective; that neutral vessels could navigate freely from port to port along the coast of belligerent nations. The remaining two principles concerned the property of belligerents in relation to contraband. Sweden and Denmark joined Russia as adherents of the League, announcing they would use their naval forces to protect their own ships under the declared terms. In the Netherlands, which had been invited to join, the League immediately became a divisive issue, setting Amsterdam against the Orangists and every faction at odds with every other. No agreement could be reached for eight months. The known unreadiness of the Dutch Navy to face British retaliation if the Netherlands opted for armed defense of neutrality was cause enough for hesitation. Amsterdam, determined to protect her commerce, was able to extract from the

States of Holland a vote for adherence, but when at first the States General accepted it, the provinces of Zeeland, Gelderland and Utrecht protested. Under their pressure and the storms raised by Sir Joseph Yorke, who denounced the vote as a violation of the Treaty of Alliance of 1678 and went into his routine of demanding "satisfaction for the insult," the States General disavowed the vote and re-opened the debate. Sir Joseph and his government were not satisfied. Clearly the Dutch were turning more inimical in their feelings and acts. The refusal of Amsterdam to require John Paul Jones to restore his prizes and the refusal of the aids and subsidies claimed under the old treaties and the hostile vote for unlimited convoy registered just at this time in April, 1780, disqualified the Dutch, Britain said, from all former privileges under these treaties. The British government, having come to a decision, was ready for a fight. Their decision had been taken at a Cabinet meeting at which Lord North fell asleep when the problem was discussed and Lords Hillsborough and Sandwich dozed — the result, it was said, of making policy decisions after dinner. It would mean, as Malmesbury wrote to a colleague, that Britain would have to contend alone against four nations — the French, Spanish and Dutch and the American rebels, "three of which after herself were the most powerful at sea." To fight against four at once seems not the most judicious choice of contest, but taking on the Dutch seems to have been welcomed by the British as a show of bravado, in spite of, and perhaps because of, their ailing performance in America. Besides, they were angry at the Dutch, never a mood for clear thinking. The need to cut off Dutch provisioning of the French fleet was felt to be even more important than supplying the Americans. The emotional feeling against the Dutch appears in the remarks of Malmesbury, who in advance of taking over from Sir Joseph Yorke seems to have imbibed the acrimony of his predecessor. The Dutch, he wrote nastily to a fellow-ambassador while still in St. Petersburg, are "ungrateful dirty senseless boors," and "since they will be ruined, must submit to their fate."

A more material motive than anger was present in British minds. Even the British, so disdainful of commerce, had joined the commercial crowd in greedily contemplating the prospect of "a new and lucrative trade with America." Malmesbury included this candidly in his letter as one of the "contributing factors" in the decision for war on the Dutch, who would be the most serious competitor for American trade. Timing was an urgent concern. One did not know what the Dutch in their peculiar politics were going to do now about the Neutrality League, but if they were to join, armed neutrality must not be allowed to be the *casus belli*, for in that case the Dutch would have the advantage of fellow-members of the League as their allies. It became apparent to the British that if they were going to declare war, they must do so before and not after the Dutch joined the League, if that indeed was their intent.

In search of a more immediate pretext, they complained of Dutch failure to grant the aids and subsidies (among them the Scots Brigade) called for by the Treaty of Alliance of 1678. But they were afraid of taking any overt action that might precipitate the Dutch into the League. At this point a curious and welcome accident that no one could have foreseen helped them out of their dilemma. The draft treaty of amity of commerce with America, drafted by de Neufville, turned up along with correspondence connected with its origin, wet from a dunking in the sea but no less useful for all that. The American who had negotiated and drafted it with de Neufville had been William Lee, a meddlesome member of the large family of Virginia Lees. Congress had appointed him an envoy to Prussia and Austria, but he had not been accredited in Vienna or Berlin because they were not ready to place themselves in trouble with Britain by officially recognizing an American minister. Lee made his way to Holland, where he hoped to block the appointment of Silas Deane (to replace Adams) and divert the post to himself. Under the wing of the Amsterdam Pensionary Van Berckel, who was steaming with plans to promote Amsterdam's trade, Lee was soon in contact with de Neufville and working with him on the terms of a treaty of amity and commerce patterned on the model drawn up for hopeful use with future allies by Benjamin Franklin and Arthur Lee, William's brother, in 1776. When it was completed, William sent it off in triumph to friends in Congress as his ticket for the diplomatic post. He had no authority to negotiate a treaty for his country any more than did Van Berckel or de Neufville for theirs, but no one worried about that for the moment. In Philadelphia the draft was submitted to Henry Laurens, a wealthy planter of South Carolina, lately President of the Congress. He was the man who had actually been appointed to The Hague to follow Adams. As he was about to sail in August, 1780, to his post, he took the draft of the treaty with him to examine the terms. Traveling not in convoy but in a lone packet (a passenger or mail ship), his ship the *Mercury* was chased by a British cruiser, H.M.S. *Vestal*, off Newfoundland. Quickly, Laurens emptied the diplomatic papers from his trunk, stuffed them into a bag weighted with shot and threw it overboard. Unfortunately, he had not deflated the air, so the bag floated, was sighted by an alert sailor on the *Vestal* and hooked on board. Boarders from the *Vestal*, on discovering Laurens' identity as "a gentleman on his way to Holland to conclude a loan for the use of the persons calling themselves the United States of America," arrested him on September 3 and carried him off to prison in the Tower of London, where he remained until the end of the war.

Discovery of the treaty in Laurens' papers, and the correspondence associated with it, excited the British as a hostile act by the Dutch perfectly suiting their need. Here was proof, wrote Lord Stormont, now British Minister for Colonial Affairs, to Yorke, that Amsterdam was in direct contact with the Americans, conduct which he luxuriously described, as "to all intents and purposes equivalent to actual aggression." Considering that the treaty was provisional and drawn by unofficial persons with no authority to act for either Holland or America, British intensity over the document was exaggerated — deliberately.

They wanted to make a commotion that would frighten the Dutch out of entering the Neutrality League, and they carried on about the Laurens disclosure as if it were a plot to assassinate the King. If the States General were found to have had a hand in it, wrote Lord Stormont to Yorke, it could be used as a *casus belli* for a declaration of war. If the Netherlands under the influence of the French party entered the Neutrality League, the Laurens papers would "justify before the whole world any measure they [Britain] wished to take" and "give the properest direction to the war, by making it a particular quarrel between Great Britain and Holland in which no neutral power has any concern." Yorke at once took up the agreeable task of conveying the British threat to the Prince. Publication of the affair, he reported, could not "fail to occasion a wonderful alarm in the country . . . and will thoroughly cool the ardour for the Northern League." But Yorke pushed the matter rather too heavily, demanding in his most domineering manner that the draft treaty must be disavowed by the Stadtholder and that Van Berckel and his accomplices must be given exemplary punishment as "disturbers of the public peace and violators of the law of nations"; otherwise His Majesty would be obliged to take measures to uphold his dignity. Adams, not yet replaced, repeated that "the arrogant English were treating Amsterdam exactly as they had Boston." With that fatal gift for the unlearned lesson, they produced the same result — unity against the oppressor, which in America had brought the fractious colonies into their first federation. Adams reported a wide expectation of war. On Christmas Day he wrote that a "violent struggle" gripped the Republic. Anti-English songs calculated to please the taste of sailors were sung in the streets. "A woman who sung it . . . the day before yesterday sold six hundred of them in an hour and in one spot. These are symptoms of war." While debate on the Neutrality League resumed, the British issued an ultimatum claiming that the Dutch had failed to fulfill the terms of the Treaty of Alliance of 1678. On their part, the Dutch replied that since the treaty's aids had been requested for a colonial revolt and not because of attack by a third party, the treaty did not apply. They rejected the ultimatum and on November 20, 1780, reached agreement to enter the League of Neutrals. Belligerents were officially notified of that decision on December 10.

Further indignity was added by the secret treaty as the case of a friendly nation treating with rebels, and also by the flow of contraband which the British could not stop, except by a drastic measure: the seizing of St. Eustatius to stop it at the source. This measure was suggested to his government, it is said, by Sir Joseph Yorke. Admiral Rodney was selected for the mission.

A rejected ultimatum requires some action by the party that issues it. On December 20, the British, as predicted, declared war on the United Provinces. They were able to convey instructions to their commanders at sea, in particular, Admiral Sir George Rodney, who was instructed to proceed against St. Eustatius, before the Dutch could notify the island to prepare for attack. In his speech to Parliament announcing the war, Lord North listed the wrongs suffered by Britain at Dutch hands. "In open violation of treaties" they had refused assistance to Britain to which she was entitled, they had furnished France with warlike stores, they had countenanced by Amsterdam an "insult upon this country by entering into a treaty with the rebellious colonies," they had allowed John Paul Jones, a "Scotchman and a pirate [apparently equal offenses], to bring British ships into their ports and refit there," they had permitted a "rebel privateer" to be saluted at St. Eustatius after it had captured two British ships "within cannon shot of their forts." While Lord North exaggerated the crimes of the *Andrew Doria,* which had not, as we know, captured any British ships, much less two, his citing the salute of the Continental flag as one in his list of causes for war showed that de Graaff's gesture rankled deeply in the British mind, not only in having given recognition to "traitorous rebels" but in treating the Americans, whom the British regarded as in some way lower-class, as equals.

Curiously, what seemed to annoy Lord North the most was the Dutch lack of preparedness, as if it made him feel guilty in taking the offensive. In spite of their provocations, he told the House, "they had not acted with any degree of prudence, made no preparation for war, in case of being attacked; and although they must have been aware that, in direct violation of every acknowledged law of nations, their merchants had constantly supplied Britain's enemies with warlike stores and provisions, of which they had made the island of St. Eustatius the depot, yet they had not thought it necessary either to take any precautions against detection, or to guard against surprise by the British naval and military commanders in those seas, of whose vigilance and activity they could not have been ignorant." Clearly, North would have felt better if Britain had declared war on a ready-to-fire opponent.

The peripheral, almost disregarded, war that followed, called by the Dutch the Fourth English War, was in world terms a small affair with disproportionate consequences. Locally, in the continued saga following de Graaff's salute, it would bring down St. Eustatius and bring in a major actor, Admiral Sir George Brydges Rodney — a central figure of British sea power, who by an act of omission was to play a critical part in the fate of the American war.

For Holland it would lead to capture by the British of colonies, trade and ships, and to the ultimate destruction of the Prince's prestige when he was blamed for neglect of the navy, for delay in joining the Neutrality League and for everything else disastrous. As a result, the French party of the *Patriotes* secured political control, the Stadtholdership was overthrown and, through the prevailing of French influence, the United Provinces were incorporated into France by Napoleon in 1795, marking for the present the fall of the Dutch Republic after less than 150 years of its hard-won independence.

SEVEN

Enter Admiral Rodney

When Admiral Sir George Brydges Rodney was given the mission to attack St. Eustatius, he was commander of the Leeward Island station of the British fleet in the West Indies and had long been angered by St. Eustatius' daily operation as the principal source of supply to Britain's enemies. A man of unforgiving character and vigorous action, he welcomed the opportunity for punishment. His orders, received January 27, 1781, when he was stationed off Barbados, at the eastern edge of the Windwards, informed him that Britain was now at war with the United Provinces and that in view of the "many injurious proceedings of the States-General of the United Provinces and their subjects, and for procuring reparation and satisfaction by attacking and subduing such of the Dutch possessions in the West Indies as the commanders of his Majesty's land and sea forces shall be of opinion may be attempted with success," the Admiralty proposed immediate action. They recommended as "first objects of attack St. Eustatius and St. Martin's, neither of which it is supposed are capable of making any considerable resistance." Rodney was authorized to consult "on procedures" with General Vaughan, commander of land forces which had been sent out a few weeks previously in anticipation of action. Material gain, the necessary justification for all warlike enterprise of the 18th century, was not overlooked: Because great "quantities of provisions and other stores are laid up there," the Admiralty pointed out, and "may fall into our hands if we got possession speedily, the immediate attack and reduction of those islands" is recommended. Strategically, as Rodney wrote to Sandwich, First Lord of the Admiralty, on December 25, Martinique, boasting the finest harbor in the Leeward Islands, "is the island most proper to attack." British possession of that island could have made a real difference in the course of the war, but Britain's immediate object was to cut off the contraband flowing from St. Eustatius to her enemies the French, as well as to the rebels in America. Two-thirds of the provisions and naval stores sent out from Britain under convoy, Sandwich had told the Cabinet in the September just past, ended up at St. Eustatius, from which they were shipped into French naval hands at

Martinique. Well knowing this iniquitous trail, which his ships had often intercepted, and angered by the island's withholding rope for repair of his rigging on a false plea of having none in stock, Rodney had conceived a hatred for St. Eustatius, and needed no prodding. He "lost not a moment's time" in executing the order, he reported to the Admiralty. Troops were embarked, ships victualed and watered, guns and rigging inspected and readied, "the whole being kept a most profound secret" so that the blow should fall like "a clap of thunder." Late in the evening of January 30, his squadron of fifteen ships sailed on its mission, reaching the harbor of St. Eustatius on February 3.

It was one of the peculiar malfunctions of technology that shore batteries on the islands were generally of inadequate caliber and range to knock out a ship approaching with hostile intent. One is moved to wonder why, if a 10-pounder gun could be mounted on the rolling deck of a sailing vessel, the same or larger could not be mounted on land? The fact is that the blind parsimony of the defense kept the shore batteries usually too few in number to equal in firepower the heavy guns of a ship of the line. When one of these big ships engaged in an exchange with shore batteries, it was more likely to knock out the land guns than vice versa. The guns of Fort Orange, like those of other islands, can still be seen mounted in the courtyard of the fort pointing right down at the harbor. If they could not defend against a landing force, what were they for? Silent, technology has no answer.

Rodney's troops were disembarked and a summons issued to the island's Governor for "instant surrender," within an hour, "of the island of St. Eustatius and its dependencies with every thing in and belonging thereto for the use of his said Majesty. If any resistance is made you must abide by the consequences." With only one Dutch warship in port and no prepared defenses against Rodney's heavy guns and his land force of 3,000, de Graaff had no choice. After firing two rounds from the fort as a show of resistance for the honor of Admiral Bylandt, representing the Dutch Navy in the harbor, he yielded St. Eustatius. Fifty armed American merchantmen in the roadstead with no chance to prepare for battle were taken. Their papers supplied more evidence, Rodney wrote, of the importance of St. Eustatius in assistance to the rebels. "All their rigging, sails, cannon powder, ammunition and stores of all kinds were sent from this island without whose assistance American navigation could not possibly have been supported," again making his point that

St. Eustatius had been essential to the colonial rebellion. Two thousand American seamen and merchants on the island wanted to fight but, being cut off from food by the British troops, had to join in the surrender and were made prisoner. British capture and occupation were effected February 3, 1781.

"I most sincerely congratulate their Lordships," Rodney wrote in reporting the success of the enterprise to the Admiralty, "on the severe blow the Dutch West India Company and the perfidious magistrates of Amsterdam have sustained by the capture of this island." He hoped it "would never be returned to the Dutch as it has been more detrimental to England than all the forces of her enemies and alone had contributed to the continuance of the American war."

The "surprise and astonishment of the governor and inhabitants," he wrote further, "is scarce to be believed." The arrival of Count Bylandt from the Admiralty of Amsterdam two days earlier had "allayed their fears of hostilities." It might be supposed that Count Bylandt would have brought at this time a more acute warning of alarm when the prospect of war with England hung darkly over Holland. Presumably he saw no use in exciting efforts for defense when he had been given nothing to use for that purpose. In any case, the "surprise and astonishment" at a British demand for surrender was understandable, because Rodney reportedly sailed into the harbor flying the French flag, a report that lacks a verifiable eyewitness source. The deception, if true, seems a surprisingly dishonorable and unlikely procedure for an admiral of the Royal Navy, who might be expected to scorn disguise under the flag of the traditional enemy. Warriors through the ages who have talked so much about the honor and glory of combat are always quite ready to act on the dictum that all is fair in war, no matter how crooked. In fact, the use of false colors was not contrary to international law such as it existed at the time, and did not excite any umbrage. Rodney was to practice another deception when he kept the Dutch flag flying over the island for several weeks after the British occupied it, as a decoy to lead unsuspecting vessels to their capture.

Rodney descended upon Statia with devastation and confiscations that were to arouse the reproof of the Opposition at home, voiced by its supreme orator and master of outrage, Edmund Burke. To begin with, the seizing offshore of 130 merchantmen of all kinds, with their cargoes valued at £500,000, was normal enough as a prize of war. There followed the plundering of private property, in shops and houses, of naval stores and goods in the warehouses, arms and ammunition in the arsenals, crates of sugar, tobacco and rice on the beaches. The total proceeds have been valued at £3 million, excluding the captured ships. Asking for a list of merchants and their inventories, Rodney singled out the Jews, who had a small well-established community on the island, and ordered them stripped for cash or precious stones or whatever might be supposed to be secreted in their clothing. Acting out a common antipathy with unnecessary zeal, he ordered the Jews expelled on one day's notice, without notice to their families or access to their homes. With more reason, French nationals as enemy citizens were all deported to neighboring French islands. With equal zeal Rodney pursued Governor de Graaff with penalties deserved by the "first man who insulted the British flag by taking up the salute of a pirate and a rebel, and who, during his whole administration has been remarkably inimical to Great Britain and a favourer of the American rebellion. . . ." Two American ships named *de Graaff* of 26 guns and *Lady de Graaff* of 18 "prove how much the Americans thought themselves obliged to him. . . . He has made an amazing fortune and, by all accounts, much by oppression. His plantation is seized for his Majesty" and de

Graaff himself taken as an enemy prisoner to be sent with all his other household property to Great Britain. With due respect for a rich man, Rodney explained further that the Governor "will be allowed to take with him his household goods, furniture, plate, jewels, linen and all his domestic servants, and he will be conveyed to Great Britain in a good ship properly fitted for his own and his family's reception."

While loot was being counted, Rodney ordered two warships and a frigate to chase a Dutch convoy of thirty ships, "richly loaded," which had sailed from St. Eustatius 36 hours before his arrival. The convoy's Dutch commander, Admiral Krull, who resisted against hopeless odds for the honor of his flag, was killed in the fight and all his convoy taken. "Not one escaped," Rodney reported with satisfaction. Three large Dutch ships from Amsterdam and a convoy from Guadeloupe came in later and were taken, and "a squadron of five sail of the line is hourly expected." When the squadron arrived with a man-of-war, the *Mars*, of 38 guns and a crew of 300, it proved no match for Rodney's squadron. The *Mars* would "now be commissioned and manned, and in a few days she will cruise as a British ship of war." He could also report the taking of five American frigates of 14–26 guns. In the first month of the Dutch war as a whole, 200 of the Dutch merchant fleet, an objective as important as St. Eustatius, were taken by the English, paralyzing Dutch shipping in the process that accelerated the decline of the Republic. Occupied on land in collecting and disposing of the island's riches and arranging for their safe convoy to England, and in pursuing the iniquitous English merchants who had been trading with the enemy,* Rodney was not at the head of his fleet patrolling the waters to intercept possible French intervention in America. While he has borne responsibility for this fateful omission, the fault did not in fact lie with him so much as in the casual management by his government and its war ministers, who did not foresee or consider French intervention as a serious concern. At no time did they issue any orders to Rodney that a primary mission of his fleet must be at all costs to prevent French reinforcements from reaching America to aid the rebels. If he or his government had been gifted with a talent for seeing into the future, and could have anticipated the fatal effect for Britain of future French pres-

*Besides trading in their own right, many were acting as agents of merchants in England, who shipped their goods across the Channel to Holland, from where they were transshipped with Dutch cargoes to St. Eustatius and thence to America.

ence at Yorktown, orders to the Admiral might have been more definitive in the Spartan tone of "Come back with your shield or on it." Rodney was given no such urgent advice because the English never seriously considered that the Americans could win the war or that French help could or would be decisive. Ministers did not act to prevent a siege of General Cornwallis' army at Yorktown because it was a contingency they never conceived of as happening.

The objects of Rodney's sternest wrath were British merchants of both Statia and, particularly, St. Kitts who had been selling arms to the enemy for use against their own countrymen. He pounced upon their records in accountants' offices, which had not been destroyed owing to the speed and surprise of the English attack, and sent them back to England to the war ministry of Lord George Germain. Two American agents of the Continental Congress, by name Isaac Gouverneur and Samuel Curzon or Courson, who had handled the purchases were sent with the papers as prisoners, in the hope of seeing them tried as traitors. Acquainted though he was with loose practice in English office, Rodney placed too much trust in government. When he needed the evidence to defend himself in court in lawsuits brought against him accused, the documents revealing the ces and profits of the British merchants trading with the enemy, which had been deposited with William Knox, Germain's undersecretary for the Colonies, and would have been injurious to the government if made public, were found to have disappeared, proving the usefulness of the right "connections." Rodney was able to produce in court only one which showed the trade at work. Goods would be shipped by English merchants across the Channel to Holland, where they would be transshipped to St. Eustatius and sold there to American agents, for use on the firing line against English soldiers. The two American agents were in fact tried for high treason, but *in camera*, and were afterward imprisoned. When the war in America was over, they were released and one of the two died soon thereafter. Their correspondence and business documents, which had been turned over for the trial to the House of Lords and might have proved embarrassing if not incriminating to important persons, could never be found. By this time the British surrender in America was embarrassment enough, leaving no one anxious to pursue the scandal of the traitorous merchants' missing papers.

In gathering up the treasure of St. Eustatius, Rodney well knew that unlike a naval prize, which was customarily divided among admiral, captain, crew and shipowner after its value had been realized at an advertised auction of ship and cargo, the spoil of territory or treasure seized in the name of the nation belonged to the sovereign. Yet, eager to feel the clink of real money in his hands, he greedily or foolishly adopted the prize-court process, and advertised auction sales of the goods seized from the inhabitants. Because the sales allowed the goods to go below cost, the owners entered claims against Rodney for the deficits, creating the lawsuits that were to sour his victorious hour and harass his life thereafter.

For the moment all was glory. "Joy to you, my dear Sir George," wrote his wife happily, "equal to what you have given your friends at home and I may say the whole nation, on your glorious successes. . . . Every countenance is lighted up with joy, every voice rings with your praises. . . . My house has been like a fair from the moment" his express arrived, on the 13th. . . . "Every friend, every acquaintance came." At the drawing room on Thursday, "the attention and notice I received from their Majesties were sufficient to turn my poor brain. In the evening I went to Cumberland House, where the congratulations were equally warm and flattering. . . . This glorious news has been a thunderbolt to the Opposition, very few of whom appeared in the House of Commons. It is reported that you are to be made a peer."

Equal and opposite was the shock in the Netherlands at the fall of St. Eustatius. "You can have no idea," wrote John Adams, "of the gloom and terror that was spread by this event," which also distressed, as Rodney was glad to report, the French West Indian islands "beyond conception. They are greatly in want of every species of provisions and stores" and he hoped "to blockade them in such a manner as, I hope, will prevent their receiving any."

By his capture of St. Eustatius, Rodney reminded their Lordships, "the loss to Holland, France and America is greater than can be conceived. . . . The capture is immense and amounts to more than I can venture to say. All is secured for the King to be at his royal disposal." By this time, in fact, the entry of France in the American war as an ally of the Colonies supplied most of their need of arms, so that St. Eustatius' role was no longer crucial. Rodney's capture of the island came too late for any larger purpose than loot.

Not a peerage but appointment as Knight Commander of the Bath was all that was forthcoming, which, considering that George III was always complaining of passive commanders and seeking bold men of action, was rather meager. Reports of Rodney's dubious methods may have been the reason. He hopes that "if His Majesty is graciously pleased to bestow any part of it between the navy and the army, that he will dictate in what manner his gracious bounty may be bestowed, that all altercations may be prevented."

The furor aroused by Rodney's confiscation of British-owned property from the merchants found to have been trading with the enemy naturally reached the government's critics at home and brought the most forceful voice of the Opposition, Edmund Burke, to his feet in the House to demand an inquiry. In denunciation, the power and passion and overflowing torrent of Burke's rhetoric could make a man believe his own mother was an arm of Satan. His theme was "the cruelty and oppression" of Rodney's treatment of the inhabitants of St. Eustatius which could provoke, he said, reprisals by their nations while "we were engaged in a most calamitous war in which we had many enemies and no friends." Pursuing the happy notion that gentler methods toward the enemy instead of "pushing war to its extremes" would, Burke claimed, "soften resentment" and bring their minds to a "favourable inclination towards peace," while neutrals "might be brought to applaud the dignity of our sentiments as a people and assist us in the conflict. But a contrary behaviour on our part was likely to provoke them to unite against us and make the protection of human nature from plunder and robbery a common cause." For so keen a political mind and so well-informed an observer as Burke of the real behavior of states at war, this was moonshine in which it is hard to suppose that Burke believed or that it changed a single vote not already determined by party loyalty. Burke could indulge and hold the attention of the House in this kind of rhapsodizing by the force of his language and the hypnotizing magic of its flow. The terms used in declaring the Dutch war, he went on, "threatened no inhuman cruelty, no uncommon severity," but "seemed rather to portend the short variance of old allies in which all their old friendship and affection would operate rather as the softener than the inflamer of the common calamities of war. It breathed expressions of kindness and long suffering" and its menaces "seemed to be torn by constraint from a heart bleeding under the affliction of unwilling strife." Then the expedition against St. Eustatius was ordered close upon the "most melancholy and general disaster" of the recent hurricane, "which had involved all the islands in common suffering and common distress."

Here he had a point. "It might have been expected that the deadly serpents of war would for a time have been hushed into a calm in that quarter of the world . . . and would not have increased the stock of their distress. . . . Surely when human pride was levelled in the dust and we saw what worms we were beneath the hand of Omnipotence it became us to crawl from our holes with a feeling of brotherly love to each other; to abate a little of our rancour and not add the devastations of war to those of the hurricane. But it was not so with Great Britain." He followed with a sobbing passage about the "unprepared, naked and defenceless" conditions of the islands, as if this were somehow Britain's fault, adding to her guilt, and then moved to a peroration about the confiscations: "Without regard to friend or foe," to neutrals or British subjects, "the wealth of the opulent, the goods of the merchant, the utensils of the artisan, the necessaries of the poor were seized on, and a sentence of general beggary pronounced in one moment upon a whole people. A cruelty unheard of in Europe for many years . . . a most unjustifiable, outrageous and unprincipled violation of the laws of nations . . . accompanied too with cruelties almost unheard of in the history of those barbarous times . . . warehouses were locked up, and access was denied to the proprietors," depriving them of the "honest profits of their labours. . . . Was there known till that moment a more complete act of tyranny than this? . . . unparalleled in the annals of conquest, but it was surpassed by what followed." The next step "was to seize upon all their letters and their private papers," which made it impossible to apply for loans abroad . . . "merchants and inhabitants plundered and robbed of all that they possessed in the world and of all the hopes that they had of having their property restored." In his compassion for the beggared merchants, living with their silver and servants and bulging warehouses, Burke seemed unmoved by their trading with the enemy. He said not a word about this aspect or the fact that the account books had been seized for that reason. Because the affair was being used to accuse the government, he made no attempt to be objective.

When, in his long speech, Burke came to Rodney's treatment of the Jews, he showed the interest of a wide-ranging mind. Speaking of the order exiling them on one day's notice, without their property and without wives and children, he described their vulnerability through statelessness eighty years before the Jews themselves were to formulate the nature of their problem. "If Britons are injured," said Burke, "Britons have armies and laws to fly to for protection and justice. But the Jews have no such power and no such friend to depend on. Humanity then must become their protector and ally." Burke perceived the problem, if not the solution in statehood. That had to wait for the next century, for Burke was not concerned with the Jewish problem but with the wrongdoing of his own government embodied by Rodney. His motion precipitated a vigorous debate about whether there was or was not a recognized law of nations.

Lord George Germain spoke as Rodney's principal defender, saying that Burke showed himself a "perfect stranger" to the conduct of war, as there was scarcely an island captured or a territory seized that had not suffered the same circumstances as the "unavoidable and common consequences of capture" which, however "humanity might recoil at them," could not be prevented; that the Dutch had made the island a very depot for the use of Britain's enemies; "that without regular supplies from this island the French could not have carried on the war," no more so the Americans; that when Rodney, in "great distress for rigging and stores" after the storms of October, had applied to purchase rope at St. Eustatius, he had been refused on the pretext that they had very little left when in fact they had several thousand tons in their store — enough to supply all the shipping that could have needed any for years to come; that as regards the confiscations, private property had been sealed and marked to show ownership to wait for disposition by the courts; that, in short, he "found nothing to blame in the conduct of the commanders."

The debate swelled into the open in heated prosecution and defense. Charles James Fox, who had a lashing tongue for invective, began. With an elaborate bow to the persons and character of Sir George Rodney and General Vaughan, for whom he was sure the honorable gentleman who moved the inquiry (Mr. Burke) professed and "felt as sincere a regard as any men upon earth could possibly do," he stated that their personal responsibility was not at issue, "but to pronounce on the great national question" — the reputation of Britain: "Would the nations of Europe wait for the slow decision of the Admiralty courts before they pronounced judgment on the case and proceeded to retaliate . . . ? without taking the trouble to inquire . . . whether it was the lust of plunder or the profligate cruelty of an insatiate military or the barbarous system of a headlong government, they would instantly and justly pronounce it to be a violation of all the laws of war on the part of Great Britain and would hasten either to punish us for the horrid renewal of these savage practises which once buried England in ashes or remain with their arms across suffering us to be extirpated by those foes which our madness or impolicy had joined against us." For this reason, Parliament must come to an immediate resolution "declaring their surprise and horror at such proceedings and condemning them in the most pointed and emphatical terms. . . ." He was glad to hear that the noble lord [Germain] saw nothing to condemn in the matter, for "now it was known and would be proclaimed all over Europe that ministers and not our commanders were the plunderers of St. Eustatius and the violators of the rights of war" and the army and navy [were] thus "rescued from the ignominious aspersion and the character of Sir George Rodney," his colleague as fellow-member for Westminster, "was rescued from the obloquy which even great and good men must have otherwise thrown upon them."

With heavy sarcasm, Fox declared he was "happy in the generous acquittal which the noble lord had given of the navy and army. The military of this country and particularly the navy was dear to him and their fame ought to be held sacred to every British heart. It was from that virtuous body of men that the empire had derived all its respect and strength and from which it must continue to receive its security and its fame. If they by some hasty act of rapaciousness or of avarice should blacken the purity of their character and stain their former deeds, Great Britain would sink to a state from which neither their future repentance nor their gallantry could be able to raise her, a state of ignominy more dreadful than disaster since enterprise might retrieve disadvantage but not restore reputation so destroyed." Fox's verbal vision of reprisals and contempt of nations flowed on with its wonderful command of words matched only by the exaggeration of its sentiments, which, one would think, would have been more likely to repel his listeners than win them. Following Fox, the Lord Advocate of Scotland entered into what the rapporteur described as a serious "defence of the proceedings at St. Eustatius," which in his mind were "justifiable on the ground of necessity, policy, and by the laws of nations," and that it was "good policy in the commanders to destroy that magazine from which the enemy were supplied with arms against us, it was in fact their duty . . . that as to the laws of war, it was a principle on which Grotius, Puffendorf, Vattel and every writer agreed, that it was just to destroy not only the weapons but also the materiels of war."

Six more speakers carried the debate to late hours, until it was concluded by Burke with more of his magniloquent rhapsodizing. Upon the vote being taken, all the words might as well have gone unspoken. Burke's motion for an inquiry was defeated by a safe government majority of 160–86. When the party system regulates, argument addresses the deaf.

Rodney's savage feelings toward the English merchants' greed and treason were genuine and profound, as would be those of any man who sees fellow-combatants facing bullets supplied by their own countrymen. He intended to remain on St. Eustatius, he wrote to the Governor of Barbados on February 27, three weeks after taking the island, until the iniquitous "English merchants, base enough from lucrative motives to support the enemies of Great Britain, will for their treason justly merit their own ruin . . . till all the stores are embarked and till the *Lower Town*, that nest of vipers, be destroyed, and lumber sent for the use of your unfortunate island and St. Lucie." He was not going to leave until this "iniquitous island may be no longer the mart for clandestine commerce."

While it is easy to say, and has frequently been said, that Rodney, mesmerized by the

217

riches lying at hand on St. Eustatius, stayed too long on the island in his desire to gather them up, outrage and desire to punish the traitors were clearly as strong additional motives. "The Chief Judge of St. Kitts, Mr. Georges, is returning to expose the villainy of the English merchants who resided in this island of thieves," he noted. "They deserve scourging and they shall be scourged," Rodney wrote with passion to Lord George Germain, and that intention remained his abiding aim. The judge from St. Kitts "takes all their books and documents," which Rodney had ordered to be seized and in which "all their base designs are brought to light. Fifty-seven English merchants of St. Kitts and Antigua were equally guilty." To a commissioner of the government he writes that he had had "daily experience" of the "iniquitous practises and the treasonable correspondence" of the British merchants in this and neighboring islands by intercepting hundreds of letters, and he is "fully convinced that had it not been for their assistance the American war must have been long since finished. . . ." They made themselves Dutch burghers who had once been Englishmen — "Providence has ordained this just punishment." Here the Admiral was succumbing to the luxurious temptation of equating Providence with himself.

The plunder of the island, packed in 34 merchant vessels, was sent home at the end of March and the Admiralty informed that a "very rich convoy" was sailing for England escorted by four ships of war: the *Vengeance*, of 74 guns, the former Dutch *Mars*, of 62 guns (renamed the *Prince Edward*), and two others, of 38 and 32 guns, all under the command of Commodore, later Admiral, Hotham, who "has my orders to be extremely attentive to their preservation." Meanwhile "the enemy's four line-of-battleships and four large frigates which still continue at Guadeloupe and Martinique are well watched. Every trick that can be devised has been attempted to induce General Vaughan and myself to leave this island in hopes of retaking it by a *coup de main* and thereby recover the stores. . . ." The treasonable merchants "will make no scruple to propagate every falsehood their debased minds can invent. . . ."

Despite all precautions, the precious convoy was lost. Having received correct intelligence of its departure and what it contained, the French had sent one of their leading admirals, La Motte Piquet, with a squadron of six major ships of the line, including one of 110 guns and two of 74, plus additional frigates to watch for it. They sighted it May 2, off the Scilly Isles, and gave hot pursuit.

Admiral Hotham signaled to his convoy to disperse and save themselves, but the faster French warships gained on the merchantmen and captured twenty-two of them, the larger part. Outnumbered by and inferior to the French, Hotham could not or did not defend his charge to the bitter end; except for a few ships that escaped to Ireland, the rich plunder, valued at £5 million, went to the French. As one of the captains who had served under Rodney in the mismanaged fight of April 17 that so enraged the Admiral, and who, with no love lost between them, had later asked without success to be transferred to another command, Hotham felt no devotion to his commanding officer. While Rodney would certainly have been aware of ill feeling, he entrusted Hotham with the convoy because his ship was the *Vengeance*, strongest and largest of Rodney's squadron.

At the same time, the Admiralty, having in its turn learned that La Motte Piquet had left the French naval base at Brest and was at sea, had sent out ships to intercept him or, alternatively, to detach frigates to meet Hotham and instruct him to return via the North of Scotland and Ireland, the old escape route of the Spanish Armada. But the searchers, after cruising for two weeks, failed to find the Eustatius convoy and send it out of danger. They put back to port in England without bringing home the expected treasure, to the sharp disappointment of ministers who would have welcomed a great prize to show off as a gain for the administration. Instead, Lord Sandwich in a letter to the King had to confess a sorry naval failure in what he calls "this unpleasant affair."

For Rodney, who after dividing with General Vaughan would have stood to gain a one-sixteenth share, or an estimated £150,000 pounds, the disappointment was considerably deeper. Lost too was the more important prize of St. Eustatius itself. It was recaptured by the French in November, 1781, a month after the British loss of America at Yorktown. Rodney and General Vaughan had determined to make its defenses impregnable "to secure this important conquest to Great Britain that she might avail herself of all its riches as atonement for the injuries it has done her." With some savagery, he writes that he and Vaughan will leave the island "instead of the greatest emporium upon earth, a mere desert and only known by report, yet, this rock . . . has done England more harm than all the arms of her most potent enemies and alone supported the infamous American rebellion. . . ." Regarding his own expectations, he writes, "If my great convoy of prizes arrive safely in England, I shall be happy as, exclusive of satisfying all debts, something will be left for my dear children." Concern and affection for his two daughters and his sons repeats itself in his letters as one of the more sympathetic aspects of his character. "My chief anxiety," he wrote to his wife after his ill-fated convoy had sailed for home, "is that neither yourself nor my dear girls shall ever again be necessitous nor be under obligations to others." The humiliations of penury, however much of his own making, sound their painful note in this letter.

Believing he had left the captured island a Gibraltar of the West Indies, with land forces on guard and repaired fortifications, Rodney sailed to Antigua and then to Barbados. When St. Eustatius was retaken by the French six months later, they found the place in ashes, empty of population. Though rebuilt and repopulated during the French occupation, it never regained its former extravagant prosperity.

The uneven career that brought Rodney to St. Eustatius and determined what he did there began with his entry into the Royal Navy at the age of twelve. He was the son of an old county family settled since the 13th century in Somersetshire, where they held the estate of Stoke Rodney. In the twenty generations leading down to the Admiral, his ancestors served in various military and diplomatic positions of no outstanding distinction, but fulfilling the duty expected of the landed gentry of England and establishing a record, as was said of them, of a family of greater antiquity than fame. In the process, they acquired a ducal connection in the person of James Brydges, first Duke of Chandos, who came into possession of Stoke Rodney through the marriage into the Brydges family of a daughter and heiress of an early Rodney. Chandos was a familiar at the court of George I and together with the King stood as joint godfathers to the Rodneys' son, who was endowed with both their names, George and Brydges. Chandos' grandson, who succeeded as third Duke in the period of Rodney's maturity, remained a loyal adherent of the Hanovers and a supporter of George III and of his American policy until about 1780, when the policy's futility became obvious enough to move the Duke gradually into opposition. He was evidently not a man impervious to change but rather one able to allow realities to penetrate. Though not belonging to one of the great Whig ruling families, Rodney could qualify as a young gentleman of "excellent connections." Connections were the key to "place" in

18th century society, meaning a remunerative post in the official world, and "place" was of the essence, especially for a younger son, which Rodney remained until his older brother died, when the younger was about twenty.

Personal characteristics were both an aid and a drawback to his career. Slight and elegant in figure, he was more than handsome; if the portrait by Joshua Reynolds, painted at forty-two when Rodney was already a widower and a father of three, does not lie, he was frankly beautiful. With a strong sensual mouth, a broad brow and impressively large dark eyes, the face was youthful and seductive and would surely have promoted his amorous pursuits, of which the busy diarist, Sir William Wraxall, makes a point. "Two passions both highly injurious to his repose, women and play [gambling] carried him into many excesses," Wraxall writes of his friend. According to Horace Walpole, the emperor of gossip, Rodney won the favor of the Princess Amelia, daughter of George III, and left of their liaison a "token." The token grew to be a pretty young lady of small stature known in her circle as "little Miss Ashe." Indefatigable investigators who edit 18th century letters and journals maintain, based on calculation of relative ages, that Rodney was too young to have been responsible for this royal fragment. Though Rodney was loquacious, Wraxall says, and particularly given to "making himself frequently the theme of his own discourse" and talking "much and freely upon every subject concealing nothing regardless of who was present," he himself left no mention, as far as is recorded, of the Princess Amelia or the "token." About his gambling, however, there is no question. He was never long absent from the gaming table at White's, where the addiction ruled, and if his debts were not as spectacular as those of the rising political star Charles James Fox, it was only because Rodney did not have a rich father to pay them. The debts remained, and as many were owed to men in office or with political influence, they were to become stumbling blocks in his professional career, besides keeping him, combined with a spendthrift character, under tight pecuniary pressure all his life. "His person was more elegant," Wraxall adds, "than seemed to become his rough profession. There was even something that approached to delicacy and effeminacy in his figure: but no man manifested a more temperate and steady courage in action." Equally "fearless" in talk, "he dealt his censures as well as his praises ... which necessarily procured him many enemies particularly in his own profession."

The year of the Reynolds portrait was 1761, when Reynolds had burst, like Byron later, into glittering overnight celebrity. Everyone of fame and fashion, equipped with 25 guineas in hand, formed a line to his door. All of London, social, political and important, met on Reynolds' canvases, from Admiral Anson, circumnavigator of the globe who had captured the richest Spanish treasure galleon and was afterward First Lord of the Admiralty, to sleepy Lord North, soon to endure his long confinement as reluctant Prime Minister, to exquisite duchesses in the gauzy gowns that exercised the brushes of Reynolds' drapery painters, to the uncouth figure and sparkling talker Dr. Samuel Johnson. The full-length portrait of a hero of naval and political battle, Admiral Keppel, attracted the most attention. Standing upright in a statuary pose before a background of storm-filled sky and heaving waves, he dominated the group, but of the male portraits there was no close-up to equal the stunning head of George Rodney.

The possessor of these handsome features has been described by one historian as "the most enterprising and irascible, able and bombastic, intolerant, intolerable and successful naval officer between Drake and Nelson." This is an exciting introduction but it is, one is obliged to say, a case of historian's hype. Irascible yes, but so was every naval commander of the time, owing no doubt to the continual test of trying to navigate as a fighting instrument a cumbersome vehicle whose motor power was the inconstant wind not subject to human control, and whose action depended on instant and expert response by a rough crew to orders governing the delicate adjustment of sails through an infinity of ropes hardly identifiable one from another. That a commander who had to bring home success in battle under these conditions should be irascible is not to be wondered at. Or it may be that there is something about commanding a ship, sail or steam — a mysterious fungus on shipboard, as it were — that brings out ill-temper. Of a great wartime admiral of another age it has been said, "He was vindictive, irascible, over-bearing, hated and feared." Not a man of the 18th century, this was Ernest J. King, Commander-in-Chief of American naval forces in World War II. Irritability was an occupational disease. "Intolerant and intolerable" belong in the same category, made no lighter by the foul physical conditions of life on a sailing vessel, with its reek of rotten meat and putrefied cheese, damp clothes, bilge water, open vats of urine in which the men were instructed to relieve themselves, on the theory that it would

227

be used to retard fire, plus the smell of five or six hundred unwashed bodies packed for sleep in their hammocks below deck or rolling in rum-soaked drunkenness or in fornication with wives and doxies who were carried on board.

The stench of a ship wafted by an inshore breeze could often tell of its approach before it reached port. Reports of the bad tempers and quarrels of captains and admirals — with the exception of Nelson — are repetitious. John Paul Jones, apart from killing a mutineer who may have deserved death, carried on a furious vendetta with a captain of one of his ships — Landais of the *Alliance* — whom he accused of betrayal in combat. "His fault finding, nagging and perfectionism coupled with his unpredictable temper made him disliked by many shipmates" is the verdict of his biographer, Admiral Samuel Eliot Morison. Admiral Hyde Parker, commander at Barbados who served on several occasions with Rodney, had a "bitter choleric temper" and was called "Old Vinegar" on account of his harsh manner and speech. Richard Lestock, whose recriminations against his commanding officer, Admiral Mathews, became public after the Battle of Toulon had historic result, was "on malevolent terms" with Mathews from the start. Mathews, who had served at the court of Sardinia, was nicknamed *Il Furibondo* by the Italians because of his violent temper. Among the French it was the same. Count d'Estaing, active against the British in American waters and against Rodney in the West Indies, is called "brusque and autocratic" and not liked by officers and men, while Admiral de Grasse, the most important of all to the history of America, summoned his captains on deck to administer the "sharpest reproaches" to express his dissatisfaction for their failure to chase and engage the enemy in an encounter off Martinique. He would rather lay down his command, he said, unless they showed better conduct in obeying signals and fulfilling their duties. Rodney's own notorious outbreak of anger at the errors and failure by his captains in the blundered battle off Martinique in 1780 — expressed in his public statement to the Admiralty, the "British flag was not properly supported" — will appear in due time. If that was irascible, it was clearly not a matter of personal temperament. "There is no set of men who understand these matters so ill as sea officers," lamented Lord Sandwich, suffering from his experience as First Lord of the Admiralty. "For it scarcely ever happens that after an action they do not call the whole world to hear what complaints they have to each other." Irascibility in the navy was a recognized phenomenon, as attested in the journal of a French officer who, in describing a case of naval noncooperation, refers casually to "the charming maritime ill-temper."

More damaging than irascibility to effective management of a warship was the raging political partisanship that divided officers, and obstructed the collective will to win. The furious quarrel of Whig Admiral Keppel and Tory Admiral Palliser, over claims by Palliser of failure in battle by Keppel, carried over into an explosive court-martial that tore the body politic apart, brought angry pro-Keppel mobs in assault on the Admiralty and left permanent animosities in the navy so deep that officers believed each other capable (and perhaps they were) of deliberate errors or failures in combat on purpose to injure a fellow-admiral of the opposite party. These animosities lasted throughout the period of the American war when the administration's belief in crushing the rebellion by force was the object of the Opposition's deepest scorn.

Rodney entered the navy at twelve, taken from school at Harrow, where he had his only allotment of formal education. Though he became an ornament of the sophisticated world, known for pleasing conversation, he must have learned the manner spontaneously or from association with other sophisticates. The early removal from school of future officers of Britain's sea power, leaving them unacquainted with the subject matter and ideas of the distant and recent past, may account for the incapacity of military thinking in a world that devoted itself to military action. With little thought of strategy, no study or theory of war or of planned objective, war's "glorious art" may have been glorious but, with individual exceptions, it was more or less mindless. Native intelligence in the Royal Navy was no doubt as good as that of any other nation, but for achieving desired ends in an exacting profession it was not always enough. Admiral Alfred Thayer Mahan, father and pontiff of the theory of naval warfare, was to write that England's failure to obtain the expected results from her naval superiority taught a lesson of the necessity of having minds of officers "prepared and stocked by a study of the conditions of war in their own time." But what stock of knowledge has an adolescent officer acquired by the time he stops learning at the age of twelve?

Long before Mahan, in the reign of Queen Elizabeth, the great voyager Hakluyt spoke of the need for education of sailors. In his classic work *The Principal Navigations, Voyages, Traffics, and Discoveries of the English Nation,* he pointed out in his dedication to the Lord High Admiral of England that the late Emperor Charles V with "great foresight established a Pilot Major for the examination of such as sought to take charge of ships" and also "founded a notable lecture of the Art of Navigation which is read to this day ... at Seville." Hakluyt was thinking of seamanship, not strategy, much less the study of history and politics. His idea of education for seafarers was not thought to apply to the quarterdeck except in France, in its academies for training officers. Whether it would have made a difference to the inept British management of the war of the American Revolution no one can assert. It was America's good fortune at this moment in her history to produce all at once, as everyone knows, a group of exceptionally capable and politically gifted men, while it has been less remarked that it was Britain's ill fortune at the same time to have just the opposite. George III, Sandwich, Germain and the successive Commanders-in-Chief in the field, Sir William Howe and Sir Henry Clinton, both men without energy, were not the best Britain has produced in a crisis to conduct and win a war.

Through the influence of his patrons, Rodney entered the navy as a "King's Letter Boy," meaning with a letter of introduction from the King, which opened a place initially as no more than a captain's servant, even lower than a midshipman, but highly desirable because it guaranteed officer's status on the quarterdeck when the candidate had climbed enough rungs on the ladder of advancement. It was peacetime in England in 1730, the year of Rodney's entry, when England and France, unable to afford the further expenses of war, were each endeavoring to stay quiet under the careful guidance of their respective ministers, Sir Robert Walpole and Cardinal Fleury, and this unaggressive condition offered an ambitious young apprentice no chance of action to start him on his climb. Peace, however, was not likely to, and did not, last long. War with Spain over control of the right to trade in Spain's West Indies broke out in 1739, precipitated by public excitement at the grievance of a merchant captain named Jenkins, who had suffered the severance of his ear in a clash with a Spanish revenue officer. This War of Jenkins' Ear, engaging France as an ally of Spain in the Bourbon Family Compact, began the period of colonial and continental conflict between France and England that was to last intermittently through Rodney's lifetime, creating the opportunities for combat that made his career.

The war had old roots. By virtue of Columbus' discoveries claimed in the name of Spain, followed by a Spanish Pope's (Alexander VI) division, in 1493, of the New World between Spain and Portugal, with the larger part to Spain, the stage was set for Europe's overseas conflicts. Needless to say, Spain after her conquest of Portugal in 1580 absorbed the whole, thus acquiring exclusive control of trade and empire from Brazil to Cuba. English smuggling into this region with the aim of breaking into the trade of the Spanish-American colonies provoked the insult to Jenkins' anatomy.

Prize money to be divided among officers and crew was a motor power for navies as important as wind, and simple booty rather than strategic purpose was a more immediate object of the sea battles in the War of Jenkins' Ear, as it was in most combats of the time. Without a clearly conceived strategic aim for dominance of the sea-lanes or land base for control of the Colonies, battle was engaged mainly for the money it would pay to the captains, who took their share in prize money, and to the state, which took a voracious bite out of the opponent's commerce. In the spectacular convoy battle off Cape Finisterre, Spain, in May, 1747, against the French East India trade, the English under Admiral Anson, annihilating the French escort, took

French warships and, out of the convoy's 40 ships, five armed East Indiamen and six or seven other merchantmen. The remainder escaped to Canada. Even so, the English haul included about £300,000 in treasure and stores, in addition to the captured ships. In a heroic defense by the French, the small 40-gun *Gloire* fought on until nightfall against three English ships of the line, until its captain was decapitated by a cannonball, 75 of the crew lay dead on the deck, masts and sails were in ruins, ammunition was reduced to the last cartridge and the hold was filling with water before the flag was struck in surrender. The obdurate refusal to yield may have owed something to the presence of an ensign of the *Gloire*, the twenty-five-year-old François de Grasse, a provincial nobleman known ever since he was a cadet for his energy and force. When the *Gloire* was captured, he was taken prisoner and held at Winchester in England for three months. Money and goods were loaded into twenty wagons at Portsmouth to be paraded through the streets to the cheers of the populace before the proceeds were deposited in the Bank of England. In a second encounter in June off Brest (often confused with Cape Finisterre because it lies in the department of the French Finistère), against a large French convoy bringing home the rich

West Indian trade, an English squadron, including Rodney in the *Eagle*, captured 48 prizes loaded with valuable cargo. Although more than that number of French merchantmen escaped, Rodney and his fellow commanders gained a wealth of prize money. In the Seven Years' War, 1756–63, the central conflict of the era, from which the English emerged sovereign of the seas, they took in the single year 1755, before even a formal declaration of war, 300 French merchantmen for an estimated total of $6 million.

Individual admirals and captains made their fortunes from their share of prize money, which was divided according to prize law of an extreme complexity that testified to its importance in the system. Ships' captains of a victorious squadron divided $3/8$ of the total value of captured ships and cargoes, depending on whether the squadron was under the orders of an admiral, with $1/8$ reserved for a captain who was a flag officer if one was on board. Lieutenants, captains of marines, warrant officers, chaplains and lesser officers divided $1/8$. Another $1/8$ went to midshipmen and sailmakers, and the remaining $2/8$, or 25 percent, to seamen, cooks and stewards. Prize law allowed an intricate adjustment based on size and armament to equalize the share of larger and smaller ships, on the theory that the stronger ships did most of the shooting and had more numerous crews. The adjusted rate was worked out by applying to each ship a factor calculated by multiplying the number of the crew by the sum of the caliber of the ship's cannon. Clearly, prize money received more serious attention than scurvy or signals.

As Captain of the *Eagle* in the battle off Brest, Rodney's share was £8,165, which enabled him to buy a country home and laid the basis of his fortune, which he was to gamble away.

From the capture of Havana in 1761, the distribution of prizes amounted to £750,000, of which Admiral Keppel, who was second in command, received £25,000 and his chief, Admiral Pocock, £122,000. Admiral Anson, the leading naval officer of the day, was believed to have made £500,000 in the course of his operations. The lure of such rewards drew young men into the navy despite its dangers and discomforts.

In the War of the Spanish Succession, ending in 1713, England had gained dominance in the Mediterranean by annexation of Gibraltar and Minorca. Colonial rivalry in America added to, even superseded, ancient conflicts in Europe. France, eager for colonial territory, had advanced overland through the American north woods down from Canada and Nova Scotia and down the Ohio to establish settlements that pushed against the English-settled colonies in the effort to block their westward movements. French colonies in India were also conflicting with the English. But France, sucked dry by the land wars of Louis XIV, had let her navy sink into shabby neglect that could not sustain a serious bid for the sea power on which trade and empire depended.

For the next fifty years, 1739–89, from the War of Jenkins' Ear to the French Revolution, war in the 18th century continued in these terms through various phases and under various names, until the issues were shaken up and rearranged by the Revolution and fighting recommenced under Napoleon. As between France and England, it was basically a maritime war for overseas commerce and colonies in America and India. This was not fundamentally changed by the intrusion of the American Revolution, though it altered war aims politically.

A strange development of the three major maritime powers, Holland, England and France, was that each should have allowed its vehicle of sea power to decay through inadequate funding and indifference and the corruption that drained available funds into the pockets of bureaucrats and dockyard managers. Moreover, the Royal Navy of Britain was halved in effective power by having two functions: offense and defense. Honored by its countrymen as the "wooden walls of England," it was also the only conveyance by which Britain's military forces could be deployed against an opponent, whether it be colonial rebels or France. As an island, Britain could use land forces against a foreign enemy only to the degree that sea power allowed. Instead of being polished and fed and kept at the peak of perfection, for instant use upon call, the navy, which had enjoyed appropriations of more than £7 million in 1762, was cut in 1766, after the close of the Seven Years' War, to £2.8 million, less than half, and cut by half again to a stingy £1.5 million in 1769. Sandwich, though he was not yet First Lord, was held to blame because he was a well-known figure detested by the public for his betrayal of the popular hero John Wilkes.

Sandwich at this time held office as Secretary of State for the so-called Northern Department, actually the department for foreign affairs. Although associated with the Admiralty because of his previous service and supposedly deeply devoted to the navy, he did not exert himself, as Choiseul was doing in France, to rebuild it as a proud and eminent fighting fleet.

Besides being splintered by politics and faction, the navy was administered not by a professional in the service, as was the army, but by a figure of political power chosen from the group known at this time as the King's Friends. For eleven years, from 1771 to 1782, the First Lord of the Admiralty was the fourth Earl of Sandwich, called by some the most unpopular man in England, known for the venality of his administration and for personal sins, ranging from laziness to debauchery. A peer who inherited his earldom from a grandfather at the age of eleven, he thereafter followed a peer's normal progress from Eton and Cambridge and the Grand Tour through a succession of government offices assigned for no particular merit other than the right "connections" and an intense loyalty to the King and support of a hard policy toward the Americans. This brought him to a place on the Admiralty Board at the age of twenty-six from which he advanced at the age of thirty to First Lord for a short term in 1748–51, and again for the longer term in the '70s and early '80s. His reputation was gained from a scandal of his own making, when he read to the House of Lords in 1768 an obscene verse entitled *Essay on Woman*, by his friend the notorious John Wilkes, who had already been arrested — illegally, as his partisans charged

— for lèse majesté in a libelous critique on the King published in No. 45 of Wilkes's journal the *North Briton*. On the obscenity charge he was now expelled as M.P. from the House and declared an outlaw, while his crony Sandwich was ever after known as Jemmy Twitcher, after the treacherous character in *The Beggar's Opera* who turns in his friend. Naval appointments under his rule were determined by patronage, which answered to the seventeen votes that Sandwich and his group controlled in the House of Commons, the source of his power. As First Lord, he presided over the Lords Commissioners of the Admiralty, who were seagoing professionals as well as politicians with seats in the House of Commons.

Spain, nearly two hundred years since the lost Armada of Philip II, was still depressed, with no appetite for maritime battle, and the French Navy was at its lowest point of neglect. It was being renovated by the strenuous energies of Choiseul, chief minister of Louis XV and the most able public official to serve France in the 18th century. He established naval academies for the design and construction of ships of war and for the training of officers, ordered an *inscription maritime* for the regular draft of seamen to fill the crews, instead of relying like the British on impressment of drunks and vagrants and the victims of misery and want picked up from the streets; a corps of 10,000 gunners was rigorously trained for accuracy of fire; dockyards hummed with the building of new ships of larger and better design than Britain's. In seamanship, the French trained for beauty of maneuvers, practicing so that the parts of a squadron would make their turns in unison or progressively with the precision of a ballet, with their sails billowing or furling in artistic design. Town by town, Choiseul organized a fund-raising campaign for shipbuilding, with each new ship, when launched, being named for the town that had donated the most. The fleet's giant flagship of 110 guns named the *Ville de Paris* was the warship that Rodney would one day bring to surrender in his last and greatest battle. A spirit of enterprise prevailed, in contrast to the lethargy of Spain and in contrast, too, to the defensive doctrine of naval warfare that governed French tactics. On going into battle, the guiding principle for a French sea captain was to adopt the lee gauge, a defensive position, and by forcing the enemy to attack, to destroy his ships while keeping his own intact. The theory, in the words of the French Admiral Grivel, was that, of the inferior of two opponents, the "one that has the fewest ships must always avoid doubtful engagements . . . or, worst, if forced to engage, assure itself of favorable conditions." In short, "circumspection, economy and defensive war" was the fixed purpose of French policy directed toward reversing the position of inferiority at sea that France had sustained by the defeats of the Seven Years' War. Logically it would seem that such a course, when consistently followed for years, must affect the spirit and enterprise of the officers imbued with it. Yet if that were true of the average, the outstanding French seaman Admiral de Grasse, in his historic decision that saved America, had little difficulty in subduing the voice of caution and allowing the impulse of bold risk to make up his mind.

Rodney's first active duty was at Newfoundland, from where he was promoted to Lieutenant and transferred to the Mediterranean and given command by Admiral Mathews of the *Plymouth*, a ship of the line of 64 guns — "of the line" referred to the largest class of warships, of 64 guns or more, powerful enough in construction and in armament to fight in the single file of ships bearing down on the enemy and firing broadside as they passed, which was the conventional and only tactical formation used in the combat of fighting sail in the 18th century. The largest ships of the line, mounting 100 guns in three tiers, were 200 feet long, built of oak at a cost of

£100,000. The largest, Nelson's H.M.S. *Victory* built in 1776–77, was crewed by 875 men, and lesser ships by crews of 490–720. *Victory*, at 220 feet, required for construction 2,500 major trees, equal to sixty acres of forest. It carried a mainmast of fir standing 205 feet above waterline and three feet thick at its base. Constructed in three sections, the three mainmasts of a ship of the line could suspend 36 sails, amounting to four acres of fabric, and make a speed of ten knots. When masts were bent by a strong wind, the strain on floorboards caused the leaks that required constant pumping. Frigates used as commerce raiders were ships of 130–150 feet, usually manned by volunteer crews seeking the prize money.

Guns, measured by the weight of their cannonballs, were 12–42 pounders (frigates carried 4–6 pounders), with a maximum range of one mile when fired by 400 pounds of gunpowder. They fired not only cannonballs but all kinds and shapes of missiles — pails of nails or sharpened pieces of scrap iron — heated red hot to burn sails. Guns were mounted on wheeled gun carriages, secured by rope tackles used to run the guns in and out of the gunports and take up the recoil. Each firing required a succession of nine or ten orders to the gun crew: "Cast loose your guns" — the ropes removed and coiled; "Level your guns" — to make them parallel to the deck; "Take out your tompions" — to remove stoppers from the muzzles; "Load cartridge" — the cartridge of black powder in a cloth bag is rammed down the muzzle; "Shot your guns" — the cannonball or other shot is rammed down; "Run out your guns" — guns placed for muzzles to protrude through gunports; "Prime" — gunpowder from the powder horn is inserted in the touchhole; "Point your guns" — the slow match is brought to the breech while the cannoneer keeps it alight by careful blowing and the gun is adjusted on its base; "Elevate" — a bead is drawn on the target through the sights; "Fire!" — when the roll of the ship brings the top sights on the target, the lighted match is applied to the touchhole; firing is followed by the order "Sponge your guns" — a sponge fixed to a length of stiffened rope and dipped in a tub of water is thrust down the muzzle to extinguish any scraps of the powder bag that might be burning. Guns were then repositioned and the loading process repeated. In Nelson's time a perfectly trained crew could complete this process at a rate of once every two minutes.

Management of sail in order to tack — that is, to shift direction or sail into the wind or to bear down on the enemy or to seize the weather gauge or to chase or fall back in any other maneuver requiring adjustment to the wind — demanded another precise set of orders governing braces, sheets, halyards set, bowlines at every edge of the square sails to keep them taut and flat, mainsails, top mainsails, topgallant mainsails, staysails, jib sheets, backstays and an infinite number of extras, whose names will offer no comprehension to the landlubber. A crew with officers or boatswain stands by each mast to haul or let go the sails while the captain, besides calling his orders, keeps in communication with the helmsman. To bring a ship about — that is, reverse or change direction — is an action keyed to a pitch of precision and excitement at the operative moment when the mainsail flaps over with a loud bang to catch the wind from the opposite side. As described by Admiral Morison — using as example a southeast wind for a turn to the southwest — it involves different orders for different sails and yardarms (the wooden poles suspended from the mast to which the sails are attached).

First, the seamen trim the yards as close as possible to the axis of the hull, and haul in taut the sheet of the fore-and-aft driver or spanker on the mizzenmast so as to kick her stern around. The officer of the deck

246

shouts "Ready, about!" and the boatswains pass the word by piping. The man at the wheel turns it hard — all the way — to starboard, which puts the helm that connects with the rudderhead to leeward, and when he has done so, he sings out, "Helm's hard a-lee, sir!" The jib and staysail sheets, which trim the headsails, are let go. As the rudder brings the ship up into the SE wind, the yards point directly into it, the sails shiver, and the lines, with tension released, dance about wildly. As soon as the ship's head has passed through the eye of the wind and is heading about, SE by S, the port jib and staysail sheets are hauled taut; and their action, added to that of the foresail, fore topsail and fore-topgallant sail, which are now back-winded — that is, blown against the mast — act as levers to throw the ship's bow away from the wind onto the desired new course. As soon as the wind catches the starboard leach (edge) of the square mainsail or maintopsail, the officer of the deck cries, "Mainsail haul!" This is the great moment in coming about. . . . All hands not otherwise employed then lay ahold of the lee braces on the main and mizzen yards and haul them around an arc of about seventy degrees until the sails catch the wind from the port side. If done

247

at just the right moment, the wind helps whip them around. By this time, unless the ship is very sharp and smart and the sea smooth, her headway has been lost. . . .

The next important order is "Let Go and Haul!" This means let go fore braces and sheets, and haul the foreyards, whose sails have been flat aback all this time, until the wind catches them on their after surfaces. The weather jib and staysail sheets are let go and the lee ones hauled taut, and all other sails are trimmed so that she gathers headway and shoots ahead on her new course. . . . In a warship with a big crew this process would take at least ten minutes, probably more. . . .

This laborious process for every change of direction, called tacking, while it made for tense and exciting moments, cannot be called an efficient form of locomotion. To tack a big ship with its billowing mass of sail might be done in good weather with a trained crew in ten minutes, but otherwise could take several hours, and in rough weather as long as half a day or in a really bad blow might become impossible. To arrive at any place not lying in the direction of the wind meant tacking zigzag the whole way, exhausting ship and crew, so that it is hardly to be wondered why both were frequently weak and unfit for service.

In the renewed strife for supremacy of the sea that filled the mid-century, the opening clash of navies took place in the Battle of Toulon in 1744. It was not a heroic combat, like John Paul Jones's against the *Serapis*, but a messed-up composite of all the troubles and defects that were to beset naval warfare in this period, and it evoked from a French minister, M. Maurepas, a disgusted dimissal of warfare with its waste of lives for some inconclusive result: "I don't think much of these naval combats. *C'est piff poff* on one side and the other, and leaves the sea afterwards as salty as before." At Toulon, England was engaged against France and Spain, allies in the Bourbon Family Compact, which suffered from the strains of most family efforts at union. Apart from colonial hostilities in America and India, which were the true source of conflict, the secondary struggle lay as usual in the complex of continental quarrels, this time known as the War of the Austrian Succession, in which remote and irrelevant Silesia was again in contention. It would be wasted effort to try to follow the twisted trails leading to this war, other than to say that in 1740 Frederick the Great had gained the throne of Prussia just as the Emperor of Austria, Charles VI, died, leaving the disputed sovereignty of his jigsaw of dominions to his eldest daughter, Maria Theresa, whose succession the European powers had guaranteed. For his own purposes, Frederick II was trying to dispossess her, and when he seized Silesia, among other inimical acts, Prussia and Austria went to war, with the several powers taking sides.

Out of this muddle, the three major sea powers, Spain, France and Britain, came to a focus at Toulon, the chief French naval base on the Mediterranean coast, located halfway between Nice and Marseilles. The Battle of Toulon in 1744 ensued, when Spain as an enemy of Austria moved to take over Italian territories ruled by Austria. The Spanish fleet entered Toulon, where it remained shut in for four months by an English blockade. When Spain applied to France for an escort to conduct her ships home, France complied, but, distrusting Spanish fighting efficiency, the French Admiral requested that the Spanish ships be scattered among his own, a proposal that the Spanish Admiral Navarro naturally refused. In a compromise, the Spanish ships kept their own group upon entering the line of warships, which was always formed in sections designated van, center and rear. With nine French in the van, six French and three Spanish in the center and nine Spanish in the rear, the Allies' line of 27 warships sailed out of port to face the British line of 29, commanded by Admiral Mathews of the Mediterranean fleet squadron. He was seconded by a man he despised, Admiral Lestock, who fully returned his commanding officer's sentiments. Their quarrel was personal and petty, not political, stemming from Lestock's failure to send a frigate to meet Mathews on his arrival from England to take over his command. Described as an illiterate, ill-mannered and domineering officer, Mathews vented his displeasure in "coarse insults" to his subordinate, causing Admiral Mahan, as historian, rather timidly to suggest that a "possible taint of ill will" between the two played a part in the "fiasco" off Toulon.

Sighting the sails coming out of Toulon toward evening, Mathews, having the weather (or windward) gauge, raised the signal for a "general chase," but when his van came up with the enemy next morning, his rear, under Lestock, was too far — some five miles — astern to join him and make the English squadron's superior numbers tell. During the previous night, Lestock had already been out of position. When Mathews signaled for the fleet to "lie-to" — that is, stay put for the night — he also signaled for "close order," which to a willing instead of a resentful subordinate would clearly suggest coming up during the night to take his position in the line. By morning Lestock was still several hours' sailing time behind. Lestock chose to obey the stationary signal to lie-to rather than to close up.

Bursting with impatience for the laggard Lestock and fearing that his prey would sail away to escape their planned destruction, Mathews struck out for independence and left the line to attack the enemy by himself, in the belief or hope that he could overwhelm the Spanish rear and the French center before the French in the van could double back to rescue them. Whether by error or in the excitement of his dare, he raised the signal to engage while keeping the signal for the line flying, thoroughly confusing his captains, who could find no guide to his intentions in the signal books or in the ruling manual called *Fighting Instructions*. They knew only that the signal for "line ahead" supersedes all others. Some of his squadron followed Mathews with or without signals, but others hung back, leaving their Admiral unsupported and their fire at ineffective range. In the disorder, the enemy escaped; only one was taken, in a spirited action by a captain of later renown, the future Admiral Hawke. By nightfall Mathews had to withdraw and regroup with nothing to show for all his audacity except the satisfaction of having Lestock put under arrest and sent home.

This sorry tale was roughly debated in the House of Commons and, following severe criticism of the Admiralty, in a series of courts-martial which, with the irreproachable logic of men in uniform, punished Mathews, the man who fought, but acquitted Lestock, the man who did not. Mathews was condemned and dismissed from the service (on the ground of his having signaled for "line of battle" while by his own action making preservation of the line impossible), whereas Lestock, on his claim of obedience to signals, was held blameless.

At this point we must meet the paralyzing dragon known as *Fighting Instructions*, a tyrannical document that required each ship of the line to follow each other at a cable's length (200 yards) and to engage its opposite number of the enemy's line, van for van, center for center and rear for rear, and never to leave the line to do otherwise. The rule, called "line ahead," was intended to prevent the confusion called a *mêleé*, in which individual ships might come under the fire of their fellows, and to give a section of the line, if closely supported by the one next astern, a chance of destroying the enemy's section opposite. *Fighting Instructions* was issued during the first Dutch wars under the regime of Oliver Cromwell, whose autocratic mentality it certainly reflected, although the instructions have also been attributed to that poor creature James I, who would not seem to have had the character to conceive a document of such intransigence. Because individual captains of the time had formerly used their own tactics, often resulting in unmanageable confusion, the Admiralty issued the *Fighting Instructions* to give a fleet greater effect by requiring its ships to act in concert under signaled orders of the commanding officer and prohibiting action on personal initiative. In general, the result did make for greater efficiency in combat, though in particular instances — as in Admiral Graves's action in the crucial Battle of Chesapeake Bay preceding Yorktown — it could cause disaster by persuading a too submissive captain to stick by the rule when crisis in a situation could better have been met by a course determined by the particular circumstances. As deviations from the rule were always reported by some disgruntled officer and tried by a court-martial, the *Instructions* naturally reduced, if not destroyed, initiative except when a captain of strong self-confidence would act to take advantage of the unexpected. Action of this kind was not infrequent, even though no people so much as the British preferred to stay wedded to the way things had always been done before. In allowing no room for the unexpected that lies in wait in the waywardness of men, not to mention the waywardness of winds and ocean, *Fighting Instructions* was a concept of military rigidity that must forever amaze the layman.

Whether Lestock at Toulon held back from the rear of the battle line out of malice toward his commander, or whether, as he claimed at the subsequent court-martial, he had put on all possible sail but could not make up the distance, was not adjudicated. To the charge that he failed to attack later when he might have done so, he used the technicalities of the *Fighting Instructions* as a defense, saying that the signal for line ahead was flying at the same time as the signal to engage and that he could not leave the line to fight without disobeying the signal to form line.

As the core of naval battle, line ahead was conditioned by the structure of the ships themselves, whose main armament necessarily fired broadside. The line was necessary because it was the only formation that allowed all ships of a squadron to turn with beam facing the enemy and at the same time ensure that no one of its own would come between gun and target. The law of line ahead conditioned a battle of formal movements as of some massive minuet played upon the sea to the music of gunfire. The warships advanced, bowed and retreated while drums beat a tattoo summoning gun crews to their posts and explosives burst from the cannons' mouths. The line advanced along the length of the enemy line drawn up opposite, each ship firing as it came into position. The English aimed at the hulls, the French at masts and rigging, loading their guns with chains and grapeshot and scraps of metal to tear the sails. Flames leapt, wood splinters flew causing nasty wounds, decks strewn with dead bodies and slippery with blood grew hazardous, the wounded lay helpless, fearful of being rolled overboard among the corpses to where sharks swarmed around the ship, their open jaws to be the sailors' unmarked graves. The destructive violence wrought upon the empty sea was loud and satisfying, if not always of strategic value. Observing the performance, the proverbial visitor from another planet would have admired the beauty of the sailing maneuvers in their white-winged saraband but would have wondered, to what purpose?

Which side was the victor in the unfixed territory of a sea battle was usually decided, even by historians, on the basis of the relative number of killed and wounded suffered by either combatant. The numbers, often 700 or 800 killed in some pointless "piff poff," were large. The only person to express any concern that appears in the records was curiously enough the King of France, Louis XVI, not known for his popular sympathies. In a speech to his Council he asked, "But who shall restore the brave sailors who have sacrificed their lives in my service?" This was a greater degree of interest than expressed by any official who received the count of losses or by any admiral who saw the bodies pile up on his decks.

The ultimate objective of any war is the gaining of political and material power, which at this period was considered to depend on colonies and commerce. Since these in turn depended upon free communication through control of the sea with bases for supply along the way — but not too many, as Mahan cautiously advises — and since holding the bases depended on their protection by the navy, therefore the objective of sea war was to prevail over the enemy's navy and find occasion to meet and destroy his fleets. To take this argument to its logical end meant that the best result would be had by staying out of battle altogether. The French, being a logical people, had reached this conclusion and followed it when they could.

The battle of fighting sail as practiced in the 18th century troubles the rational mind. Clearly, line ahead depended on the enemy presenting himself in an equivalent line as target or opponent. But suppose he did not, refused to form a line, maneuvered for the weather gauge and, if successful, sailed away to a friendly base or home port. The French often did just that, or did not come out to meet the enemy at all, leaving the English with the frustration of empty claws.

A paradox of the 18th century, so admired for reason and enlightenment, is the senselessness it often exhibits, as in the case of the futile shore batteries on the islands and the unchanging tactics of line ahead, a maneuver which everyone on the ocean knew as well as he knew his own name, an old story that could have no surprises, although surprise is the sharpest weapon in the military arsenal.

Since medieval days of the sixty-pound suit of armor, in which, for the sake of combat, men roasted and could not arise if they fell, no contrivance for fighting has matched in discomfort and inconvenience and use contrary to nature the floating castle called a ship of the line in the age of fighting sail. With its motor power dependent on the caprice of heaven and direction-finding on the distant stars, and its central piece of equipment — the mast —

dependent on seasoned timber that was rarely obtainable, and control of locomotion dependent on rigging and ropes of a complexity to defy philosophers of the Sorbonne, much less the homeless untutored poor off the streets who made up the crews, and communication from commander to his squadron dependent on signal flags easily obscured by distance or smoke from the guns or by pitching of the ship, these cumbersome vehicles were as convenient as if dinosaurs had survived to be used by cowboys for driving cattle. The difficulties men willingly contend with to satisfy their urge to fight have never been better exemplified than in warships under sail. Not a few contemporaries were bemused by the curiosities of naval warfare that had inspired M. Maurepas' conclusive judgment as "piff poff."

Hardly designed to invigorate naval spirit, the verdicts of the Toulon courts-martial succeeded in tightening the grip of *Fighting Instructions* while mystifying the public and deepening public suspicion of government. Eleven out of twenty-nine captains were accused and tried, of whom one died, one deserted and was never heard of again, seven were cashiered from the service and only two acquitted. Damage and discouragement in the navy, not unnaturally, followed.

In 1777, the Admiralty's report of 35 ships of the line in the Grand Fleet was shown to be fiction when surveyors reported the majority unfit for sea and only six fit for service, and these, when inspected by the new Commander-in-Chief, Admiral Keppel, "no pleasure to his seaman's eye." Little had improved since the survey of 1749, when the inspector discovered lax and ignorant officers, crews left idle and unskilled, stores disorganized, equipment shabby and decaying, ships dirty, unseaworthy and inadequately manned. Leaving untouched the central problem of corrupt management at the top to which these deficiencies could be traced, the authorities were moved to enact a sterner version of the *Fighting Instructions* under the title *Additional Fighting Instructions*, or, more formally, the Naval Discipline Act of 1749, which added "negligence" in the performance of duty falling short of the last ounce of fighting effort as a punishable offense. Under this legislation was staged the navy's most notorious act of the century, the execution in 1757 of Admiral Byng on being tried and convicted under the death penalty of negligence in what was judged to be a halfhearted fight to relieve Minorca. In the actual combat that made Byng's tragedy, when ordered to relieve Minorca, the Admiralty had underestimated, as it so often did, the strength of the enemy and had sent Byng with a small inadequate and ill-equipped squadron to the defense. The enemy had already landed and overrun the island when he reached Gibraltar. The Governor of Gibraltar, supposed to assist with troops, refused to release them, on the ground that they could not be spared from his garrison. Although Byng had already complained at the inadequacy of his squadron, he made no protest and proceeded against the French, whose ships were larger with heavier guns than his own, but were keeping to the defensive. When the two fleets came within sight, the French were to leeward and Byng had the wind. He raised the signal for line ahead but did not follow it at once, while he had the advantage, with the signal to bear down (engage) because his ships had not yet completed the line formation. He was cramped by the effect of the Mathews court-martial, which had punished Mathews for engaging without his full force in line. Having himself sat on the bench in the Mathews-Lestock case, Byng cited the verdict to his flag captain, "You see, Captain Gardiner, that the signal for the line is out," and he pointed out that two ships were still out of place. "It was Mr. Mathews' misfortune to be prejudiced by not carrying down his force together, which I shall endeavor to avoid." When Byng did raise the signal to bear down, his ships, still in some disarray, came in at an angle with the van taking the full blows of the French guns. The center and rear were still too far apart from the enemy to bring their firepower to bear in support. The van was crushed. The fleets separated as night fell. Byng, making no effort to regroup, summoned a war council and readily accepted the advice given under his command that nothing further could be done and Minorca must be left to its fate. Accordingly, without further action he returned with his fleet to Gibraltar, where he was superseded and sent home under arrest. He was charged under No. 12 of the Articles of War with not having done his utmost to relieve the garrison of Minorca or to seize and destroy the enemy's ships as was his duty. Article 12 refers to failure of duty "through cowardice, negligence or disaffection," and since Byng was explicitly acquitted of cowardice or disaffection, negligence was left as his implicit guilt. The verdict left *Fighting Instructions* more twisted than ever, for it meant that while Mathews had been court-martialed for leaving line ahead to bear down on the enemy, Byng was punished for refusing to do so. Admirals were in a forked stick. Command, deprived of personal judgment, can win no battles, and the most important one that would decide the fate of America was still to come.

Uproar at the death sentence was vociferous. Ministers were content to let Byng bear it, to cover their own failure to send adequate force to the defense. King George II, a stranger to the quality of mercy, granted no pardon. Rodney, always independent-minded, who could tell absurdity from utility when it stood in front of him, joined with the champion of Byng's cause, Captain Augustus Hervey, in a campaign to solicit petitions for his pardon, in vain. The death kept discussion alive, one more bitterness to divide the navy. Byng was duly shot by a firing squad of brother officers for no discernible purpose except to "encourage the others," as remarked by a mean-minded Frenchman. Voltaire's comment would immortalize the act, whose peculiar excess was another aberration of the enlightened century. The execution could accomplish nothing, for even then nobody supposed that men can be made brave by enactment or deterred from weakness by fear of punishment.

If to no purpose, why was the death penalty imposed? Because it was there, on the statute books, decreed by the lawmakers in their wisdom for the particular failing for which Byng was judged and held guilty. Because it was there, offering no alternative punishment, it must not be evaded. The court's discretionary power had been removed and it claimed to have no alternative. Exercising choice, however, is one of the burdens of being human and having a mind. Not to exercise it may be easier, but if unused it is likely to become sluggish, which may be one of the reasons British performance in the American war was not brilliant.

Byng suffered for his time. This was a period when the British went in fear of the wild assaults of the gin-soaked poor and feared anarchy rising from the so-called criminal class, which they believed to exist as an entity. To suppress it, they enacted laws of ferocious penalty, and no matter what suggestion of reason or compassion or common sense might be advanced against transporting for life and separating from home and family a boy of eleven for stealing a stocking, it would not be heard; the law must not deviate. In a sense, this non-thinking severity was a development of the very political liberty of which the British were the progenitors and had done so much to foster by their own revolution in establishing the principle of a government of laws not men, of constitutionalism not dictate. This was now what Britain's children, the Colonies, were fighting for, and which the British insistently ignored, pretending that the American rebellion was some kind of misguided frenzy and thereby losing any chance of winning back allegiance or reconciliation.

Byng's judges pronounced the death sentence expecting that the King or ministers would pardon him. In fear of the mob, angry at the loss of territory — Minorca, taken from Spain in 1708, had been British for only forty-eight years — and, shouting for blood, the government proffered no pardon; Byng was left to be shot as a scapegoat. The firing squad barked on command; the crumpled figure of the Admiral lay in a heap on the quarterdeck of the *Monarch,* a mute witness to one of the atrocities of law, the guardian of human conduct.

Given the angle of fire, line ahead may have had no alternative, yet innovative minds might have devised tactical variations or surprises, as Rodney himself was one day to do. But the navy was not a home for innovative minds, being considered the place to dispose of the unteachable or stupid son of a family whose more promising brothers qualified for the army or clergy. While breaking the line was the most radical and important contribution to tactics of the time, after which they were never the same again, it was the idea not of a professional seaman but of a schoolboy of

Edinburgh, who made a hobby of sailing homemade toy boats in a pond as a child and eventually worked out his plan in a treatise, which Rodney had the nerve to employ when the chance offered. The boy, John Clerk, was first drawn to the ways of seagoing vehicles by the tale of the shipwreck in *Robinson Crusoe*. Studying the movement of ships in response to the wind blowing through Leith, Edinburgh's harbor, he began experimenting for himself with a schoolmate's model boat. Soon he was making model boats of his own to watch as they sailed across his father's pond. Meanwhile, public attention had fastened on the Keppel-Palliser court-martial, and as he followed the testimony the boy learned about "line ahead" and the problems it raised in naval combat. Possessor of that alert Scottish intelligence that so often caused uneasiness below the Border, Clerk noticed the major flaw in line ahead: that if the enemy did not offer himself in a comparable line, there could be no fighting that day under the rules of *Fighting Instructions*. As he watched his little ships move as directed by the breezes, he evolved the solution for breaking the deadly grip of the line. It was to allow the full line to concentrate against one section of the enemy, instead of each ship against its opposite in line, thus smashing a gap through which to penetrate and "double" the enemy while it was caught in the slow process of coming about and sailing back into the wind to assist its companions. Drawing charts to accompany his text, John Clerk explained his thesis in a small book entitled *An Essay on Naval Tactics*, which, circulating among friends and naval enthusiasts, found a publisher and soon came to the notice of navy professionals, among them Admiral Rodney. Investigators were later to find that he had come into possession of a manuscript copy, which he had annotated and was to put to use at Cape St. Vincent and in the aborted battle off Martinique in 1780, and most distinctly in his ultimate triumph in the Battle of the Saints of 1782, in which he was to win a decisive victory over the French that restored British self-confidence after the loss at Yorktown. The battle's name refers to two islands so named marking the channel between Guadeloupe and Dominica where the action took place.

Conditions that kept half the manpower of a ship in illness most of the time as a result of living between decks for months on end in fetid and stale air, on rotten food and brackish water in a hot climate, were other lazy submissions to old ways that could have been changed if the authorities had had the wit or the will to permit the entry of a ray of enlightenment. For two centuries, from 1622 to 1825, the official diet of the Royal Navy consisted of beer, salt pork and salt beef, oatmeal, dried peas, butter and cheese, usually rancid, and biscuit that walked by itself, as Roderick Random tells in Smollett's novel, by virtue of the worms that made it their home. Since the diet supplied nothing of the body's need of vitamin C, the result was widespread scurvy, whose symptom after the telltale skin lesions was generalized weakness deepening into exhaustion followed by death. It took the Admiralty forty years to adopt the known remedy of citrus fruit discovered within the navy itself by a ship's surgeon, James Lind, who obtained wonderful cures by issuing oranges and lemons and limes to dying men and who published *A Treatise on the Scurvy* in 1754, prescribing a ration of lime juice for all. Because this was judged too expensive, it was not made compulsory until 1795. Enlightenment had not suggested that the burden of carrying and even minimally caring for a crew too weak to work was more costly than a keg of lime juice, which may account for the thought attributed to a legendary "philosopher" of 600 B.C. that there are three kinds of people in the world: the living, the dead and those at sea. Is it possible that admirals became resistant to change through some effect of life at sea? In the 20th century, hidebound inertia still ruled the flag deck. As First Lord in 1914, Winston Churchill, according to the authoritative naval historian Richard Hough, regarded "the professional hierarchy of the Royal Navy of the First World War as tradition bound, unadventurous, and underendowed with initiative and intelligence."

Atypical, Rodney possessed both, in addition to abundant self-confidence that never deserted him. When he saw a condition clearly in need of improvement, he was an activist, prepared to innovate, in one case to his own detriment. During his service in Jamaica, he installed a system of piping water from reservoirs to the ships, sparing the sailors the long laborious work of rolling barrels all the way. Their blessings turned to resentment when they discovered that under the new system, the task was done so rapidly that it gave them no time for shore leave. As the sailors' annoyance was one reason for denying Rodney the governorship of Jamaica, his innovation unhappily demonstrated the greater safety in inertia.

Tolerance of disgusting living conditions accepted with no effort at improvement bespoke a mental lethargy that underlay the general reluctance to change old habits. Alternatives were not beyond reach. To find friendly ports of call where fresh food could be obtained would have been difficult among so many belligerent relationships, but not impossible. Fresh air could have been introduced by opening hatches without the danger of the sea pouring in, if care had been taken to open them on the port side when the ship was heeling to starboard, or vice versa, but so much thinking in advance for the sake of comfort was not part of the plan. Preservation of food from rot may have had no alternative, but human filth was not incumbent. Given sweat, vomit, defecation and urination, sexual emission and the menstrual flow of women, the human body is not a clean machine, and when people are crowded together in an enclosed space, its effluents can create a degree of unpleasantness raised to the extreme. Means of improving hygiene and sanitation could have been devised if they had been wanted, for men can usually work out the technical means to obtain what is truly desired unless the refrain "it can't be done" becomes their guide.

Innovations occasionally broke through — not for comfort, but to improve the functioning of the ships. The most important was copper sheathing of the hulls to prevent infestation of crustaceans and worms and plant growth that rotted the bottoms, slowing speed and often rendering a ship unusable altogether. Rodney was always asking for coppered ships, which, in the Admiralty's rare moments of spending money were sometimes forthcoming. A wheel on the bridge connecting by pulleys to the rudder and giving the helmsman mechanical control was another advance that by its sheer efficiency managed to introduce itself against the overwhelming power of inertia. Even the time-honored "castles" used by archers in medieval combat were eliminated to lower the center of gravity and make room for more sail. Triangular jib sails to catch an elusive wind were added, over the jeering of the old salts.

In 1742 on board his first ship, the *Plymouth*, in the Mediterranean, Rodney made his mark at once by bringing in safely an unwieldy convoy of 300 merchant ships of the Lisbon trade through the haunt of enemy privateers at the western end of the channel. This feat brought him to the attention of the public and of thankful merchants of London and Bristol as well as to the Lords of the Admiralty, by whom he was promoted to Captain and later given command of the *Eagle*, a ship of the line of 64 guns.

Active in commerce-destroying aboard the *Eagle*, Captain Rodney was not present at Toulon, where he might have supplied the needed vigorous action that he was to show in the second Battle of Finisterre three years later in October, 1747, and the earlier fight off Brest. That year Rodney was with a squadron under Admiral Hawke which the British had dispatched to cruise the Atlantic in search of French trade convoys. In the first engagement, Rodney's unit under Commodore Thomas Fox fell upon four French warships escorting some 150 merchant sail coming from Santo Domingo, heavily loaded with sugar, coffee, indigo and other goods of the West Indies. During two days of chasing the widely dispersed convoy, Rodney took six ships, escorted his prizes home and put back to sea. He had rejoined Hawke when orders came to attack an outward-bound convoy of 250 French merchantmen, escorted by nine ships of the line. When the English intercepted the French in the waters off Finisterre in Spain, the westernmost point of Europe, there was nothing passive or negligent in the battle that followed. The French Admiral l'Etenduère, in order to give the ships he was escorting a chance to escape, placed himself between them and the English and fought for six hours, inspiring in his captains a fighting spirit as determined as if they were carrying the Dauphin himself on board. The French suffered terrible damages. On the 70-gun

Neptune, seven officers and 300 men were killed before she was given up. Rodney fought for an hour against the more powerful *Neptune* and a second Frenchman on his other side, until, disabled by a broadside that destroyed the steering wheel and tore sails and rigging, the *Eagle* drifted clear. Despite heroic resistance, six of the French warships had surrendered by evening. Only two escaped, pursued into the night by Rodney — who, after some repairs, was eager for further action — and by two other ships of the English fleet. The convoyed French merchantmen escaped.

Rodney's captures raised him another rung in reputation, especially as the spirit shown at Finisterre helped to dispel the cloud of shame of the Toulon courts-martial and more especially as the English loot amounted to over £300,000, paraded, this time through London, for the customary delight of the citizens.

As the begetter of this happy fortune for the government, Rodney was taken up by the Pelhams — Henry Pelham, the First Minister, and his brother the Duke of Newcastle, who were the two ruling patrons of "place." By them he was made a protégé of the governing party, and supplied with that equipment felt to be a necessity as the path to personal advancement by every man of ambition — a seat in Parliament. He was presented by Admiral Anson, overall commander of the fleet at Finisterre, to King George II, who was much impressed by Rodney's youth, remarking, as attendant courtiers hastened to take note, that he had "not before imagine[d] that he had so young a man a captain in his navy," to which Lord Anson replied, "I wish your Majesty had one hundred more such captains, to the terror of your Majesty's enemies."

"We wish so too, my lord," replied the King with ready repartee.

As disciples of Robert Walpole, the Pelhams wanted an end of the war, and after the rich haul at Finisterre, fighting was nominally brought to a close at the peace of Aix-la-Chapelle in 1748. The peace treaty exchanged various territories, but was in reality only a temporary truce which resolved nothing in the struggle for colonial supremacy, because the powers were reluctant to negotiate carefully for fear of prolonging the war. The boundaries of Canada and Nova Scotia and the rights of trade and navigation vis-à-vis Spain were left unsettled, and belligerence continued in the West Indies and North America.

The next year, in 1749, with the smile of royal favor Rodney was named Captain of the *Rainbow*, carrying with it command of the

Newfoundland station and title as Governor. In 1753, he married a sister of the Earl of Northampton, and even before taking on this domestic status he assumed what he saw as his proper place by building a handsome mansion on the grounds of an old manor house in Hampshire and, with due appreciation of the best in the business, had it landscaped by Capability Brown, just as he had selected Reynolds for his portrait. At the same time, he acquired, with rather lordly outlay for a naval captain, a private house on Hill Street in London.

On his return to England from Newfoundland, in 1752, he had to be carried ashore at Portsmouth and turn his ship over to his lieutenant owing to a severe case of gout, the first of the many attacks of illness that were to afflict and sometimes disable him for the remaining forty years of his life. At age thirty-three he was young to be gout's victim, but the heavy drinking of the 18th century that was a cause of the disease was even heavier on shipboard, to suppress the sickening smells and distract the boredom of long empty days at sea. As gout destroyed the health of the Elder Pitt, Earl of Chatham, England's greatest statesman of the century, it was to wreck Rodney's eventually, too, though not until he reached 74. On his homecoming, his ill health was useful, for though ordered to sit on the court-martial of Admiral Byng in 1756, he was excused on the ground of a "violent bilious colic," and, by an even more fortunate stroke of luck, when the execution was scheduled to take place on his own ship, the *Monarch*, he was transferred to the *Dublin* shortly before, and did not have to give the order to "fire!" to a firing squad on his own deck. Luck did not stay with him long, for in February, 1757, his wife, Jane, who had borne him two children, died in the childbirth of the third, a baby girl who survived. Without a wife, Rodney was eager again for action and was soon to find it in the "wonderful year" of 1759 in the full tilt of the Seven Years' War, when England overcame her enemies in every encounter.

The Seven Years' War, fought mainly between France and Britain in rivalry for sovereignty of the seas and for colonial dominion in America and to a lesser extent in India, was the central war of the century. In America it was known as the French and Indian War. With hindsight, later historians have seen it as the first real World War because of its subsidiary conflicts in Europe in the web of territorial and dynastic disputes and tangled alliances centering around the duel of Prussia and Austria for dominance. France on

Prussia's side was opposed to England allied with Austria, with Sweden, Spain and the United Provinces variously involved.

The outcome of the war confirmed Britain's rule of the seas, and her maritime supremacy was soon taken for granted. Horace Walpole, reporting the return of a convoy from India, could calmly assert that it sailed homeward through "the streets of our capital, the ocean." On land, the major gain was the ceding of Canada by France and the acquisition of Florida in exchange for the return of Havana to Spain. In succinct summary, Admiral Mahan was to state the results in one sentence: The "kingdom of Great Britain had become the British empire."

Justifying Pitt's confidence, British sea power during the Seven Years' War secured an increase of trade reaching 500,000 tons, about one-third that of all Europe, carried by 8,000 merchant vessels filled with the products of new industry journeying to new markets. Convoy of delivery was sacred. Trade was power. It provided the income to maintain the fleet and 200,000 soldiers and mercenaries on British pay, including 50,000 in America. Britain's priority was, in fact, trade and the income it provided. So much British trade traveled the sea-lanes that the inroads by French commerce raiders and privateers had no appreciable effect on the balance of the war. The West Indies, with their valuable produce, made a centerpiece of commerce directly re-represented by a number of West Indian planters who held twelve to fifteen seats in Parliament and exerted their influence through their wealth and connections rather than through numbers. The most prominent was Sir William Beckford, the largest landowner in Jamaica and twice Lord Mayor of London in the 1760s. How secondary were the colonies of North America was seen after the Revolution had become an armed struggle, when in 1778 Philadelphia was stripped of 5,000 troops for transfer to the West Indies to ward off French recapture, followed by a second convoy of four regiments to the Leewards and four more to Jamaica in 1779. When General Clinton in New York at this time was crying for reinforcements and England was scraping Ireland for recruits and mobilizing the inmates of prisons, a total of 22 battalions had been sent to the West Indies since the beginning of the American war.

The most significant feat of the "wonderful year" of 1759 was General Wolfe's defeat of the French at Quebec, an indirect victory of the British sea power that Pitt had believed in and prepared as the instrument that would enable England finally to prevail over France in their centuries-old struggle for supremacy. Wolfe's 9,000 troops were transported to Canada through the British control of the sea, and before they scaled the cliffs to the plains of Abraham the way had been opened by preliminary victories at Ticonderoga and Crown Point. Even at the cost of the loss of a hero, in General Wolfe's death in the battle on the hilltop, the victory brought a decisive result, for it was followed by the occupation of Montreal, which in turn assured the British conquest of Canada. The French were thereby eliminated from a territory that had allowed them to dispute possession of America. Facing attack on Montreal from below and from behind by General Amherst's forces coming from Lake Ontario, the Marquis de Vaudreuil, French Governor of Canada, in September, 1759, surrendered the Province of Quebec, or New France, to the English. French presence as a Catholic power and French collusion with the Iroquois, who were hostile to the settlers of the New England colonies, were always seen by both British and Americans as factors that would hold the Colonies loyal for the sake of British protection against the threat from the north. By one of the tricks that Fate likes to use to show the vanity of human expectation, the British by their own victory at Quebec and its removal of the Catholic threat gave the Americans the freedom for rebellion.

Although Rodney sailed in 1758 with the fleet under Admiral Boscawen that was sent against Louisburg, his vessel, the *Dublin,* was an unhealthy ship, with a crew laid low by an epidemic of fever. It was left behind at Halifax, with the men installed in sheds hastily erected on shore by the ship's carpenters. Owing to the *Dublin's* debility, Rodney missed the assault on the great French fortress whose capture opened the way to Quebec. He joined the victors just before the surrender and sailed home with them to England. He missed, too, in November, 1759, Admiral Hawke's crushing of the French main fleet, intended for the invasion of England, in the Battle of Quiberon Bay, on the coast of Brittany. Called "the greatest victory since the Armada" by an unidentified enthusiast, it added more laurels to the "wonderful year." Rodney was engaged at the time on a mission against another aspect of the invasion plan, commanding a squadron ordered to destroy by means of bomb ships a flotilla of flat-bottomed boats gathered at Le Havre as landing craft. These boats were 100 feet long, capable of carrying 400 men each. Promoted in May, 1759, to Rear Admiral of the Blue (blue, white and red were colors originally indicating squadron position in the line, and carrying minor progression in grade from blue through white to red), he took his 60-gun flagship, the *Achilles*, with four other gunships, five frigates and six bomb ketches to bombard the harbor of Le Havre and burn its boats. While Rodney received from the shore batteries a "very brisk fire indeed," he inflicted damage on the French boats that left all masts gone and the "boats to all appearance broken-backed" and the port itself believed ruined as a naval arsenal for any further annoyance of Great Britain during the continuance of the war. His bombardment finished off what was left of the invasion plan after the smashing of the French at Quiberon Bay.

Upon his return from the fiery mission to Havre, Rodney found a new King in England. In October, 1760, George III had come to the throne. The first English-born native of the Hanover line, he was infused by belief in his own rectitude and by his mother's prodding, "George be a King." He wanted to be a good ruler to his country and a firm sovereign to his empire, especially to those restive Americans, so ungrateful for the war fought on their behalf against the French, as King George and most of his countrymen thought of it. American objection to being taxed for the cost of the war and for future defense was regarded as thankless ingratitude, not as a basic constitutional issue of taxation by a British Parliament in which they had no representation. Whether or not George III comprehended this view of the matter, he was determined to affirm the right of Parliament — or, as he saw it, of the Crown — to tax the Colonies, and he wanted action and active commanders.

A critical area of defense that the King did comprehend was the West Indies. "Our Islands," George III wrote to Lord Sandwich twenty years later, in 1779, when the American Revolution had become a war, "must be defended even at the risk of an invasion of this island." George was given to extreme statements, and "even at the risk of invasion" was certainly not a sentiment with which ministers would have agreed. But the navy could not be everywhere at once, and if held in home waters to repel a French invasion, it could not be in sufficient strength in the Caribbean to secure the islands there. "If we lose our Sugar Islands," the King's letter continued, "it will be impossible to raise money to continue the war." While this too seems extreme, it had some basis in the revenue that flowed to the government from the abundant fortunes of the rich planters and merchants of the West Indies. Sandwich agreed that as the French grasp at sea power imperiled the Sugar Islands, Britain's principal naval effort should be made in the Caribbean. Although the state of the fleet in the Leeward Islands in 1779 was "very deplorable" and needed reinforcements, a successful operation against Martinique was "the most to be wished," because if it were taken, the other French islands would fall and the French would feel the blow so sharply that "it would probably put an end to the war." Sandwich also was to recommend, in this 1779 memorandum to the King, action against St. Eustatius, from which the French could supply their West Indies fleet with provisions. If French sea power could be broken in the Caribbean and French islands taken, the full force of the British Navy and Army could be turned upon America and the rebellion put down. While in 1759 the Americans had not yet taken up arms against the mother country, and the letters of the King and the First Lord reflect the strategy of a later situation, they show the overriding importance that the West Indies held in British thinking. Always wanting "bold and manly" efforts and offensive operations to thwart the French instead of the "cautious measures" of his ministers, the King, in October, 1761, the year after he ascended the throne, was happy to approve the appointment of Rodney as Commander-in-Chief at Barbados of the Leeward Island station for the purpose of conducting the naval part of a joint land and sea attack on Martinique. The most populous and flourishing of the French islands, Martinique was the largest island of the chain sometimes called the Windward and sometimes the Leeward group. The nomenclature, as one historian of the region laments, "lacked precision." Regardless of being nominally grouped with the Leewards, Martinique dominated the windward position. At Fort Royal it had the finest harbor and, as the most flourishing of the French islands, was the capital of the French West Indies and seat of the French Governor-General and the sovereign Council with jurisdiction over all the French Antilles. Barbados, further down the chain and further into the wind, had no good harbor. The English used English Harbor on Antigua, further up the chain from Martinique.

When Rodney on October 21, 1761, taking up his new command, sailed from Plymouth to join the fleet in the West Indies, plans for the attack had already been made, originally by Pitt when First Minister.

Touching at Barbados on November 22, a thirty days' sail of the westward crossing of the Atlantic, Rodney joined the land forces of General Monckton. Together they reached Martinique on January 7, and the operation, despite the surprising strength of the defense, was a routine West Indian landing. Having "silenced the forts of the coast," the fleet anchored in St. Pierre's Bay with the loss of only one ship, not from enemy gunfire but from striking a reef of rocks. "We have saved all her people, all her stores, and I hope soon to get all her guns," Rodney reported. The fleet having secured the landing and an excellent harbor, a squadron with two brigades was dispatched to the bay of Petite Anse to take up station there, and another squadron to Grande Anse. When Captain Hervey of the *Dragon* had silenced the battery, Rodney's marines and seamen attacked and took possession of the fort. "On January 14th I followed with the whole fleet and army," having again destroyed the enemy's batteries on shore. After reconnoitering the coast here, he determined with General Monckton to attack Fort Royal on the 16th. And having "very successfully and with little loss silenced the batteries [which seemed to have registered on this occasion a more than ordinary record of uselessness], I landed General Monckton with the greatest part of his forces by sunset; and so the whole army was on shore a little after daylight next morning, without the loss of a man," with all necessary supplies, and "all ships and transports anchored as much in safety as this coast will admit of." Two battalions of marines of 450 men each were then landed and proceeded to ascend the heights from which they proposed to lay siege to the fort. On February 10, Rodney was able to congratulate their Lordships on the surrendering of the important citadel of Fort Royal, which had "given his Majesty's forces possession of the noblest and best harbour in these parts." He has also taken fourteen "of the enemy's best privateers" and expects many more from other parts of the island to be delivered to him under the terms of the surrender. He is happy to report "the most perfect harmony" between the army and navy, each vying to serve King and country best. A lively account by an infantry officer with the land forces tells how the sailors dragged cannon and the heaviest mortars up the hills to secure the position, "and," Rodney reported, "the service they did us, both on shore and on the water, is incredible." Freedom from the miseries of their ships doubtless lent energy to the rugged pulling.

The surrender of Martinique, leaving the Lesser Antilles defenseless, caused the surrender to Rodney's fleet of three islands, Ste. Lucie lying south of Martinique, St. Vincent, and Grenada at the bottom of the chain. These were valuable stations, on whose "peaceable possession" Rodney congratulated the Admiralty. Ste. Lucie, largest and considered loveliest of the British Windward Islands, which Rodney had long felt to be particularly desirable, abounded in good ports, while the "important island" of Grenada would provide a safe port in the hurricane months and a very strong citadel.

Meanwhile Jamaica sent him an urgent call for help against an expected combined French and Spanish attack. Anticipating lucrative prizes from this venture, Rodney prepared to go to the relief of Jamaica on his own responsibility, without orders from England, even though General Monckton more submissive to authority, was not willing to detach forces to go with him without instructions from home. Rodney informed the Admiralty of his intention, on the ground that he believed himself "authorized and obliged to succour any of His Majesty's colonies that may be in danger," and assuring their Lordships that he had "no other view but the good of His Majesty's service." The Admiralty suspected otherwise and, to Rodney's angry disappointment, orders arrived instructing him not to pursue his design, because a secret expedition was in preparation for which "everything else must give way" and which he must assist by remaining at his station. Sullen at being deprived of an opportunity of the kind from which fellow-admirals had made fortunes, he prepared his fleet to join the forces for the coming action at Havana, fulcrum of Spanish trade. In the successful outcome at Cuba, Admiral Pocock, who commanded the naval force in the attack, did indeed come away with a fortune in prize money, while Rodney in bitterness gained nothing. In his chagrin, he quarreled with General Monckton, with whom he had worked in such "perfect harmony" at Martinique, and now claimed the General had divided the prizes taken there unfairly.

A more general disappointment was felt next year, in the Peace of Paris of 1763, because of Britain's softheaded yielding by treaty of almost every advantage she had won by arms in the Seven Years' War. Martinique, jewel of the Antilles so newly won, and its neighbor Guadeloupe and Ste. Lucie were given back to France, in return for France ceding all of Canada with Nova Scotia and Cape Breton and islands of the St. Lawrence. Like England, France put the valuation of the West Indies over that of Canada. She was willing to cede Canada in exchange for retrieving Martinique, Guadeloupe and Ste. Lucie because she believed the loss to Britain of those islands would do more than anything to injure the commerce necessary to Britain's life, which the French, like King George, believed was vital to her. The exchange was viewed with disgust by the British public as putting concern for the Colonies ahead of the immense wealth and commercial advantage of the Indies. A similar negative view was taken of the arrangements with Spain by which Cuba and the Philippine Islands were restored to Spain in return for her guarantee to Britain of Florida and all Spanish territory east of the Mississippi except New Orleans. As an exchange designed to safeguard the southern colonies, this too was seen as preferring the interest of the American Colonies before every other.

The British public viewed the Seven Years' War as having been fought to protect the Colonies from French encroachment against which the Colonials were supposed not to have lifted a finger in their own defense. The fact of the Continentals having opened Wolfe's way through Ticonderoga to Quebec and having launched the first siege of Louisburg and defended their own settlements against French-sponsored Indian attacks was ignored. As the British had emerged from the war in the strongest position and as unquestionably sovereign of the seas, the giveaway at Paris seemed all the more unnecessary. The fact that Britain obtained under the treaty virtually total control of the North American continent was not recognized as any great gain. The government was seen as placing a higher value on a wild uncleared land, thick with brush and trackless forest, than on the ready revenues of sugar and trade, an exchange that seemed absurd to contemporaries. If it meant a dimly grasped potential of America's future, that was perhaps a first sign of common sense in the enlightened century — and, as such, thoroughly unpopular to the British citizen.

To persons of extra perception, the prospect presented by securing the Colonies from further encroachment by France or Spain was not favorable. When they "no longer required the protection of Great Britain," "from that moment," wrote Rodney's biographer and son-in-law, admittedly with hindsight, "they may be said to have obtained independence." He was hurrying history, for eventful years had to pass before a movement for independence took root. But insofar as the Colonies were freed from fear of French and Catholic rule, a turning moment had indeed come. For Rodney, who was promoted to Vice-Admiral of the Blue in October, 1762, the cessation of war meant a period of slowing advancement and frustration and involvement in debt leading to a strange and decisive episode in his life. For the moment, on his return to England after the Peace of Paris, his fortunes progressed quietly, if penuriously, while on half pay, the common fate of all officers and crew of a ship when it was paid off. In recognition of his addition of three valuable islands to the British Empire, he was made a Baronet in January, 1764. In the next year, after being a widower for seven years, he remarried — a lady named Henrietta Clies, about whom very little is told except that in due course she bore him his second son and three daughters. A land post was offered him in November, 1765, as Governor of Greenwich Hospital, a shelter for disabled and indigent seamen and a place affording many openings for jobbery (the contemporary term for bureaucratic graft). Rodney's tenure was marked by a notable rebuke to his Vice-Governor for refusing to grant greatcoats to the pensioners in winter, especially as the Vice-Governor wore one himself when sitting by a good fire. His own rule, Rodney said, should be "to render the old men's lives so comfortable" that younger visitors would say: " 'Who would not be a sailor, to live as happy as a prince in his old age!' " Greatcoats were accordingly ordered.

Without a ship and in proximity to London and the fashionable man's life, the lures of gambling enveloped Rodney again, although it was less these than the lures of Parliament that were to be his undoing. He had held three seats in the gift of political patrons, but in 1768 Northampton, which he represented, was suddenly contested by an outsider and an election campaign had to be waged in order for Rodney to retain it. Even without television and modern expenses, the cost of a contested election for entertainment, drinks and direct payment for votes was ruinous. The mystique of Parliament was so powerful that Rodney was willing to spend £30,000 for an illusion of power where he exercised no influence and from which he obtained no benefit and which plunged him even more deeply in debt. In 1771, he was named to the honorary position of Rear Admiral of Great Britain and appointed Commander-in-Chief of Jamaica. Since half his designated salary as Rear Admiral was withheld until he had accounted to the Navy Board for expenditures of public money in Jamaica and to other claims upon his salary, he asked to retain his Greenwich Hospital post, as, he pointed out, three predecessors had been allowed to do before him. Lord Sandwich, showing signs of some unexplained grudge, refused to allow this and when, after his service in Jamaica, Rodney asked to be appointed Governor of that island, this too was refused. Embittered and resentful, he faced coming to the end of his three-year commission with the prospect of returning to England on half pay unless he was given another post. Advised upon his return in September, 1774, that he should leave the country rather than face a possibility of debtor's prison, he fled to Paris. Here the pleasures of elegant life and sociable companions who admired the handsome English Admiral overcame him once more, until the burden of new debts he had incurred imprisoned him in the French capital, if not within stone walls. The French police made it plain that he would not be allowed to leave the city until his Parisian creditors were paid.

At this moment the shots at Lexington and Concord announced the American rebellion and put Rodney in a frenzy of impatience to take his part in action at sea. He was held immobile, however, for in spite of urgent letters to Lord Sandwich offering his service for active duty and his readiness "to go on any enterprise . . . at a moment's warning," no recall came from the Admiralty and nothing more than a formal and official reply from the First Lord, who in his fulsome correspondence had always professed himself Rodney's true friend.

Rebellion against England of her primary

colony was now a fact, bringing a foreboding of international conflict. That was realized when in February, 1778, France entered into alliance with the Colonies after the stunning American victory at Saratoga in October, 1777, that brought with it the nearly unbelievable surrender of General Burgoyne's army of 5,700, who were shipped home as prisoners under oath not to resume arms against America. Four months later, in March, 1778, the French informed the British government that they recognized the independence of the United States of America, and had concluded treaties of alliance and of amity and commerce with the Continental Congress upon condition that neither party should make a separate peace before England acknowledged American independence. The alliance changed the war, putting a major power on the side of the rebels and embroiling Britain once more against her ancient enemy.

EIGHT

The French Intervention

To make alliance with rebels necessarily put France at war with Britain as the governing power, which was of course the French intention. Bourbon policy was not formed out of sympathy with the Jeffersonian principle that a time comes when a people must "assume among the powers of the earth the separate and equal station to which the laws of Nature and Nature's God entitle them." That was not a monarchical idea, although enunciated by the ally whose cause the Bourbons now embraced. Less philosophical, the French motive was simple hostility to Britain, grown out of seven centuries of rivalry since 1066, and desire to redress French losses in the Seven Years' War. Thus it was a power struggle of the Old World, not a concern with America, that brought about the French intervention that would make it possible for the American Colonies to win their separation from Britain. The alliance was composed of two treaties, one of commerce and friendship, and the other contingent upon both parties binding themselves not to make a separate peace with Britain before she acknowledged American independence.

In July, 1778, five months after signing her treaty of alliance with America, France declared war on Great Britain, to be followed a year later by Spain, in renewal of the Bourbon Family Compact. Spain's price was a French promise to help her recover Gibraltar and Minorca.

The greatest French dread was that the Colonies would reconcile themselves with the mother country and re-establish her trade and her colonial and maritime position, restoring Britain to the pre-eminence which it was France's chief war aim to reduce. Benjamin Franklin's deliberate hints to the French about a possible reconciliation, and supporting signs and portents which the French thought they detected, had led them to make the treaty of alliance in the first place. Its pledge against a separate peace barred the way to French fear of settlement between Britain and the Colonies — for the moment. It was soon to revive when the British themselves proposed a settlement with the Colonies.

Seventeen days after the French entered the war, the opening fleet action that had nothing to do with America, yet that would in the long run seriously damage the British war effort, intangibly if not physically, was fought in the Channel near the island of Ushant, off the French coast. The French objective was to gain control of the Channel preparatory to invading England. Having intelligence of the sailing of two French squadrons from Brest and Toulon, the British objective was to prevent their juncture, and in case the two squadrons did join and proceed up the Channel, to attack them unless their force was "markedly superior," and in that case to return for reinforcements. Admiral Augustus Keppel, the British commander of the Channel fleet, on sighting two frigates, outriders of the French fleet, opened fire in eagerness to bring on a battle. The usual practice of the time was for the admiral to be in the center of the line, where he had the forward and rear extremities of his fleet equally visible, or equally invisible, as the case might be. For successful action, a perfect understanding must exist between the admiral and his second in command, who directs the rear. In this case, Admiral Keppel and his third in command, Admiral Hugh Palliser, belonged to different political parties. Again occurred a misapprehension of signals, whether from misunderstanding or malice was afterward disputed by partisans to the point of blows. Either way, the signal table was inadequate for its purposes. The British code had no signal that allowed a captain to indicate a failure to see or understand a given instruction, nor any by which an admiral could indicate that a second signal superseded the first or other change of orders. No better system of communicating could be worked out except the use of light dispatch boats as messengers, like a general's aides on land galloping forward with spoken instructions. This was not practical, because ships of the line could not stand still awaiting orders as brigade or divisional commanders could on land. The alternative of placing the admiral in a frigate at the head of the line, so that he might show the path he wanted by his example rather than by signal, was later attempted by Nelson but never generally adopted.

Thirty ships of the line fought on either side at Ushant; none was taken or sunk and both fleets returned without glory to their respective ports. The British public — expecting to see the home fleet return with the French scalp hanging from its belt, having driven the enemy from the seas — looked for someone to blame and fell into furious dispute when charges were raised by Palliser against Keppel, and vice versa, culminating in courts-martial of first one and then the other, fiercely dividing opinion in the public and the navy. Popular sentiment favored Keppel, who was a Whig attached to the Opposition and who, in 1775, had announced that he would not serve against the American Colonists. Only after the French entered the war had he accepted command of the home fleet. Now, charged by Palliser with having thrown away victory at Ushant by ordering his fleet to withdraw when the French were fleeing, he demanded a court-martial to clear him of the accusation. Palliser was a protégé of Sandwich and a loyal supporter of the government. His attack upon a superior officer and a Whig aroused the antagonism of colleagues, of whom twelve admirals signed a protest against his conduct, so that he too took his turn in court. The trials and testimony by witnesses aroused public passion even further. Opinion in general laid the fault for the navy coming home empty-handed on Sandwich, who was believed to have sent Admiral Keppel to sea with an ill-equipped fleet in the hope that he would suffer defeat and thus discredit the Opposition which Keppel openly supported. Jobbery in the yards had, in truth, left ships unseaworthy, underequipped, unprovisioned and undermanned. Opposition members in Parliament charged Sandwich in a "fierce torrent of invective as was ever heard in the House" with "gross incompetency and criminal neglect" of naval affairs. As a stick to beat the administration, his dismissal was moved by Charles James Fox. The motion was defeated by the government's safe majority of 103 votes. Sandwich remained.

Excitement rose when the court-martial at Portsmouth enthusiastically acquitted Keppel. The London mob celebrated by looting Palliser's house and smashing all the windows at Lord North's. The easy-tempered Prime Minister, a master of survival, climbed to the roof and equably remained there until the rioters dispersed. Unsated, they rushed on to assault the Admiralty gates and howl for the downfall of Sandwich. After Palliser too was acquitted, he resigned his commission in the navy and was later recompensed by the government for his loss of income by appointment to the post Rodney had held as Governor of Greenwich Hospital. Keppel, with a louder gesture, declared that he would not serve again in the navy while Sandwich was First Lord. The withdrawal of the two antagonists in no way quieted the quarrel. A train of dissension and intramural hostility now pervaded the senior service, from officers to dockyard workers, just at the time when Britain's need of an able, self-confident navy for offense and defense in four theaters of war at once — in America, in home waters, in the West Indies and in India — was at its most critical. Rallying to Keppel, Whig flag officers took up his example and made it a point of honor for opponents of the government to decline service under Sandwich. Divided against itself by party faction, the navy was now deprived of many of its forward-looking officers. Naval officers were Whigs almost to a man.

The navy was ruled at the top by the Lords Commissioners, who were professional seamen exercising political power from seats in Parliament and among whom the First Lord held a seat in the small national governing Cabinet of eight or nine ministers. It was a vast institution administering several hundred warships, with enough cannon to equip an army and enough personnel to man its ranks, dockyards, victualing yards and storehouses around the world. The harm done by the rampant politicizing following the default of Ushant is recorded by Rodney's friend Wraxall, drawing on Rodney's private letters. "So violent was the spirit of party and faction in his own fleet, as almost to supersede and extinguish the affection to their Sovereign and their country . . . " and of such "inveterate an animosity to the Administration . . . particularly to the First Lord, as almost to wish for a defeat if it would produce the dismission of Ministers." Naval officers themselves confirmed these sentiments. As Commissioner of the Portsmouth dockyard, Admiral Hood declared in a letter to his brother that "such a want of discipline and order throughout a fleet was never known before, and such a want of regard and attention to the good of the King's service. The negligence of officers in general is really astonishing, and God knows to what extent the mischief will go." Admiral Samuel Barrington, who had entered the navy at the age of eleven, commanded a ship at eighteen and whose brother was one of the Lords Commissioners of the Admiralty, when declining the Channel command, spoke of the "total relaxation of discipline" and said that the "strain and anxiety" would kill him. "Had I been in command, what I have seen since I have been here would have made me run mad." He had no confidence in Sandwich or in the Admiralty, who were the "wickedest herd that ever good men served under." The lesson was not yet clear in the 18th century, as America was to learn to her cost in our own century, that the presence of disunity in the military about method and strategy, and among the nation's people about the rightness of the war aim, makes it impossible for a war of any duration to be fought effectively and won.

A modern historian, Geoffrey Callender, has offered the provocative thought that the stalemate at Ushant had historic result, for if the French had been beaten and shut up thereafter in their ports, they could not have come to the aid of the Americans, with the probability that the British might then have defeated the Revolution, leaving America to remain part of the British Empire. However interesting may be this prospectus for the history of the world, it is not realistic, for it would have depended on British will and capacity to undertake and maintain a blockade of French Atlantic ports. To tie down the fleet in a static role when protection of trade and defense of far-flung positions from Gibraltar to Ceylon was considered the warships' primary duty would not have been at all likely, even had there been a victory at Ushant.

The accepted view that inadequate naval force was the primary reason for Britain's defeat in the War for American Independence leaves an open question. Disunited and ill-disciplined the Royal Navy certainly was. Its numbers were too few for its tasks, and as a result of profiteering at the dockyards and the carelessness of the Admiralty's Commissioners, the ships were in such poor condition that one liner, royally named the *Prince William* for the King's son, actually foundered and sank at anchor in the Thames. Its governors were men of limited intelligence, limited experience, no coherent strategy and unlimited assurance of winning. The open question is whether the persistence and will of the enemy in such men as George Washington and the Reverend Daggett of New Haven (whom we shall meet further on) and the geographical logistics of the American continent, where every one of the 50,000 British troops in North America and every bullet and every biscuit of his supply and every letter of instructions to his commanders had to be transmitted over the six-to-eight-week width of the Atlantic Ocean, would not have made the war unwinnable by the British anyway. A larger navy, it is supposed, could have made a major difference by allowing ships of the Channel fleet or the West Indies to be diverted for blockade of France's Atlantic ports, preventing French maritime intervention in aid of the Colonies, but that could have happened only if the British had thought blockade sufficiently important. They did not, since at no time in the war did they take seriously the possibility of the Americans winning. Blockade of the French ports would have required immobilizing a large number of ships while their bot-

*Admiral Sir George Brydges Rodney at
forty-two, by Joshua Reynolds, 1761*

ABOVE: *St. Eustatius,
copperplate engraving by
C. F. Bendorp, Dordrecht,
Holland, 1782*
RIGHT: *Southeast view of New
York Harbor in the years just
preceding the Revolution, by
an unidentified artist, 1757*

ABOVE: *Sir Joseph Yorke, by Perroneau*
RIGHT: *Admiral François Joseph Paul de Grasse at*
Yorktown, from London *magazine, 1782*

ABOVE: *Action between the* Serapis *and* Bonhomme Richard, *September 23, 1779, line engraving by Lerpinière and Fittler, 1780*
OPPOSITE BOTTOM: *The Battle of Cowpens, 1781, by Frederick Kemmelmeyer, 1809*

*ABOVE LEFT: Sir Henry Clinton in 1787,
miniature by Thomas Day*
*ABOVE RIGHT: General Count de Rochambeau,
by Charles Willson Peale*

AMERICA TRIUMPHANT and BRITANNIA in DISTRESS

EXPLANATION.

I. America sitting on that quarter of the globe with the Flag of the United States displayed over her head; holding in one hand the Olive branch, inviting the ships of all nations to partake of her commerce; and in the other hand supporting the Cap of Liberty.

II. Fame proclaiming the joyful news to all the world.

III. Britannia weeping at the loss of the trade of America, attended with an evil genius.

IV. The British flag struck, on her strong Fortresses.

V. French, Spanish, Dutch, &c. shipping in the harbours of America.

VIA view of New-York, wherein is exhibited the Trator Arnold, taken with remorse for selling his country, and Judas like hanging himself.

"America Triumphant and Britannia in Distress"

I. America sitting on that quarter of the globe with the Flag of the United States displayed over her head; holding in one hand the Olive branch, inviting the ships of all nations to partake of her commerce; and in the other hand supporting the Cap of Liberty.

II. Fame proclaiming the joyful news to all the world.

III. Britannia weeping at the loss of the trade of America, attended with an evil genius.

IV. The British flag struck, on her strong Fortresses.

V. French, Spanish, Dutch, &c. shipping in the harbours of America.

VI. A view of New-York, wherein is exhibited the Trator Arnold, taken with remorse for selling his country, and Judas like hanging himself.

(American print published in Weatherwise's Town and Country Almanac, 1782) toms grew foul from marine growth, and would have depended on a concerted decision by the war Cabinet, which could never make up its mind whether concentration of naval forces in one place for blockade was worth weakening the forces available for convoy of trade and for defense of the Caribbean and East Indian colonies and of the home islands.

As in older and later empires, resouces were not equal to the overextension of the imperial reach. Inadequacy of decision-making was a primary defect. Lord Sandwich begged the King to require that "meetings of the Cabinet" should reduce its decisions to writing, "and when a question is agitated it ought to be decided one way or another, and not be put off as now most frequently happens, without any determination." Failure to focus available resources on a single objective and give that objective absolute priority was a major failure in strategy. Notwithstanding common opinion, human beings can and sometimes do learn. After Pearl Harbor in 1941, the American decision, previously agreed with Britain, to give priority of defense to Europe and defeat Hitler first was what made his defeat possible.

In 1778, Britain had no one capable of a decisive determination of that kind. Not the King. While George III had no trouble making up his mind, it contained only one idea — to conquer, but not how. Pitt was gone, felled by a stroke in April at the time of the French alliance, and dead a month later. The King's two chief war ministers, Germain and Sandwich, were emphatic enough, but not usefully, having no clear plan of strategy and sloppy about implementing any plan they conceived. Saratoga, the most stunning British defeat before the end, was the result of simple carelessness to ensure that two armies, Howe's and Burgoyne's, which according to the plan of campaign were supposed to meet to form a pincer, were both informed of the design and timing of the movements planned for them. As it turned out, they were not; moreover, the plan approved by Lord Germain was based on the "wildly fallacious premise," in the opinion of William Willcox, Clinton's biographer, that Howe's main field army could operate through Pennsylvania while a substantial part of it was immobilized in New York and that Burgoyne's could move independently in the North without reference to Howe. Professor Willcox assigns the responsibility of the "worst" British planning of the war to "intellectual shortcomings" of the three architects, Howe, Germain, Burgoyne, and to the "almost complete lack of communication between them." The basic fault was complacency rather than mental incapacity.

Complacency is an attribute of long-retained power like that of the Chinese. Throughout her history, China conceived of herself as the center of the universe, as the Middle Kingdom surrounded by barbarians. Outsiders whose misfortune it was "to live beyond her borders" were inferiors, required, if they wished to approach the Emperor, to assume the kowtow position, prone with face on the floor. If not quite so explicitly, Britain carried the same feeling in her soul, a sense of being the world's moon that pulled the tides of international affairs.

The danger in complacency is that it causes the possessor to ignore as unimportant the local factors and conditions that govern other people with whom it deals. Britons faced with the American Revolution were not interested in Americans or in their magnificent continent reaching from ocean to ocean. No British monarch had ever seen his domain across the Atlantic, and no British minister in the fifteen years, 1760–75, when insurgency was brewing to a boil visited the Colonies to learn what was exercising the unruly subjects or what kind of people they were. The consequence was ignorance, which is a disadvantage in war.

"Know thy enemy," the *sine qua non* of successful military operations, was entirely lacking in the war with America, and complacency allowed no room for effort to make good the lack. Lord Sandwich, for example, employed no proper means to obtain intelligence of French naval movements, according to a charge in Parliament by Lord Stormont, the British Ambassador in Paris. His "negligence" was "inconceivable" in that it allowed French warships to leave their ports to sail for the West Indies without an alert to the British at sea who were watching for them. "We have no intelligence," the Ambassador told the House of Lords. Stormont said he had done his utmost repeatedly to arrange for cutters to lay off the French ports to get information, but could not prevail on Lord Sandwich to grant them.

More fundamental was the attitude of the chief war minister, Lord George Germain, who had won his position through the King's favor by advocating the "utmost force of this kingdom" to finish the rebellion in one campaign, which should conclude with an offer to the Colonies of submission or ruin. That was the extent of his government's understanding of the rebels.

Planlessness followed from the start of the war, when the British assumed that no plan was needed to suppress a rebellion — only hard blows. Carelessness followed from the assumption that the superiority of British force was so great that it made taking pains in performance unnecessary. A more basic deteriorating factor was dissension at home.

Politics as much as anything defeated the British in the American war. The British have always been obsessed with politics, not so much in terms of opposing systems of belief as in terms of who's in and who's out. Transmitted to the navy by the Keppel-Palliser quarrel, it cut like a carving knife through the solidity of the senior service. "So violent was the spirit of party and faction" in the fleet, as Wraxall has told us, "as almost to extinguish every patriotic sentiment."

Mistrust of Sandwich after the Keppel affair was virtually total except for the King, who relied on him and who, knowing nothing of the nuts and bolts required to keep a fleet serviceable, accepted what he was told and dutifully believed in the navy as a British eagle which would pounce upon and destroy his enemies. Constitutionally unable to change ministers for fear that the unknown would be worse than the known, he held on to Sandwich as he had held on to Bute and now Lord North, as a sinking swimmer might hold on to a post when the waters are closing over his head.

The Opposition despised the First Lord. One of its leading figures, the Duke of Richmond, wrote to Keppel when he was first offered command of the Grand Fleet, before Ushant, that he did not think it a matter for congratulation. If Sandwich has a "bad fleet" to send out, he would "be glad to put it under the command of a man whom he does not love." He advised Keppel to have each ship examined by himself and his officers and "not to trust Lord Sandwich for a piece of rope yarn."

Britain's greatest dread, the belligerency of France in alliance with the American rebellion, was now a fact. It put odds heavily in the balance against her and convinced many of the government party that the immediate necessity was to relieve Britain of a war both costly and profitless in order to free her to meet the French challenge, and the only way to do that was a settlement with the Colonies, as the Whigs had long been urging. Slowly the discouraging truth that the war was unwinnable was forcing itself on the notice of what Edward Gibbon called the *"thinking* friends of government," meaning others like himself.* Chatham, formerly Pitt, the great Prime Min-

*Gibbon had been elected to Parliament as a supporter of the government in 1774.

ister, was the first to have pointed this out, in a speech on November 20, 1777. Before he knew of the American victory at Saratoga, he had told the House of Lords, "I know that the conquest of English America is an impossibility. You cannot, I venture to say it, you cannot conquer America. . . ." The war was "unjust in its principles, impractible in its means, and ruinous in its consequences." The employment of "mercenary sons of rapine and plunder" (meaning the Hessians and other German mercenaries) had aroused "incurable resentment." "If I were an American as I am an Englishman, while a foreign troop was landed in my country, I never would lay down my arms — never — never — never." By insisting on submission, Britain would lose all benefit from the Colonies through their trade and their support against the French, and gain for herself only renewed war against France and Spain. The only remedy was to terminate hostilities and negotiate a treaty of settlement.

The logistics, Charles James Fox added, pursuing the argument, made military success impossible. On land, generals were placed too far apart to aid each other, while America's immensely long coast with its innumerable bays, estuaries and river mouths and her self-sufficiency in food, if not in arms, made her virtually impervious to sea power. Indeed, hostilities worked the other way around, by depriving Britain of the tall white pines from America for her masts, and of seasoned timber, tar and other naval stores for ship-building. Whereas in a European land war siege of a capital city usually led to surrender, the separateness of colonial regions meant that capture of New York or Boston or Philadelphia brought no finality. And there was a final problem that Chatham had also remarked. Even if you could conquer the Americans, you could not make them willing partners.

Failure to quell rebels by conventional military action was humiliating to Britain, and the failure to arouse active support by the Loyalists, who had been expected to rise up and overwhelm their misguided countrymen and had been counted upon as a primary component in the military suppression of the rebellion, was a major disappointment, which the British seemed not to realize was their own fault. In their persisting attitude of scorn for colonials, they made no effort to recruit Loyalists for an organized force of their own, or form Loyalist divisions or even brigades, or to offer them commissions as officers in the British Army. If the Loyalists had wished to fight as an organized force and do more than protect themselves from harassment and persecution by the patriots, what military command could they join? The British government, while paying German mercenaries at increasingly disagreeable cost and adding a few miserable results from Irish recruiting, did not use what they had at hand and complained unhappily when a Loyalist army did not arise out of the earth spontaneously. Loyalists, who mainly belonged to the propertied class, had in fact stronger feelings about the war than the ruling British. Their sentiments sprang less from devotion to the Crown than to their privileged position, which the Revolution threatened to overturn. Although the revolutionary leaders were landowners like Washington and Jefferson and men of wealth like the Morrises, they were felt to represent a spirit of subversion rising in the world. As against the Loyalists, the Revolution was essentially a class war which, like all conflicts that threaten the loss of property, arouses the fiercest feelings.

Britain had based her calculations on ending the rebellion by the spring of 1777; instead, in 1778 a successful conclusion in America was as far off as ever. The entry of France added force to the arguments that the war was unwinnable and brought about an astonishing reversal by Lord North's government — an offer of peace terms and of conciliation to the Colonies, which it was hoped would bring them back to the house of the parent and break off their betrothal to France. The Conciliatory Propositions, as they were called, were submitted to a stunned and unbelieving Parliament in February, 1778. Their purpose was rather to placate the Opposition than to negotiate peace with the Americans. The Opposition, which enjoyed the Commons' most eloquent and effective speakers, Fox and Burke, continually denounced the war as unjust, and as certain to be ruinous to Great Britain by the ever-increasing cost of maintaining enlarged armies and fleets at the price of increased taxes.

To stem the disaffection, the government made its peace proposal for the sake of its own hold on office, the primary concern of every government, regardless of policy. A Peace Commission was appointed in March, headed by Frederick, fifth Earl Carlisle, a young man of great wealth, scion of the Howards and owner of the regal Castle Howard. Known chiefly as a fashion plate, he was otherwise qualified mainly as the son-in-law of Lord Gower, a prominent member of the Bedford Gang, a political group faithful to the King and Lord North. Ample wealth and great estate are not attributes that as a rule accustom the possessor to walk softly and adjust to compromise. Life had not trained the Earl of Carlisle to be a negotiator, especially not vis-à-vis followers of Samuel Adams and Benjamin Franklin.

Except for one missing element, the peace terms proposed by Britain appeared to be a package of everything the Americans wanted: exemption from taxation by Parliament, membership in the House of Commons accepted as a principle (method and numbers were to be worked out in discussion), recognition of Congress as a constitutional body, repeal of the tea duty and other punitive acts — in short, everything except the grant of independence, on which the Americans insisted as a prior condition of, not a subject for, negotiation. Upon this rock of independence the mission foundered, nor was there any mention of withdrawal from the country of British troops and ships, another American condition; and without these conditions, members of Congress would neither meet nor talk with the peace commissioners. In any event, the peace overture had come too late. Having pledged to France to make no separate peace, the Americans could not have come to terms with the British even if they had wanted to. "The pride of men," Edmund Burke noted, "will not often suffer reason to have any scope until it can be no longer of service."

To end a war and restore peace in its place needs delicacy. The tactics of Carlisle and his colleague on the commission — Governor Johnstone, so called because he had formerly served as Governor of West Florida — were so heavy-handed as to suggest that they were intended to fail, as perhaps they were. The British government, hating and rejecting the thought of independence, had, as was suspected, planned the Peace Commission as a gesture to quiet the Opposition, without wanting a positive result. They were not likely to get one by Governor Johnstone's methods, which were as counterproductive as possible, as we shall see. Before his service as Governor of West Florida, he had been a naval officer of the aggressive, dictatorial and quarrelsome kind. Given to dueling, he had been found guilty by court-martial of insubordination in a duel, but not sentenced except by reprimand because of personal bravery in action. In Florida his staff had officially protested his autocratic conduct. He was not the ideal selection for a peace mission. Carlisle, as noted, knew nothing of negotiation. William Eden, the third commissioner, had been confidential secretary to the Board of Trade and Plantations, which governed relations with the Colonies, and, as a member of both the English and later Irish parliaments, had to deal with both Americans and Irish, two troublesome peoples. During the war with America, he served as the director of secret intelligence. In these positions he might be supposed to have learned the utility of tactful procedures, though if he had, he seems not to have been able to convey them to his colleagues.

The British government itself had nullified the mission before it could act, by ordering the evacuation of Philadelphia for transfer of command to New York, giving an effect of British withdrawal just as the peace commissioners were due to arrive in America. The appearance of yielding was enhanced by the transfer of 5,000 troops, which had held Philadelphia, to the West Indies to counter expected French attack on the islands. Philadelphia was thus rendered indefensible and Carlisle deprived of his theorem that "gunpowder or guineas will fix the business."

An offer of peace terms by one belligerent will always give an impression of a weakening of purpose and will to victory. The other party, sensing weakness, will be less disposed to accept terms. This is one reason why ending a war is always more difficult than starting one. The Peace Commission and the Conciliatory Propositions unavoidably gave an impression that British enthusiasm for the war was fading, which was indeed the case and which naturally gave the Americans reason to reject terms or even to discuss them.

Frustrated and affronted in America by the refusal of Congress to meet with him and his colleagues, Johnstone's idea was to persuade individual members by worldly rewards to move the recalcitrant Congress to enter negotiations. He made his proposals in writing, offering to bribe Robert Morris of Philadelphia, one of the richest men in America and a devoted partisan of the Revolution, and also Joseph Reed, the Pennsylvania patriot, who was offered £10,000 if he could reconcile the Colonies with Britain. Johnstone suggested that peerages could be arranged for other members who might succeed in promoting a settlement. Among those he approached was Henry Laurens, President of the Congress. When Johnstone's letters were given by their indignant recipients to the press, public outrage forced the overenterprising commissioner to resign from the Peace Commission and return to England. Eden, more circumspect, took no part, unless private and undocumented, in his colleague's too zealous maneuvers, writing only to his brother at home that if "my wishes and cares could accomplish it, this noble country would soon belong once more to Great Britain." His chief of mission, Lord Carlisle, was left to resort to a tactic of threats of terror and devastation. In a public manifesto of October, 1778, which he ordered distributed to all members of the Congress, to George Washington and all American generals, to all provincial governors and assemblies, to all ministers of the Gospel and commanders of the British forces and prison camps, he proclaimed in the name of the Peace Commission that the Colonies having made alliance with the enemy of Britain, it became Britain's duty "by every means in her power to destroy or render useless a connexion contrived for her ruin"; in short, to replace the "humanity and benevolence with which she had hitherto pursued the war" by sterner practices. Carlisle's notion of benevolence addressed to people who in every colony had already suffered pillage and destruction, the burning of villages and the laying waste of farms, fields and timberlands, did not lend him credibility. Taking advantage of his threats, Congress recommended to local authorities that the British text should be published in gazettes of their districts, "to convince the good people of these states of the insidious designs" of the Peace Commission.

Military ill success and the personal humiliation of the Peace Commission had prompted the commissioners to issue the manifesto known as the Carlisle Proclamation. Its expressed threats were modest compared to the intentions of its first unpublished draft, proposing "a scheme of universal devastation," to be applied by the army and fleet, which its author fondly believed "will have *effect.*" A test came in Connecticut. Whether or not taking its cue from the Carlisle Proclamation, a short campaign of terror was carried out by Governor Tryon of New York in July, 1779. Compared by Henry Laurens to the operations of the Duke of Alva, in dreadful memory of the Spanish Terror, the Connecticut raid was no massacre, but vicious enough to stimulate rather than subdue resistance, a well-known effect of such measures, and to induce residents to record the events in many journals.

Apart from geographical convenience, Connecticut was chosen because it had made itself obnoxious to the British in and around New York by manufacturing munitions for the colonials and furnishing more troops for the rebel cause than any other colony except Massachusetts, and by launching frequent raids on land and water that interfered with the military plans of Sir Henry Clinton, the British Commander-in-Chief. Moreover, its population was counted as three-quarters disloyal. Clinton had decided upon "severe punishment" to be inflicted by a force of 3,000 troops coming from New York under the command of Major General Tryon, Governor of New York, and to be joined by 2,000 sailors and marines crossing from Long Island in 48 transports with tenders escorted by two warships. The largest collection of ships that had ever entered Long Island Sound, the armada made an impressive sight as it came up to New Haven and anchored in the early light of dawn July 5, 1779.

On the previous day, July 4, Tryon had issued an eloquent proclamation distributed in printed copies evidently thought to be truly persuasive, for although their effect, he reported, "cannot be discovered until further operations and descent upon their coast," he expected his words to awaken "terror and despondency" among the people of the coast, whom he believed to be "already divided and easily impressible." He told them that their lives and "the existence of their habitations on your defenceless coast showed Britain's for-bearance and lenity in its mild and noble efforts." He urged the population to give up their "ungenerous and wanton insurrection into which they had been deluded by design-ing men for private purposes." In this plea, General Tryon reflected the enduring British belief, which held Britain to the expectation of an early victory around the corner, that the mass of Americans were basically loyal and only waiting to overturn demagogues and agitators to come back to their old allegiance. "Can the strength of your whole province," continued the proclamation, "cope with the force of Great Britain? You are conscious it cannot. Why then, will you persist in a ruinous and ill-judged resistance? We hoped you would recover from the frenzy which had distracted this unhappy country and we believe the day will come when the greater part of this continent will blush at their delusion."

How was it possible for Tryon, Governor of a colony, to know so little of the people he was fighting? Only the year before, giving firm notice of their intent, Connecticut and six other colonies — two from New England, two from the mid-Atlantic and two from the South — signed the Articles of Confederation that were to be the foundation of the United States of America.

At sunrise on July 5, a gunshot from the ships of Tryon's raid sounded the signal for landing. Instantly, a string of boats filled with redcoats was seen dropping astern from every transport and pulling directly for shore. They were met by a biting blaze of musket fire from a people who proved less "impressible" than supposed. Warned in advance by compatriots in New York of Tryon's coming, defenders armed with ancient long-range Queen Anne muskets poured into New Haven from nearby towns to a total of several thousand. Knowing every tree and fence, and fighting for their homes and rights, they fired upon the invaders from the protection of the tall Indian corn now at its full July height. As excellent marksmen, they severely damaged General Tryon's assumptions, but they could not repel his numbers nor save their homes and neighbors from pillage, fire and murder. The sharp crack of musketry and the smoke of burning buildings marked the invaders' line of march. Smashing their way into every house, they tore and trampled on furnishings, piled up furniture to set it in flame, beat, raped and savaged the residents, and in one case murdered an aged and defenseless victim. He was Mr. Benjamin English, who, according to an account in the *Connecticut Journal* two days later, reproved a group of drunken redcoats for rough and insulting behavior to his daughter when they broke into his house demanding refreshments. They ran him through the body several times with bayonets. His daughter, on entering the room where he lay on the floor bleeding as he died, cried out, "Oh! How could you murder my poor old father so cruelly?" One of the soldiers asked "Is he your father?" and at her reply of "Yes," he stamped upon the old man's chest and upturned face, crushing his nose.

In the midst of the skirmish in New Haven, a body of students from Yale College, marching to meet the enemy, raised a cheer as they saw their former president, the Reverend Dr. Naphtali Daggett, astride his old black mare and carrying his fowling piece ready for action, riding furiously to the attack. Professor of divinity and president of Yale for nine years, he galloped past and soon was seen standing alone on a nearby hillside, firing upon the advancing British column. Coming up, the officer of the column shouted, "What are you doing there, you old fool, firing on His Majesty's troops?" Firmly, Daggett replied, "Exercising the rights of war." Asked whether, if his life were spared, he would do such a thing again, he answered, "Nothing more likely. I rather think I should." Cool defiance can invite respect, if only temporary. Instead of shooting him, the soldiers permitted Daggett to surrender and marched him back to town at the point of their bayonets, wounding him with small stabs as they pricked him forward under the burning midday sun of the hottest day, one observer said, he had ever known. "The stoutest man almost melted in the heat." When the Reverend's strength failed and he was ready to sink to the ground in exhaustion, the soldiers drove him on with blows and bruises from the barrels of their guns and stripped his shoes from him to take their silver buckles, while they called him a "damned old rebel" and a thousand insults. Bleeding from his wounds, he was finally left where neighbors took him in and cared for him, but the battering had been too much. He died within the year — as everyone firmly believed, from the treatment he had received.

Two churches and a meetinghouse were burned at New Haven, which Tryon excused on the ground that they had caught fire accidentally from houses burning nearby. Papers and manuscripts taken from Yale College were not recovered, despite the indignant protest of President Ezra Stiles to Tryon, telling him that a war "against science" had been "reprobated for ages by the wisest and most powerful generals." As the Duke of Alva would not have done, Tryon actually replied, saying that an inquiry had turned up no information about the papers. It was an insignificant item amid tragedy that did not end at New Haven. Governor Tryon's forces moved on to pillage and burn Fairfield and Norwalk and destroy the salt pans at Horse Neck before they re-embarked for New York.

What could they have thought to gain by this persecution of civilians — to persuade Americans to give up their cause and return obediently to the sovereignty of Britain? To be worth the effort, war requires a rational objective, political and, in the short run, military, not just foolish aggression. Ultimately, the end sought is surrender of the enemy and the giving up of his purpose, whatever it may be, by the military destruction of his armed forces and his supporting resources, by penetration and occupation of his territory, by fear and despair induced in the population by terror. From the days of the Tarquins on the banks of the Tiber to the Germans in Belgium in 1914 and again at Lidice in Czechoslovakia in 1942, when every adult of the town was collected in a group and shot dead in retaliation for some act of resistance, this method has rarely brought the desired results, unless it is total and undeviating. Did Clinton and Tryon expect otherwise? More likely they and their soldiers were simply moved to vent violence by the angry frustration of unsuccessful war, which is what usually generates atrocity — as in the case of the Americans at My Lai — except when it is authorized and organized from above, as in the case of the Spanish in the Netherlands, the Japanese in China and the Germans in both World Wars. It is always possible to say, and is always said afterward, that the agents were merely acting on orders of higher authority, but when does normal inhibition in the common soldier or other agent cry stop? If inhibition has been systematically weakened by prevailing policy, it does not operate.

Given the firm intent of the British to hold their empire of the American Colonies and the equally strong intent of the Colonies to achieve independence, there was in fact no solution to the conflict. From King George down, every Englishman, including most of the Opposition, was convinced that Great Britain's greatness depended on the possession of colonies and that to give up America would mean the fall of Britain as a world power and her reduction, as Walpole wrote, "to a miserable little island as insignificant as Denmark or Sardinia." "If American independence were recognized," declared Shelburne, a leader of the Opposition, "on that day, the sun of Great Britain is set." Even if she won, trade and useful connection with an angry defeated people would dry up, unless measures were taken to recover their friendship. The Tryon raid did not seem the surest way to recover friendship.

Without trade or colonies, Britain's ruin seemed foretold. "Like Carthage she will fall when the commerce on which she is founded is no more," an official said, a prophecy that found an echo in the sage of Strawberry Hill. "She will lose her East Indian Colonies next," Horace Walpole predicted, "and then France will dictate to us more imperiously than ever we did to Ireland." France had every such intention, but history had laid out a different path. The challenge of Napoleon, thirty-odd years later, stimulated Britain to a revival of her energies and her will, and when her recovered navy under Nelson turned the challenger back at the Nile and at Trafalgar, Britain, instead of sliding as predicted to the level of Denmark or Sardinia, regained her dominant place as a world power and retained it for another hundred years until the crash of 1914.

In America, the Carlisle peace overture had brought only failure to finish a humiliating and interminable war. Faced with the absolute refusal of members of Congress to meet for talks, Carlisle and his fellow-commissioners went home in November, 1778, emptyhanded. Their visit, like the Tryon Raid, had been an exercise in futility.

At the same time, American fortunes suffered a graver exercise in futility in the fiasco of the first military assistance produced by the French alliance — the more disappointing because it was naval assistance, the kind wanted most. Early in July, 1778, when the French first entered the war, a French fleet of 12 ships of the line and 3 frigates, under Admiral Count d'Estaing, had arrived on the coast of Virginia and moved up to New York. The plan of action contemplated a joint offensive on New York by the French fleet together with American land forces, but the large French warships found themselves unable to cross the bar at Sandy Hook in New York Bay. At Washington's suggestion for a combined attack on Newport, Rhode Island, d'Estaing then sailed north. A British fleet under Admiral Howe from New York moved after him, but a series of frustrations intervened, culminating in a furious storm that dispersed both fleets. Battle was averted when, in the gale, d'Estaing's flagship suffered the loss of masts and rudder, forcing him to retreat into Boston under a makeshift jury rig for repairs. From Boston he sailed away without action, leaving soured hopes and no love. Americans in their disappointment claimed they had been "deserted in a most rascally manner as if the Devil himself were in the French fleet." To smooth over a riot of bad feeling took earnest effort by Washington and others, but to no great purpose, since d'Estaing was not fortune's favorite. From Boston he sailed to the West Indies and returned the following year for another joint venture with the Americans: to recapture Savannah, which had been taken by the British the year before. In the fighting, Count d'Estaing was wounded and this assault, too, failed in its purpose. The cherished hope of naval superiority, which should have shut the British off from their supply line, vanished with the last sight of d'Estaing's masts as they disappeared over the horizon, taking the frustrated Admiral back to France.

NINE

Low Point of the Revolution

Interned in Paris, Admiral Rodney, Britain's ablest naval officer, was moored far from mast or sail, an admiral without a sea. Frantic in disuse, he tried through friends to be recalled for a private audience with the King, in vain. He wrote to his wife urging her to plead his cause with Sandwich in person and to send his son to speak to Lord North. Sandwich refused to receive Lady Rodney, replying to her letter that it would be politically impossible to give her husband active employment until he had discharged his debts to private creditors and to the Exchequer, referring, it may be supposed, to expenses like the greatcoats for the Greenwich Hospital pensioners, charged to the navy. In an unnecessarily mean letter to the King, Sandwich wrote, "If Sir George Rodney should from his indigence have any temptation to make advantage of purchasing stores or anything else of that sort, he will have no means of doing it at present, as there will be a Commissioner on the spot through whose hands all that business must be transacted." It was this kind of action that formed his contemporaries' dislike and generally low opinion of Sandwich as a man. When Rodney was later recalled to active duty, an Admiralty Commissioner was indeed assigned to him to make sure he did not use his post for personal enrichment. No one knew more about taking advantage of purchasing than Sandwich himself, up to his elbows in jobbery throughout his career. Since graft was a way of life to English officials, it is hard to understand why, if the Navy Board found indebtedness so shocking, they made it virtually incumbent on Rodney by paying only half the salary due his rank, possibly on the pretext of his residence abroad. If the Navy Board would "deliver but half of what is due to me as Rear-Admiral of England," he wrote to his wife in April, 1778, "it would be sufficient to satisfy every body and there would be money to spare besides." In his letters, he pointed out rather logically that employment was the only method by which he could both serve his country and honorably discharge his debts. Certainly Sandwich seems to have borne some kind of grudge. To leave in disuse at this juncture of renewed war the most dynamic sailor in the

Royal Navy, as Rodney was soon dramatically to prove himself, and one moreover willing to serve under Sandwich as First Lord, when most officers at this time, owing to the Keppel affair, were not, was hardly in the national interest. The given reason was that Rodney was too bellicose and likely to allow himself some action that would add Spain to the war, but this seems not to have been a very real fear, for the British were always making slighting remarks about Spain's lack of enterprise and avoidance of any offensive action in the Channel when, having numerical superiority in combination with France, she had the opportunity for it.

In Paris, Rodney — receiving no messages or remittances — wrote in agony of mind to his wife, "Delays are worse than death, especially at this critical time when every hour teems with momentary expectation of war." A French squadron, he reports, has sailed at the end of January for America along with a convoy of 13 sail and 2 ships of war "belonging to the Congress of twenty-eight guns each who saluted the French Admiral under Congress colours and had their salute openly and publicly returned, by which France seems to own them as a Republic — the greatest insult they could offer us."

Besides the agony of inaction, Rodney was

now in acute embarrassment for living expenses. At this moment an unexpected hand of friendship was extended to him, so unexpected and from so unlikely a source as to seem unreal. A French nobleman, the Maréchal Duc de Biron, Marshal of France, Colonel of the Gardes Françaises and commander of the troops of Paris, having heard of his enforced detention, proposed, Rodney wrote, "that his purse was at my service," saying that "whatever sum I might want, even to £2,000 he would immediately let me have," and the English friends in whose home the proposal was made would be asked to inform certain bankers to advance the sum which the Maréchal would pay. After Rodney's initial reluctance to accept such astonishing generosity, the Duc de Biron assured him in the hearing of the English guests present "that it was not a French gasconnade but an offer of pure friendship and regard," that "all France was sensible of the services I had rendered my country and that the treatment they all knew I had received was a disgrace to the nation and to its ministers" and that the Maréchal would be extremely happy if he were allowed to make this proof of his "esteem and good will" in order that "I may leave Paris without being reproached." The Frenchman's offer was made in May, after the French alliance was concluded with the American rebels but before France's actual declaration of war on Britain. Biron certainly knew that he was releasing a formidable opponent, for he was reproached by many of his countrymen for doing so when his intervention became known. It was on this occasion that he consulted the French Chef de Cabinet Maurepas, who thought the matter of no great consequence because naval combat in his opinion was "piff poff." Biron also went to Versailles to ask the King's permission to give Rodney his freedom. *"Je vous envie d'avoir eu cette idée,"* the King replied, according to Biron family records. *"Elle est Française et digne de vous."* (I wish I had had your idea. It is French and worthy of you.) If it was French, it was perhaps a reflection of medieval chivalry in which fellow-knights felt joined by brotherhood in the transnational chivalric order and more obligated to each other than to any other loyalty.

The Duc de Biron belonged to the Gontaut-Lauzun family, one-time partisans of the usurper Henri Quatre of Navarre. An ancestor, Charles de Biron, was named Admiral and Marshal of France before he suffered the common fate of prominence too close to a King. On being accused of conspiracy and tried for treason, he was beheaded by order of the erratic monarch he served. The family nevertheless prospered in royal service and by Rodney's time had acquired an excess of riches, judging by the startling expenditures of Biron's nephew Armand Louis de Gontaut, born 1747, who took the title Duc de Lauzun. He is recorded as having bought a colonelcy for 1.5 million livres (then worth about $400,000). His mansion was the present Ritz Hotel. He spent 1,337 livres and 10 sous for half a box at the opera, 1,500 for half a box at the Théâtre des Italiens and the same for a box at the Comédie Française. In between theatrical distractions and keeping count of amours that seemed likely to match Leporello's proud record for Don Giovanni in Spain of "a thousand and three," he applied himself to the subject of the day by writing a treatise on *The Defenses of England and All Her Possessions in the Four Quarters of the World*. Whether or not impressed by his subject, he became one of the young nobles who volunteered to fight in the American Revolution and was to take an active part in the Yorktown campaign. Elected in 1789 a deputy to the Estates General as a partisan of the Revolution, he commanded the Revolutionary Army of the Rhine but, in the course of factional struggles, suffered the fate of his ancestor and met death on the guillotine in 1793.

Because Rodney had been heard to boast that he could deal with the French fleet if free to go back to England, and because English newspapers were implying that the French were keeping Rodney from the front because of his military talent, it has been suggested that Biron's generosity may have been moved as much by national pique as by chivalry. Whatever his motive, the sense of warmth and esteem it offered Rodney after the neglect by his own compatriots, and the prospect of release from Paris, came at a critical moment, for, as he writes, his passport had expired and the creditors had grown so "clamorous" that he risked being sued or worse, for they were only held back by the police and by the visits of "those great families whose attentions kept my creditors from being so troublesome as they otherwise would have been." "For more than a month past," he wrote to his wife on May 6, he had not had a letter from anyone "but Mr. Hotham and yourself." Such astonishing neglect by his friends at home seems to suggest that Rodney was not very popular in his own circle in England, which makes all the more striking the puzzling contrast with the remarkable kindness and generosity of the Duc de Biron's offer and the hospitable attentions of the "great families" of Paris — unless the explanation may be that the French

derived a perverse pleasure in finding themselves aiding an enemy in distress, especially
an English enemy.

On the same May 6 on which he acknowledged the absence of any message from England, Rodney, understandably depressed,
dropped his scruples and accepted Biron's
offer to advance him 1,000 louis, satisfying all
creditors. On his return to England in May,
1778, money to repay the loan was raised by
Drummond's Bank, whose director Henry
Drummond was a relative of Rodney's first
wife. When this gentleman learned the circumstances, he arranged to cancel the debt.
Rodney's more pressing need of active employment was left hanging for yet another
year, on the ground that the major commands
in America and the West Indies and of the
Grand Fleet had been filled. In fact, this was
not true. At a time when Spain's belligerency
was anticipated and the combined Bourbon
enemies were preparing for assault, Rodney
was passed over as successor to Keppel for
command of the Grand Fleet in favor of Sir
Charles Hardy, one of the superannuated admirals whom Sandwich was scraping from the
bottom of the barrel like last season's dried
apples when more active flag officers would
not accept appointments, fearing to be made
scapegoat if anything went wrong. Taken out

of comfortable retirement at Greenwich Hospital, Hardy had not been at sea for twenty years. "Does the people at home think the nation in no danger?" wrote a senior captain of the Grand Fleet to a colleague while under Sir Charles Hardy's limp command. "I must inform you the confused conduct here is such that I tremble for the event. There is no forethought . . . we are every day from morning to night plagued and puzzled in minutiae while essentials are totally neglected. . . . My God, what have you great people done by such an appointment?" Political division in the navy, besides setting comrades against each other, had injured the service by narrowing the choice of flag officers, and even of the Navy Board, to old and tired veterans, weak in health and spirit, the relics of better days.

Nature took care of the problem, when in May, 1780, after a year of the too heavy responsibility, Sir Charles Hardy died. The sigh of relief was short, for Hardy's successor, when Admiral Barrington refused the command, was the seventy-year-old Admiral Francis Geary, another withered apple, whom an officer described as "wholly debilitated in his faculties, his memory and judgment lost, wavering and indeterminate in everything." In three months Geary was not dead but exhausted, reporting that he could not get out of bed in the morning and sending his doctor's opinion confirming his request for leave. When Barrington, who was second in command, again refused to move up, the Admiralty searched its own premises for an officer not likely to collapse, and found a member of the Admiralty's Board in his fifties, Vice-Admiral Darby, willing to take the command.

While Rodney had been held idle, a scramble in the West Indies had taken place when the French, after the stalemate at Ushant, redirected their offensive against British commerce from the Caribbean. By aggressive troop landings, they captured Dominica, lying between Martinique and Guadeloupe, giving them a strong position in the middle of the Leeward and Windward islands. At the same time, the British took back Ste. Lucie, which Rodney always considered the key base from which to observe Fort Royal in Martinique. In the following summer of 1779, more islands fell with the French capture of St. Vincent near the middle of the Windward chain and of Grenada at the bottom.

When Spain joined France against Britain in June, 1779, both powers had reached the conclusion that defeat of their common enemy could best be realized by attack on the heart rather than on the limbs; by direct invasion of the home islands rather than assault on her sea-lanes and wide-flung colonies, reaching across the world from Ceylon to Jamaica. The invasion was planned for the summer of 1779 with a combined fleet of 66, far greater strength than the 45 ships that Britain could muster in the Channel for defense. What saved her was a worse case of French ministerial indecision and sloppy management than her own. Correspondence between Versailles and Madrid had been under way since December, but coordination of the fleets and commanders was on paper, not in practice, which proved a serious flaw. D'Orvilliers, the French commander, sailed for the rendezvous under hurried orders the first week in June and was not joined by the main Spanish fleet until July 23, by which time he had been cruising for six weeks doing nothing, with ships already short of provisions and water. They were poorly manned, he complained, with "mediocre captains," of whom there is "a still greater number on this cruise than in the last one." Sickness, which had already taken a terrible toll among the Spaniards, was spreading among his crews. Further time was lost in the translation of signal books and orders which had not been prepared in peace time. Conscious of too little joint experience to expect good maneuvering, D'Orvilliers wrote that he would have to place his hopes on "bravery and firmness."

Alarm gripped England as people caught sight of the white-winged herd of enemy sails coming up the Channel. A Royal Proclamation ordered horses and cattle to be withdrawn from the coasts, booms to be placed across harbors, troops to be encamped on the south coast. Weather again came to the aid of the English, not like the storm that had scattered the Armada of Philip II but its opposite — a calm that held the enemy motionless within sight of Plymouth. The situation of the French fleet, D'Orvilliers reported, "becomes worse every day" because of the epidemic of sickness and the dwindling water supply. On top of this, a frigate arrived bringing a total change of orders for a landing at Falmouth, on the coast of Cornwall, instead of on the Isle of Wight as was the original plan. Furthermore, D'Orvilliers was told that the King wished the fleet to remain at sea "for several months" and that a supply convoy was "about to leave" Brest to meet him. To change a vast plan of operations at the last moment when army and navy were already at sea was hardly a sensible procedure. To postpone action when supplies were running out and "this terrible epidemic" was weakening his ships was, D'Orvilliers was forced to say, "very unfortunate," and to expose fleets at sea during the autumn and winter was likewise. It was clear, wrote a personage of the court, the Duc de Chatelet, to the commandant at Havre, that the ministry had decided to "risk at all hazards . . . some sort of expedition against England in order to fulfill the engagement to Spain." The court had been unable to come to a decision, reflecting the same "ignorance and vacillation" of our ministers who have "behaved like weak-minded people who never know what they want to do until the moment comes to do it. . . ." Under these circumstances, with the death rate on the Spanish ships leaving them virtually helpless, the invasion was called off in the fall of 1779 and the combined fleet dispersed. England was spared by act of God, if not by the navy, from what might have been the first invasion since the Normans of 1066.

At this late stage, in October, 1779, at a time of many threats, when Spain together with France was besieging Gibraltar and the Armed Neutrality League was showing hostility and the Dutch were considering adhering to it, Rodney, because of his reputation as an aggressive sailor, was taken back into active service. Since he did not belong to the political Opposition but supported the government in believing that "coercion of the colonies was perfectly just," he had obtained his long-awaited audience with the King, who promised him an early appointment. Now, having been left to molder a year in London when no other officer of repute would serve under Sandwich, he was offered command of the Leeward Islands station and Barbados. Relief of Gibraltar, near exhaustion of its last supplies, was to be his immediate mission.

Anxiety for the great gate of the Mediterranean, England's most important foothold on the Continent, was acute. With time pressing at his back, Rodney hastened at once to Portsmouth to prepare the fleet to make sure of seaworthy ships and full crews. He found working conditions and discipline there revealing, according to his biographer, an "extraordinary want of diligence in the different public departments," and an "absence of proper zeal and activity in the officers of his fleet who were almost all strangers to him; and many of whom behaved to him with a marked disrespect and want of cordiality."

Their attitude was political, for Rodney was known as a supporter of the government and of the war against the Americans. Feelings on this subject had become heated and divisive to the point of a civil war in opinion, strongly felt in the navy. In a recent diatribe, Opposition speakers in Parliament denounced the "pernicious system of government" as having brought the navy in home waters to a condition "superlatively wretched" and Britain, as they claimed, to "confusion, discord and ruin." More than wretched, the navy was very far from the level prescribed by the unwritten rule that the British Navy must be kept at least as strong as the combined forces of France and Spain. As First Lord, Sandwich bore the blame.

Feeling the cold wind of public disfavor and threat of losing office, Parliament responded to the King's plea in his speech from the throne in November, 1779, for more vigorous prosecution of the war by voting added subsidy for mercenaries and a draft of 25,000 seamen and 18,000 marines for the navy. Through a shower of complaints about delays and indiscipline, Rodney was able at least to put together a fleet fit for sea. He suffered a final frustration from westerly winds followed by a "stark calm" that held him in port for about two weeks, while Sandwich nagged when he felt a breeze in London: "For God's sake go to sea without delay. You cannot conceive of what importance it is to yourself, to me and to the public that you should not lose this fair wind." At last a wind blew through Portsmouth and on December 24, 1779, Rodney was able to sail to the encounter that would make him the hero of the hour.

He led a great fleet of 22 ships of the line, 8 frigates and 66 storeships and transports loaded together with a convoy of no fewer than 300 merchantmen bringing the trade to the West Indies. With his long train of followers that stretched over miles of ocean, he sailed south into the Atlantic, heading for the coast of Spain. En route he came upon a Spanish convoy on its way to supply the besieging force at Gibraltar. When the Spaniards in greatly inferior force surrendered without a fight, he took over the 54-gun escort, 6 frigates and 16 supply ships, which, with their cargo, were added to his train. Sailing on, he sighted on January 16 a Spanish squadron off Cape St. Vincent, on the coast of Portugal just north of Cádiz. It was lying in wait to intercept the Gibraltar relief force, of which the Spaniards had been warned. With only 11 ships of the line and 2 frigates, half the size of Rodney's fleet, the Spaniards should have run for safety to Cádiz. Now, facing Rodney's numbers, they chose to seek shelter in some harbor of the Cape.

Rodney, commanding from his cabin where he was lying ill with gout, chased them through the night under a rising moon until 2 a.m. Not to be deprived of a triumph while bedridden, he took a decision of instant boldness that few but he would have dared. With a hard gale blowing, giving promise of a storm, he raised the signal to engage to leeward — that is, to come between the enemy and the land, with the object of preventing the Spaniards from running to safety into a harbor. Leeward was a helpless position that every captain would normally avoid, with the added danger, in this case, of darkness and being dashed on the rocks by the rising storm. No council of war in advance had prepared his captains for any such unorthodox action, apart from his giving them all notice "upon my approaching the said Cape to prepare for battle." Unlike Nelson, Rodney did not believe in holding conference and making friends with his officers. The risk he took in the moonlight depended on his own seamanship and his officers' belief in him. Considering their attitude at Portsmouth, this appeared less than solid. Perhaps his boldness now inspired belief. They followed him, hoisting all their canvas for maximum speed and jettisoning barrels and lumber overboard to lighten weight.

The "brilliant rush" of the English fleet swept toward the shore while the light of the now full moon showed the fleeing Spaniards "flying for Cadiz like a shoal of frightened porpoises" pursued by sharks. Rodney told his sailing master to pay no attention to the smaller merchantmen but to lay him alongside the largest, "the admiral if there be one." The Admiral's ship proved to be the 80-gun *Fenix*, flagship of Don Juan de Langara, the Spanish commander who struck his flag along with five others. Another Spanish ship blew up with a tremendous explosion and four were taken, entangled with the English in the shoals. With the twilight falling in the short light of January, and the wind at gale force, Rodney had to put crews aboard the prize while keeping his fleet off the rocks. In the morning he could count possession of six enemy warships of the line, including the Admiral's flagship and the Admiral himself as prisoner. Three more of the enemy line were wrecked on the rocks. Only two of Langara's squadron escaped. Not forgetting his relief mission, in the midst of his triumph Rodney sent frigates to inform the consul at Tangier that Britain now held the Straits and provisions must be sent across to Gibraltar at once. Through storm wind and a heavy sea he reached the Straits, drove off the blockading squadron and anchored off the Rock, where he found the garrison and inhabitants on short rations close to starvation, with sentries posted at every store to prevent assault on the last produce on the shelves. After supplying Gibraltar and, beyond it, Minorca, with two years' supply of stores and provisions, Rodney sailed for the Caribbean while cutters hastened back to London with the glorious news of Gibraltar's relief and the tale of the moonlight battle.

Rodney's numerical superiority at Cape St. Vincent reduced the victory from the heroic scale, but it was intrepidity and perfect command that brought him glory. Horace Mann, Walpole's faithful correspondent, wrote from Florence that Rodney's victory "caught like wild fire about the town" and Mann received congratulations from everyone he met. Rodney was greeted at home as the rescuer not only of Gibraltar but of the honor of the navy and, more than that, the honor of the flag. Guns were fired from the Tower of London and fireworks blazed for two nights running. "Everybody almost adores you," wrote his eldest daughter, "and every mouth is full of your praise." It was impossible to describe, wrote his wife, "the general applause that is bestowed upon you; or to mention the number of friends who have called to congratulate me on this happy event." Many of them without doubt were the same friends who had left him without a word when he was down and out in Paris. How quick is the leap to catch on to the coattails of success! Rodney's reward was the rather ephemeral gift of the thanks of

Parliament, voted by both Houses, and the freedom of the City of London presented in a gold casket. More gratifying was his election unopposed on the floodtide of his victory as M.P. for the borough of Westminster.

Later, Rodney's flag captain, Walter Young, claimed that he himself had given the order to chase and engage to leeward and that Rodney, because of the ill state of his health and his "natural irresolution," had tried to call off the ships from the chase. Confined to his bed, Rodney had obviously had to rely on someone else's sight of the situation, but Sir Gilbert Blane, the fleet physician, testified that the Admiral had discussed the leeward course with Young at sunset, when it was then decided on. Irresolution was not a characteristic that could credibly be attributed to Rodney. The order for a leeward course would have had to come from the Admiral and the action be his responsibility. That there had been no confusion and no hanging back by the captains indicated that much. In his report, Rodney expressed himself highly pleased by the promptitude and bravery of "all ranks and ratings" and by the advantage of coppered bottoms, which made it possible to bring the enemy to action. "Without them we should not have taken one Spanish ship."

Sandwich wrote congratulations on the

naval combat in terms which, in view of his earlier abandonment of Rodney, can only be described by use of the modern word "crust": "The worst of my enemies now allow that I have pitched upon a man who knows his duty and is a brave, honest, and able officer." Having been informed by one of Rodney's captains, Sir John Ross, that our expedition "in nine weeks [had] taken from the enemy 36 sail of merchant ships valued by them at a million sterling and nine sail of the line [and] have supplied the garrisons of Gibraltar and Mahon with two years' of provisions and stores of all kinds," Sandwich at least had the decency to add that he hoped "to prevail on his Majesty to give some more substantial proofs of his approbation." This he did, and the coming reward was to be ample.

News of the victory of Cape St. Vincent evoked from Horace Walpole an odd comment that does not quite seem to fit the occasion. "It is almost my systematic belief," he wrote to the Reverend William Cole, another of his regular correspondents, "that as cunning and penetration are seldom exerted for good ends, it is the absurdity of mankind that . . . carries on and maintains the equilibrium that heaven designed should subsist." Inapplicable to the Moonlight Battle, as it was soon everywhere known, Walpole's remark was presumably intended as a philosophic maxim on human affairs rather than a reference to Rodney. "Adieu my dear Sir," he concluded, "shall we live to lay down our heads in peace?" John Adams, too, felt peace to be elusive. With a bold and enterprising naval captain in action, he saw the British desire for a settlement receding, because "naval victories excite them to a frenzy." Adams, as he often did, put his finger on the spot, for what Rodney achieved by the Moonlight Battle and the relief of Gibraltar was to invigorate British self-confidence, which was fatally to become overconfidence in the American war.

The prizes from Cape St. Vincent were sent back to His Majesty while Rodney himself, with four ships, set course for the Caribbean and his Leeward Island post at Ste. Lucie. He arrived in the same week that a French fleet under the Comte de Guichen came into Fort Royal at Martinique, intending with France's revived naval powers to bring the war to the West Indies.

In this stage of the conflict, England was at a disadvantage that had not been so in the Seven Years' War. Now she was militarily bogged down in war against the Colonies in North America, which drew strength away from support of the navy, while the reverse was true of her enemy. France, after the Peace of Paris, was relieved of continental war, which before 1763 had drawn her major strength to the army, keeping her maritime effort weak, but since then she had been pouring men and supplies, training and ship-building into the strong navy by which she hoped to prevail over Britain. In 1778, when France formally declared war, she had 75 to 80 ships of the line and 50 frigates, ships that were newer, better designed and faster than the British. Spain added 60 more of the line, although, like Italy in World War I, Spain's uncertain will to fight made her as an ally as much a hindrance as help. Against the Bourbon allies, Britain had 69 ships of the line of which only 35 were seaworthy and 11 were in American waters, far from parity with the combined fleets of France and Spain.

Aggressive French designs on the Leeward Islands were to bring Rodney within a few months of his triumph at Gibraltar to the most disappointing battle of his career. Happily, to balance the blow, although it never obliterated the sting, great good fortune met him at Ste. Lucie when he returned to the Antilles after Gibraltar in March, 1780. The good news was a letter of congratulations from Lord Sandwich officially informing him that the King had conferred on him an annual pension of £2,000 and, more important, that after his death the pension would continue in the form of annual payments of £500 to his widow, £1,000 to his eldest son and £100 each to his other son and four daughters "to continue during each of their respective lives." Relieving him of his worst anxieties for his family, the award also removes from history the force of the frequent argument that the money of St. Eustatius afterward bewitched Rodney into forgetting his duty at sea. The pension gave him ease of mind, he wrote to his wife rather too confidently. "All I want is to pay off my debts as soon as possible . . . Let me be clear of all demands, and our income will be more than sufficient to live as we ought, and to save money." It was not to be that easy, for in the end the several lawsuits brought against him by the merchants of St. Eustatius and St. Kitts whose goods he had confiscated were to keep him in financial need for the rest of his life. That distress, however, could not be foreseen to spoil his newfound good fortune. At first notice, the pension reawakened the old yearning for membership in the one Club above all others, the House of Commons. Not yet informed of his election for Westminster, he raised the question with Lord George Germain. "To be out of Parliament," he wrote, "is to be out of the world, and my heart is set upon being in." And to

Sandwich he confessed the same desire, writing that "the happy situation in my affairs" would not only discharge his debts but be sufficient "to spare a sum of money if necessary to bring me into Parliament."

While he was en route from Gibraltar, news had been learned from escaped British sailors who had been prisoners in Brest that a strong French squadron of 15 to 20 sail of the line, with transports carrying 15,000 troops, had sailed for the West Indies. The object, after picking up one or two extra sail at Fort Royal, was to deliver Barbados where the British held 2,000 French prisoners and to recapture Ste. Lucie. Rodney saw an opportunity for a major, perhaps decisive blow. Never content with the parade tactics and ceremonious duels of his era and never a slave of *Fighting Instructions*, he believed in fighting for serious results. "The objective from which his eye never wandered," as Mahan appreciates, "was the French fleet," the organized force of the enemy at sea. This was indeed the crux. As long as French naval power had access to America as an ally and was able to furnish the rebels with men, arms and especially money, they would not be defeated. From the hour of the French alliance, British strategy should have made the blocking of France from America her primary aim. There was no cabinet decision that ever made this explicit nor orders to seagoing commanders to make it a primary concern. Ultimately the time came when the private loot of St. Eustatius and the public duty of protecting the overvalued West Indies, for which as Commander-in-Chief of the Leewards Rodney felt responsible, blurred his vision. Rodney's eye did waver, and in a critical moment of bad judgment, strategic purpose was set aside.

Rodney's plan for action in the West Indies in 1780 was a plan for breaking the line as envisaged by John Clerk in the harbor of Edinburgh. It was an unorthodox movement in which all of his ships at once, instead of section by section down the line, would fall upon and destroy the French center and rear before the van was engaged. The plan was explained to his captains in advance, but as it was contrary to *Fighting Instructions*, it was evidently not understood or else, as Rodney was later to charge, deliberately disobeyed for sinister political reasons.

Once again, the unregenerate signaling system that had not been changed for a hundred years was to ruin what could have been a decisive fleet action. On the theory that, for the sake of comprehension, flags should be kept as few and as simple as possible, the system was primitive. The rule was that signal flags should be hoisted only one at a time, so that varieties of meaning could only be indicated by adding pennants or by the flag's position on a mast or to which mast it was attached. Given these limitations, a flag usually called by a number for one or another of the *Fighting Instructions*. Unless his plan were very carefully explained, which was not his habit, Rodney could not count on prompt and accurate response when discipline was lax.

On April 17, 1780, the English and French fleets sighted each other off the coast of Martinique. Gaining the wind in the morning, with his ships in close order while the French were strung out, Rodney, believing himself on the edge of a crushing victory, prepared to execute his surprise. Instead of the grand design he had laid out, the British system of signals virtually ensured that the captains would be bewildered. To indicate his intentions, Rodney had to raise signal 21, from *Additional Fighting Instructions*. A sport in regular tactics, signal 21 meant for each ship to bear down and steer for her opposite in the enemy line. It was made by flying the signal flag from the main topgallant mast in conjunction with firing a gun, not the most precise message when in the midst of action. The tired captains, puzzled by unorthodox maneuver, took off in individual disorder, some bearing down on the van as would have been normal, others, unsure of what to do, following each other against the wrong section in the French line, leaving their Admiral unsupported and his plan a shambles. For an hour he fought alone until his flagship was so hurt — with eighty shot in her hull, three below the waterline, with main- and mizzen-masts broken, sails gaping with holes, her main spar dangling uselessly like a broken limb — that for the next twenty-four hours she could barely be kept afloat, and Rodney had to shift to another ship of the rear division. Others of his ships were so badly damaged in the mêlée that two of them sank afterward in the bay. Neither fleet having gained its object, they separated. In the fury of his disappointment, Rodney in private correspondence accused his subordinates of "barefaced disobedience to orders and signals" in a plot to discredit him and, through him, the government in the hope of turning them out of office. At long distance it seems possible that the disobedience arose as much from misunderstanding of unusual procedure so contrary to the sacred rule of line ahead as from politics.

More restrained in his official report to the Admiralty, Rodney felt compelled to inform their Lordships, "with concern inexpressible mixed with indignation," that the British flag "was not properly supported." Even that was too much for the Admiralty, which deleted this passage from publication of the report in the *Gazette*. Rodney's private charges of outright disobedience quickly circulated, raising an unwanted prospect, after the Keppel disruptions, of more courts-martial. Sandwich promised the "shame and punishment" of those "who have robbed you of the glory of destroying a considerable part of the naval force of France." Rodney, loath to reopen further damage to the navy by pressing for a public inquiry, chose rather to warn his officers that no rank would screen from his wrath anyone who disobeyed signals, and that if necessary he would use frigates as messengers to ensure compliance.

In the bitterness of being deprived of his great chance that "in all probability," as he believed, would have been "fatal to the naval power of the enemy," Rodney was determined that the French should not get away. Guichen, his opponent, had retreated to a base at Guadeloupe and would be sure, Rodney felt, to make an early effort to regain the shelter of Fort Royal, where Rodney, despite his own damaged ships, intended to keep guard and force him again to battle. Guichen, however, holding the windward position, was not to be lured from his advantage. When sighted again some fifteen miles off Martinique in the strait between Guadeloupe and Ste. Lucie, he could have initiated action if he had wished, but avoidance was rather the French game. Intent on conserving their vessels under the French doctrine of seeking strategic results without tactical risks, the French took evasive action, the more so as they recognized in Rodney's actions an opponent ready to adopt unexpected battle movements that they thought best to avoid. In fickle winds, each admiral engaged in trying to outmaneuver the other. Guichen, with expert seamanship, managed to put himself in position either to enter Fort Royal or attack Ste. Lucie, while Rodney's endeavor was to gain the wind in order to bring him to combat before Guichen could do either. To carry out his threat of closer command over his captains, he shifted his flag to a frigate. He believed they were "thunderstruck" by this resolution. "My eye was more to be dreaded than the enemy's cannon. . . . It is inconceivable," he told Sandwich afterward, "in what awe it kept them." He was never shy in appreciation of his own efforts. Not content, he informed his captains more directly of the nature of command. "The painful task of thinking," he told them, "belongs to me. You need only obey orders implicitly without question."

For fourteen days and nights, with cannon loaded and slow match lighted, the opponents maneuvered for position, so near to each other that "neither officers nor men could be said to have had sleep. . . . The greatness of the object," Rodney wrote to Sandwich, "enabled my mind to support what my strength of body was scarce equal to." He did not go to bed during the fourteen days and nights: Only "when the fleet was in perfect order, I stole now and then an hour's sleep upon the cabin floor." Rodney liked to dramatize himself; in fact, when his ship was stripped for action, his furniture would be stored in the hold and his cabin transformed into an extension of the gun deck.

Further endeavors during the next six weeks to bring the French to action were unavailing.

Despite his own damaged ships with top masts shattered and leaking hulls, Rodney persisted in his pursuit, discovering as he sailed that Guichen, under orders to bring the trade convoy back to Europe, had withdrawn his fleet from the West Indies to return home. In one more "piff poff," the campaign of 1780 in the West Indies had closed ahead of the hurricane season in early fall with no great advantage to either side, except that the presence and imminent threat of Rodney's fleet checked the French from further offensives against the islands.

The withdrawal freed Rodney from anxiety for the fate of the Leewards under his command but not from his rage over the blundered battle, which had spoiled "that glorious opportunity perhaps never to be recovered of terminating the naval contest in these seas." He craved a renewed opportunity for decisive action. Just at this time he learned from a captured American ship that a French squadron of 7 liners escorting troop ships had been sent to America to aid the rebels. This was de Ternay's squadron bringing Rochambeau's army. Perceiving that the added enemy would outnumber the British at New York and gain superiority in American waters, Rodney decided he must go to New York to save the situation. During his enforced idleness in Paris, he had kept his mind at work in studying a strategy for America, where he believed the war was being badly mishandled. He had formulated his thoughts in a letter to Sandwich in 1778, soon after France had entered the war. No copy is extant, but references by himself and others indicate that, first of all, Rodney believed in the necessity of viewing Britain's conflicts as a whole, as a single war with a united plan for all its forces and a specific aim. Based on his recognition that

French aid to the rebel colonies would now be a decisive factor, he advised that England's effort should be to keep the French busy in the West Indies, so that they could not spare ships or men to intervene in America, and that during the hurricane months, when operations in the Caribbean were static, he should take his fleet to the American coast and, by uniting all available resources there, crush the rebellion. Sandwich had acknowledged and approved, or wrote Rodney a letter to that effect, but in fact England did not have enough ships to spare for action in the West Indies to keep the French busy.

While Rodney prepared for his venture, his friend Wraxall, who spent much time with him at his residence in Cleveland Row just before he left for America, found him "naturally sanguine and confident" and repeatedly prone to talk too much about himself.

The only change the British war ministers made was to name a new Commander-in-Chief of British forces in America. Sir William Howe, whose heart was not in the fight, was replaced by Sir Henry Clinton, who was not an improvement. The appointment of Clinton — a cousin of the Duke of Newcastle, manager-in-chief of political patronage — was not unrelated to his having the right "connections." It gave direction of the war in the field to a man of neurotic temperament, whose constant hesitation always made him reach decisions too late for the event that required them.

Within three months of his appointment in May, 1778, Clinton's survey of the elements of the situation — its immense geography, the fixed resolve of the rebels on nothing less than independence, as the Carlisle Commission was just then discovering, and the absence of active support by a large and eager body of Loyalists which the British had counted upon — left the new Commander-in-Chief with little enthusiasm and no illusions. Almost his first act, as he tells in his postwar narrative, was to solicit the King for leave to resign, on the ground of the "impracticability" of the war. Refused in his request, Clinton became as unhappy in his function as Lord North was in the premiership, not so much from North's sense of personal unfitness for the post as from recognition, like Pitt's before him, that the war was unwinnable. The means were too limited for the task. He complained of delay in promised reinforcements, which left him without adequate forces and "without money, provisions, ships or troops adequate to any beneficial purpose," while being constantly prodded for more vigorous action here, there, or anywhere by Lord Germain, the war minister at home, his ministerial chief whom Clinton disliked and distrusted.

"For God's sake, My Lord," he wrote in one exasperated outburst, "if you wish me to do anything, leave me to myself and let me adapt my efforts to the hourly change of circumstances." By September, 1780, he writes flatly to Germain his opinion of the "utter impossibility of carrying on the war without reinforcement." This was wishing for the moon. Imperial Britain did not have the population to match the extent of her dominion, nor the funds to spend on more mercenaries, whose further employment would, in any case, have risked rancorous fury in the Opposition. Reinforcements would not be forthcoming. It was the old — and ever new — condition in war of ambitions outreaching resources.

Believing his field army in New York to be too few in numbers (which seems to have been a case of nerves, since he well knew that Washington's army, suffering from shortages and mutinies, could not attack), and alarmed by "threatening clouds . . . which begin to gather in all quarters," Clinton became prey to "the deepest uneasiness" and, like Lord North, repeatedly peppered the King with his wish to be relieved of the chief command and to turn it over to Lord Cornwallis, who was conducting the campaign in the South. Now in his uneasiness he not merely asked, but "implored" His Majesty to be relieved of the high command, and on a third occasion, his plea becomes a "prayer" for release. Though he was clearly not a general for the bold offensives wanted by the King, he was retained. King George, in his passionate conviction of righteous conquest and confidence in bold action, was left to depend for his chief lieutenants, one in the political and one in the military field, on a pair of reluctant coachmen, each of whom wished only to let go of the reins and descend from the coachman's box. That is not the way wars are won.

The most active fight in America at this time was in the southern states, where the British campaign was intended to regain the area that contained the greatest number of Loyalists in the hope of mobilizing their support. Here the most active British Army leader from whom the most was expected, Lord Cornwallis, wrote ruefully to a fellow-officer in Virginia, "Now my dear friend, what is our plan? Without one we cannot succeed." Clinton, he told his friend, has no plan "and I assure you I am quite tired of marching about the country in quest of adventures." Supposed to advance northward through Virginia, the campaign was halted by the capacity of Nathanael Greene, Washington's most reliable general, to stay in the field despite defeats and to wear down the British deployed against him. Greene was carrying out a Pyrrhic strategy foreseen by an enemy, General Murray, Wolfe's lieutenant and Governor of Quebec, who had predicted that if the business was to be decided by numbers, the enemy's (Americans') plan should be on the Chinese model "to lose a battle to you every week until you are rcduced to nothing."

While land warfare in America tottered along inconclusively, Rodney felt he must play a personal hand at trying to infuse some purposeful motion. He undertook the mission to America on his own authority. His commission as Commander-in-Chief of the Leeward Islands and the seas adjoining gave him virtually a free hand in the Western Hemisphere. "I flew on the wings of national enthusiasm," he wrote to a friend, "to disappoint the ambitious designs of the French and cut off all hope from the rebellious and deluded Americans." If delusion was anywhere, it lay with the British in their belief, which Rodney clearly shared, that the Americans had somehow been deluded into rebellion by self-serving agitators. Recognizing no fundamental movement for independence, they failed to take the Revolution seriously.

On his arrival in America in September, 1780, Rodney swept the coast of the Carolinas and moved on to New York, where his hope of reviving unity of purpose and fresh spirit was balked by Clinton's inertia and by the resentment of the elderly and prickly Admiral Arbuthnot, commander of naval forces in America, at Rodney's taking precedence as his superior. Arbuthnot at age seventy was another of the relics dragged out from the bottom of the barrel, and was said in one comment to be "destitute of even rudimentary knowledge of naval tactics." Already on bad terms with Clinton, he quarreled with all the orders issued by Rodney, who found the whole southern coast exposed, with "not a single frigate to be seen from that coast [Carolina] to Sandy Hook," while the shores were swarming with American privateers. Rodney ordered ships to be stationed off every province, "by which means 13 sail of rebel privateers have been already taken, and the trade of his Majesty's subjects effectually protected." A torrent of orders and counterorders flowed between the two Admirals while their angry, if beautifully phrased, complaints of each other, addressed to the First Lord, made no great gain toward the hoped-for unity.

In 1780, with the rebels' loss of Charleston,

the treason of Arnold, and the lack of funds to keep an army in the field, the British had every reason to expect the Americans to give up, and the burdensome war at last to end. Clinton thought Rodney's arrival in America an additional calamity for the rebels, which, he stated, "has thrown [them] into a consternation" by showing Washington's "repeated and studied declarations of a second French fleet and reinforcement to be groundless and false," with the result of spoiling his recruitment, "for under the influence of these invented succours" he had been able to collect large numbers. Washington wanted the addition of a second division of French ships and troops to make an attempt on New York. "Your fortunate arrival upon this coast," Clinton wrote to Rodney, has "entirely defeated such a plan. . . . The rebels have grown slack in their augmenting the Washington army which on the contrary has diminished very much by desertion. Thus, Sir, in a defensive view of things your coming on this coast may have proved of the most important consequences." Clinton regretted that he could offer no encouragement for an attack on the enemy position in Rhode Island, now too strongly fortified. Instead, he thought better of an expedition into Chesapeake Bay, "as to the necessity and importance of which we both agreed," an interesting proposal at this time that might have changed the course of the war.

It was hardly likely to come. Clinton, who was no fire-eater, preferred to blame the inactivity on the aged incapacity of Admiral Arbuthnot. With a competent admiral, he wrote a friend in England, "all might have been expected from this Campaign, but from this Old Gentleman nothing can: he forgets from hour to hour — he thinks aloud — he will not answer any of my letters." His heart might be in the right place, "but his head is gone." To this state the British Navy, in time of need, had reduced itself by the political quarreling that left the quarterdeck to antiques.

Prize money, so often the source of contention, appeared again as a divisive factor, because Rodney's advent as the superior officer in the naval command in America meant Arbuthnot's loss of the chief share in the division of prizes. "I am ashamed to mention," Rodney reported rather sanctimoniously to the Navy Board, "what appears to me the real cause and from whence Mr. Arbuthnot's Chagrene proceeds, but the proofs are so plain, that prize money is the Occasion." And he forwarded verifying documents. When submitted to the King, His Majesty adjudicated the Admirals' quarrel in favor of Rodney, whose conduct, he said, "seems as usual praiseworthy . . . [and] the insinuation that prize money" was the cause "seems founded." Although both Clinton and Rodney threatened to resign unless Arbuthnot were withdrawn, the Navy Board made no move, apparently unwilling to make another enemy. Only when Arbuthnot himself offered to resign by reason of age, and perhaps also the hostility of his colleagues, was he relieved, to be replaced in 1781 in the naval command in America by a cousin of Lord North. Unable to acknowledge even now that the hour was dark, requiring something more than the husk of an ancient mariner, the Navy Board could do no better in its limited range of choices than delve into its collection of old men of the sea and select Sir Thomas Graves. At sixty-seven, considered old age in those days, he was well past his prime and past the prime, too, of combat seamanship. Graves's main characteristic was a highly developed caution, and his career had already skated within a hair of the court-martial verdict of "negligence" such as condemned Admiral Byng, but which in Graves's case had judiciously settled for "error of judgment." That too can be fatal. If negative qualities can ever be said to be determining, Graves makes the point.

The worst mistake in America, in Rodney's opinion, had been the "fatal measure" of the evacuation of Rhode Island, which Clinton had given up in October, 1779, for the sake of concentrating his forces on the southern campaign — or, as he later claimed, under the "enforced" advice of Admiral Arbuthnot, who said Rhode Island "was of no use to the Navy and he could not spare a single ship for its defense." British departure left Newport to the French, with the serious loss of Narragansett, which Rodney called "the best and noblest harbour in America, capable of containing the whole navy of Britain" and from where, he added in a grand vision, the navy "could blockade the three capital cities of America, namely Boston, New York and Philadelphia" in 48 hours.

Rodney's greatest frustration was the failure of his "most strenuous endeavours" to persuade his associates Clinton and Arbuthnot to undertake an offensive for the recovery of Rhode Island. Arbuthnot would not put the navy at such a risk and the animus between him and Clinton precluded any agreed-upon action. "The fleet would never see Rhode Island," asserted a naval officer, "because the General hates the Admiral." Clinton said it was now too late, the French on reoccupation having strongly fortified it, and while it might have been taken before with 6,000 men, it would now take 15,000, which he could not spare for fear of an expected attack by Washington's army on New York of which he had learned from intercepted letters delivered to him by Loyalist agents. The same story of intercepted letters is told in relation to Allied plans for the final campaign. For many years, statements have circulated that they were a deliberate plant by Washington to keep Clinton paralyzed, but subsequent researches have disproved this deception by the Commander-in-Chief.

Rodney had an idea, inventive and outrageous and characteristic of his readiness for independent action without reference to orders, of how to dislodge the French from Rhode Island. In a discussion with Clinton of which Clinton kept a record, he proposed — on the assumption, as everyone believed, that another French squadron was on the way to join de Ternay, commanding the French naval forces at Newport — to let some British ships under French colors appear off Block Island at a time when the wind was fair for de Ternay to emerge, and let them be engaged in a sham fight with Arbuthnot's ships. De Ternay would certainly come out to assist his supposed compatriots and, once lured into battle, could be effectively demolished by the combined force of Rodney's and the New York squadrons. Clearly this was not a man who would have hesitated to use the French flag in attacking St. Eustatius. Doubtless the plan was too much for the safe turn of mind of Clinton and Arbuthnot, for nothing more was heard of it and the "noble bay" of Rodney's visionary sweep remained in French control.

On departure from America, Rodney wrote to Sandwich to report that the war was being conducted with a "slackness inconceivable in every branch," and taking particular note of Clinton's inertia. Washington's intercepted letters, whether genuine or a plant, affected Clinton like a too strong sleeping pill, holding him in a paroxysm of inaction during the next critical months, when by sending prompt reinforcements he might have blocked the coming fatality at Yorktown. But at the moment the British were not worried, because American fortunes were so low as to point to an early collapse.

The period 1779–80 that followed the sorry disappointment for the Americans of d'Estaing's naval intervention, the loss of Charleston, and the terrible privations of the winters at Valley Forge and Morristown, deepened by the miserly aid of Congress and the absence of vigorous popular support, was the worst year of the war when the Revolution sank to its lowest point.

In discouragement close to despair, Washington wrote in December, 1779, "I find our prospects are infinitely worse than they have been at any period of the war, and that unless some expedient can be instantly adopted, a dissolution of the army for want of subsistence is unavoidable. A part of it has been again several days without bread." Battle in the Carolinas and Georgia, in spite of local victories, had brought reverses which now threatened to split the South in fatal division from the northern colonies. Misfortune augmented in May, 1780, when the fall of Charleston, with the capture of 5,000 American soldiers and four ships, marked the heaviest defeat of the war.

In September, 1780, Washington sustained a sharper personal blow in the treason of Benedict Arnold, whose planned betrayal to the British of West Point, key to the Hudson Valley, was foiled by the chance arrest of his go-between with the British, Major André, Clinton's aide, only hours before the keys and plans to the fortress were to be handed over.

Winter quarters of 1779–80 at Morristown, New Jersey, were more severe even than the year before at Valley Forge. Rations were reduced for already hungry men who had been shivering in the snows to one-eighth of normal quantities. Two leaders of a protest by Connecticut regiments demanding full rations and back pay were hanged to quell an uprising. In January of 1781, Pennsylvania regiments mutinied and, with troops of New Jersey, deserted to the number of half their strength before the outbreak was suppressed. At the frontiers, Indians out of the woods guided by Loyalists were burning farms and homes and massacring civilians. Even to keep an army in the field was problematical, because soldiers of the militia had to be furloughed to go home to harvest their crops, and if leave were refused, they would desert. Fighting a war in such circumstances, said General von Steuben, the army's Prussian drillmaster, "Caesar and Hannibal would have lost their reputations."

Washington's desk overflowed with letters from his generals in the field, pleading their shortages of everything an army requires: food, arms, field equipment, horses and wagons for a regular system of transportation, all of which had to be taken by military requisition from the local inhabitants, rousing antagonism toward the patriot forces. "Instead of having everything in readiness to take the field," Washington wrote in his diary of May 1, 1781, "we have nothing and instead of having the prospect of a glorious offensive campaign before us we have a bewildered and gloomy defensive one — unless we should receive a powerful aid of ships, land troops, and money from our generous allies and these, at present, are too contingent to build upon."

To rise above, and persevere, in spite of such discouragement required a spiritual strength, a kind of nobility in Washington rare in the history of generalship. It had something of the quality of William the Silent, making the possessor the obvious and only choice for Commander-in-Chief. This quality, conveyed abroad by another genius of America, Benjamin Franklin, and by the warmth of Lafayette, persuaded Louis XVI, last leaf on the dry stem of the old regime, to attach the monarchy's faith and fortunes to the struggle of backwoods rebels against authority and royalty, the very props that supported Louis on the throne. In the wake of Lafayette — whose charm won Washington to love him like a father and Congress to appoint him Major General, and American recruits, who did not like to serve under foreigners, to fight willingly under his command — the young nobles of France flocked to volunteer in the American battle. Restless in the boredom and vacuum of court life, where the only excitement lay in vying for a nod from an overfed King in a powdered wig or a languid wave of his hand inviting their presence at the morning ritual in his dressing room, they craved manhood in military exercise, traditionally the path to reward, and a chance to devote their valor to the magic goddess Liberty, who was opening hearts of men in the tired and quarrelsome realms of the Old World. "Government by consent of the governed," that magic phrase promised by the American Declaration of Independence, thrilled the minds and hearts of subjects ruled for generations by the dictatorship of monarchs and nobles. The promise seemed personified by the young new nation fighting for birthright in America. Her appearance in the world, they felt, would herald a new order of liberty, equality and the rule of reason for old Europe. What higher task could there be for men of liberal mind than to dedicate their arms and fortunes to aid the coming of that event?

A more mundane desire to retaliate for the loss of Canada revived the old impulse to fight the British that had stirred in their bones ever since William the Norman found a reason for quarrel in the 11th century. The King and Vergennes, his astute and hard-driving Minister for Foreign Affairs, thought rather of keeping the Colonies' battle alive as a military cat's-paw in France's power struggle against

Britain. By strengthening and augmenting the rebels' resources, they could blunt the British sword, gain for themselves the advantage in North America, and by harassing British sea power and seizing a sugar island or two, they might even break down those wooden walls to invade the British hearth.

French purpose as conceived by Vergennes was not to assist the Colonies to victory or strengthen them to a level that might lead Britain to offer a reconciliation, leaving her once more free to knit up the torn fabric of empire and again concentrate her forces against France. Rather, it was to reinforce the Colonies enough to keep their battle going and keep Britain occupied in its toil.

So it was that out of desire to replace Britain as top dog, Bourbon France, placing a large block of irony across the path of history, lent her finances, fighting men and armaments in aid of a rebellion whose ideas and principles would initiate the age of democratic revolution and, together with its drain on the French budget, would bring down the *ancien régime* in the tremendous fall that marked forever the change from the Old World to the modern.

TEN

"A Successful Battle May Give Us America"

If the French did not recognize the significance to themselves of what they were doing in aiding the rebels, neither did the British as a whole consider what place their conflict with the American Colonies had or would have in history. They thought of it simply as an uprising of colonial ingrates which had to be put down by force. To those with a larger world view, it was an imperial power struggle against France.

Ideologically, in the eternal struggle of left and right, the rebellion was seen as subversive of the social order, and the Americans as "levelers" whose example, if successful, would set alight revolutionary movements in Ireland and elsewhere. The British government and its partisans, as opposed to Whigs and radicals, felt themselves to be the upholders of right and privilege who should be receiving Europe's support instead of hostility in their fight for existence. With France and Spain as enemies and Holland about to be another, and with the prospect of the Neutrality League contesting sovereignty of the seas, Europe in not coming to Britain's aid, or in actively aiding the Americans, was seen as cutting her own throat; if the Americans won, she would herself experience the tramp of radicals and hear the shout of "Liberty!" across her lands.

Of all people, the somnolent Prime Minister Lord North, who was always begging the King to let him resign because he felt inadequate to the situation, perceived the historical context of the conflict in which his country and its colonies were engaged, and the historical consequences of an American victory. "If America should grow into a separate empire, it must cause," he foresaw, "a revolution in the political system of the world, and if Europe did not support Britain now, it would one day find itself ruled by America imbued with democratic fanaticism."

The mutinies and privations of Mr. Washington's army (the British could not bring themselves to accord him the title of "general") offered a gleam of hope that the American Revolution was lagging, as could be seen in its want not only of material and finances but of fresh recruits. Encouraged, Clinton told himself comfortably, "I have all to hope and Washington all to fear." Logically he was right, but a detached observer would have drawn no encouragement, for "hope" to Clinton meant further reason not to act, and "fear" for Washington meant a factor that existed to be overcome.

So certain were British managers of the war in their superiority of force that they remained convinced the rebels would have to give in and make peace. As Lord Germain, the King's chief adviser, expressed it, "So contemptible is the rebel force now in all parts . . . so vast is our superiority that no resistance on their part can obstruct a speedy suppression of the rebellion." Settled complacency allowed no other thought. Expectation of the rebels' early collapse was all the more intense because it was sorely needed — for despite complacency, British resources were badly strained; recruiting was poor, victualing inadequate and finances on stony ground. The British clung to the belief that if only they could keep the war going, the Americans would have to surrender. Congress' authority would fade and public opinion turn back to the mother country. Most cogent in their thinking was belief in the Americans' early financial collapse. "I judge," wrote General Murray from Minorca, "that the enemy finds the expense of this war as intolerable as we do." A civilian skeptic was Walpole's correspondent Horace Mann: "Unless some decisive stroke," he wrote to his friend, "can be given to the French fleet either in America or in Europe, perseverance of the rebellious colonies and the *point d'honneur* of France will prolong it and wear us out." George III himself could contemplate no such outcome. He insistently believed that victory was just over the hill, that the truly loyal people were about to rise and that with one or two hard blows the rebellion would collapse.

What made the difference in expectations on both sides was French intervention. The sinking to its lowest ebb in 1780 of the American cause prompted joint Franco-American planning to keep the Revolution alive and fighting. Washington had asked the French for money, for troops and, despite the mortifying results of d'Estaing's campaign, above all for naval aid. He was absolutely convinced that without command of the coasts and freedom of the sea, the Americans could not win and that only by this means could Britain be defeated. The British arch in America rested upon New York and Virginia where Chesapeake Bay opened a long coastline on the Atlantic; communication between New York and Virginia, while the Americans held Pennsylvania and New Jersey in between, could only be had by water. Nor could the British Army live off the land, because of the hostility of the inhabitants; their supply and deployment within the country depended on transportation by water and control of ports and estuaries. If this could be blocked or wrested from them, the British would starve. Indeed, Clinton was to note afterward, of the period when he was afraid of losing naval superiority to d'Estaing, "Army three times in danger of starving." If the statement was anxiety more than reality, it reflects Clinton's sense of the deplorability of everything in the self-justifying account he wrote after the war.

Conversely, only if water transportation were made free to the Americans could the movement of troops make possible an offensive. This was the basis of Washington's insistence on naval superiority. As he explained it to Colonel Laurens, son of the former President of the Congress, who was on a diplomatic mission to France, the British could not maintain "a large force in this country if we had the command of the seas to interrupt the regular transmission of supplies from Europe. . . . A constant naval superiority upon these coasts would instantly reduce the enemy to a difficult defensive." Naval superiority "with an aid of money, would enable us to convert the war into a vigorous offensive." Washington's desire was for attack on New York, keystone of Britain's military base in America. Recapture of Long Island and Manhattan from the British might, he believed, be the decisive blow. Because of the obstacle presented by the shallow draft of the waters at Sandy Hook at the entrance to New York, which had already barred the way to d'Estaing, and because of the better entry to Chesapeake Bay and its wider scope for action, his French ally Rochambeau, on the contrary, believed a campaign in the Chesapeake region would be more practical and more effective. Besides, it was here that the British Army under Cornwallis was the most active and menacing enemy force in the war.

Washington and other generals of the army deeply wanted America's cause to be fought by her own people, but their hardest discouragement was the fainthearted patriotism of the country at large insofar as tangible support by the populace was evidence. At Valley Forge, Washington painfully acknowledged, failure of supply meant that there were men in his ranks "without the shadow of a blanket," and they "might have been tracked from White Marsh to Valley Forge by the blood of their feet." When levies were called for operations in the summer of 1780, fewer than thirty recruits had straggled into headquarters six weeks after the deadline. Civilians who volunteer generally wish to escape, not to share, privations worse than their own. They were not anxious to join the emaciated ill-clad ranks of the Continentals. Farmers' contributions of wagons and teams to carry supplies were no more forthcoming.

After the d'Estaing fiasco, the army began to deteriorate, grumbling in their grievances against Congress for leaving them unpaid and in contention among themselves over ranks and seniority, and threatening resignations. Even General Greene, the steadiest of them all, now serving as Quartermaster General, complained bitterly that Congress gave him money no more equal to his needs than "a sprat in a whale's belly." He became so enraged by the negligence of Congress when he was trying to plan an offensive for the recovery of Savannah that even he talked of resigning.

On New Year's Day of 1781 Pennsylvania troops, quartered in Morristown for a second hungry and shivering winter after the bitter one at Valley Forge, reached outrage at being left in misery and want and unpaid, while civilians sat tight in comfort. Lack of clothes and leather for shoes, of horses and wagons for transport, of meat and flour and gunpowder in all units, of fresh recruits and of the confidence and support of the country, had left an army barely able to stand up. Generals' letters reporting their shortages flowed over Washington's desk. Even when provisions were on hand, they could sometimes not be brought to hungry companies for lack of transport. The troops took their only recourse to make their case: mutiny. Connecticut and New Jersey troops no less neglected joined the Pennsylvania line in its action and the outbreak was only contained by the example of the two from Connecticut who had been executed. "I have almost ceased to hope," Washington had confessed in 1780 shortly before the mutinies. "The country in general is in such a state of insensibility and indifference to its interest that I dare not flatter myself with any change for the better."

In France a change for the better was preparing. Vergennes, the Foreign Minister, though he did not appreciate being lectured by an American, was impressed by John Adams' insistence that only naval power could decide the war in America, and that there was no use in France spending her forces on taking sugar islands in the West Indies or besieging Gibraltar or collecting an assault force for the invasion of Britain, because the place to defeat the English was in America. Pleas from the Continental Congress to the same purpose were having effect. From George Washington himself came a letter to La Luzerne, French Minister to the United States, stressing the need of naval superiority and asking for a French fleet to come to America. As forerunner, seven ships of the line under Admiral de Ternay, d'Estaing's successor, came into Newport in July, 1780, bringing a man and a small land army who were to become essential partners in the final campaign. The man was General Jean Baptiste Rochambeau, age fifty-five, bringing three regiments under the command of the Marquis Claude-Anne de Saint-Simon, whose younger cousin Count Henri de Saint-Simon was the future founder of French Socialism. Both were related to the illustrious Duc de Saint-Simon, chronicler of the court of Louis XIV. The young count had volunteered to come with his troops to America to serve under Rochambeau's orders. His regiments were then stationed on Santo Domingo in the West Indies, on loan to the Spanish. This happy addition was held in unhappy inaction for nearly a year because of the British blockade outside Newport. Without land transport, Washington could find no way to employ them. Without the means to move, Washington could not take the offensive, and to fight on the defensive, he knew, could never lead to victory. With money to pay for food, Rochambeau's army remained at Newport, eating and flirting, militarily a blank — now, but not forever.

Rochambeau, a short stout figure of amiable disposition and solid military experience, proved an ideal ally, a strong supporter and loyal partner, willing to put himself second to the Commander-in-Chief without being subservient or a mere junior lieutenant. He had ideas of his own, which he was ready and able to advocate. Though sometimes engaged in sharp dispute with senior officers, he commanded the respect and unbroken discipline of his men. Despite the want and hardships of the coming joint campaign in enforced intimacy with Americans of alien speech and habit, no serious frictions marked the partnership. When the time came, the French soldiers marched through America in better order and discipline than either the English or the Americans had ever shown.

In the Rochambeau army was the Duc de Lauzun, the extravagant nephew of Rodney's benefactor in Paris, soon to prove a dashing fighter in the Yorktown campaign. At Newport he "rendered himself very agreeable to the Americans by his prepossessing manners," which we may easily understand to mean his free-spending habits. In a memoir, he relates that upon the departure of the French force from Brest, only half the promised transports were on hand, "forcing us to leave behind one brigade of infantry, one-third of artillery and one-third of my own regiment." Clearly, the management of the French Navy had not improved since the muddled invasion effort of the year before. The most interesting thing about Lauzun's memoir of his venture to a new world to attend the revolutionary birth of a new nation is the absence of any thought given or notice taken or comment of any kind about the historic events in which he was taking part, or about the country, people or politics of the war. As Lauzun was considered the archetype of young ornament of the French court, he may reflect his class and kind and the characteristics that brought them to extinction. Or, without making *too* much of it, he may merely have had a firm grasp of his personal priorities. These were his amours, which fill the first half of the memoir devoted to his life in France in the last years of the pre-Revolution aristocracy. For 140 pages we have a kiss-and-tell catalogue of his mistresses and their degree of "marked preference for myself" on first and growing acquaintance, with every name stated without regard for position, family or husband. When published under the Restoration, a time when émigrés of the former nobility wished to show the morality and rectitude of their lives, the book created a supreme scandal engaging two ruling critics, Talleyrand and Sainte-Beuve, in an angry controversy as to its authenticity. As the book's only interest could be to contemporaries who knew and may have shared the favors of the ladies mentioned, it remains for posterity an empty shell with only a faint murmur of the glittering sea from which it came.

When, on August 25, Washington learned from Rochambeau the news brought by a French frigate, that the promised French Second Division on which he had counted to reinforce Lafayette and Greene in the South was blockaded at Brest and could not arrive until October at the soonest, by which time the army would have consumed all the provisions the region could supply, his iron endurance of disappointments was allowed to crack in a letter to his brother Samuel. "It is impossible for any person at a distance to have an idea of my embarrassments or to conceive how an army can be kept together under any such circumstances as ours is." Within days came news of the defeat at Camden in South Carolina, exposing Virginia to invasion from the South. Washington could only patch the hole by sending a regiment from Maryland to Greene and summon the confidence to meet his French allies for a conference at Hartford on a plan of campaign.

On their arrival at Newport, de Ternay and Rochambeau marched down from Rhode Island (100 miles) through Connecticut to the meeting at Hartford on September 20–22. Washington brought with him old reliable General Henry Knox, the onetime bookseller from Boston who had made himself an artillery officer and had dragged the captured guns from Ticonderoga over ruts and hills to drive the British out of Boston in 1776. No one arrived with good news. Lafayette came fresh from the fighting in the South where in August, 1780, only three months after the fall of Charleston, the Americans had suffered the crushing defeat at Camden. Here the pugnacious General Lord Cornwallis was pursuing a campaign to conquer the whole of the state. At Camden he had thrashed General Gates, the hero of Saratoga and, afterward, a conspirator in the Conway Cabal that attempted to discredit and supplant Washington by a whispering campaign of insults designed to provoke him to resign. Conscious that he was indispensable, Washington refused to be drawn, but he could not prevent the malcontents in Congress from engineering the appointment of Gates to take command in the South. Under Gates's clumsy generalship at Camden, the Americans lost 800 killed and 1,000 taken prisoner, and were further embarrassed by the hasty departure of their General in a retreat so far and so fast that it carried him by the evening of the battle seventy miles to Charlotte, and did not stop until he reached Hillsboro in the mountains. According to a statement by Alexander Hamilton, Gates in his craven abandonment covered 180 miles in three and half days, an unlikely distance in the given time, even with relays of fresh horses, which obviously could not have been prepared for a retreat. Whatever the actual fact, the shameful retreat was enough to plunge Gates into disgrace and suspend him from the army. An official investigation was ordered but never took place.

The victor, after fastening the British yoke on South Carolina, was now moving north through North Carolina toward Virginia, the Old Dominion and richest state of the South. Narrowed at its waist by the indentation made by Chesapeake Bay, it was the place, in Cornwallis' opinion, to cut off the richer resources of the South from the North and achieve the decisive stroke to end the war. "A successful battle may give us America" was his favorite dictum. The gleam of that single battle lured every commander on either side in the hope of finishing off a miserable war that would not end.

Ending a war is a difficult and delicate business. Even intelligent rulers, when they exist, often find themselves unable to terminate a war, should they want to. Each side must become convinced at the same time and with equal certainty that its war aim is either not achievable or not worth the cost or damage to the state. The certainty must be equal, for if one side perceives a slight advantage or disadvantage it will not offer terms acceptable to the other. In the Hundred Years' War that dragged France and England through the 14th century, both sides would have liked to quit but could not, for fear of losing power and status; hate and mistrust fed by the war prevented them from talking. In the ghastly toll and futility of 1914–18, no end could be negotiated short of victory for one side or the other, because each felt it must bring home to its people some compensating gain in the form of territory or a seaport or industrial resource to justify the terrible cost. To come home empty-handed might mean a revolt against the rulers at home — or at least the loss of their position and place in society, as the Kaiser and the Hohenzollerns were thrown out in 1918. Common soldiers are not rulers and do not have to worry about losing thrones or office so why, when in hunger and rags, do they go on? The answer is a complex of many factors: because they have absorbed a sense of the goal, because giving up in desertion or mutiny carries the ultimate penalty, because of comradeship, because if they leave the army they would have nowhere to go and no way to go home. For rulers to stop short of the declared war aim, thus acknowledging their own as well as their party's and their nation's incapacity, is as problematic as the camel's passage through the needle's eye. Short of absolute defeat, would the leaders of the American cause have given up their fight for liberty and independence or the British King and ministers have given up their imperial control? "Forbid it, Almighty God!" would have been the answer, and so each side in America fought on for the gleam of that successful battle and the "decisive stroke."

Clinton, with uncharacteristic optimism, wrote to the government after the capture of Charleston, "A few works if properly reinforced will give us all between this and Hudson river." In London, Germain caught the gleam, stating, "One more campaign would reduce all the southern provinces." No matter how the fortunes of war fluctuated, he continued to believe that suppression of the rebellion would be easy, a happy assumption of British strategists based on their total lack of acquaintance with Americans. They could not believe that farmers and woodsmen untrained as soldiers — "these country clowns," as a Hessian officer spoke of them at Trenton — could ever stand up to the well-drilled British and German professionals. They forgot the extra weapon that is possessed by those who are fighting for a cause. Training is usually the criterion of military effectiveness, but not this time.

The American fighting style of firing from concealment behind walls and trees while wearing dull-colored homespun or fringed Indian tunics, in total contrast to the spit and polish of the brightly uniformed European armies who advanced in solid ranks to shoot and be shot at, was the major cause of the persistent British underestimation of the rebels. The very first opening fight at Lexington, when redcoats were killed all along the road back to Boston by the bullets of minutemen skulking behind stone walls, instead of in the decent well-drilled order of the soldiers of the King of France (or, alternatively, of the Duke of York) in the nursery rhyme who with 40,000 men marched up the hill and then marched down again, fixed the image of peasants, not to say savages — unfit to meet the infantry of Europe. When, not long after Lexington, the British marched up Bunker (Breed's) Hill and then, much reduced, marched down again, they did not learn to change their estimate.

But despite the advantages of the American fighting style, at the Hartford Conference the outlook was bleak, and Rochambeau was pessimistic and Lafayette even more so. Because of the great decline in American credit since the taking of Charleston, the "very unfavorable" news about Camden and the fall in the finances of Congress, Lafayette pronounced "this campaign" at rock bottom. "We are still more destitute of clothing, tents and wagons for our troops," he reported to Washington. It was essential to have provisions sent to them, "were it possible to find means of transportation. Despairing of this, as much is sent as possible northward on navigatable rivers." His report was not one to encourage anyone, but the goal ahead was stronger than discouragement. The Hartford Conference was occupied mainly by the two commanders, Washington and Rochambeau, taking each other's measure and discovering what comradeship they might — or might not —develop, and in discussion of what should be the locale of their joint action. Between Rochambeau, a knowledgeable soldier, and Washington, who inspired a touch of worship merely by being, mutual respect came easily; an agreed plan of campaign less so. They agreed that assault on New York, Washington's dearest object, could not be accomplished without French command of adjacent waters, which de Ternay's squadron could not by itself establish. Moreover, Rochambeau could not offer a firm plan of campaign because he had been instructed that the French fleet and army were to act together, and until additional French naval forces arrived, he felt obliged to remain in support of de Ternay's force at Newport. Not until a year later when a second contingent of French land forces arrived under Admiral de Barras to replace the deceased de Ternay, and along with de Barras the promise of a French fleet coming to give the Americans the naval power they needed so badly, was the daring plan of envelopment by sea and land conceived that was to win the war.

But the American General's mind was still fixed on New York. Washington did not like Rochambeau's alternative of a campaign in the Chesapeake region to cut off the British threat from the South, because he believed the French soldiers would sicken in the summer heat of Virginia, and his own New Englanders despised the South for its snakes, heat and mosquitoes and had the deepest suspicions of the climate as unhealthy, not to say poisonous and rife with fever. Fever, undifferentiated by name because its sources in germs and infections were not known, could include malaria, pneumonia, yellow fever, typhoid, typhus and dysentery. Its prevalence in Virginia arose less from the climate, which was always blamed for all ill health, than from swamps and mosquitoes combined with unsanitary conditions of men living in military groups. Eight out of ten deaths in the 18th century were ascribed to "fever."

To bring an army to Virginia would mean a journey of about 500 miles, which would have to be made on foot, as the only available sea transport was the eight-ship squadron at Newport under Admiral Count Louis de Barras, now the French naval commander there. Against the superior strength of the British fleet off New York, de Barras refused to transport troopships packed with soldiers down the coast to Virginia. The overland march appeared to Washington too risky and costly and likely to lose a third of the army to sickness and desertions, and he did not think the campaign could bring much benefit so long as the British controlled the offshore waters of the Virginia coast. He believed that an attack on New York, as a diversion causing

Clinton to call up troops from the South, would do more to relieve Lafayette than direct action in his behalf. Most compelling was his emotional attachment to New York as his first major defeat of the Revolution in the early Battle of Long Island. It had left him with a yearning to retrieve the city. According to the alliance, Washington was Commander-in-Chief and Rochambeau, under his orders, giving the final decision to Washington, but Rochambeau, skillful as he was amiable, knew the art of supporting his flanks. Soon, in response to his persuasions, La Luzerne, the French Minister, and de Barras and others primed by Rochambeau were advocating the advantages of a campaign at the Chesapeake in their letters home.

What was the Chesapeake and why all the focus on it? Great Chesapeake Bay formed the coastline of Virginia, stretching for 200 miles along the Atlantic to Maryland and New Jersey. With its many doorways facing Europe and its many ports and estuaries facing inland and giving access to the interior, it was the widest opening to the southern section of the country. The Bay's upper waters came within twenty miles of meeting the Delaware River near Philadelphia, thus forming a natural waterway connecting the South with the mid-Atlantic states and creating the strategic neck

course of events as do larger impersonal forces like economics or the climate. Lord Cornwallis was one such individual. His seat was the borough of Eye in Suffolk, which his family had represented in Parliament off and on since the 14th century. He was born in 1738, the same year as George III. After school at Eton, having shown a military bent, he obtained a commission as ensign in the Grenadier Guards. At eighteen, while on a European tour with his tutor, a Prussian Army officer, he enrolled in the Military Academy of Turin, considered one of the best in Europe. In the relaxed Italian atmosphere, its curriculum had a charming irrelevance to the subject at hand. The students took ballroom dancing from 7 to 8 a.m., presumably on awakening, followed for contrast by the German language from 8 to 9 and for relief by two hours for breakfast from 9 to 11. Military instruction occupied one hour from 11 to 12, plus two hours for mathematics and fortifications from 3 to 5 in the afternoon. At five o'clock came more dancing lessons, visits, and attendance at the opera until supper. On two days a week students owed a duty of attendance at the King of Sardinia's court. Turin, formerly a possession of Spain and then of France, was the residence of the Kings of Sardinia, whose royal title passed to the

Dukes of Savoy and by them to the royal family of Italy at the time of the Unification of 1860.

If their studies did not deeply instruct Turin's students in the science or the art of war, they provided a gentlemanly introduction to the military profession. War soon engaged Cornwallis in service with the Grenadier Guards as an ally of Prince Ferdinand of Brunswick in a continental offshoot of the Seven Years' War. In 1762 he inherited his title on the death of his father. On returning to England in that year to assume his seat in the House of Lords, he took up a surprising position by associating himself with the Whigs, the Opposition party which vigorously opposed the King's and the government's coercive policy toward the restive Americans. Whether the unwarlike Turin program played some part in his choice or he was following a bent of his own mind, or was influenced by his good friend the Whig leader Lord Shelburne, is not apparent. Though superficially an orthodox Guards officer, he was a more ambivalent character than he appeared. In spite of his Whiggism, he was respectable enough to be made colonel of his regiment and an aide-de-camp to the King. He is not recorded as taking any part in debates in the Lords.

More emphatic than if he had spoken up, he stood with a brave little minority of four peers in support of Lord Camden's motion in March, 1766, opposing the Declaratory Bill. The Bill was a government measure to assert Parliament's right of taxation of the Colonies, intended to counteract what was seen as appeasement of the Americans by the repeal of the Stamp Act. As far as was reported, Cornwallis did not open his mouth in the debate on the Bill, but the remarks in the House of Lords by Lord Camden, for whose position he voted, were unequivocal. The Declaratory Bill, Camden said, was "absolutely illegal, contrary to the fundamental laws of this constitution," itself "grounded on the eternal and immutable laws of nature," because "taxation and representation are inseparably united. . . . this position is founded on the laws of nature for whatever is a man's own is absolutely his own; no man hath a right to take it from him without his consent. Whoever attempts to do it attempts an injury, whoever does it, commits a robbery; he throws down and destroys the distinction between liberty and slavery." These words could have been spoken by Tom Paine or Patrick Henry if not John Adams, who would never have allowed himself so romantic a view of "natural law." They were presumably approved by Lord Cornwallis, since he voted with the speaker. Yet he did not refuse to take a command in the war, as did Lord Jeffrey Amherst and Colonel Ralph Abercromby, a hero in the Brunswick war and an outstanding soldier in the army, and others who disapproved of coercing America. On the contrary, Cornwallis volunteered for an assignment when the Americans took up armed rebellion and the British Army needed reinforcements in America. Governed by an exacting sense of duty, he felt that as a soldier holding the King's commission it was his duty to help suppress rebellion. Yet either duty worked slowly or else ambivalence was already operating, for it was seven months after the Americans fired the shots at Lexington before he decided to accept a command in the suppression of the rebellion. The lag was due in part to the pleas of his wife, to whom he was deeply attached. In February, 1776, however, he departed for America in command of seven regiments, which he took to Halifax where General Howe had retired after yielding Boston. Cornwallis saw action in the battles of Long Island and White Plains. He captured Fort Lee on the Jersey shore of the Hudson and afterward pursued Washington across New Jersey to Trenton. Here he frustrated Washington's advance in the Battle of the

Brandywine and went on to occupy Philadelphia.

Cornwallis does not appear to have been too strongly gripped by the duty that had brought him to America, for war against a tattered colonial militia did not appeal to him as likely to add to a Guard officer's reputation. Accordingly, he took the long voyage home on leave in 1777. Promoted to Lieutenant General, he returned to duty in America in 1778, sailing on the same ship with the Carlisle Peace Commission. His concern that his suite might be crowding the space wanted by the commissioners for their own use was outweighed by the enjoyment of the two earls' friendly games of whist. In America he found himself named second in command to Sir Henry Clinton, who had been appointed Commander-in-Chief to replace the inglorious William Howe and who soon showed himself even less aggressive than his predecessor. When given command of the southern front, Cornwallis, despairing of Clinton's inaction and convinced, like Rodney, that the war was being mismanaged, made his attempt to resign that was not allowed.

The French alliance had now intervened, convincing Cornwallis that the doorways by which the French could enter, bringing men, money and arms to the rebels, must be closed, in particular those of Chesapeake Bay. The Chesapeake ports were in regular use by the Americans for the shipping of tobacco and cotton and export goods to European traders to finance the purchase of arms and ammunition. Cornwallis envisaged a major offensive to subdue the South and make an end of insurgency there, for which Clinton was obviously disinclined. What Clinton wanted was for Cornwallis to settle contentedly at a permanent base and lend his army for operations in Pennsylvania or for defense of New York. Cornwallis thought this was pointless and wrote to his colleague General Phillips the shocking suggestion that "if we mean an offensive war in America, we must abandon New York." Instead, we should "bring our whole force into Virginia" where "we then have a stake to fight for" and where his refrain "A successful battle may give us America" might be realized.

Proof of the dogma was not making much progress. The fighting at this time was conducted for the British by two hated and dreaded figures, the cavalry Colonel Banastre Tarleton, valued highly by Cornwallis as the spearhead of his army, and the traitor Benedict Arnold, who, having sold himself to the British for £10,000, as he thought, and fringe benefits, had to prove by his violence

410

the value of what he had sold. (He had asked for £10,000 but received £6,000, calculated on a basis of 2 guineas per man of the West Point garrison.) Tarleton's heavy dragoons trampled fields of corn and rye while his and Arnold's raiders plundered and destroyed the harvested tobacco and grain in barns, spreading devastation. Tarleton was charged with driving cattle, pigs and poultry into barns before setting them afire. He was known as "no quarter Tarleton" for his violation of surrender rules in the Waxhaw massacre, where he had caught a body of American troops that held its fire too long before firing at fifty yards, too late to stop the charging cavalry. After surrender, they were cut down when Tarleton's men, let loose to wield their knife-edged sabers, killed a total of 113 and wounded 150 more, of whom half died of their wounds. Enmity flared higher when the tale of the Waxhaw spread through the Carolinas, inflaming hatred and hostility and sharpening the conflict of Loyalists and patriots.

Owing to his wife's serious illness, Cornwallis hurried home a second time, to be met by the misery of her death shortly after he reached England. Profoundly depressed, he wrote to his brother that the loss of his wife had "effectually destroyed all hopes of happiness in this world." He could find nothing to live for save the army. The personal tragedy, leaving him alone and unoccupied, brought him back to the war once more, in July, 1779.

In August, 1780, Cornwallis defeated Gates in the battle of Camden. Though the English saw Camden as a pronounced victory, rebellion was not reduced and American militia and Continentals did not dissolve and leave the field to the victors. "We fight," as Greene wrote to Luzerne, "get beat and rise to fight again." As this was all too true, a victory in the field for the British did not appear to bring the contest any nearer to victory in the war. Greene's simple formula kept the nucleus of an army and the coals of rebellion alive in the South, while the defeat at Camden proved almost a benefit because it led to the replacement of Gates and Washington's appointment of Greene and Steuben to reform and command the southern army. All they had left was a remnant of the Continental militia, whose members would join together to fight for a few days or weeks and then return to care for their crops and fields, plus a saving addition of a few formidable partisans or guerrilla leaders, like the Swamp Fox and Andrew Pickens and Thomas Sumter, who kept the fighting hot and resistance to the British alive. Intensified raids of destruction by Tarleton's men, whose cavalry gave them extra mobility, and the outrage aroused by the Waxhaw massacre stirred desires of revenge and augmented the feud between Loyalists and patriots. Their strife as much as anything kept the fires of rebellion hot in the Carolinas. In South Carolina, Cornwallis had to admit that the Swamp Fox "had so wrought on the minds of the people partly by the terror and punishments and partly by the promise of plunder that there was scarce an inhabitant [in the region] that was not in arms against us." His diagnosis of the hostility, ignoring the raids of Tarleton and Benedict Arnold, who were plundering homes, burning flour mills and dragging off civilians as prisoners to the lethal prison ships, reflects the willful blindness of the invader who assures himself that the natives are only made unfriendly by some other provocation than his own. Cornwallis was convinced that after so crushing a defeat as the Americans had sustained at Camden, they could not maintain the Revolution in the South except with help from the North. To him this meant one thing — that he must wipe out the rebel forces in North Carolina and take control of that province. The one necessity for victory — to destroy the enemy's army — proved beyond his reach. Exasperated by the partisans' warfare that erupted whenever districts were thought pacified, Cornwallis' commander in the province, Major Patrick Ferguson, resorted to the threat of terror. He issued a proclamation in September, 1780, to patriot officers that if they persisted in resistance to British arms, he would march over the mountains, hang their leaders and lay waste to the country with fire and sword. Ferguson was not a tyrant but ordinarily a humane and temperate individual. He had entered military service at fourteen, when his family purchased for him a cornetcy commission in the Royal Scots Greys. After a study of military science, more technical than ballroom dancing and the opera, he invented a rapid-firing breech-loading rifle capable of four shots a minute while hitting a target at 200 yards. As more efficient than anything the British Army possessed, it was, of course, not adopted; only 200 were manufactured. Ferguson was one of the few English officers to treat the American Loyalists with equality, sitting and talking with them for hours on the state of affairs and the ruinous effects of rebellion. As a local hero to the back-country people, he was chosen to lead a campaign to stamp out the patriot fires. Nevertheless, his ill-advised proclamation had the normal effect of such things. Used by the partisan leaders to call "over-mountain" men to throw off the iron heel of the oppressor in defense of their homes and lands, it brought in more than 1,000 mounted volunteers with their sharpshooting rifles. Clad in buckskin, they assembled at Sycamore Shoals in Tennessee. Ferguson sensed their dangerous mood and sent for reinforcements to Cornwallis, who was camped with his army only 35 miles away at Charlotte in North Carolina. His message, expressing urgency, read "something must be done," but the help did not come. Taking the road to Charlotte that passed by a high ridge called King's Mountain, and sharing the usual assumption that the Americans would be beaten, Ferguson decided to confront his pursuers on the ridge, though he might have reached Cornwallis in a couple of hours. He took his stand on a cleared oval space that crowned the ridge whose slopes were thickly wooded by tall pines from top to bottom, creating, as he believed, an impregnable position. The frontiersmen, informed of his location by spies, marched through a night of rain with rifles wrapped to keep them dry and their ears alert for sounds of ambush. As the weather cleared, they reached King's Mountain at three in the afternoon, where they dismounted and circled the base of the hill. Having no commander, they elected a Colonel William Campbell to take command. Then, with war whoops and barking rifles, they charged up the hill, crouching behind tree trunks as they climbed. The height above, which had seemed a daunting obstacle, proved an advantage, for the British fire from the ridge "overshot us altogether, scarce touching a man except those on horseback." Ferguson's Loyalists, with bayonets bared, came charging downhill under the frontiersmen's deadly rifle fire which felled them in rows. The redcoat ranks wavered and fell back. Attempting to rally the assault, Ferguson rode forward on a white horse, slashing with his sword at two flags of surrender already raised among his troops by men in panic. Target of fifty rifles, he was pierced and torn by their bullets and blasted from the saddle to a dead heap on the ground. The ridge was captured; the Battle of King's Mountain was over in half an hour. His blood-stained riderless white horse plunged in abandon down the embattled slope where Ferguson died. News of the defeat at King's Mountain sped through the region, causing Loyalist adherents to blow away like dust clouds. "Dastardly and pusillanimous" in Cornwallis' words, they refused after King's Mountain to aid the British while the rebels turned more "inveterate in rancour." Seven hundred of the Loyalist force that fought with Ferguson were taken prisoner. Of them, twenty-four were tried for treason by the rebels at a drumhead court-martial, and nine found guilty and hanged, heating the feud of Loyalists versus patriots.

In this situation Cornwallis was persuaded he must abandon the campaign for North Carolina and fall back to winter in South Carolina. Accordingly he set out for Winnsboro, about fifty miles south of King's Mountain and thirty miles from Camden, where his fortunes had been so high. The retreat, though the distance was short, proved a ghastly ordeal and the winter at Winnsboro his Valley Forge. In continual rain his men marched without tents and with food so scarce that they subsisted on nothing but turnips and Indian corn scratched from the fields for a yield of five ears a day for two men. With no rum and no beef, they pulled their wounded in wagons jouncing over rough fields. Rivers were the worst, with half-starved horses barely able to reach the other side through rushing icy waters. The last reverse was loss of a single blockhouse, made of strong logs, on a hill which had been fortified by Colonel Rugeley of the Loyalist militia with earth piled at the base and a circle of stakes defying it to be taken except by cannon. The American cavalry officer Colonel William Washington fashioned an imitation cannon from a tree trunk and, pulling it up, though not too close for inspection, summoned the blockhouse to surrender. Colonel Rugeley yielded without firing a shot.

For the patriots, the small triumph at King's Mountain was offset by the difficulties of trying to prepare for a winter without the suffering of Morristown and Valley Forge. Pennsylvania had 5,000 horned cattle growing too thin to serve for beef. They could not be slaughtered anyway, because there was no hard money to buy salt to preserve the meat and merchants would not salt anything for paper money. Shortage of everything persisted — of cash first of all, of clothes, shoes, blankets, ammunition and, less material but more important, of popular support. Lethargy in prosperous Virginia was notable. While he believed that "the views and wishes of the great body of the people are with us," Greene wrote to Jefferson, then Governor of Virginia, "they are, except for the influence of a few, a lifeless and inanimate mass without direction or spirit to employ the means they possess for their own security." Washington felt chagrined to have the French witness the poverty of his army and the "paucity of enlistments." When the French came to find "that we have but a handful of men in the field," he feared that they "might sail away." Washington was sadly discovering the frailty of his fellowmen. "It is a melancholy thing," he wrote, "to see such a decay of public virtue and the fairest prospects overcast and clouded by a host of infamous harpies who to acquire a little pelf, would involve this great continent in inextricable ruin. . . . Unless leaders in the states bestir themselves, our affairs are irretrievably lost." Yet he never for a moment believed them lost. Through it all he had "no doubt but that the same bountiful Providence which has relieved us in a variety of difficulties before will enable us to emerge from them ultimately and crown our struggles with success." In the face of the piling up of frustrations and disappointments — the mutinies, the fall of credit, doubting officers and failing army — Washington was still able, when he learned from Laurens that de Grasse was bringing part of his fleet to America, to state to a member of Congress with the confident assurance that made him unique, "The game is yet in our hands . . . a cloud may pass over us, individuals may be ruined and the country at large or particular States undergo temporary distress, but certain I am that it is in our power to bring this war to a happy conclusion." If it was the need of the hour that produced a man so firm in purpose, so unshakable in faith, the same need had not yet produced a nation to match him.

Despite Cornwallis' recent setbacks, the crushing of Greene's army, engine of rebellion in the South, was still his overriding objective. On New Year's Day, 1781, the year of so many decisions, Tarleton, in the van of Cornwallis' force, received orders from the General "to push Morgan [in Greene's army] to the utmost. No time is to be lost." Tarleton had a force of disciplined dragoons, light infantry and five battalions of British regulars and a small artillery unit, altogether about 1,100 men. General Daniel Morgan commanded 1,600 Continental infantry, the Maryland and Virginia, and other state militias, 200 Virginia riflemen and a cavalry unit of his own, numbering 160 horsemen. Alerted by local partisans of Tarleton's advance, Morgan took up position in a thinly wooded camp in the bend of the Broad River near the northern border of South Carolina. No Alamo or Argonne with heroic overtones, the site bore the plain domestic name Cowpens because cattle were customarily penned there when awaiting delivery to market. Morgan, crippled by painful arthritis, made camp at the base of a hill flanked by woods to prevent surprise penetration. Expecting his untrained militia to run at the charge of the dreaded Cavalry Legion, but knowing they could not run far because of the unfordable river behind them, he limped among the campfires, encouraging the men to stand firm next morning, long enough to fire three volleys. "Just hold your heads up, boys, three fires and you are free," and he told them how the girls would kiss them and the old folks bless them when they returned home. As the first British infantry line marched forward with heavy tread and fierce shouts, Morgan called, "They are giving us the British halloo. Give them the Indian halloo, by God!" and was answered by wild cheers and shouts from his own lines. Calling to the men to aim for the epaulets of officers, he mounted and rode for the place of his tethered horses, to which he could see a militia unit was fleeing. When the runaways reached the horse park, the General was there ahead, waving his sword and barring their way, and crying to them to "Form again! Give them one more fire, and the day is ours!" Behind the lines, Virginia sharpshooters were picking off the riders from Tarleton's saddles. Suddenly the dragoons were met in turn by a charge of American cavalry, under Colonel William Washington, swinging their sabers with no less vigor than the enemy. Pursued by the Americans for nearly a mile, the British line lost cohesion. "Give them one fire," ordered Colonel Washington, "and I'll charge them." Below the hill, riflemen and Continentals were pouring fire on the British infantry, and at the order "Give them bayonet!" swept down upon them. Seeing their infantry broken and running, Tarleton's horsemen, despite his furious orders, refused to make another charge, and turned and galloped from the field, shortly followed by their commander. Surrounded by vengeful rebels, his Legion, his dragoons, his light infantry and regular foot soldiers surrendered — all but a few obdurate artillerymen, who refused to yield and were killed or captured defending their guns. The British lost at Cowpens 110 dead, 700 prisoners, 800 muskets, 100 horses and Tarleton's entire baggage train of 35 wagons with ammunition. Except for 300 who escaped, virtually the whole of Tarleton's force was killed or captured — a substantial portion of Cornwallis' army. "The late affair," he was to say, "has almost broke my heart." General Greene could take more satisfaction. "After this," he said, "nothing seems difficult."

Determined to allow the rebels no chance to exult over their victory at Cowpens, Cornwallis was seized by a passion for pursuit, to catch up and annihilate the enemy and take from them any encouragement his reverse might have given. The army's intention, as

General O'Hara, Cornwallis' deputy commander, wrote to the Duke of Grafton, Lord Privy Seal in the North ministry, was almost fanatic: "Without baggage, necessaries or provisions of any sort for officer or soldier, in the most barren, inhospitable unhealthy part of North America, opposed to the most savage inveterate perfidious, cruel enemy, with zeal and bayonets only, it was resolved to follow Greene's army to the end of the world." Cornwallis needed a victorious battle not only for public effect but to gain control of the region, for as long as Greene remained in the Carolinas as a center of resistance, the rebellion would not be stamped out. Morgan was no less anxious to bring his company with booty and prisoners out of the pursuer's way. Still determined to eliminate Greene and reclaim the South, Cornwallis was soon joined by reinforcements of 1,500 men, under General Leslie, sent by Clinton, who had received an addition of Irish recruits to fill their places in New York. With these reinforcements he intended to pursue his offensive into North Carolina.

Recent heavy rains had made high water in the rivers and turned the roads into troughs of mud that sucked at the marchers' boots and slowed progress. Morgan, aching from his ailments, could not trot his horse and could hardly sit astride. Greene, aware of Morgan's condition, was anxious to bring him safely out. With his usual care, he had ordered preparation of wheeled platforms on which improvised pontoons could be hauled with the army for crossing rivers. By this foresight, he was able to ease and speed Morgan's flight and put his own army across flooded rivers, now grown too deep for fording. Cornwallis' large army, plowing heavily through the mud churned by Morgan's passage, was slowed, and delayed at every river, but kept on coming. In steady rain mixed with snow, they were making no more than six miles a day. Recognizing that at this rate he would not catch his fox, Cornwallis decided he must lighten his wagon train to speed his pace. On January 25, in midwinter, 250 miles from the nearest point of resupply at Wilmington, North Carolina, he ordered the discarding of what the Romans, knowing the problem, called *impedimenta*, all but a minimum of provisions and ammunition, and all "comforts" — that is, tents, blankets, personal baggage and, to the horror of his troops, several hogsheads of rum — the whole burned in a consuming conflagration as if to burn away the greatest British humiliation since Saratoga. To set an example, Cornwallis threw his own baggage into the flames. In the midst of nowhere, the extremism of the act seems almost suicidal, as if some premonition of the end, like the chill shadow of a cloud that darkens the earth, had turned his every prospect black. At first, free of its heavy wagons, the column made up speed, only to find itself blocked by the Dan River at flood stage with naked banks from which all boats had been pulled away by the Americans. The radical stripping of impediments had been in vain, leaving Cornwallis now with no choice but to retreat in the hope of rallying Loyalists' support in the countryside and reaching a point of resupply. By scouring the country and slaughtering draft oxen for meat, he made it with an exhausted and hungry army back to Hillsboro, at that time the capital of North Carolina, supposedly a Loyalist center, where he raised the royal flag and issued a call to citizens to take up arms with his forces. On the principle that to declare a thing done can have the same effect as doing it, he added a proclamation that North Carolina had been recovered for the Crown. It was not persuasive. So few responded to the call to arms as to amaze General O'Hara at his government's deceived expectations, "Fatal infatuation! When will government see these people thro' the proper medium? I am persuaded never." It was now February, 1781, and the British were no nearer a secure hold on the South or the "battle [that] will give us America," though Cornwallis was still bent on achieving it by a battle with Greene that would eliminate him as the fulcrum of resistance in the South. Greene's ever-reviving force was to Cornwallis what Gaul was to Caesar: it had to be conquered, not merely to avenge his defeats but because there was no point in his operations unless they were directed toward restoring royal government in the South as a basis for its restoration in America. Only this could justify the lives lost at King's Mountain and Cowpens and comfort the shades of the men who had died there that they had not died emptily.

With his losses restored by the reinforcements, Cornwallis felt fit for battle again.

In pursuit Cornwallis was always at his most vigorous, though harassed by rebel partisans and Marion's men and hampered by poor intelligence. He could get nothing from the local Loyalists. "Our friends hereabouts," as he wrote to Tarleton, "are so timid and stupid" as to be useless. Supplies, supposed to reach him from New York via Charleston, often failed because of the partisans' disruption of the roads. Absent rum after a day's cold wet march was the worst privation, leaving many of the men, weakened by malaria, to be kept alive on opium. The underfed horses were sometimes too weak to pull the artillery, and men weakened by fever and shaking with ague often had to substitute for them. Their General while keeping his army moving had to organize protection of the supply line and push his way through to confront Greene. Rivers at flood stage in the winter rains had to be forded. Delayed for two or three days at a time at the banks of swollen rivers, Cornwallis fumed as he waited for the waters to subside. At the Catawba, broad, deep and rapid, and filled with "very large rocks," Cornwallis, deceived by faulty or false intelligence, was led to the wagon ford of "swimming water" instead of to the shallower horse ford. The strongest men and horses were swept downstream in the swift current. Leading the van on a spirited mount, Cornwallis plunged in. His horse was shot in midstream by North Carolina militia posted behind timber at the fords. With a general's spirit, the horse managed to clamber to the banks before it went down. General O'Hara's horse fell on the rocks and was rolled with his rider forty yards in the torrent. The river was a mass of struggling redcoats, as reported by a Loyalist observer, "a-hollerin', a-snortin' and a-drownin', a-snortin', a-hollerin' and a-drownin'." With their knapsacks weighted with powder and ball, and their muskets across their shoulders, the redcoats could not fire, but in the heavy fog hanging over the river the North Carolinians could not get accurate range for general slaughter.

Greene, certain that Cornwallis would not stop until he had avenged his defeat at Cowpens and recovered the prisoners, pushed on as hard as his pursuer. His strategy was to keep Cornwallis moving, luring him northward in his pursuit away from his supply bases until, without supply train, he would be exhausted and isolated. He himself had received reinforcements from Steuben, giving him an army of about 4,000, of whom a third was militia, and he would have liked to turn and face his foe in a pitched battle, but against the enemy's augmented force he was not going to allow himself to be caught at a time and place of the enemy's choosing. Facing better trained troops, the best he could do was to deploy at his own time at a site to his own advantage. Traveling light, with his men carrying small portions of dried beef and corn and salt in wallets and guided by partisans who knew the bypaths through the swamps and forests, he kept well ahead of Cornwallis until, early in March, he came to Guilford in the center of North Carolina. A place he had previously reconnoitered, it was located on the main north-south road where it met at right angles an east-west road running along a wooded ridge. At the junction of the roads stood Guilford's courthouse at the base of a gradual slope where the main road ran up to the top of the ridge. Halfway up the slope was a broad clearing flanked by thin woods, open enough to permit visibility for rifle fire. The site was similar to Cowpens, and here Greene decided to make his stand. He sorely missed Morgan, whom he had sent on his way home to Virginia in a litter, but he possessed Morgan's shadow in a careful report that Morgan had written out for him after Cowpens. Knowing that Cornwallis would pursue for a finishing fight, Morgan had advised Greene to place his least reliable militia, the North Carolinians, in the center in a line interspersed with troops picked for firmness, and with a line behind of veteran Continentals to "shoot the first man who runs." On either side of the front line would be placed Virginia riflemen and small cavalry units of sixty horsemen each, and with them on the slope two of Greene's four guns to command the approach along the main road.

Informed by scouts, Cornwallis knew that his desired moment had come. The clash that followed was a textbook example of the seemingly senseless 18th century tactic in which brightly uniformed infantry march in compact phalanx against the muzzles of the enemy's firearms. The expected effects of the tactic duly took place on both sides. The glistening steel of fixed bayonets advancing relentlessly upon them struck terror in the hearts of the defenders, who scattered into a stampede for escape while the point-blank target made by the British absorbed the lethal fire of the Virginia riflemen. In the platoons the well-drilled guards and grenadiers dropped down, hardly falling out of line. For two and a half hours of units moving forward and back under fire in recovery or counterattack, the exhausted armies fought, until both commanders, each seeing a line near collapse, called almost simultaneously for withdrawal. The Battle of Guilford Courthouse was ended. Cornwallis was left in possession of the field and a technical victory, but his admitted casualties of 532 (killed and wounded), about 25 percent of his army, were double Greene's at 261. The victory, as Cornwallis recognized, was "rendered without utility" because without provisions he could not hold the ground. In unkind assessment afterward, Charles Fox, at a civilian's comfortable distance from the blood and bullets, was to say "another such victory would destroy the British army."

Pyrrhic or not, the fortunes of Guilford

Courthouse could not subdue Cornwallis' instinct for aggressive action nor arrest his drive to Virginia, which he still thought, as he wrote to Clinton, "the only possible plan, even if it meant abandoning New York, for until Virginia is in a manner subdued, our hold on the Carolinas must be difficult if not precarious." Though he could hope for no support from Loyalists, he intended to go on to carry out the mission assigned to General Phillips, who was dying from a fever, to establish a naval base more central to the country than Charleston, which the British campaign required.

The Americans in the winter of 1780–81, following the Hartford Conference, were in no better case, although the British did not fully realize to what low ebb the rebellion had sunk. The mutinies in the army and the catastrophic fall of the financial credit of Congress, with every prospect, as Rochambeau expected, of the currency falling shortly "to total non-value," darkened the outlook even more. In Virginia, Benedict Arnold, acknowledged on both sides as a general of the highest capacity, was conducting "thundering excursions" of destruction at the head of 2,000 men (largely southern Loyalists) on behalf of the enemy. Defense was weakening. Under the pall of accumulating misfortune, Congress determined to send a special envoy, in the person of Colonel John Laurens, to inform the court of France in the "clearest light the state of distress of this country." To save the sinking cause of the Revolution, fresh help from France was essential. Benjamin Franklin was already in France as congressional commissioner, but it was felt that a fresh voice was needed to supplement the old philosopher's finesse. The younger Laurens, who knew the privations in the field from shared experience, had an added personal reason to fight the British in the cause of his father, who, captured at sea with the incriminating Dutch treaty, was still a prisoner in the Tower of London. His son could be counted upon to be a forceful advocate. John Laurens had fought with Washington at Brandywine and Monmouth and afterward, and had been employed by him in a number of secret missions. Commissioned a colonel by Congress, he had fought a duel for what he considered insults to Washington with the troublesome Charles Lee, whose order for retreat at Monmouth in the New Jersey campaign of 1778 had so infuriated Washington, and who ever after had been trying to discredit the Commander-in-Chief in the hope of supplanting him. Since the duel, Laurens had been serving as Washington's secretary, being credited by him with a character for "intrepidity bordering on rashness," which would be useful for cutting through the diplomatic niceties established by Franklin in his relations with Vergennes. Engrossed in the female charms and admiration of Paris, Franklin as envoy had acquired more celebrity than tangible aid.

Before Laurens departed, Washington drew for him a dark and frank appraisal of conditions. He thought a point of crisis had been reached. The people in general had lost confidence and regarded the impressment of supplies as "burdensome and oppressive." The system had excited "serious discontents" and "alarming symptoms of opposition." The army had suffered "calamitous distress" and their patience was "nearly exhausted." With money, the Allies could make a "decided effort" to secure America's liberty and independence; without such aid, "we may make a feeble expiring effort" which could well be our last. In a letter of April 9 to Laurens in Paris, Washington put the case as starkly as he could: "We are at the end of our tether, and now or never our deliverance must come."

Franklin, humiliated by the dispatch of a special envoy to his post while he was present, was galvanized by Laurens' coming to make a more emphatic approach of his own. In letter and interview with Vergennes, echoing Washington's "now or never," he told the Foreign Minister he must face the dire fact that unless America received the "most vigorous aid of our allies, particularly in the article of *money*," she might have to yield and sue for peace, leaving Britain to "recover the American continent and become the terror of Europe." He asked Vergennes point-blank what Congress might be told it could expect in French aid. Vergennes answered that the King was prepared to make an outright gift of 6 million livres, to make up for the promised Second Division.

Laurens, on arriving, opened a campaign as direct as bullets. He promptly asked Vergennes for a loan of 25 million livres in cash (about $6 million), plus supplies of arms, ammunition, clothing, equipment and tents. Vergennes replied that the King could not make a loan for the kingdom, but as proof of friendship he would make an outright donation of 6 million livres. Knowing that this had already been promised to Franklin, Laurens said bluntly that without the supplies this was not enough; that France was in danger of losing all her past efforts in favor of America, unless all his requests were complied with. The interview, recorded by Laurens' French-speaking secretary William Jackson, horrified

Franklin, who was present and who reported home that Laurens "brusqued" them too much. Laurens followed brusquerie with shock. He said to Vergennes that the "sword which I wear in defense of France as well as my own country," unless the help were forthcoming, "I may be compelled to draw against France as a British subject." Not content with this thunderclap, he betook himself to the royal levee next day and, making his way up to the King, handed him a scroll explaining his requests. At this intrusion of business at a court formality, the King said nothing, merely handing the scroll to the Comte de Ségur, Minister of War, who was standing nearby. Next morning Laurens, expecting to be shunned, found himself invited to an interview with M. Necker, Minister of Finance, who promised a good portion of the supplies and immediate delivery of a good part of the cash. On the basis of the Minister's word, Laurens was able to collect 2 million livres' worth of supplies and 2 million livres in cash and arrange for four transports to carry them to America, and eventually to negotiate a loan underwritten by France of 10 million from the Dutch.

At the same time as the Laurens mission, Rochambeau by careful maneuvering was able to get a frigate through the English lines to carry his son Colonel Rochambeau to France with a report of the Hartford discussions and a complete account of the troops, vessels and money that were needed, which the son committed to memory in full, lest he be captured. In correspondence with Admiral de Grasse, Rochambeau could offer him no encouraging prospect, but this seemed not to deter the French Admiral or his countrymen.

Laurens' and Franklin's prospect of the Colonies falling away from the fight against England frightened the French. Until now they had believed that England's defeat might be accomplished on her periphery by seizing her sugar islands and breaking into her trade. Now they were persuaded that more effective harm could be done by assisting American independence and the loss to Britain of the American continent. During Laurens' visit, the decision was taken to go forward, and to commit French sea power in a major effort to resolve the American war. After the failure to invade England, France was ready to take offensive action in both America and the Antilles, where her intention was to deliver 2,000 French prisoners being held on Barbados, and to take Ste. Lucie from the English.

Louis XVI, putting his finger on one of the individuals that history chooses for agent, issued orders to Admiral François de Grasse to take a strong fleet of supply to the Leeward Islands and from there, after giving what aid was required by the Spanish under the terms of the Bourbon Family Compact, to proceed to America to cooperate with the generals of the Revolution in whatever military action they planned. It was the most positive act of his reign.

Emphasizing the importance of the operation, de Grasse was promoted to Rear Admiral, carrying with it the title of Lieutenant General in the army. At the same time, the young Claude-Anne, Marquis de Saint-Simon, cousin of the future founder of French Socialism, and a relative of the illustrious Duc de Saint-Simon, chronicler of the court of Louis XIV, notified Rochambeau that he was ready to join him in America with his three regiments from Santo Domingo. De Grasse sent word to Rochambeau that he had received orders from the King to undertake the American mission and that he would arrive on the coast at the earliest by July 15 of the coming summer, 1781, with money and men-at-arms. He added that, owing to the promise of help to Spain, he was under orders to stay for only six weeks.

With matchless energy de Grasse appeared every morning at five o'clock in his quarters in the arsenal at Brest to oversee repairs and provisioning of his ships, and kept everyone jumping thereafter for a full day's work. Born in 1722 — ten years older than Washington, three years younger than Rodney — he came of a family ennobled in the 16th century. At the age of eleven he had received an appointment in the Garde de la Marine, which gave candidates an education at the Naval Seminary of Toulon, where young noblemen were trained to be naval officers and where at the edge of the seawall they became familiar with all the activity of the waterfront. From the windows of the school they looked out on the forest of masts, with its myriad rigging and flapping flags making patterns against the sky, and rows of black spokes thrusting the noses of cannon through holes in the ships' sides. After a year at the seminary, twelve-year-old de Grasse, as young as Rodney had been when he first went to sea, won a similar first appointment as a page to the Grand Master of Malta. The Knights of Malta, who included many naval officers in their ranks, administered a fleet that was active in convoying merchantmen through the Mediterranean to guard them from corsairs sailing out of Tunis and Algiers and the doorways of Morocco. On convoy duty, young de Grasse met action and combat from the start of his career, culminating in the heroic resistance on board the *Gloire* in the Battle of Finisterre. In 1781, the year fateful for so much in this history, he was named Commander-in-Chief of French naval forces in the West Indies. This was the two years after Rodney was named chief of the British command in the Leeward Islands. In physical contrast to the slight Rodney, de Grasse was a tall, heavily built man six feet two in height and six feet six on deck in time of combat, in the words of an admiring junior officer. He was considered "one of the handsomest men of the age," although his appearance when angry was "grim" and his manner "brutal," according to a Swedish lieutenant, Karl Gustaf Tornquist, who served on his ship in these critical years and wrote a memoir of the experience.

While Franco-American plans were in the making at Hartford and in the correspondence crossing the Atlantic, Rodney in September, 1780, was in New York, thwarted in offensive action by Clinton's refusal to spare any forces from the defense of New York and also by his wordy dispute with Admiral Arbuthnot over which of them was the superior in command. Rodney concluded that he could accomplish little against these obstacles and that it was more important to return with his fleet to the Leewards to defend the islands in case the

French should take advantage of his absence. He prepared for departure. Losing a strong-minded associate, Clinton saw him go with regret, writing to say goodbye and to express the hope of seeing him again, concluding wistfully, "should you be appointed Commander-in-Chief here as well as in the West Indies for which God grant." God had not chosen to stand at the British elbow at this hour. To leave the decrepit and petty Arbuthnot in command of American waters at a time when the great Western continent was slipping from British hands, when Britain could have replaced him by a man of Rodney's energy and enterprise, was another in the train of ill-thought if not plainly foolish decisions that infected British management of the American war. Clinton and Arbuthnot, incapable of concerted action while they despised each other, were left in position, while Rodney's superior boldness and skill were retained in the West Indies, still considered a more important possession than America. With his fleet of fifteen ships of the line Rodney left New York in November, 1780. A violent gale, blowing for 48 hours while he made his way south, scattered his ships but carried no warning of the fearful wreckage that would greet him in the islands, nor of the tremendous fuss the home government was then making over their quarrel with the Dutch and the perfidy of Amsterdam in negotiating a treaty of commerce and amity with the rebels. He reached Barbados on December 6 to find a scene of devastation from one end of the Leewards to the other, as if some avenging army had passed through, bent on ruin. For once the wrecker had been no human enemy but an October hurricane, the most terrible in memory. A tidal wave raised by a titanic wind starting on October 9 had flooded Jamaica; then, blowing with ferocious force through the next day and night, the winds tore off the roofs of Ste. Lucie, beached and destroyed ships at anchor. With relentless sheets of rain and thunder and lightning, the storm roared through the night until 8 a.m., blasting house walls and windows, lifting cattle off the ground and the bodies of men to rooftops, crushing houses to rubble while the cries of the helpless people trapped in the ruins could not be heard through the crash of the elements and tumble of walls. Trees were torn up by the roots and the bark stripped from their trunks by the violence of the wind. The part of Rodney's fleet that had been storm-scattered outside New York had come in, "dreadfully crippled," while eight out of the twelve of his warships at Barbados were a total loss and only ten members of their crews saved; 400 inhabitants of Barbados were killed. Water sources and food, never plentiful on the islands, were reduced to dangerous scarcity; care and shelter for the homeless, repair of roads, wells, homes and every facility mounted to an overpowering burden, on ships of the fleet no less than on the towns. Supposing the ruin to have made no exception of forts and shore batteries, the British chose this moment, two months after the hurricane, to declare their war on the Dutch, with accompanying orders to Rodney to seize St. Eustatius and such other islands as they believed would be unable to offer resistance.

Receiving the orders at sea off Barbados on January 27, 1781, Rodney immediately prepared his ships for attack on St. Eustatius and coordinated measures with General Vaughan. He was ready to sail in three days and to appear on February 3 below Fort Orange, where, just over four years before, the *Andrew Doria* had received the fort's salute to the flag of the Continental Congress. Rodney's rampage of confiscations and evictions executed by Vaughan's soldiers followed, leading to the accusations of Burke and Fox and to satisfaction in Tory quarters. Recording a report that 6,900 hogsheads of tobacco valued at £36,000 were stored in Eustatian warehouses before Rodney came, Captain Frederick MacKenzie

— the most observant and active diarist on Clinton's staff — gloated, "The loss of one half of it is enough to ruin all the rebel merchants in America."

Rodney's successful seizure of the island confirmed his value in the otherwise shaky company of the navy. Whether to restrain or strengthen him, the Admiralty sent him a vigorous second in command, Admiral Sir Samuel Hood, who had once served as midshipman under Rodney during his early convoy duty in the Mediterranean and had been with him again as a captain in the burning of invasion boats at Havre. From service in two campaigns and acquaintance over a period of forty years, they knew each other well — perhaps too well, with some of the disrespect familiarity is said to breed. They were now joined in the critical mission to stop de Grasse from crossing the ocean to reinforce the Americans. Mutual confidence would have been useful, but relations were, at best, ambivalent.

On being offered the post under his old chief, Hood at first wrote to the Admiralty asking to refuse, and two days later wrote again hoping it was not too late to change his mind. On his side, Rodney wrote to say, "I know no-one whatsoever that I should have wished in preference to my old friend Sir

Samuel Hood." That seemed unequivocal. But in private he is reported by one of his staff to have grumbled, "They might as well have sent me an old applewoman." Here again was the pervasive animosity among commanders that seemed to grow from an ill-managed war.

Rodney's sneer is startling, in view of Nelson's future fulsome praise of Hood in the Napoleonic Wars as "the greatest sea officer I ever knew, great in all situations which an admiral can be placed in." As Hood was to play a significant role in coming events, this remarkable difference of opinion of him, by two persons whose judgments were both based on personal experience as his commanding officer, is a matter of interest. Nelson was habitually overkind to his officers, and in this case rated Hood more highly than he deserved; his tribute cannot apply to situations in America in which Hood, on a number of occasions, was not only not great but something less than adequate.

"It has been difficult to find out proper flag officers to serve under you," Sandwich informed Rodney rather tactlessly, although the difficulty, he said, was not personal but because some officers were unfit politically (which Sandwich referred to as "their factious connections") and others because of "infirmity or insufficiency, and so we have at last been obliged to make a promotion in order to do the thing properly." Rodney, as we have seen, professed himself well pleased by the choice of Sir Samuel Hood, although developing tensions were to break apart an old friendship and deprive the fleet at an important moment of cordial cooperation between its chiefs.

Hood arrived expecting to lead an expedition to capture the two Dutch colonies of Surinam and Curaçao, from which he anticipated rich booty, but on the basis of a false intelligence report that a large French fleet was on its way to the West Indies, Rodney felt obliged to keep all his forces ready for defense of the islands and called off the Surinam-Curaçao expedition. This was the first of Hood's discontents. They then fell out over preferments to two places in the navy, one of which Hood believed Rodney had promised him for his first lieutenant while Rodney now said he must first fulfill promises made to a peer's son belonging to "one of the first families in the kingdom." Hood wrote to the Admiralty some very nasty letters about Rodney's "instability" and his primary desire to stay on St. Eustatius to safeguard the proceeds of his capture. The two English fellow-officers were now in greater disaccord than ever occurred between the French and Americans despite their differences.

The real trouble was that Rodney, burdened with supervising the disposal of the property confiscated at St. Eustatius and with arranging for its loading on thirty transports and designating the proper ships for its safe escort back to England, was miserably ill with gout and with a urinary stricture that now added its torment. His one thought in his discomfort was to obtain leave to go home for relief. He had several times written to Sandwich for leave, without avail. "The continual mental and bodily fatigue," he wrote on March 7, "that I have experienced for this year past preys upon me so much that unless I am permitted to leave this climate during the rainy season, I am convinced it will disable me from doing my duty to His Majesty and the state in the active manner I could wish and have been used to." He entreats Sandwich to lay before the King that "in case my health should be such at the end of this campaign as to require a northern climate to restore it he will permit my return to Great Britain during the three rainy months." It pains him "to request one moment's respite from the public service but I have a *complaint,* owing to too much activity and exertion which I am told by my physician will absolutely require my leaving the torrid zone. . . ." The warm humid climate of the summer months was in fact a disease breeder. Hundreds of soldiers and sailors were too sick to move and Rodney had been warned that if his stricture were left untreated it could develop to fatality. His urgency to return to England was understandable. Sandwich replied in May that he had made Rodney's request an "official letter" and had apparently gained for him the King's permission for leave, but hopes that "you will not avail yourself of your permission to leave your command in the present critical situation of our affairs. The whole government, and the public in general, are satisfied while you retain your command." The war, Sandwich asserts with the benighted self-confidence of a minister who knows nothing, nor had ever bothered to learn anything of the field or the opponent, "cannot last much longer." About French intervention, Sandwich was relaxed and casual, offering his opinion that "it is most probable that the French fleet in your seas will go to North America in the hurricane months. . . ." This demonstrated a poor sense of timing, for the hurricane months were still five months off, and the French, who had heard the urgency of the American call, had no need to wait until then — nor did they. "No one can so well judge," Sandwich concluded, "of the propriety of following them as yourself," and he leaves Rodney to be guided "by your own feelings." Rodney's feelings, as confided to his wife on March 18, were simple: "I must leave this country in June at farthest." He mentions his severe gout as the reason plus "a very painful complaint" (prostate trouble). It was at this time that he gave vent to his vengeful feelings about the traitorous traders on St. Eustatius: "I cannot express the fatigue I have suffered on this island. Had I not stayed here, every villainy would be practiced by the persons who call themselves English." It was now, in the irritable distress of his illness, that he issued his wrathful threat to leave the island "a mere desert." He added the sad hope that would soon miscarry: "If my great convoy of prizes arrive safe in England, I shall be happy as, exclusive of satisfying all debts, something will be left for my dear children."

On March 21, Sandwich forwarded an intelligence report to Rodney telling of a fleet of 25 sail about to leave from Brest, though Sandwich could not say where it was destined; probably, he suggested, to the West Indies and afterward to North America or to join the Spanish at Cádiz to "check your conquests." His supposition was correct, if not alert, for this was de Grasse departing with his fleet on the first leg of his journey to America, which was already public knowledge. Mme. du Deffand, Walpole's faithful correspondent on all the gossip of the French capital, had already written to him about a regiment in Saint-Simon's command "which is one of those destined for America. *Voilà nouvelles publiques.* " (This is public news.) Public as it was, the report of the enemy's approach, which was important for Rodney to know, did not reach him until a week after de Grasse had already arrived in the Leeward Islands and had met Hood in combat.

The Admiralty's dispatches were sent by the cutter *Swallow*, evidently under an impression of speed derived from her name. Though fast for its size, a cutter, a single-masted vessel, carried only a small portion of the sail area of a frigate in which to catch the propelling winds. In contrast, the Americans, for the urgent correspondence between Rochambeau and de Grasse, used the French frigate *Concorde*, which zipped back and forth between Boston and the Leeward Islands in rapid transits of sixteen and eighteen days. The difference in sailing time was not simply a matter of ships but because the British, certain they knew best about everything oceanic, persisted in bucking the Gulf Stream. Flowing in a peculiar northerly circular course, the current slowed progress from Europe to the

Caribbean while its swift current in the Atlantic shortened mail time from Europe to America. Traced first by whalers of Nantucket who followed the track of the whales, the course and speed of the stream was made known to Benjamin Franklin when he was Postmaster General by his cousin Captain Timothy Folger of Nantucket for use by the masters of mail packets crossing the ocean. Folger explained why American captains of merchant ships made faster time from London to Rhode Island than English captains of mail packets from London to New York. It was because American captains, advised by the whales, understood the location of the Gulf Stream and crossed over it, instead of running against it for days. From Folger's chart and written directions instructing shipmasters how to track the stream by dropping thermometers at regular intervals and measuring the speed of surface bubbles and noticing changes in the color of the water, Franklin in 1770, before the war, offered the information to Anthony Todd, Secretary of the British Post Office. British sea captains, not inclined to take advice from American colonials and fishermen, ignored it. Franklin himself made a test on a voyage in 1776, dropping his thermometer two to four times a day from seven in the morning until eleven at night.

His report on the Gulf Stream was withheld until after the war, when it could no longer help the British, but Folger's map, the first map of the Gulf Stream, was published in 1768, before the outbreak of overt hostility and revolution.

With the West Indies as his first concern, Sandwich wrote again to Rodney saying that unless he could intercept de Grasse before he reached Martinique, the French would have a superior number of ships, so that England must depend "on the skill and conduct of our commander in chief and the bravery of the officers and people under him," as there was no possibility of sending him reinforcements. Expecting the French any day, Rodney detached three sail of the line to Hood with orders to cruise windward of Martinique on the lookout for the enemy. Shortly afterward, Hood was moved inshore to keep a close watch on Fort Royal, in order to prevent four French liners stationed there from emerging to add their numbers to de Grasse when he should arrive, and to prevent de Grasse from entering to take possession of the "noblest and best harbour," as Rodney had named it. Hood did not like the inshore position and repeatedly asked Rodney to let him go back to his former place, which Rodney refused. Strong disagreements about the proper position from which to watch for and intercept the enemy added to their quarrel.

On St. Eustatius, Rodney had appointed a commission to superintend disposal of the seized property and documents. The more he learned of the business operations of the traitorous British merchants, the more it fed his anger. The whole of the confiscated property "I have seized for the King and the state and I hope will go to the public revenue of my country. I do not look upon myself as entitled to one sixpence nor do I desire it. My happiness is having been the instrument of my country in bringing this nest of villains to condign punishment. They deserve scourging and they shall be scourged." Whether or not this entire lack of interest in personal gain should be taken at face value, Rodney's desire to bring the villains to judgment and wield the whip of their scourging was clearly what held him at St. Eustatius through the month of March and early April while his opponent was advancing toward him across the Atlantic.

With a strong fleet of twenty ships of the line, three frigates, and a swollen convoy of 150 transports bringing supplies and men to the West Indies, de Grasse sailed from Brest on March 22 aboard his huge flagship, the three-decker *Ville de Paris* of 110 guns, monarch of the French fleet, and the largest ship afloat. He expected to meet Hood or Rodney in combat in the West Indies. After supplying the needy islands, he was to give what aid was necessary to Spanish forces in Cuba and Santo Domingo and then, at the approach of winter, move on to America. Joined by an East India squadron of forty merchantmen, which were slow sailors and had to be taken in tow by the warships, he reached the offshore waters of Martinique at the end of April, 1781.

In America news came to Newport on May 8, like an arrow piercing the curtain of discouragement, that de Grasse was actually on his way, headed for the West Indies with America as his next destination. Coming just a month since Washington had confessed "We are at the end of our tether," the news promised to give renewed life and new hope to the American fight. Ten months of impatient frustration had passed since Rochambeau and his infantry of 5,700 had come to Newport in the previous summer, held there ever since by the Americans' lack of mobility and by Arbuthnot's blockade outside the bay. De Ternay, the French naval commander, had died of a fever in the interim, to be succeeded in command by Count Louis de Barras, who had come via Boston bringing the report to Washington that de Grasse was on his way. A Council of War among Washington, Rochambeau and de Barras (who was unable to come) was immediately summoned to meet at Wethersfield, a town adjoining Hartford, on May 21. In the course of the discussions, Washington's plan of campaign against New York was seemingly accepted, with reservations by the French on condition that de Grasse would cooperate in assigning his land forces to a joint offensive with the Americans. In spite of the twice-failed effort under d'Estaing for combined operations by French naval and American land forces, the conferees agreed to make the attempt again. Rochambeau, evidently sharing the opinion of a number of 20th century historians that Washington was no strategist (which fails to measure the more important quality of generalship), contradicted promptly the Wethersfield plan by writing to de Grasse on May 31 his own recommendation, that the offensive should be made at the Chesapeake. He enclosed copies of the Wethersfield agreements, saying that de Grasse must make his own judgment of the problem of the Sandy Hook shallows and suggesting that on arrival he look into the Chesapeake, and if he found no occasion for action there, to come to New York. He asked to borrow for three months the regiments arriving under Saint-Simon.

He wrote two more letters, on June 6 and

11, reporting frankly that American affairs were in a "grave crisis." With no money or credit, these people "are at the end of their resources. . . . I must not conceal from you, Monsieur, that Washington will not have half the troops he is reckoned to have and that I believe, though he is silent on that, at present he does not have 6,000 men and that M. de Lafayette does not have a 1,000 regulars with militia to defend Virginia and nearly as many on the march to join him. . . . And that it is therefore of the greatest consequence that you will take on board as many troops as possible, 4,000 or 5,000 will not be too many, whether you aid us in Virginia or in seizing Sandy Hook to aid us afterwards to lay siege to Brooklyn. . . . There, Monsieur, are the different possibilities you have in view and the actual sad picture of the affairs of this country. Whichever, I am quite persuaded you will bring us naval superiority." In closing, he re-emphasized the need to bring troops, and money to pay them. While it was hardly a report calculated to inspire an ally to invest his fate in a losing game, it evidently had the desired effect. We do not know what de Grasse thought or felt, and can only judge by his subsequent dedication of himself and his fortune to a faltering cause not his own. In relationship with allies and neighbors, the French can often make themselves exceedingly difficult and even disagreeable, but there was something in the destiny-filled air of 1781 that brought them to their most admirable. They were not ready, if they could help it, to let the American fight for independence be dissipated in the smoke of burned-out liberty and in the renewed imperium of their ancient rival.

Rochambeau's preference for the Chesapeake in his letters to de Grasse was endorsed by other French envoys in America, who believed an assault on New York would be too hazardous and costly and the ability of Washington to hold New York after de Grasse had left very uncertain. The French court, as Rochambeau's son reported when he returned with de Barras, was not prepared to invest the men and money required for a protracted siege of New York. The French were counting on a decision of the war in 1781 and had scheduled only six weeks for de Grasse's action in America, after which he was supposed to return to the West Indies for action against the British in that sphere. In the planning with Rochambeau, the place along the American coast to which he would come and the site of the offensive campaign were left open for de Grasse himself to determine, a measure of confidence which may have been advised by

Rochambeau's knowledge of the man. Yet, considering how much was at stake, it represented a large deposit of confidence and trust in good luck that had not so far been the American portion. It left a wide area open for misadventure in coordinating naval forces and land forces under different national commands which had already failed for d'Estaing, not counting the hazards of transoceanic communication, subject to winds, weather and enemy action. That such matters were almost certain to bring a default of the kind that kept Howe and Burgoyne from coordinating the campaign that died at Saratoga, neither side seemed seriously concerned. In the result, the wheel of fortune — or Providence, in which Washington firmly trusted, with a helping hand from himself — turned upward on the American side. Faultless timing and good luck at every fork were to bring about the rarest of military operations — a campaign in which everything coordinates and no one of a hundred chances takes the wrong turn in the road.

While en route from Brest to the Caribbean, de Grasse made his choice. He wrote the letter informing Rochambeau that he was coming on the King's orders and, as a foretaste, he detached a squadron of thirty ships with 700 soldiers to join Rochambeau at New-

457

port. Contrary to Washington's wish, he chose the Chesapeake for the scene of action, for a sailor's reasons: because of the shorter sailing distance from the West Indies, its deeper waters and easier pilotage and the advice he had received from de Barras. The same frigate that had brought the Wethersfield letters turned around to carry his reply, so that the American command might have it as soon as possible. His request for American pilots to guide him in the Bay gave proof of serious intention.

Washington, at the same time, turning aside from New York, was coming around to Rochambeau's preference for the Chesapeake. Changing his emphasis from ships to troops, he was now thinking of marching the army down on foot. Reports from Virginia, where Cornwallis had now penetrated, were "alarming," and he was deeply disturbed by the devastations inflicted on his native state by the raids of Benedict Arnold. For a more positive reason, the possibility of trapping Cornwallis now offered itself, convincing Washington that a campaign in Virginia could be more decisive than continued inconclusive operations in the Carolinas. If Cornwallis and his army were to overrun Virginia, he warned Congress, they would soon be north of the Potomac. Moved for once to react, in fear of their own safety, Congress was induced to send militia from Pennsylvania, Delaware and Maryland to reinforce Greene. Writing to La Luzerne, Washington urged the French to send troops from the West Indies, so that by "one great decisive stroke, the enemy might be expelled from the continent and the independence of America established." This opened a far more positive view of the outlook than Rochambeau's depressing report of "grave crisis" and dwindling forces. It indicates that the Commander-in-Chief was beginning to think in terms of action at the Chesapeake against Cornwallis, and contemplating the march on foot to Virginia that was to bring him to Yorktown. The assured coming of de Grasse, and the report of Rochambeau's son confirming that the Admiral's purpose was to bring his fleet to establish naval superiority in American waters, swung the decision for the Chesapeake, which was reaffirmed when a probe of Clinton's defenses of New York showed them to be of formidable strength.

The Americans' strategic plan was the obverse of Britain's. They too saw the South as the place to defeat the enemy. What they hoped to gain from a campaign at the Chesapeake would be to enclose Lord Cornwallis and the last important British army in

America between a pincers of the Allied army and the French fleet, which would block him off from the sea and thus from help from New York and from overseas supply, while Allied commanders in the South, Lafayette and Greene, would take care of closing off his escape by land. In short, his army was to be enclosed in a squeeze where he would be forced to surrender or stand and die. The French fleet to close the sea exit was, of course, necessary to the plan. Cornwallis had not yet established himself at a base on the Chesapeake when the Allies at Wethersfield were discussing him as the destined target. He was just at that time on the way to placing himself there, where it was essential to the Allied purpose that he remain; otherwise the trap would have no occupant when the Allies arrived.

For the British, on their part, to reach victory, it was clear they needed a naval base more central to the country than Charleston. After evacuating Newport, all they had left was New York and Halifax, in Nova Scotia. New York was not a good port because of the bar at Sandy Hook. Their choice fell upon Portsmouth, in Virginia, at the southern end of Chesapeake Bay. But Cornwallis, as field commander, did not like what he saw of it, because the place was hot and unhealthy and could not provide protection for an anchorage of ships of the line. Surveying the area, he preferred Yorktown, a more attractive town about 100 miles further north on the "beautiful blue estuary," a mile wide, of the York River where it emptied into Chesapeake Bay at the foot of Cape Charles. Then simply called York, it was only twelve miles from Williamsburg, the capital of Virginia, which consisted of a single street "very broad and very handsome," as described by Blanchard, "with two or three public buildings pretty large." Once an important business center with handsome Georgian brick houses, settled at the beginning of the century, York had greatly declined to a population of only 3,000 with 300 houses, because the tobacco culture had moved to new ground and British raids had forced merchants and farmers to move away. A town of 300 houses, York was situated on a plateau bordered by ravines. Swampy land and a 500-acre farm lay beyond. The Williamsburg road ran alongside. Across the James River, which ran more or less parallel to the York River, was Jamestown, the first city built by the English in America, and producer, says Tornquist, of the "best tobacco in the whole world." On the same side, opposite York, was the promontory called Gloucester Point, held by Cornwallis as a part of his defense position. York's entrance to the

Bay still provided the only deep-water harbor for major ships and gave access up the Atlantic coast to New York. Because of its easy access to the enemy, Admiral Arbuthnot considered the Chesapeake vulnerable, but as just another of the old Admiral's tired negatives, his warning received scant attention.

In May, 1781, the month when Rochambeau at Wethersfield was urging an offensive at the Chesapeake, Cornwallis had decided, with the approval of his naval advisers, to make his base at York instead of Portsmouth. He chose it because other ports of the region were too shallow and because York's location was central to the labor supply of the area, which would be needed for work on fortifications. Establishment of the base with a ring of fortified earthworks around the town would take three months, a lapse of time that was useful, although they did not know it, for the Franco-American transatlantic planning of their offensive. Cornwallis completed his move to Yorktown on August 2, three days before de Grasse sailed from the West Indies for the coast of Virginia.

Because of its fate, the choice of Yorktown has been much disputed. Clinton certainly authorized it with the proviso that Cornwallis detach a portion of his army as reinforcement for the defense of New York. A dispute arose over this point when Cornwallis claimed that York could not be defended with less than his full force, in which he may have been right, although to maintain the full complement would have made the problem of provisioning more acute. Charges and countercharges developed which have obscured the issue of responsibility. In keeping with his habit of off-again-on-again letters, Clinton assured Cornwallis in July that he could keep as large a force as he needed for defense of the base and was "at full liberty to detain all the troops now in Chesapeake — which very liberal concession will I am persuaded convince your lordship of the high estimation in which I hold a naval station in Chesapeake." The responsibility for the decision was clearly enough for both to share and to permit Cornwallis authoritatively to make the move to Yorktown and settle himself there a month before the French fleet arrived to lock the door.

ELEVEN

The Critical Moment

Admiral Count de Grasse, by virtue of his appointment to bring naval aid to America, was now a key figure in the American war. When in March, 1781, he sailed with a great fleet from France for the West Indies, on the first leg of his journey to meet Washington for the all-important joint action that was to be Washington's final stroke, the departure of his great fleet from Brest made news in the maritime community. Word soon reached the British that an important intervention was on the way. The challenge, coming geographically from the West Indies, put it up to Rodney to intercept the massive fleet before it reached America to alter the balance of power in the war. Confrontation between the two admirals, Rodney and de Grasse, rose in prospect before both. Their lookouts, clinging to the swaying crow's nests, peered anxiously over the glimmering water to identify any mark on the horizon that could mean a mast, and warn of coming junction.

When de Grasse reached Martinique on April 28, he found Hood cruising to leeward of the island with an inferior force of seventeen ships of the line and five frigates, on instructions to intercept the French and blockade Fort Royal to prevent four French warships coming out to join de Grasse and to prevent him from entering and taking possession of the "noblest and best" port of the area, as Rodney called it. Besides gaining the key harbor, de Grasse would there be able to join the aggressive Governor of Martinique, the Marquis de Bouillé, and combine with his land forces in attack on one or more of the British-held islands.

When sighted from Hood's mastheads, the French were to windward, apparently heading north. Unsure of what they would do during the night, Hood elected to come to a standstill until morning, with the unfortunate result that his ships were at the mercy of the wind and had by dawn been blown to leeward and drifted so far downwind as to become becalmed. While Hood was collecting them, the enemy reappeared with his convoy pressed close inshore and his battleships to seaward. As both fleets were forming their lines of battle, the French convoy slipped into Fort Royal. At long range the battleships opened fire. De Grasse kept his distance, endeavoring to draw his opponent away until the convoy was safely in port. His broadsides inflicted heavy damage and casualties. Two of Hood's ships suffered holes below the waterline and, after pumping continuously for 24 hours, could no longer keep station; others had shattered masts and were in no condition to fight. Before dark, the main topmast of the *Intrepid* came crashing down, and the *Russell*, with water gaining on the pumps, was in dangerous condition and ordered to St. Eustatius, where she brought news of the battle with its cost of 37 killed and 125 wounded. By nightfall of the second day, the fleets were seventy miles from Fort Royal and Hood decided to quit. By next evening the fleets had lost sight of each other, but the French were inside Fort Royal. In the exchange of *ex post facto* accusations, which had now become habitual with the British, Hood and his partisans blamed the result on Rodney for not allowing Hood to cruise to windward at the outset, but the clear fact was that de Grasse had outmaneuvered and outfought Hood.

Rodney, increasingly ill and irritable, held his fleet at Barbados to take on desperately needed water and the fresh vegetables that warded off scurvy. Of no great importance itself, Barbados, easternmost of the Windward chain and nearest to Europe, was the island longest in British possession, fertile and well-cultivated and reputed producer of the finest rum. In the midst of the victualing, an alert was brought to Rodney that French troops were invading Tobago 200 miles to the south. A relief force was sent with a regiment of volunteers only to find that Tobago had surrendered before they arrived. The whole French fleet was sighted heading north during the afternoon. In a critical moment of decision-making, Rodney rejected the temptation to chase, lest he be drawn to leeward where he would be unable to come to the relief of defenseless Barbados if it were attacked. He showed lights during the night in the hope of luring de Grasse to fight the next day, but the French Admiral had other plans. The consequence of Rodney's failure to pursue was that de Grasse was not halted, and reached America according to plan.

Since Rodney was deeply conscious of the seriousness of French naval intervention in America, his failure to give priority to stopping de Grasse was partly due to his need to go home for medical treatment and partly to his belief that Hood would do as well. Especially it was due to the fact that the Admiralty itself gave the matter no priority, reflecting, in turn, the absence of any coherent strategy on the part of the government.

These operations occupied the month of May and early June, 1781. After taking Tobago, de Grasse returned his fleet to Fort Royal, the splendid harbor of Martinique, where he could assemble ships from surrounding islands and take on water, wood, cattle and other provisions for the campaign in America. In July he moved to Cap-Français, the port of Haiti-Santo Domingo, called for its elegance "the Paris of the Isles." In its ample roadstead, capable of harboring 400 ships, de Grasse found waiting for him the thirty American pilots he had asked for to take him into the Chesapeake. Also waiting for him were Rochambeau's letters from Wethersfield stating frankly the "grave crisis" in American affairs and advocating his own preference for a "grand stroke" at the Chesapeake. A letter from de Barras at Newport came in the same mail, saying, "The most necessary article needed here is money." The letters, and others from the several French envoys, all emphasized the dangerous military situation in the South and the need for aid as quickly as possible. Undiscouraged, de Grasse together with a Captain Charitte of his squadron promptly offered to pledge their private property and plantations on Santo Domingo as security to the inhabitants for loan to the Crown of 300,000 piasters (equivalent to Spanish dollars) to float the expedition. Although the value of the properties pledged "greatly surpassed" the proposed loan, the government rejected the offer, to de Grasse's resentment. He did not sulk, but instead paid with his own money for fifteen merchant ships to carry his provisions. His commitment was total.

Here at Cap-Français, de Grasse came to two decisions that were to be critical to the military outcome of the American Revolution — first, to take his whole fleet, rather than dividing it; and second, to take it to the Chesapeake. With a negotiating talent equal to his combative spirit, he obtained the Spaniards' agreement that, as they planned no action in the West Indies, they could hold the Antilles without French help, leaving him free to take all his ships with him to America. To employ the whole fleet on the mission to America, which to the shortsighted — who are always the majority — was secondary in value to the West Indies, was a decision of great boldness and risk. It meant abandoning the duty of convoying the current French trade back to Europe, inviting censure for disregarding the vested interests of merchants. It was the act of a man who had either lost his heart to the venture in liberty or had a more farsighted view than most Europeans of what

America would become. History had given de Grasse the task of carrying forward the Americans to completion of their break with Britain. He seemed to know it, to feel as if appointed to it, to have listened, even as a foreigner, to the call by the Declaration of Independence for a pledge of lives, fortunes and sacred honor to the cause. A great imperative imparts a wonderful impulse to the spirit. It touched even the Spanish governor of Santo Domingo, who agreed to release to de Grasse's force of Saint-Simon's three regiments of 2,500 which had been lent for Spanish use. Spain may have disliked the cause of liberty, but she disliked the British even more.

On July 28, de Grasse wrote the conclusive letter that was to reach Rochambeau and Washington on August 14, informing them that he was coming with 25 or 26 ships, bringing three regiments, and would leave on August 3 for Chesapeake Bay. Speeding directly by the *Concorde*, this letter did not pass through diplomatic channels to be read and copied by agents in English pay. In the early 20th century, the American Secretary of War Henry L. Stimson objected to establishment of a "Black Chamber," on the ground that "gentlemen do not read each other's mail." In the 18th century, the practice was customary. Foreign ministries maintained regular clerks who, through long familiarity, learned the codes, and read and copied the correspondence of officials of foreign countries. Although the English were soon made aware that a French fleet was on the way to aid the Colonies, they did not know in what strength or to what destination.

Rodney learned of Hood's encounter with de Grasse when the damaged *Russell* crept into St. Eustatius. Leaving the plunder still in legal limbo and the English traitors still not brought to justice, Rodney sailed at once to join Hood at Antigua, a British island and naval base in the chain north of Martinique, from which he could protect Barbados, where he expected a French strike. The three chief actors in the conflict that was advancing upon the North American coast were now collected in the Leeward Islands — de Grasse bent on reaching the goal, Rodney and Hood assigned to stop him. With Hood's flagship and others of his squadron out of action, and with de Grasse's additional ships from Fort Royal, the French now had 24 warships to the British eighteen,* a surplus that ordinarily advised against challenge — the more so as the French were to windward, leaving the British,

---

*Fleet numbers are often inexact, depending on whether frigates are counted and on liners that may join or leave the main body.

471

if they were caught to leeward, helpless to come to the aid of defenseless Barbados, which might then be taken by assault. As commander of the Leewards, Rodney felt that British honor and interest, as well as his own, must not suffer the loss of another island. Moreover, because there were 2,000 French prisoners on the island, an attempt to free them could be expected. When Rodney arrived at Barbados, he found the British flag still flying; Ste. Lucie, where de Grasse with land forces from Martinique had struck next, had successfully repelled the invaders with the aid of shore batteries, which the defenders, with surprising enterprise, had reinforced with the more useful guns of a dismantled ship.

Mortified by the surrender of Tobago, Rodney brimmed with intention "to lower French pride," as he wrote in his dispatches, provided "they give me a proper opportunity." They did not oblige. When he sighted the French at sunset on June 5, Rodney drew near enough to count a fleet of 29 sail — 24 of the line and five frigates — against his own twenty as now counted. Under the necessity of holding his fleet in readiness to defend the islands and protect incoming convoys from Britain and Ireland, he decided not to engage. Suckled like all English seamen on the doctrine not to open combat without the wind, he stationed frigates to keep watch. Early in July, one of them cruising off Martinique was able to capture a frigate of a French convoy coming out of Fort Royal and to learn from the master that he belonged to a fleet commanded by Count de Grasse, that it consisted of 25 sail of the line and nearly 200 merchant ships collected from the different French islands and that it was reportedly bound for Santo Domingo. Rodney sent a warning notice to Admiral Graves in New York, now commander of British naval forces in America, saying that a French fleet of 28* of the line had appeared at Martinique and that "a part" of the fleet is reported to be destined for North America. He believes it will sail "in a short time," though he cannot learn whether it will call on the way at Cap-Français in Santo Domingo. "I shall keep as good a lookout as possible on their motions by which my own shall be regulated," he wrote. He added that Admiral Hood, with 14 sail of the line and 5 frigates, will be ordered to follow the French to the coast of Virginia and proceed along the coast to the Capes of the Delaware, and from

*The number is variously reported at various times by various observers. As near as can be made definite, de Grasse's fleet numbered 26–28 liners plus some extra frigates and armed merchantmen.

thence to Sandy Hook to place himself under Graves's orders. Graves should station cruisers at the Capes of the Delaware to keep watch for Hood, he told him, "so that they may combine their forces to intercept the French who are coming from the West Indies." He adds that Graves may depend upon his squadron being reinforced, "should the enemy bend their forces that way." To Germain in London, Rodney promises to "watch the enemy like a lynx" and to Arbuthnot in New York he promises to "send you every reinforcement in my power." His expectation and plan, as he specifically describes it in a separate letter to the Earl of Carlisle at this time, was not to allow the enemy [de Grasse] to take advantage "of superiority on the coast of America," but rather for Hood "to arrive on that coast before the French squadron from Cape François" and to effect a junction with the English already there [namely, with Graves] "to defeat the enemy and all their projects." At the same time, Rodney sent a convoy of five liners and five frigates to accompany the trade to Jamaica, with orders to Sir Peter Parker, the commander there, to dispatch the ships at once to North America where, together with Hood's, they would give the British in America a clear naval superiority and provide Graves with the promised reinforcement.

Rodney assumed, as did everyone else, that de Grasse would divide his fleet. Sir Peter Parker, for whatever reason, did not carry out his orders.

Rodney took French intervention more seriously, telling Hood that if he saw the French ships, to "please acquaint me thereof with all the despatch possible . . . this being of the utmost importance." Appearing to have been the only one who realized in advance how definitive de Grasse's intervention might be, he felt he must go himself in pursuit, and before leaving on August 1, he wrote to his wife, "The enemy when they leave these seas will go to America. Wherever they go I will watch their motions and certainly attack them if they give me a proper opportunity. The fate of England may depend upon the event."

The warning notice to Graves, and his other dispatches of the same days, show Rodney in possession of the whole picture, identifying the place, the problem and a plan of appropriate action. Dealing with slower minds, Rodney was not content to leave Graves with anything less than precise instructions. In a supplementary despatch of July 31, he put his finger on just what might be expected. Repeating the intelligence he had learned that de Grasse was sailing for America, he added that he had sent Hood to the Capes of Virginia, *"where I am persuaded the French intend making their grand effort"* (italics added). This was no magic vision. Rodney had learned of the pilots who had joined de Grasse at Cap-Français, and he drew the natural inference (not always a normal practice) that if de Grasse had asked for pilots for the Chesapeake, that was doubtless where he intended to go.

Unfortunately for the British, Rodney's warning notice to Graves went undelivered, in one of those quirks of war that inspired Clausewitz a century later to make it a basic principle that all war plans should be formed in expectation of the unexpected. The warning to Graves was sent by England's *Swallow*, with less speed than a frigate, not nimble enough to evade capture by three American privateers on Long Island Sound, leaving Graves unalerted to the approach of de Grasse. The anonymous privateers should have a niche in the history books. Hood too sent a warning letter which was also captured at sea, with the result that Graves knew neither of the English help nor the French menace that was on the way. When Hood arrived in New York Bay on August 28, he rowed over from his ship to Long Island the same day to confer with Admiral Graves, without result. They did not combine forces to sail into Chesapeake Bay in order to be ahead of de Grasse, as Rodney had planned. Although they agreed at their conference to sail in combined force for the Bay, they stayed in place for three days doing nothing. Even had they moved promptly, they could not have been in time to fill the Bay with British ships before de Grasse arrived there on August 30. It would have taken Graves, who was anchored inside New York harbor, the usual three days to come out across the bar at Sandy Hook. The fact is they did not move at all until August 31, but stayed where they were to wait for events.

Rodney's plan to establish naval superiority on the Virginia coast either by the Hood-Graves combined forces or by the ships of Sir Peter Parker disintegrated, as the best-laid plans will when human agency is deficient. Graves, as he was to show, was never in a hurry, and Hood was not venturesome in America, no matter what Nelson said of him later.

Here was a situation in which the contingency was foreseen and the correct preventive prescribed, yet not taken. The question of English refusal to see their opportunities becomes insistent. Were they in a do-nothing trance because they were caught in a war they did not know how to win? Pessimism is a primary source of passivity.

As the only one of the English who took seriously and had long taken seriously the threat of active French intervention in America, why did Rodney not attempt, together with Hood, to intercept the French when they were in his own territory in the Leeward Islands, instead of leaving them to be intercepted after they had already reached America? This was the moment of vacuum. Rodney's non-pursuit was not due to a desire to stay in St. Eustatius in order to take in as much as possible of the plunder, as his accusers, then and now, have charged. All that had been taken care of, as far as it was possible for him to do so; his booty from St. Eustatius had already sailed for England in Hotham's convoy in March. Why did he not send frigates on reconnaissance to ascertain precisely where de Grasse had gone after he left Fort Royal, how many ships he was taking and a more exact date of his departure than "in a short time"? With that information, the combined forces of Rodney and Hood could very likely have crippled or stopped de Grasse before he crossed the Atlantic.

Rodney did not make that attempt because he felt his primary duty was to keep his ships at hand to defend the islands, because the time needed for repair of Hood's crippled ships left him with inferior numbers and, most of all, because his physical miseries drained the spirit of enterprise that normally would have carried him to seek out and destroy the French in his own vicinity. A negative mission lacks the propelling impulse of a positive one. He made no search and found no combat. He determined nevertheless that he must join Hood in pursuit of de Grasse, with the lingering hope that in the sea air of a northward voyage his illness would recede. His orders to Hood to sail in search of de Grasse were issued on July 25. Sixteen days followed of repair and provisioning before Hood was ready to depart. In the interim, Rodney, in the severity of his ailment, felt that he could at last take his promised leave to go home for treatment of his stricture. (The word "prostrate" was not then in use for the condition.) After signing orders on July 25 for Hood to pursue de Grasse, Rodney followed on August 1 accompanied by Dr. Blane, the fleet physician, with the hope that after leaving the torrid zone he would be well enough to continue on to America, resuming his place as an active admiral. In case of combat, he took with him the *Gibraltar* and the *Triumph*, two of the larger liners, both in need of repairs, and the frigate *Pegasus*, which he hoped, if his health permitted, would carry him on to America.

His condition did not improve on the voyage as he had hoped, and when he passed the latitude of the Bermudas with no relief, he realized he must make for home. As a result, the two warships he had with him were not present to add to the British naval force which was soon to contest naval superiority with the French fleet in American waters. To Carlisle he describes his distress, when about to proceed to America "with a force sufficient to curb or defeat" His Majesty's enemies, "to be deprived of that honour by a severe distemper which reduced me so much as to render me incapable of taking charge of the fleet destined for that service." He returned to England on September 19.

Apart from rejoining his family, his homecoming was not entirely joyous, for sixty-four legal actions had been entered against him by St. Eustatius and St. Kitts merchants, and the political Opposition were prowling on the heels of Burke and Fox in readiness for parliamentary attack in a chorus of condemnation. Hints of a coming peerage receded* under the cloud of disfavor, and when on his arrival he hurried to Windsor Castle to request an audience with George III to present his case, he

*To be later bestowed, in 1782, at the lowest rung of the peerage, a mere barony, after his victory in the Battle of the Saints.

was put off to another day. Worse was the news that Hotham's convoy, with the bulk of the produce of St. Eustatius, had been captured by the French, causing a storm of abuse to fall upon the much-abused Sandwich for failure to provide adequate ships to protect the homecoming treasure.

To the public, Rodney still emitted rays of glory for the relief of Gibraltar and the Moonlight Battle. Dockyard workers cheered him at Plymouth and garlands were hung at the door of his house in London. He hastened to Bath to submit to the untender mercies of 18th century surgery for his condition. For the next month (September–October), while he was in surgery and recovery, he was entirely out of affairs while the terminal crisis was reaching its climax in America.

The surgeon, Sir Caesar Hawkins, appears to have had a good result and to have "cured his patient," according to Rodney's biographer, although on November 4 Rodney himself writes to Jackson of the Admiralty Board that "my complaint has been and still continues." His spirit, in spite of the "misery of a surgical operation," was as ardent as ever. The government, once so neglectful, was now eager for his services. In November he was offered the post of Vice-Admiral of Great Britain, with promise of the 90-gun three-

481

decker *Formidable* as his flagship. He accepted at once, though his friends found him thin and ill but "determined to serve again." Sandwich wrote him letters virtually pleading with him to rejoin, insisting, "Our loss will be great if we are deprived of your assistance."

This raises a question: if he was so invaluable, why did the Admiralty not give him leave to come home for treatment of a "severe stricture . . . so serious and painful that I must soon return home" when he first asked, on March 2? Treated at that time, he instead of Graves, future loser in the crucial Battle of the Bay, might have been employed in America. Hood later generously acknowledged, referring to Rodney, that if "that Admiral had led His Majesty's squadron from the West Indies to this coast, the fifth of September [date of the Battle of the Bay] would I think have been a glorious day for Britain."

Judging by Rodney's sensational victory over de Grasse a year later, in the Battle of the Saints, Hood was probably right. Rodney would certainly not have made such a muddle out of the Battle of the Bay as to lose its control to the French. If the British had held the Bay, they would, or might, have rescued Cornwallis, in which case Washington's last chance would have failed; mediation by Catherine the Great might have been the only recourse, and under Imperial Russian influence, with Britain in the opposite corner, American independence and a constitution would have been unlikely to emerge. Rodney's own judgment of the Battle of the Bay was unequivocal. "In my poor opinion," he wrote to Jackson on October 19, "the French have gained a most important victory, and nothing can save America." He was right on both counts. The day he wrote the letter was the day of Cornwallis' surrender at Yorktown, though it would not be known for another month in London.

In the West Indies during July, de Grasse completed his preparations for the campaign, except for the last necessity of money. The loan he had hoped to raise from the inhabitants of Santo Domingo having been thwarted, he turned to another local Spanish source, the population of Cuba. By speedy frigate he sent a letter to the Governor of Havana explaining his need for a sum equivalent of 1.2 million livres. While official Spain was not eager for the success of the American rebels for fear of its effect on her own colonies, the population of Havana, remembering the assault on their city by the British less than twenty years before, were glad of the opportunity to retaliate. By popular subscription, the money for de Grasse is said to have been raised in less than 48 hours, with the help of Cuban ladies who contributed their diamonds, and was promptly delivered to his flagship. Less romantically, Tornquist states that "Cuba" issued a cash order for 700,000 piasters, which was delivered in cash in five hours. On August 5, 1781, missing his expected departure date by only two days, de Grasse sailed from Cap-Français for America and Chesapeake Bay with the money, the three Saint-Simon regiments and all 28 ships of his fleet.

To escape British notice, de Grasse took a difficult and little-used route through the Bahama Channel between Cuba and the Bahamas, a course of many obstacles which made for slow sailing. In spite of the American pressure for haste, his choice of the Bahama Channel proved wise — or lucky. Admiral Hood left Antigua on August 10, only five days behind de Grasse, failed to find him on the wide ocean and, because he took the most direct route for the American coast, arrived in America five days ahead of him. When he looked into Chesapeake Bay, he saw no sign of foreign sail, for de Grasse was still beating his way up from the Bahamas. By relieving the British of anxiety about the advent of de Grasse and confirming them in the belief that if he was coming at all, he was coming to New York, the mischance of missing him at this point was more significant than a physical clash.

Hood dutifully went on to a conference on August 28 with Graves and Clinton. The attention of neither was focused on the coming of de Grasse. Rumors of a French fleet coming to the American coast from the West Indies were probably the work, Graves assured Clinton, of a "heated imagination" or, insofar as mention was found in intercepted French letters, it was French "gasconading," the favorite word for any French statement, threat or promise. Hood certainly knew it was more than that, having himself only recently seen action against de Grasse in the West Indies. He knew the size of the French fleet and, with any strategic sense, could have judged, as Rodney did, its destination, and though junior to Graves in rank Hood might have made a strong case for their sailing together to maintain control of Chesapeake Bay before the French occupied it. Had they done so, they would have changed the course of the war, but Hood did not argue for it, owing no doubt to the mischance of finding no enemy in the Bay when he first looked in. Judging by his subsequent inaction in the developing crisis over the rescue of Cornwallis, he seems to have caught the contagion of paralysis from the moment he set foot in America.

Clinton shared the complacency of Graves and Hood, having been assured by Lord Germain that he had nothing to fear from de Grasse because Rodney with a superior fleet was keeping careful watch of his motions. Old Admiral Arbuthnot, before his retirement, had suggested to Graves that it was quite impossible for Rodney, "be his vigilance ever so great," to send reinforcements to America in time enough "to be here before them," and that de Grasse, if he came, would have superiority in American waters, endangering Cornwallis in his vulnerable position on the Chesapeake. The prospect envisioned by the weary eyes was to come true to the letter, but the old man was gone at last and the New Yorkers felt no need to worry about the southern theater, which they saw as secondary. Their worry was for their own position, for everyone was certain that the French fleet, if it came, would be coming to New York. What Graves and Clinton feared was a descent by de Barras' French squadron from Newport to join with de Grasse and gain supremacy over British sea power in America. Why did Graves never venture to neutralize de Barras by an attack at Newport instead of waiting passively for attack at New York? "Throughout the course of the war," de Lauzun writes, in the nearest he ever came to critical thinking about war, "the English seemed to be stricken with blindness. . . . They refused to seize the most obvious and most golden opportunities." He cites the occasion still to come; when the Rochambeau army would leave Newport to join Washington for the final campaign, "the British then had only to attack the French fleet off Rhode Island to destroy it. This never occurred to them." In fact it did occur to them, but Graves, fearing to be outnumbered, would never agree to the venture.

On the day when Hood, at the end of his fruitless pursuit of de Grasse, came into New York, report arrived from Newport that de Barras had in fact sailed, destination unknown. When tested, the British blockade of Newport, which was maintained at Gardiners Island fifty miles away, not surprisingly had proved less than solid. All the New Yorkers' fears revived, although the scene of action they envisaged and the scene de Barras had in mind were not the same. Obsessed with their own position, the English thought he was coming to join some action against New York. In fact, de Barras was bringing forward the transports and siege train in support of the Franco-American march to Virginia, of which Clinton and Graves were sublimely ignorant.

Washington's allies were coming. His planned junction with them would be a last chance. Since the exciting prospect raised at Saratoga, the French, who had put large expectations in the abasement of Britain that American success would cause, had been disappointed by the weakness of the American military effort. Instead of an aggressive ally, they were tied to a dependent client, unable to establish a strong government and requiring transfusions of men-at-arms and money to keep its war effort alive. The war, like all wars, was proving more expensive for the Bourbons than planned. Since the alliance, France had advanced to the Americans over 100 million livres, about $25 million, in loans, supplies and gifts, and before it was over the cost of the American war for France would amount, by some estimates, to 1.5 billion livres, an historic sum that was virtually to bankrupt the French national budget and require the summoning of the Estates General in 1789 that led to the arrest of the King and the sequence of eruptions that became the French Revolution. The Americans were notified that the French government had already spent more than "Congress had a right to expect from the friendship of their ally." Vergennes made it clear that no more troops or ships or infusions of money would be forthcoming after 1781. This time, Washington knew, the Allied reinforcement must be made effective. But to march an army of sufficient strength for a major American role to meet the French in Virginia was not a project to be organized on air. It had to be fed, shod and supported by field guns.

In the American wilderness of want, the first angel to appear to revive offensive capacity was Robert Morris, richest of the merchants who had profiteered from the war and who in 1781 was elected by Congress to the post of Superintendent of Finance. In its abiding fear of centralized power, so like the Dutch, Congress for five years had avoided the submission of finances to a single governor. Only in 1781, when the state was sliding toward a collapse of credit, did it admit the necessity of a financial director. Morris, whose opinion of mankind grew worse "from my experience of them," and who believed that public office exposed an honest man to envy and jealousy and to the "malicious attacks of every dirty scoundrel that deals in the murther of reputations," nevertheless accepted the post and, by virtue of the funds he generated, did as much as anyone at this hour to preserve the fight for independence. The rich have their uses; although assumed to be knaves, they can prove to be pillars of the state like anyone else. Virtue and patriotism are not a prerogative of the humble. Through the influence of his personal credit, Morris obtained contributions from the various states, reduced government spending, laid the foundations for a national bank and persuaded a group of Philadelphia bankers to make a substantial loan in cash. Altogether, he borrowed from Rochambeau and from the Philadelphia businessmen a total of $40,000, which provided the ragged half-fed Continentals with their first touch of hard cash since enlistment, cut down desertions and even brought in recruits. More than that, the money enabled Washington to move to the offensive.

On August 14, Washington received, like a burst of fireworks in the dark, a letter from de Grasse to Rochambeau, written from the West Indies, to say he was coming with 28 ships and 3,000 soldiers to the Chesapeake. Without fussing further over his lost dream of regaining New York to make an end of the war, Washington at once set about preparing a campaign at the Chesapeake to make an end of Cornwallis.

He wasted no time in a judicious balancing of pros and cons that often prolongs the taking of difficult decisions, for if he were to meet de Grasse's demand for "immediate cooperation" upon his expected arrival of September 13, he had only a month to select and prepare troops for the campaign, provision the line of march to cover a distance that over local roads amounted to about 500 miles, arrange for boats to meet him at river points for transportation and provide for local food supply to keep his army alive when they reached their goal. Rochambeau's army, which had already marched 200 miles from Newport to join him at White Plains in the first week of June, also had to be prepared. The venture was a long chance and a formidable operation. To bring off a long trek in heat to a disliked destination with troops in an uncertain temper, with a mixed army of French and Yankees with opportunity for antipathies and quarrels, and a chance of attack on the flank by Clinton's forces, was to place ultimate reliance on very long odds. To make good the "decisive stroke," the army after a month on the road must meet the French fleet after its ocean crossing in the hour of its arrival, after each had traveled an obstacle course of perils and mischances that could spoil the timing and ruin the plan. Exact timing was required in order that they should not meet the enemy with divided forces, nor by a separate arrival give him warning to escape. The longest chance was whether Cornwallis would stay where he was in position to be trapped; otherwise the great effort would go for nothing. This worry was very much on Washington's mind. He wrote to Lafayette to make sure that he did not allow Cornwallis to move back into North Carolina, and to keep him informed of all the enemy's movements.

Still the problem remained of how the joint armies were to be fed when they had dug in at Yorktown for a siege. Fifteen hundred barrels of salt beef, originally brought in with Rochambeau, were stored at Newport, which would supply the need, but the beef, too, de Barras had refused to transport. He was sulking because the appointment of de Grasse over his head had lost him the independent command he had expected to hold, permitting him to adventure off Newfoundland, promising prizes, just as Hood had been deprived of prizes from the aborted expedition against Surinam and Curaçao. Now the urgent pleading of Washington and Rochambeau persuaded de Barras to change his mind and agree to transport the salt beef down the coast along with the siege guns, too heavy for overland transport, when de Grasse should have cleared the way.

To fight at the Chesapeake required a firm and daring decision grounded in a sense of no alternative, a recognition that this was the last resort. Washington was not a man to reduce himself to a miasma of hesitations. He made up his mind on the very day of receiving de Grasse's letter. "I was obliged," he wrote in his diary for that day, "from the shortness of Count de Grasses promised stay on this coast, the apparent disinclination in their Naval officers [of the French] to force the harbour of New York, and the feeble compliance" of his own country to his request for recruits and the "little prospect of greater exertion in the future, to give up all idea of attacking New York; and instead to remove the French troops and a detachment from the American Army to Virginia." He was the more willing to give up New York because the military probe of Clinton's defenses led by the Duc de Lauzun in July had shown them to be very strong and requiring a greater assault than Washington could dispose.

The American troops, for too long orphans of the battle, unkempt, underfed and unpaid while Congress rode in carriages and dined at well-laid tables, would not march without pay. Here the lubricant of Morris' and the French funds overcame the obstacle. It put coins into empty pockets and restored the Quartermaster to business. Food would not be the problem it had been before. An army moving from place to place each day would not be the devouring incubus that a stationary force quartered on one spot through a long winter must be, consuming every last ounce of pork and grain to the destitution and alienation of the countryside. Washington was now able to store supplies of meat, flour and rum along the line of march. French silver and the credit of the Philadelphia bankers put the army in motion, but it needed de Grasse's unhindered crossing of the Atlantic, bringing him to his planned junction with the Americans, to keep the Revolution on its feet and supply the necessary strength for an offensive. By itself, the American army was too small and riddled by every deficiency to have kept the field alone in 1781. Congress had no reserves. At the same time, British capacity was unequal to successful offensive action at this stage. Without the coming of the French fleet to precipitate a crisis, Britain and the Colonies would have floundered into some miserable compromise, for private sentiment on both sides was ready for mediation. Already in England stocks rose six percent in two days when news spread in March, 1781, that the Emperor and Empress of Russia had offered mediation and that all parties had accepted and that Sir Joseph Yorke was to depart, as Walpole reported to Mann, on the "wings of winds to Vienna to conclude the peace." The stock market sadly sank back when the rumor proved unfounded and Sir Joseph stayed home. The same rumor of Russian mediation excited hopes in America, too, for war weariness was present in many places. Again, in September, the British were cheered by a rumor that the King had employed Yorke to seek a separate peace with Holland, removing Britain from at least one war. The Whigs, though in favor of peace, carped at the supposed overture, complaining, according to Walpole, that "it was the contemptible conduct of the court, to bully itself into war, and then meanly solicit a peace underhand." This rumor, too, proved without substance. In all the flutter of peace talk, a public desire to be done with war, and a readiness to compromise through mediation, was revealed. Pursuing the gleam of the "successful battle" and the "decisive stroke," the generals in the field, as always, played a stronger hand, perhaps fortunately, for a compromise would have produced no United States of America and given no impulse to the development of a democratic age. The West Indies held the determining event on the night of June 5, 1781, when Rodney chose defense of Barbados over pursuit of de Grasse.

TWELVE

Last Chance —
The Yorktown Campaign

Miraculous is a term often applied to the Yorktown campaign. The opportunity to combine his land forces with French naval power to enclose Cornwallis in the vulnerable position he had chosen at Yorktown would be, Washington realized, his one chance to defeat the enemy and bring a culmination to the long struggle. To conduct his own forces into place to do the job would be a task of extraordinary difficulty and would involve a serious risk of failure — of his own reputation, of his army and of the cause of independence. It required a decision as bold as Hannibal's to cross the Alps by elephant. Washington took it without visible hesitation. He, not Cornwallis, popularly called the English Hannibal, was the Hannibal of his time. The first necessity was to arrange the meeting of French naval and American land forces on the Virginia coast at a specified time and place. The junction in

496

Virginia had to be coordinated by two different national commands separated across an ocean without benefit of telephone, telegraph or wireless. That this was carried out without a fault seems accountable only by a series of miracles.

Rochambeau's army from Newport had marched from Rhode Island to join Washington on the Hudson in the first week of July, 1781. Dispersed through the White Plains area, their joint camp was centered at Philipsburg (Philipse Manor) in Yonkers, four miles from White Plains and less than twenty miles from where the British forces occupying New York were quartered in former American barracks on the grounds of King's College, near Trinity Church, in the Wall Street section.

The offensive planned by the Allied army of French and Americans for a union with de Grasse would require a march from the Hudson of approximately 500 miles, measured over local roads down through New Jersey, Pennsylvania, Delaware and Maryland, to Virginia. The army would be a mixed group of two newly acquainted allies speaking different tongues, with arrangements to be made along the route for food and drink and river transportation. Foraging and bivouacking at night, they would have to rely on come what may. Despite the obstacles and hazards involved in organization of the march, once Washington had taken a decision, it remained firm, not subjected thereafter to second questions.

In the midst of dispiriting frustrations and shortages and the sneers and plots of jealous generals seeking to oust him, and disappointed in having to give up his desire to retake New York, Washington was yet able to respond to a new hope and summon his energy for a new campaign. On August 15, one day after receipt of de Grasse's letter stating his choice of the Chesapeake, Washington notified the Continentals to make ready to march. On this day he issued general orders to the Continentals: "the army will hold itself in the most perfect readiness to move at the shortest notice." He followed these by a letter to Rochambeau specifying the route of the first stage of the March to Trenton and a letter to de Grasse requesting him to send all his frigates, transports and other vessels to convey the troops down the Bay. The troops selected to go were some 4,000–5,000 French of Rochambeau's army, consisting of regiments of old repute — the Saintonge, the Soissonnais, the Deux-Ponts, the Bourbonnais, the one-time Auvergne — plus armed marines of the fleet and some 2,000 American

Continentals — so named to give a sense of national unity to units coming from different colonies — of the New York, New Jersey and Rhode Island lines. In the French group was the Duc de Lauzun's cavalry legion, astride tiger-skin saddle blankets and wearing scarlet breeches, pale blue coats and fur hats. A garrison of 4,000 militia units and the rest of the American army remained to guard the Hudson forts and cover the main army's crossing of the river. A planned program for the long march had to be prepared. Arrangements for food and forage depots to be placed across New Jersey were made possible by French money. Letters went to the governors of Maryland and Virginia requesting their aid for provisions and for shipping to transport the American and French troops down the Delaware and the Bay to their rendezvous with the French fleet. Not yet knowing whether de Barras with the artillery and beef and extra naval force would come to form a junction with de Grasse and hearing nothing of either of the fleets, "you can readily conceive," Washington wrote to Greene, "that the present time is as interesting and anxious a moment as I have ever experienced."

The news from Newport that de Barras had agreed to come and a letter from de Grasse saying he was going "to do the impossible by sending to meet you" six or seven men-of-war of shallow draft followed by frigates and generally every ship fit to ascend the river together with siege cannon from his ships, 1,800 troops, and 1,200,000 francs promised that the great envelopment was moving toward actuality.

Destination at the camp in New York was kept tightly secret even from the Allied troops, so that Clinton should not learn of the proposed envelopment of Cornwallis and be moved to send reinforcements to Yorktown. The Comte de Deux-Ponts, one of the French regimental commanders, was himself in the dark. We "are in perfect ignorance whether we go against New York or whether we are going to Virginia to attack Lord Cornwallis," he recorded. Bets were being placed in camp on New York versus Virginia.

From where the Allies were situated on the edge of the continent, their first and largest obstacle would be a crossing of the Hudson. Too deep to be forded, too wide to be bridged, the great North River, as it was called, in contrast to the Delaware or South River, could only be crossed by ferryboat. To carry over 6,000–7,000 men with equipment, provision wagons, draft animals and artillery when the enemy was within striking distance was a vulnerable and perilous operation that could not be accomplished in a day, and during embarkation would expose the army to attack. The tension for the French and Americans, as they prepared for the journey by ferry was great. Would the British appear from lower New York to fire on the ferries from shore — or, worse, on the encumbered men while they were boarding?

Dobbs Ferry, at the present Tappan Zee Bridge, was one of the two crossing points. The other, considered the more secure, was King's Ferry further up the river where the stream was narrowest opposite West Point. Here in 1778 a chain had been pulled across the river to prevent the passage of British warships.

The ferries for transport across the majestic river were broad-beamed one-masted schooners of shallow draft, the famed sloops of the Hudson, carriers of the river traffic north and south and across the stream for over a century. Dutch-built, the sloops at an average of 100 tons were 65–75 feet long, with rounded stern and wide decks, a large mainsail and small jib. The cross-stream passage from bank to bank made use of the long experience of Dutch skippers, more skilled than the English. Leaning on long heavy tillers, they took advantage of shifts in winds and tides and of every twist of the current around river bends that could advance their progress. They usually sailed at dark to take advantage of the moon's tides and night breezes.

In heavy rain on August 19, 1781, Washington's and Rochambeau's armies broke camp to march to the ferry crossings. One regiment crossed first at Dobbs Ferry, where the river is a mile wide, while the rest of the Americans and the more heavily loaded French with all their horses and equipment were to cross at King's Ferry. Here, although the river was only a quarter of a mile wide, the ferry route followed a diagonal and longer course from Verplanck's Point on the eastern shore to Stony Point, the western terminus, where one of three landings connected with the main road going south.

Apart from the protection the militia could offer, the only safeguard was Clinton's known difficulty in bringing himself to act. Would that be enough? Washington had laid several false trails pointing to Staten Island, which lies at the mouth of the Hudson where the river enters New York Bay, to give an impression that he was planning to use Staten Island as a base for assault on New York City. He had ordered that all boats moored along the lower Hudson and the shores of the Bay be collected as if in preparation for such an assault, and local patriots had been told to ask pointed questions about Staten Island in the taverns and in talk with neighbors.

Clinton accepted these indications, which were eagerly collected and conveyed to him by Loyalist agents, convincing him in gloomy solipsism that he himself as Commander-in-Chief, together with New York, was the intended target of the rebel forces assembling in his back yard. He spent his days momentarily expecting assault and, while enduring the anxious wait, dared not move a man or a gun of his defense forces out of position to act against the enemy who were so plainly gathering with purposeful intention. A new anxiety reinforced his paralysis. Rumors were circulating of a French fleet coming to America from the West Indies, and they spoiled his sleep with the thought of his being robbed of naval superiority. The possible threat to his associate in Virginia did not trouble him, for, as he wrote to London on May 30, "Cornwallis is safe enough unless a superior fleet shows itself in which case I despair of ever seeing peace restored to this miserable country." The "superior fleet" that he feared was, as he wrote, already in the West Indies on its way to America.

By "peace," Clinton meant, of course, suppression of the rebellion, and he was more aware than his naval colleagues of the danger to the British in relation to food and other supplies if naval superiority were gained by the enemy. Britain's position in the Colonies depended on maritime control and active support by the Loyalists. One of these was already lacking and if she lost the other, her army and civil authorities would have to live on air. Clinton's appreciation of this factor was particularly acute because, judging by the accounts that survive in his papers of orders for food and liquor, he lived high. He ordered brandy in 10-gallon lots. His food orders were equally generous, including beef, veal, mutton, tongues, beef rumps, fish, crabs, tripe, sweetbreads, eggs. On August 24, while the rebel army were in the midst of their crossing of the Hudson, Clinton ordered 43 pounds of beef, 38 pounds of veal, an illegible number of "birds," crabs and turkeys and two calves' heads (perhaps he was giving a party). He also ordered his boots from London and his stable-boys' shoes soled in London and a steady supply locally of lavender water and "Hemet's dentifrice" and scented powder and, on August 27, a comb. One does not know how many persons of a very large headquarters staff dined at his table, but whatever the number (one mention refers to 148 general officers), they certainly ate and drank heartily. Could it be that all that brandy by the gallon helps to explain the slack performance of the British command? Were they dulled by alcohol?

While the army was billeted downtown, Clinton's place of residence was at the Beekman House, at the present 52nd Street and East River. Clinton himself actually occupied four different houses, perhaps to deceive a would-be assassin. "In and near New York," according to a political journalist, "Sir Henry Clinton has no less than four houses; he is quite a monopolizer. At times, when he is visible, he is seen riding full tilt to and from his different seats; in this, he is the Ape of Royalty." The possession of this multiple real estate and the existence of a longtime mistress, Mrs. Baddeley, by whom he had several children, were no doubt related to his obsessive desire to hold on to New York.

Unimpeded by Clinton, Washington's forces, a day after leaving camp at Philipsburg, reached the ferry crossings.

Down the cobblestone slopes leading to the docks the procession of the Allied army came; provision wagons were hauled aboard the ferries, followed by the rank and file of foot soldiers as they crowded over the gangways, while reconnaissance officers kept a tense watch for approaching redcoats. No shots or sudden charge of cavalry with flashing sabers

505

broke into their orderly progress. The ferries filled with men, ropes were uncoiled and flung over the side to waiting dockhands, sails were hoisted and the boats slid into the water.

From an observation platform erected for him by the French on a plateau overlooking Haverstraw Bay, a bulge in the river five miles wide, Washington watched the ferries bearing his soldiers over the water on the journey to the last, best hope of victory in the long fight for independence. The Americans started crossing on August 20, and all were across by the next morning. Claude Blanchard, the French Commissary or Quartermaster General, standing next to the Commander-in-Chief on August 25 (the date given in his diary), as he watched the crossing, could feel the emotion stirring behind the impassive exterior. He sensed that as Washington surveyed the pageant moving across the broad stream "glittering in the sunlight," he seemed "to see a better destiny arise, when at this period of the war, exhausted, destitute of resources, he needed a great success which might revive courage and hope. He pressed my hand with much affection when he left us at two oclock and crossed the river himself to rejoin his troops." "I have the pleasure to inform Your Excellency," Washington wrote to Rochambeau in a letter dated August 21 from

King's Ferry, on the far side, "that my troops arrived at the ferry yesterday and began to pass the River at 10 oclock in the morn and by sunrise of this day, they were all compleatly on this side of the river." His date does not fit with Blanchard's because Washington apparently came back after his first crossing and went over a second time with the French. The last of his troops landed after dinner in the darkness of the western shore at the foot of the Catskills, where the wail of the wildcat drifts through the undomesticated hills, and the rumble of thunder means that the ghosts of Henry Hudson's crew are playing at bowls.

The French, slowed by their longer march to their ferry and a heavier train of equipment, embarked several days later, and they too crossed safely without incident. The calm of the Hudson crossing had remained untroubled except for Rochambeau's order to unload surplus burdens for storage in Peekskill, which "made *the rank and file* complain loudly," as reported by Rochambeau's aide, Ludwig von Closen. Closen had a happier piece of news for his journal when a message of crucial importance to the campaign was delivered on the day of the American crossing by an officer returning from Newport to say that de Barras, the French naval commander, was now agreeable to bringing down the transports with the troops, meat and siege guns, which "greatly eased" Rochambeau's mind. All the French were across the river by August 25. The absence of British interference puzzled the Allies. "An enemy of any boldness or any skill," wrote the Comte de Deux-Ponts in his diary, "would have seized an opportunity so favorable for him and so embarrassing for us as that of our crossing the North River. I do not understand the indifference with which General Clinton considers our movements. It is to me an obscure enigma." Even Clinton's intelligence officer, William Smith, was conscious of the inertia. "There is no spirit of enterprise," he wrote on September 3, immediately after the crossing of the river, "the general dulness kills the spark that happens to rise in the mind of any man. . . . Washington's present movement from the Hudson is the severest censure upon the British commanders in this quarter." It may have been partly due to the fact that Clinton, at the time of the crossing, was absent on Long Island at the conference with Graves that ended in the same spirit of inertia as governed New York. Admiral Hood had just come into Sandy Hook on August 28 after his vain pursuit of de Grasse from the West Indies. He had rowed over to Long Island to confer with Graves and Clinton, and they had agreed that Graves should sail to the Chesapeake with the combined English fleet of nineteen ships to seek and defeat the expected squadron of de Barras from Newport with his eight ships before de Barras could join his strength to de Grasse. Presumably, Clinton left someone in command back in New York capable of giving orders in the emergency he was always expecting. One cannot suppose that preparation for the Hudson crossing passed unnoticed by everyone in the area, or that Clinton's headquarters was so naked of intelligence agents that none came a distance of fifteen miles or so to report. In fact, spies were constantly arriving at headquarters relaying in detail every move of the rebels' advance, even to the report by a woman who claimed to have penetrated the camp and located Washington's quarters. One can only speculate that headquarters was so relieved to see the enemy moving away from New York that it had no wish to interfere with their passage, or that lethargy and lost impetus had so far taken possession that the command no longer really cared about the war. A sense that the powers at home are not really interested in a war diminishes offensive spirit in the field, and just such a suspicion pervaded the mind of the British Commander-in-Chief, expressed in an extraordinarily revealing letter to his patron, the Duke of Newcastle. The letter complains of "reinforcements to every place but this," and asks pointedly, "Is it because America is become no object? If so, withdraw before you are disgraced!" That was hardheaded advice that few would have ventured, and, like most displeasing advice, it was given no hearing. If Clinton's "no object" is the clue to the British attitude in the war, it presents another enigma, for it does not fit with the predictions of the doomsayers at home that the loss of America would mean the decline and fall of the British Empire. People rarely take seriously reports of their own decline, and Britain's war leaders were no different from the normal run. Dire prophecies of decline and fall to follow loss of the American colonies did not penetrate their thinking nor make them fight more effectively.

Chiefly, Clinton's passivity was the result of his fear to move any of his defense forces out of position lest they might leave a hole open for the enemy to enter. Afterward, in his postwar apologia, he claimed he could not have attacked the Allies after the river-crossing because their forces, as he calculated extravagantly, far outnumbered his own. In fact, after the arrival of 2,400 Hessians, who had joined him on August 11, more than a week before the crossing, the reverse was the case. More to the point, he did not move because he was transfixed by the notion of imminent assault on New York. One would think this was the moment to attack first, ahead of his opponents, but that would have required a quick hard decision, which was not Clinton's way. He did nothing, as Washington had hoped, permitting the Allied army to walk away without hindrance. When a staff officer suggested to him that he might follow the rebels' march on the other side of the Hudson, he demurred, "for fear that the enemy might burn New York in his absence." Agents had reported to him that Washington had cached food dumps all across New Jersey, and other informants were citing evidence that indicated a march headed south rather than against New York. It is very difficult for a recipient of secret information to believe its validity when it does not conform to his preconceived plans or ideas; he believes what he wants to believe and rejects what does not verify what he already knows, or thinks he knows.

Meanwhile Hood and Graves had not yet sailed for Chesapeake Bay. Neither of them had Rodney's instinct for perceiving the shape of enemy strategy. Clearly the great effort of transferring an army across the Hudson would only have been undertaken by the rebels for a major strategic purpose which it would be important for the English to frustrate. That the plan was for the envelopment of Cornwallis to be carried out by the rebels' combining with de Grasse in Virginia seems not to have been envisaged by the two admirals who, as seamen, did not concern themselves with land movements, nor did they even grasp the crucial naval necessity of preventing the French from gaining superiority in Chesapeake Bay. They were locked into two fixed assumptions: that de Grasse was coming to New York, not the Chesapeake, and that he would not be coming with more than an inferior number of ships — perhaps twelve. Besides, everyone assumed that bold Rodney in the West Indies, who had been emphatic in his assurances, would take care of de Grasse in the Caribbean or, at the least, arrive at the same time to equalize naval forces. Preconceived fixed notions can be more damaging than cannon. The assumptions about de Grasse were probabilities, not certainties, and not an excuse for the British failing to place themselves in the best position possible to meet the French fleet if it came, whether or not Rodney was just behind. Hood, who knew the extent of Rodney's incapacitating illness and had himself been designated to substitute for him as the pursuer of de Grasse, could have disabused his colleagues of their expectation but did not; in his several inactions during this period, he is not easy to explain.

The inability of all three British commanders, Hood, Graves and Clinton, to envisage the envelopment of Cornwallis by a combination of the rebel army and the French fleet on the Virginia coast was simple obtuseness, the more so as the destination of Washington's march had been revealed by deserters and, so it is said, by an American girl, mistress of Rochambeau's son — inadvertently, one hopes. As usual with clandestine information, Clinton and his staff did not believe it, and, as always, underrated their opponent. They could not believe that Washington would undertake so Herculean a task as a march to Virginia, or would leave the Hudson forts denuded of his main army. If there was to be a junction with de Grasse, it seemed obvious to Clinton it was planned for Staten Island, for attack on New York.

In truth, a month of paralysis took hold of the British command in America when the French fleet entered the situation, as if each of the three — Clinton, the Commander-in-Chief; Graves, the Naval Chief; Cornwallis, General of the Army on the spot — had been administered a sedative. It began when a dispatch from Rodney reached Clinton on September 2 reporting that de Grasse's destination was the Chesapeake, as he had learned from the pilots who came to meet de Grasse at Cap-Français. Though the news threatened Cornwallis and not directly himself, Clinton realized that a fateful moment was at hand. "Things appear to be coming fast to a crisis," he wrote to Germain. "We are therefore no longer to compare forces with the enemy, but to endeavour to act in the best manner we can against them. With what I have, inadequate as it is, I will exert myself to the utmost to save Lord Cornwallis." In short, he recognized at this point that Cornwallis had to be "saved." On this day, too, he learned from Philadelphia, where the marching army he had thought on its way to Staten Island had arrived to a rapturous public greeting, that the land forces of Washington and Rochambeau were headed for a union with de Grasse at the Chesapeake. Clinton now had in his possession the full outline of the enemy's scheme, and although he was by nature the most hesitant of the three commanders, he did act at once to order Graves to take on board 5,000 reinforcements to relieve Cornwallis, for departure on October 5, with the qualification, "as soon as the way is clear" — as if expecting that de Grasse, if indeed he had come, would obligingly move out of the way. De Grasse had, in fact, arrived. After crossing the Atlantic without interception by Rodney or Hood, and after escaping Hood's notice by the maneuver through the Bahama Channel, he entered Chesapeake Bay on August 30, while Graves and Hood were still considering the matter at New York. Graves was anchored in the harbor inside the bar and Hood outside. For three days they remained in place. It was not until August 31 that they hoisted sail for the Chesapeake, and no sense of urgency impelled them because they expected to retain numerical superiority in any event — provided they could block de Barras from adding his strength to the French fleet. But de Barras had already left Newport, on his way to the Bay on August 25, well before Hood and Graves left New York.

Anxious to be on time for the rendezvous with de Grasse at the Chesapeake, Washington had ordered the Allied armies, as soon as they disembarked on the Jersey shore, to supply themselves with three days' rations and be ready to move at four o'clock in the morning, with the New York First Regiment leading, followed by the artillery and the Rhode Island Regiment and the French First Division. The march to Virginia had begun. The journal of Rochambeau's aide, Baron von Closen, is an invaluable record of the journey.

Von Closen was a native of the Palatinate, the Rhineland district lying between France and Germany. He had adopted France as his country, and entered military service at fourteen as a "pleasing, industrious, extremely intelligent, especially well informed" young officer. Rapidly promoted, he obtained a commission with the Royal Deux-Ponts regiment, who came to America in 1780 with Rochambeau. The Deux-Ponts wore sky-blue uniforms with lemon-yellow collars and facings. Closen was among the foreign diarists of the expedition who, unlike the Duc de Lauzun, were interested observers of the scenes and persons of American life and studiously recorded their observations in journals which, after 200 years, give us glimpses of what America looked like where they passed, often with unexpected views and comments.

Because of the limited and primitive roads of the period, and to ease the pressure of foraging on the countryside and to add to Clinton's uncertainty about the objective, the Allied army, in two groups, took separate routes along two parallel lines. Foot soldiers covered fifteen miles the first day, a distance that over the next two weeks remained about the daily average. Officers rode, including the

French who had brought their own horses. Washington's army marched in three columns, arriving at scheduled destinations at different times. On the way, Washington, further to implicate Staten Island, ordered the construction of hardtack ovens at Chatham, New Jersey, to suggest the establishment of a permanent camp and, in addition, the collection of thirty flat-bottomed boats on wheels, both for use on rivers going south as well as to imply a crossing to Staten Island.

Von Closen's route passed through the well-cultivated lands of long-settled New Jersey, where imperturbable cows under old gnarled apple trees lazily lifted their heads to stare at the riders. He finds pasture fences arranged like fence rails in France, "five of them, one on top of the other." Describing a "very beautiful small valley" along the river road between Chatham and Elizabethtown, he thought it "a land of milk and honey, with game, fish, vegetables, poultry," where the inhabitants — of Dutch origin, he thinks — "have kept it neat" in contrast to New York state "where misery is written on the brows of the inhabitants" — one of von Closen's odd remarks of now buried import. The riders continue on a "beautiful route" to Pompton, passing several large residences and fine cattle. At a "grandiose residence" in Whippany they are served a "sumptuous dinner," not repeated next day when at Bullion's Tavern at Basking Ridge they eat a "rather mediocre supper," balanced for von Closen by happiness in learning he is to have a bed, although he has to share it with Colonel Smith, an aide to Washington. They come next to Princeton, described in Blanchard's *Journal* as "a pretty village where the inns are handsome and very clean. A very handsome college is also to be seen there, [having] 50 scholars, [with] room for 200." So much for Princeton. After a "very good American breakfast" they push on to Trenton, having covered 45 miles that day. They dine with Washington and hear his account of past battles. Half a mile from the Delaware, Trenton is a "charming site in spite of the ravages of the Hessians (who made themselves hated)." The district is still rich in large villages reminding von Closen of his native Palatinate, though it has no good Rhine wine. Instead the people drink a delicious "Pery," or pear cider.

During the army's march through Jersey, a courier brought news on August 29 causing profound anxiety. An observer at Sandy Hook — a general of the New Jersey militia known to be trustworthy — reported the appearance of a fleet of eighteen ships, identified by their flags as British. Later the count was modified to fourteen, but either way the combination of the newcomers, which were thought to be Rodney's ships from the West Indies, with Graves's fleet would, they feared, give the enemy the most dreaded weapon, naval superiority over any number that de Grasse was expected to bring. The ships were not of course Rodney's but Hood's, now part of Graves's fleet, which was not animated by any great offensive energy in its Admiral.

Crossing the Delaware on September 1, the marchers arrived in Philadelphia the next day, having covered so far 133 miles. At Philadelphia the generals, who had entered the city three days in advance of the army, were met by the cheers of spectators and an ovation when they stopped at the City Tavern. Ecstatic applause greeted the dazzling spectacle of the French as they passed in review in their bright white uniforms and white plumes. Wearing colored lapels and collars of pink, green, violet or blue identifying their regiments, they were the most brilliantly appointed soldiers in Europe. The gold and silver thread in the facings and hats of their orderlies and the gold-headed canes the orderlies carried made them all look like generals. The artillery wore gray with red velvet lapels. Extravagant sartorial display had a purpose: it created an impression of wealth and power on the opponent and pride in the wearer, which has been lost sight of in our nervously egalitarian times. It seems a puzzle how the white uniforms could have been kept clean and pristine after one or two days' march along dusty or muddy roads. No women were on hand for laundering, for Washington had expressly forbidden camp followers to accompany the march, giving orders that wagons must not give them space nor food rations be issued. Cleaning, as far as it went, would be accomplished by covering stains with talc or white powder of one kind or another used to whiten wigs. Major Gaspard Gallatin, a staff officer of the Royal Deux-Ponts Regiment who kept a journal of the New York campaign, tells us that on reaching Philadelphia, the French Army, "having halted to burnish its arms and dust its white uniforms," and in the case of some units to change into dress uniform, "made a most impressive entrance in the City." In contrast, the American troops, grim-faced because they had not been paid, were in no very agreeable mood and were thought by some to be on the edge of mutiny, leaving some doubt whether they would continue to march. Nevertheless, they duly saluted as they filed past the flag, and past Washington, Rochambeau, Luzerne and the members of Congress assembled on the balcony of the State House. As the soldiers marched by, the congressmen doffed their thirteen hats in response. The brass instruments that accompanied French regiments excited the utmost enthusiasm of the crowd, who were accustomed only to fife and drum. The perfect marching in step to the music and the colorful regimental flags augmented the delight of the spectators who, von Closen thought pridefully, "could never have imagined that the French troops could be so handsome." The ladies watching the review from Minister Luzerne's residence are "enchanted to see such handsome men and hear such good music." Rochambeau and his staff are housed "like Princes" by Luzerne. With Washington and his generals they enjoy an "excellent repast" at the home of Robert Morris, with "all the foreign wines possible with which to drink endless toasts" to the United States, to the Kings of France and Spain, to the Allies and to the Count de Grasse. Afterward, the city was illuminated in Washington's honor.

The Allies spent the next day sightseeing in the "huge" city, which, with its large harbor and convenient piers for loading and unloading ships that come up the river, is "as commercial as Boston," having shops filled with fine merchandise. Merchants of the city, von Closen notes, "profited greatly" by the occasion because everyone "stocked up." The city had 72 straight, wide and well-built streets and sidewalks. The Congress meeting hall has the "finest view imaginable," and there is a "very famous College with the title of *University*" (the present University of Pennsylvania). At the home of Joseph Reed, "President of the State [sic] of Pennsylvania," the visitors are entertained at a ceremonial dinner of which the main feature was an immense ninety-pound turtle with soup served in its shell.

Toasts and ovations and honors did not compensate for lack of transport ships expected at Philadelphia. Morris, more familiar with obtaining money than boats, had been able to supply only a few. These were enough to carry the heavy field guns, but hope of water transport for the troops had to be abandoned.

From Philadelphia, the army moved on toward Chester, in Pennsylvania, on the way to its destination at Head of the Elk, at the top of the northernmost inlet of Chesapeake Bay. The anxiety that now rode with Washington like a physical pain can be judged in a letter he wrote on September 2 to Lafayette. "I am distressed beyond expression to know what is become of the Count de Grasse, and for fear the English fleet, by occupying the Chesapeake . . . should frustrate all our flattering prospects in that quarter." He added that he was anxious, too, about de Barras, who was supposed to be coming down to the Chesapeake with the guns and beef for the army. If Lafayette learned anything "new from any quarter," he was to send it *"on the spur of speed for I am almost all impatience and anxiety."* These words from General Washington, for so long a rock against an ordinary man's anxieties, reveal his agony on the march to Virginia. Would all the planning and the alliance and the hope come to nothing? Was he leading his army to futility at the end?

On September 5, as he rode into Chester, the agony was banished in a heart-stopping moment when a courier from de Grasse's fleet came riding up to tell him that the Admiral had actually arrived in the Bay with no less than 28 ships and 3,000 troops, and that they were already being disembarked in contact with Lafayette. The Cornwallis trap was laid! After announcing the stunning news to his troops, Washington turned his horse northward to inform Rochambeau, who was coming down by barge. As Rochambeau's boat neared the dock at Chester, he and his staff saw the astonishing sight of a tall man acting as if he had taken leave of his senses. He was jumping up and down and waving his arms in sweeping circles, with a hat in one hand and a white handkerchief in the other. On nearing the shore they could see that the eccentric figure was undoubtedly General Washington, ordinarily so grave and self-contained. Rochambeau jumped from the barge to be embraced as the wonderful news was conveyed. No one had ever seen the General so unrestrained and joyful and almost childlike in his happiness. A single worry remained. What about de Barras? Had he been intercepted in the Bay, and the food and guns he carried possibly lost to the Allies at the very brink of the ultimate encounter?

On the day that Washington heard the report about de Grasse, the same news was delivered in Philadelphia when a courier entered the hall where Minister Luzerne was entertaining Comissary Blanchard and eighty guests. All the guests fell silent as the messenger's document was taken to Luzerne, who, after hasty scanning, and in excitement almost equal to Washington's, read aloud the announcement that Admiral de Grasse with a reported 36 ships (an exaggerated count) was in the Bay, with 3,000 troops being disembarked to join Lafayette. The company was transported, and the courier overwhelmed as the guests crowded around him. In the city when the news was made public by Luzerne, the population raised cries of "Long live

Louis Sixteenth!" and mounted scaffolds and platforms to deliver funeral orations for Cornwallis and lamentations for the Tories.

As if to allow the joy and relief at Chester no unalloyed hour, Washington and Rochambeau, as they rode southward, heard a distant rumble of gunfire from the Bay. It carried a somber message: that the fleets of de Grasse and the British had met and opened combat. Stricken in suspense, the generals looked at each other, not daring to speak aloud their question. Which fleet had prevailed?

The outcome was, in fact, to be the turning point of the war and, it might be said, of the 18th century, for it proved to be the enabling factor of the rebels' Yorktown campaign.

In the Bay both fleets had made their entrance at the foot of the Capes. De Grasse, arriving on August 30, had anchored his main fleet in Lynnhaven Bay, off Cape Henry. Graves, entering on September 5, had come in at the foot of Cape Charles where the mouths of the York and the James rivers flowing down past Yorktown open onto the Bay.

Aghast upon entering the Chesapeake, Graves saw, instead of the twelve to fourteen ships he had expected de Grasse to bring, the great array of de Grasse's fleet of 28 ships of the line plus some frigates and gunboats. Against this superior force, Graves had, however, the superior position in that he was sailing in regular procession with the wind behind him, while de Grasse, after the knotty business of landing his troops to join Lafayette, was trying to maneuver his ships out of the harbor into the open sea where he would have room to form a battle line. In seeking combat, his purpose was to deny the Bay to the British and prevent the entrance of a force to aid or rescue Cornwallis. Graves's purpose was, of course, the reverse: to keep the sea-lanes open to Cornwallis. His opportunity to overwhelm the French was, according to naval critics, ideal. He was running down before the wind in good order, while the enemy in straggling succession was laboring to negotiate the uneasy passage around Cape Henry to the open sea. If he had attacked the disconnected French van one by one, he could have destroyed them. But that was not the tactical formula of *Fighting Instructions,* and Graves was a conformist to the code, and a product of the Royal Navy's greatest self-inflicted wound, the lost initiative left by the execution of Admiral Byng and the court-martial of Admiral Mathews. He knew that his duty under *Fighting Instructions* was to form line ahead in a battle line parallel to that of the enemy. Because the enemy had no line, Graves was at a loss. From one o'clock to 3:30

p.m., with the wind in rapid changes of direction, first in favor of the French and then of the English, Graves struggled to fulfill the formula, and by the time he raised the signal to engage, he had lost his advantage. While hoisting the blue-and-white-checkered flag that signaled "bear down," meaning that every captain should turn toward the enemy and attack the nearest individually, he kept the line ahead signal, which supersedes all others, still flying from his mizzenmast. "Bear down" would mean there would be no line, while the superior signal said to stay with it. The puzzled captains obeyed the superior signal. Keeping their line, they were brought up against the French at an angle instead of parallel, with the result that only their lead ships — part of Graves's force, instead of the whole — could engage. Cannon boomed and French gunnery told. Four of Graves's ships were so badly damaged as to be useless to him for renewing action next morning. For the next two days, September 6 and 7, while carpenters and riggers made what repairs they could at sea, the two fleets watched each other without engaging. They broke contact next day with no clear-cut victory or defeat discernible, yet with import that would place the Battle of the Bay among the decisive sea combats of history. Graves's fleet was damaged and dispersed; de Grasse's fleet held command of the Bay. The old culprit, "misunderstood" signals — the word was Graves's in his subsequent explanation to Parliament — had mangled yet another naval battle, although in fact the signals had been understood only too well.

On September 9, de Grasse precipitated a resolution by sailing his fleet back into the Bay to make it his domain. At the same time, de Barras, the critical addition to the contest, slipped in from Newport with his siege guns and his beef and his eight fresh ships.

Again at a loss, Graves, as senior naval officer, asked for a Council of War, which gave its opinion that, under the circumstances of his damaged ships and the enemy's increased numbers, he could not give "effectual succour" to the garrison at Yorktown. Admiral Hood, as Graves's junior, rashly advised that Graves should re-enter the Bay himself to contest the French dominion, although his persuasion was not eloquent or forceful enough to take effect.

Faced with the question often met by commanders in a tight spot, whether discretion is not the better part of valor, Graves concluded that it was, and decided that his proper course was to take his fleet back to New York for repairs to fit it for return to Yorktown. This he did, leaving the French by sea and land holding closed the gateways for either aid or exit to Cornwallis.

Cornwallis' reaction to the enemy landing at his doorstep was no less static than Clinton's at the Hudson. The same absence of combative response, almost of laziness, marked both occasions. When de Grasse first arrived in the Bay, his initial act, before the naval battle with Graves, had been to ferry his 3,000 land troops up the river to be disembarked to join and reinforce Lafayette's force facing the British stationed on Gloucester Point, across the river from Yorktown. Cornwallis had seen in the Bay the size of the fleet sent against him, which he overestimated at thirty to forty ships. As they detached one by one to come upriver to disembark their troops, and the French were caught in the scramble of landing when it would have been difficult for them to defend themselves, Cornwallis, whether in lassitude or absurd overconfidence, did not attack. "It was a pleasant surprise for our troops on landing," recalled Karl Gustaf Tornquist, the Swedish lieutenant serving with de Grasse, in his memoir, "that Cornwallis did not move in the least to hinder them, since indeed a single cannon could have caused much damage in the narrow and in many places winding river. Instead he was content to draw nearer to York, destroying everything which lay in his way, not sparing defenceless women and children." Even when the newcomers were combined with Lafayette's force of 5,000, Cornwallis' 7,800 men approximately equaled them. His inactivity at this point was due to his expectation of relief from New York, assured in Clinton's letters, though his failure to attack the hampered foe seems strangely unenterprising.

Without an observer stationed on the Capes with a prearranged signal, the outcome of the Battle of the Capes (as the combat in the Bay is sometimes called) remained unknown to Washington and Rochambeau for four silent days until scouts reported that the French fleet was still afloat in the Bay and the English had vanished over the horizon. Even then the generals could not rid their minds of a possible British return, which might cancel the rising hope that if pressed on land, Cornwallis' surrender was now a realistic possibility, bringing American victory with all its Allied objectives.

The army, still slowly trudging along its rough thoroughfare, would take another week before the vanguard could reach Williamsburg and complete the last ten miles to stand before Yorktown.

During these crucial days, Cornwallis, too,

had caught the strange contagion of passivity so foreign to him that lately had afflicted his colleagues. After learning of the outcome of the Battle of the Bay he had the time, which he did not use, during the slow approach of the enemy to open a land retreat for his about-to-be beleaguered army. The least reconnaissance of Lafayette's little army standing opposite to him at Gloucester would have shown that it was not overpowering.

A hard-hitting offensive could have broken through. He did not attempt it. As William Smith, Clinton's intelligence officer in New York, perceived, a spark had gone out. What quenched it is hard to say, unless it was a developing sense that America was slipping from the British grip and would not be arrested. Cornwallis' surprising inaction may be charged to Clinton's repeated assurance of reinforcements coming to his aid, for it was military tradition that a commander did not enter combat before an awaited reinforcement should arrive to add to his strength. After learning of Washington's passage through Philadelphia, Clinton corrected his first mistaken assumption that Washington was headed for Staten Island to attack New York. He wrote again to Cornwallis, on September 2, to say it was now clear that the army was marching southward with attack on Yorktown in mind. "You may be assured," Clinton wrote, that if Yorktown were attacked, "I shall either endeavor to reinforce the army under your command *by all the means within the compass of my power* or make every possible diversion in your Lordship's favor." An even more specific promise, dated September 6, came by express boat. "I think the best way to relieve you is to join you as soon as possible with all the Force that can be spared from hence which is about 4,000 men." These were the reinforcements he had put aboard Graves's ships when in August he had received the boatload of 2,400 Hessian mercenaries, which relaxed his obsessions about the defense of New York and allowed him the startling generosity of offering to let go 4,000 of his own men. "They are already embarked," he wrote, without mentioning that they were still in port. He added an assurance that anyone might have been justified in taking as definite from any commander other than the hesitant Clinton. They would sail "with large reinforcements on October 5" . . . the instant he was notified by Graves that "we may venture."

No hesitations or "maybes" qualified these commitments, and however little confidence Cornwallis had in Clinton as a bold or venturesome commander, he had every reason to expect prompt and effective support. Knowing Clinton's vacillation, his reliance on the promises may have been ill-judged, but even before he received these assurances, which took two weeks to come down from New York, Cornwallis, strangely for a soldier known for his pugnacity and verve, had not taken or prepared any offensive action against the slow pedestrian approach of the enemy, and none to open a path for an escape route for his own army in the event that siege was in store for him.

When the Allied army marching down from Philadelphia arrived at Head of the Elk in Maryland on September 6, they found only empty wharves, once again. No boats awaited them, only more miles of sore feet. Washington had written ahead to Maryland friends and officials to collect fishing boats and everything else available, but he was told when he came that British cruisers had seized or destroyed every vessel of useful size on the Chesapeake. In bitter conference, the generals agreed to embark on the few boats at hand about 2,000 troops, 1,200 French and 800 Americans, and send the rest of the army on foot down the road to Baltimore 55 miles away. A greater asset than boats was money. Hard money came from Robert Morris, borrowed from friends and from the French on the pledge of his personal credit and shipped from Boston and Philadelphia. The sight of the money in silver half crowns rolled out of the kegs so that the men could see it won over the mutinous troops, wrote von Closen, "and raised spirits to the required level." According to a Major William Popham of a New York regiment, "this day will be famous in the annals of history for being the first in which the troops of the United States received one month's pay in specie." Covering twenty miles a day on this stretch, the men reached Baltimore on September 12. Here at last they found water transport — in ships sent by de Grasse and in some others at Annapolis. Five frigates and nine transports took them down the Bay to be disembarked at Jamestown, on the James River just across from York.

At this point the pressure of the last days and weeks caught up with Washington. In spite of the felt need for haste, lest Cornwallis escape or make the attack on Lafayette that he should have made long since, Washington gave himself a holiday to visit his wife at Mount Vernon, his treasured home and lands sixty miles up the Potomac, which he had not seen, nor his wife, in six and a half years. The pull was one he could not resist, although delay added to his abiding fear that Cornwallis might move out of the trap before it could be sprung. This was Washington's greatest anxiety. From Mount Vernon he wrote to Lafayette, "I hope you will keep Lord Cornwallis safe without provisions or forage until we arrive." Lafayette maintained the barrier, though not against any test by Cornwallis, who made no move to break out at this time when he could have done so or, indeed, as General in command of the position, he should have done so. Washington wanted to show off his fine place to the French and return the hospitality they had given at their tables to the Americans at Newport. To anyone else a hurried ride of sixty miles each way would have seemed too far, but for Washington's energetic spirit it was feasible. With his personal servant and an aide, accompanied by Rochambeau and his staff, Washington left Head of the Elk on September 8 and galloped most of the way, reaching Baltimore in one day. Rising at dawn the next morning, the General and his two companions reached their destination as twilight dimmed the pillared white house on the hill. Unable to keep up the pace, the French followed behind. After Washington entertained the French company for two days, they rode back, stopping for a night's rest at Fredericksburg. On September 14 they reached Williamsburg to meet Lafayette and Saint-Simon's regiments and a vanguard of American Continentals encamped there. Here the good news that de Grasse was in command of the Bay and the British fleet gone was confirmed, mixed as always with trouble in the old problem of American shortages. Both food and ammunition for the army had dwindled to thinnest levels. As so often before, the foot soldiers who fought the war for American Independence were going hungry, and the prospect rose of the guns falling silent for lack of ball and powder just when they were needed to sustain a steady fire on the British garrison. Despite a good harvest in Maryland and Virginia, provisions lacked, owing to disorganized transportation and an incompetent quartermaster. Tornquist described the Williamsburg country when he passed through it as "very fertile, an average crop-yield gives sufficient sustenance for its owner the next year. Except for this advantage these inhabitants could never have withstood a six years' war; for although 12,000 acres in the neighborhood have been fallow each year for lack of farmers, who at the age of fifteen were sent to camp; yet now during a severe siege they had sufficient provisions to supply an army of 15,000 men and a fleet of 45 sails, in spite of all the ravages a bitter enemy had perpetrated during his march through the country."

The ravages Tornquist saw were as horrid as any to be found in any war. "On a beautiful estate a pregnant woman was found murdered in her bed through several bayonet stabs; the barbarians had opened both of her breasts and written above the bed canopy: 'Thou shalt never give birth to a rebel.' In another room, was just as horrible a sight five cut-off heads arranged on a cupboard in place of plaster-cast-figures which lay broken to pieces on the floor. Dumb animals were no less spared. The pastures were in many places covered with dead horses, oxen and cows. A store-house of tobacco which had been collected from Virginia, Maryland and Carolina for many years, containing 10,000 hogsheads of the best tobacco, was laid in ashes. Such was our first sight on landing in this unfortunate country. We did not find a single trace of inhabitants, for those who had been unable to flee lay on the ground as a token of the Godless behaviour of their enemies." The atrocity of the slaughtered mother of course spread rapidly through the vicinity. According to another account, which Tornquist evidently could not bring himself to mention, the unborn baby had been torn from the womb and hung from a tree. Tornquist makes no attempt to identify the murderers except by implication, in that it is entered in his memoir immediately following the statement that Cornwallis' troops on their way to York destroyed "everything which lay in his way, not sparing defenceless women and children."

Happily for the Allied army, the gold of the generous Cubans, brought by de Grasse, was on hand to subsidize farm wagons as a means of local carriage. At the same time, Washington issued a proclamation prohibiting all masters of vessels and "all persons whatsoever" from "exporting any beef, pork, bacon or grains — wheat, corn, peas, flour or meal made from same . . . by land or water," under stated penalties. The fear of useless guns remained to torment the Allied command.

A greater worry besetting them was de Grasse's approaching deadline for departure before the "decisive stroke" had been achieved. Washington asked for a conference with the French Admiral. Delighted to meet the revered Commander-in-Chief, de Grasse in a nice gesture sent a captured British ship, the *Queen Charlotte*, to convey Washington and Rochambeau down the James River to meet him aboard his flagship, the *Ville de Paris*, anchored at the foot of Cape Henry. On September 18, the two generals, together with General Knox, the American artillery commander, and their aides, climbed the ladder of the huge vessel to meet the Admiral awaiting them on deck in his blue and scarlet uniform with the broad red ribbon of the Order of St. Louis stretched across his chest. De Grasse welcomed his American visitor, almost as tall and imposing as himself, with an embrace, two kisses on his cheeks and, according to report, the enthusiastic greeting *"Mon cher petit général!"* causing Knox almost to choke in his effort to suppress an explosive laugh. Surely no one had ever addressed the Roman dignity of the American chieftain as "My dear little" anything since his mother in his infancy.

What the visitors learned from de Grasse was only semi-satisfactory. Systematic in his habits, Washington had written out his questions in advance. His French-speaking aide, Colonel Tench Tilghman, who had been educated abroad, recorded de Grasse's replies. Opening with an eloquent statement of the issue that engaged them as "big with great events and the peace & independence of his country, the general tranquility of Europe," Washington spoke of the vital importance of the French fleet remaining in place to block the river mouths until "the reduction of Lord Cornwallis' position [is] assured." He asked if the Admiral's orders named a fixed time for his departure and, if so, could he name the date; and whether he was required to return the regiments of Saint-Simon by a certain time and, if so, could he detach a portion of his fleet as their convoy while keeping his main fleet in the Bay "to form a sufficient cover to our operations, preventing the enemy from receiving supplies by water and any attempt by the British to relieve Lord Cornwallis." He also asked if de Grasse could force the passage of the upper York to control the river and its shores in the stretch above Yorktown so as "to complete the investiture of the enemy's posts," and finally, whether "your Excellency be able to lend us some heavy cannon and other artillery — powder also — and in what number & quantity of each." In the Admiral's replies, the main point was partially gained. He agreed to prolong his stay until the end of October, and since his ships would not depart before November 1, Washington "may count upon" Saint-Simon's troops "to that period for the reduction of York." As regards cannon and powder, because of the amount used in the combat against Graves, he could not spare more than "a small quantity," and he could not commit himself to control of the upper York because that depended on wind and tide, and he did not think it very useful in any case. His real reason for this negative, which he did not mention, was that he did not have enough small ships able to navigate the creeks and upper river — "crooked as a snake in motion," in the words of an American boatman. But he would stay; that was the main point, allowing time for the process of siege to take effect.

On their return, the two generals did not find the *Queen Charlotte* a lucky ship. First she was becalmed in the Bay, and then blown off course by a gale, and when at last pushing up the river, she was so slowed by winds and currents that her passengers had to transfer to rowboats and commandeer sailors to row them upstream. They did not step ashore at Williamsburg until September 22, after five days' absence. Time was racing. As they landed, it was a rare encouragement for Washington and Rochambeau to see the ships from Baltimore and even a few from Philadelphia coming in, bringing the troops from the laborious march to be reunited with the command.

As von Closen recorded it, his detachment had reached Wilmington, capital of Delaware, in a location "one of the pleasantest and most favorable on the whole continent." Here they visit the site of the Battle of Brandywine in 1777 and learn from an officer of the enthusiasm "impossible to imagine" that greeted the news in Philadelphia of de Grasse's arrival in the Chesapeake. This moment of wonderful hope is quickly blasted at Head of the Elk, "an uninteresting little place" where troops of the New Jersey, New York and Pennsylvania lines refused to march further without receiving back pay. Rochambeau dispelled the dark memory of mutiny by a gift to Washington of 50,000 livres, a third of all he had left in cash, which inspirited the troops enough to make them resume the march. Washington wrote urgently to Morris saying he needed at least a month's pay as soon as possible and that $20,000 was not nearly enough.

Coming to the Susquehanna, the marchers were obliged to make a "diabolic crossing," as von Closen recalled it, at a wide ford through "very rapid water over very large stones," and although the river was only one and a half feet deep, the horses stumble at every step but carried them across without accident. Finding no river transportation at Baltimore, they determine to "rely on the strength of our horses" and go ahead independently without waiting for boats. Here they meet trouble. Advancing without a guide, they lose their way in the woods, crash through brambles and thorns, fall over fences and ditches until torn and bruised and, lost in the dark, they come upon a house which proves to be the home of some hospitable people named Walker, who care for the horses and whose two daughters prepare a supper and offer shelter for the night. In the morning they are astonished by Mr. Walker's refusing any payment except for a few shillings for the horses' oats, all the more remarkable, von Closen wrote, "since the Americans occasionally do not scruple to bleed us as much as they can" and, when they present a bill, add a charge in addition to that for food and forage of four to six crowns *"for the trouble."*

On their way the travelers find good inns and clean beds but no such generosity as Mr. Walker's. At one place a bill was presented for $21.

On September 16 they hear with "unparalleled joy" the good news that after a successful outcome of the naval battle in Chesapeake Bay, de Grasse had remained in possession of the Bay. On the 18th they reached Williamsburg to meet joyfully with Lafayette, and on the 22nd they welcomed the return of Washington and Rochambeau from their initial visit to de Grasse on the *Ville de Paris.*

Informed of the coming of this enlarged enemy force, Cornwallis too began to weigh valor in the balance against discretion. Commanding the last effective army in America, and the last Britain was likely to be able to raise, he had to think of its preservation. To leave Yorktown before envelopment was the problem. If he could break through the blockade maintained by de Grasse with one ship of the line and two frigates at the mouth of the York, the British, using transports they had tied up at York, might on a dark night, if unseen by the Allies, sail past the enemy and across the Bay to the Virginia coast on the far side. To break up the blockade, their means would be fire ships, a nasty weapon. Empty boats filled with tarred faggots and sticks and set alight by red-hot cannonballs heated almost molten would be released in the river to be carried downstream by wind and tide. As living torches, they would set fire to and destroy the blockaders, creating such panic and confusion on the French ships as would cause their captains to cut their cables and sail away. If that was Cornwallis' hope, it seems farfetched; nevertheless, the attempt was made on the night of September 22. Four schooners were converted to fire ships and given to the command of four volunteers, one the captain of a Loyalist privateer. With the wind aiding, they were advancing down the river "with every probability of success," according to one captain's journal, when the privateer captain set his ship alight too soon. The French, at this vision of moving fire, "fired 20 or 30 shots at us" before retreating "in a precipitate and confused manner." Adding to the fire storm, the other fire ships had set themselves alight; the "whole river was now aglow" and muscular tongues of flame licked the sky. With sails and flag blazing, one boat blew up and the heat that was felt as it passed by a companion ship was so great that the pilot ran his ship aground. In the end, the only result was the loss to the British of four vessels, leaving Cornwallis no nearer to a way out.

On September 28, the clink of bridles and the rhythmic clomp of horses' hooves and tramp of marching men were heard in the British camp in Yorktown, announcing the approach of the enemy army from Williamsburg. The next night, Cornwallis astonished his army by ordering withdrawal from the outer defense line, the better to consolidate his forces for a compact defense. He believed that the expenditure in lives in a fight for the outer lines was not worth making when he was in expectation of early relief. Reasonable and compassionate, his decision was the most unfortunate he could have made. The abandoned redoubts — these were earthworks shaped like sections of a wall, built to absorb the impact of shells and to act as barriers to the assault of troops — were promptly occupied by the Allies when they found them empty in the morning, and made duck blinds for their artillery, soon to be rulers of the siege. When good fortune for once had descended in the form of de Barras' arrival from Newport with the siege guns, 1,500 barrels of salt beef and a contingent of French troops, the former British redoubts were ready-made foundations for the American batteries. Landed six miles up the James, de Barras' guns had to be tugged and dragged over streams and muddy roads at tortoise pace to position at Yorktown. Installed to the satisfaction of the engineers, they were to become, like de Grasse's ships in the Bay, "masters" of the situation.

In their new forward positions, donated by Cornwallis, the Allied generals were enabled to obtain a closer view of the terrain and the British defenses and to begin construction of their own siegeworks.

Impenitent fortune at this moment had a new blow in store for the Allies. During the generals' absence on the visit to de Grasse, a report had circulated that a British naval reinforcement under Rear Admiral Digby of the home fleet was coming to support Admiral Graves. The news made de Grasse nervous no less than Washington. It "alarmed and disquieted these excitable gentlemen of the Navy," wrote von Closen, who had carried the Digby report to de Grasse and found his reaction disquieting indeed. Trained in the French doctrine of avoiding a battle that threatened loss of ships, de Grasse had no desire to wait around to encounter the approaching Admiral Digby. Baron von Closen returned from his interview at first glance with appalling news. At the moment when the components of victory — the French fleet and the land army — had joined, fulfilling the plan for the "decisive stroke" and bringing it near enough to touch, de Grasse declared himself prepared to hoist sail and move away from his blockade of the York. In the Allies' extreme hour of high hope, the blow seemed like a grenade tossed at a wedding; after the first horrified reaction, it was made clear that de Grasse did not intend total departure nor abandonment of the blockade. In a dispatch to Washington, he explained that "the enemy are beginning to be almost equal to us, and it would be imprudent of me to put myself in a position where I could not engage them" effectively. He would leave two ships (two!) at the mouth of the York, and sail with the rest to "hold out in the offing so that if the fleet come to force the entrance [to the Bay] I can engage them in a less disadvantageous position. I shall set sail as soon as the wind permits me." Stunned by the words to "hoist sail," Washington and Rochambeau hardly noticed, or else put little reliance on, de Grasse's declared intention to "hold out in the offing" where he could still engage the enemy effectively if they attempted to enter the Bay. His proposed move still appeared as desertion. Washington wrote back a letter as frantic as his temperament ever allowed, speaking of the "painful anxiety" which he had suffered since being informed of de Grasse's intention of renouncing, as he thought, an enterprise . . . "after the most expensive preparations and uncommon exertions and fatigues" and "entreating" the Admiral to consider that "if you shd withdraw your maritime force from the position agreed upon, that no future day can restore to us a similar occasion for striking a decisive blow." He added that it could hardly be Digby's intention to "engage in a general action with a fleet whose force will be superior." Appalled by their ally's seeming desertion, Washington and Rochambeau agreed that the only man who might persuade de Grasse to reconsider was Lafayette, just recovering from the agues and fevers of a bout with malaria. Bearing Washington's letter, he was sent by frigate, still shaking from his illness, on the desperate errand to Lynnhaven Bay off Cape Henry. To his horror, he found the anchorage empty, not a mast nor a sail to be seen. The frigate-master assured him that the Admiral could not have sailed away or he would have been notified. After a twelve-hour search of the Bay, de Grasse was discovered anchored where he blocked the mouth of the York, though leaving the entrance of the Bay on the ocean side still open to British intrusion. De Grasse's own flag captains, as it proved, unhappy at the proposal to leave, which they said in a conference with the Admiral "did not appear to fulfil the aims we had in view," had refused, or showed an intention to refuse, to hoist sail. Admiral de Grasse now agreed to remain, and confirmed his change of mind in a letter to Washington and Rochambeau on September 25 in which he agreed to maintain his anchorage at the foot of Cape Henry, blocking the entrance to the Bay, and also to blockade the mouth of the York. The letter was received on September 27.

On arriving at Yorktown on September 28, Washington, after reconnoitering the position, spent his first night in the open under a spreading mulberry tree. The next morning he began the deployment of his forces for the siege. The French and their batteries were placed on the left to command the ground between the York River and the town, while the American infantry and artillery took up position on the right. Additional French batteries were mounted above the town on the same side. Lauzun's legion and the Virginia militia held an inland strip across Gloucester Point, blocking movement by the British stationed at the point's tip protruding from the York riverbanks opposite Yorktown. Cornwallis was lodged at the rear of the town, while Washington's and Rochambeau's respective headquarters faced the town directly. In front of their headquarters two parallels, or trenches to receive the besiegers, were to be dug 200 and 300 yards apart. Cornwallis' only reaction until now had been entirely defensive. After learning of the Allied approach to Virginia and knowing the outcome of the Battle of the Bay, he set about industriously fortifying his perimeter by the construction of redoubts.

During September, engineers drove the work force — including several thousand Negro slaves who had deserted to the British in the hope of gaining their freedom — in constant hard labor on the redoubts.

On September 30, the Allies felt that Yorktown was "completely invested" and that the two main objects of a siege — to prevent the defenders from receiving aid or from making their escape — had been accomplished. No passage was left open except upriver leading into the heart of the country, and Cornwallis was not expected to attempt escape by that path. Yet a lurking fear remained that he just might try, in the hope of leading his army in a *sortie* or breakout through the besieging lines, to make his way in a raid through the farming country of Maryland and Pennsylvania back to Britain's base in New York. Washington continued to worry about this stretch of the upper river, which he had tried and failed to persuade de Grasse to occupy with his warships. That escape by Cornwallis would vitiate the whole campaign which Washington had brought to this stage, was a gnawing anxiety, and exerted on him a compelling pressure to let loose a barrage of all the firepower he could throw. Because he knew that until he could employ really heavy artillery to be followed by a well-prepared assault by troops, anything less might fail, he restrained his fierce desire.

On the day de Grasse entered Chesapeake Bay to complete the envelopment of Cornwallis, William Smith, Clinton's intelligence officer in New York, asserted, "A week will decide perhaps the ruin or salvation of the British Empire." Within that week, the Battle of the Capes indeed brought a decision — neither ruin nor salvation, but room for the power that would ultimately take Britain's place in world affairs. Clinton did not have Smith's prophetic bones. "You have little to apprehend from the French," he had assured Cornwallis in his letter of September 2. Despite the information he had by now received, he could not conceive of losing control of Chesapeake Bay to the French. He, no more than anyone, had expected de Grasse to strip the Antilles and his convoy duties for the sake of America. In fact, the battle did not arouse much concern or convey its significance until Graves himself wrote, a few days later, the terrible words that no British ear ever expected to hear about a sea area under British sovereignty: "The enemy have so great a naval force in the Chesapeake that they are absolute masters of its navigation." All the dooms predicted by the Whigs could be contained in the two words "absolute masters," and even if they did not go beyond Clinton's desk, the sense they carried may explain why the energy went out of the mission to save Cornwallis.

Much of it had already faded. On September 13, the day before Graves's grim letter was received, another Council of War of general officers in New York was summoned. In frustration at the failure to launch a rescue, Councils were being held every few days. William Smith privately thought the staff officers "servile . . . not a man of business or enterprise among them." At the Council on September 13, a forceful plea for action was made by Major General James Robertson, military governor of New York, who was considered an administrative officer rather than a man of war. He was a sport among the servile insofar as he took seriously the subject they were met to consider. For the sake of making haste and for the greater chance of bringing the relief force through the enemy lines, he proposed that the expedition sail without transports, but instead that all the 5,000 men be crammed aboard the *Robust,* the only ship of the line available in New York.

Thoroughly shocked at the thought of a procedure so unorthodox and even dangerous, Clinton and the Council vetoed the idea. Robertson nevertheless put it in writing for the next day. Inaction leading to the loss of Cornwallis, he claimed, could bring down the whole cause in America. The reinforcements, if brought to bear, would enable Cornwallis to attack the enemy with his whole force. Dangers were probabilities, whereas doing nothing was certain death.

He did not carry the day. Instead, Clinton convened another Council, on September 14, at which the letter from Graves was read, and put to it a leading question with the answer built-in: whether the relief should be hazarded during "our present naval inferiority," or, given that the enemy has mastery of the

Chesapeake and that officers recently returned from Yorktown when questioned have asserted that Cornwallis could hold out until the end of October and could feed 10,000 on full allowance for that time — indeed, it was their opinion he could defend the post "against twenty thousand assailants," Clinton claimed — whether it would be better to wait until receipt of "more favourable accounts" from Admiral Graves or until he had made a junction with Admiral Digby. The Council, taking its indicated cue, declared in favor of waiting.

Cornwallis' own spirit had gone slack. For an interval of ten days after the Battle of the Bay, when he knew that its outcome had left the French in control of the seacoast with the resulting odds against his own rescue, he made no move to prepare to escape from the pocket he was in before the Washington-Rochambeau troops arrived to close his back door. When the Bay was known to be lost, this was the time when he might still have fought his way out by land — if not all the way to New York, at least through Maryland to the mouth of the Delaware. Unless he could count on Clinton's promise of relief as a sure thing, the risk of a march through semi-hostile country, with Tarleton to cut a path, was less than the certain disaster to come if he were enclosed. From September 6, when Washington's army had passed through Chester and Head of the Elk, unless intelligence was nil, Cornwallis must have known they were coming. On what day he learned of their advance we do not know, but it was doubtless at about the same time he learned of the naval outcome which elicited Admiral Graves's dismaying report on September 9 that the French were "absolute masters of navigation" in the Chesapeake. Recognizing the prospect of siege, Cornwallis wrote Clinton as Commander-in-Chief on September 16–17, "If you cannot relieve me very soon, you must be prepared to hear the worst." The "worst" was left ambiguous. If the "worst" meant defeat or surrender, it must be inferred that Cornwallis, without a ready source of provisions, had no intention of fighting his way out by land. When that letter was received in New York, on September 23, a War Council was summoned the next day to consider this sudden drawing of the curtain and its purport.

Clinton, to whom ambiguity was second nature, took the worst to mean retreat, which would have relieved his soul, for it would have lifted from him the burden of having to risk breaking through the de Grasse barrier to bring relief to York. As he was to acknowledge in his revealing postwar apologia, he "would not have been greatly displeased to have heard that Lord Cornwallis had made his escape to Carolina with everything he could take with him." Why, as Commander-in-Chief, he did not at this point order Cornwallis to make his escape was a failure which Cornwallis was later to cite as his excuse for not doing so.

Graves was no more eager to head back to the Chesapeake to challenge de Grasse again. With several of his ships crippled by the engagement in the Bay, he arrived in New York for repairs on September 24, nineteen days after the battle, five days having been consumed in maneuvering across the bar at Sandy Hook. Now it was up to him to put his fleet in shape to confront de Grasse or somehow to slip past him with relief forces for Cornwallis in York. Yet in New York, where ten ships were discovered in need of repair, he obdurately refused to move unless every one of his ships was fully repaired from hull to rigging, every damaged mast replaced and every vessel in seaworthy condition to join the squadron. At first he had appeared full of spirit and pugnacity, informing Clinton that everything would be done to restore his ships as rapidly as possible and that he was prepared to break through the French barrier to land troops at the mouth of the York. He proposed a scheme whereby de Grasse, being located in an area of strong tides, would find it difficult to maneuver to fire his broadsides, whereas he himself could take advantage of the tide to slip by under cover of darkness to anchor in the York River and disembark there. This castle in the air was to remain a phantom. On the basis of reports from the dockyards, Graves said he would be ready to sail by October 5, twelve days hence. This was the first of many creeping deadlines which came and went with no departure. For three weeks troops and crew had been embarked on motionless ships. The delays and postponements gave rise to impatient and puzzled muttering. Generals had not come to join their contingents, nor admirals their ships. Their absence elicited from an astute observer, Captain Frederick MacKenzie of the Adjutant General's office, a remark that could stand for the whole conduct of the American war: "Our generals and admirals don't seem to be in earnest about this business."

Here was the problem as an empire slid from under their feet: the problem of making do with faulty processes and broken parts, of misunderstood signals, of the useless rigidity of *Fighting Instructions*, of a scurvy-producing diet, of political quarrel among combat

557

officers, of employing worn-out and withered naval commanders, of putting the protection of trade ahead of strategic operations, of poor and too often false intelligence of enemy movements and intentions and, embracing all these, the problem of not knowing or caring to know the nature of the enemy and undertaking to suppress a major rebellion on the assumption that the rebels could be described, in the words of Lord Rawdon, a respected British officer, as "infatuated wretches."

When, at the end of their long march, the last of the Allied army tramped into Williamsburg on September 26, everything for Cornwallis now depended on how soon Clinton would expedite the relief he had so firmly promised. The mood in New York had not been vibrating with urgency, except with regard to the expected arrival of a naval addition coming under Admiral Digby. "Digby, Digby!" was the cry circulating in the army among officers who would have to go with a relief force. As it was known from a message brought by frigate that Digby was coming with a total of three ships, he could not be thought likely to perform a marvel, but it was believed he would add to the Hood-Graves complement of nineteen just enough to give superiority over de Grasse. The vision of two or three extra ships immediately caused the gleam of victory to shine anew. "Should our fleet beat theirs," wrote Captain MacKenzie, "we have a fair prospect of ending the rebellion."

With his three ships, Digby duly arrived on September 24, bringing one element to brighten the situation in the person of Prince William Henry, the King's son and future successor as King William IV. Under some happy ministerial illusion, he had been chosen, according to a rumor picked up in Rochambeau's camp, to visit America with the intention that he would eventually take office as Governor of "opulent and prosperous" Virginia. A 21-gun salute boomed rather emptily in greeting. How many people it made unhappily conscious that the guns were booming here but not at York, we cannot know. The visit of the Prince showed that New York still had energy, if not to galvanize a relief mission, at least to entertain royalty. Lethargy vanished in a burst of parties, receptions and parades for the visiting Prince. Tours of the city and reviews of German and English regiments, dinners with distinguished citizens and an evening concert by a military band, with General Clinton in attendance, took minds off anxiety about Cornwallis while evoking a nice show of loyalty to the Crown.

While the bands played in New York, Cornwallis watched the horizon in vain for masts to appear. A dispatch from Yorktown told how he was "in daily expectation of the appearance of the British fleet to relieve him, and without them has no great hopes of withstanding the great force collected against him." War Councils summoned by Clinton in New York conferred futilely, unable to decide what to do.

Cornwallis waited while the guns pounded for the promised reinforcements, but no sail appeared. While in New York the navy hesitated and councils vacillated, the painful procrastination of the relief force rose from fear of risking the navy, Britain's wooden walls and defender of empire around the world. In Graves's spiritless hands after the Battle of the Bay, the navy lost its function like a candle without a flame. While the navy remained static for six empty weeks waiting for the wind and for courage, down on the blue estuary where the York flows into the Chesapeake an empire disappeared.

Councils followed each other like the fall of autumn leaves. At these meetings, participants agreed that the relief expedition must be hazarded and would probably get through, but they questioned how, having lost surprise, would it come safely out? Without a clear answer, the Council agreed again on the oft-repeated sailing date of October 5, of which Cornwallis should be informed. Clinton's letter to this effect was what decided Cornwallis, in anticipation of the relief, to withdraw on September 29 from his front lines for a consolidation of his forces. Because repairs at the New York dockyards were not complete, Graves's intended sailing date of October 5 was not met. Departure dates for October 8 and 12 likewise went by, with no ships hoisting sail.

By now the New York chiefs well knew that Cornwallis' situation was precarious and delay was dangerous. Worried by Graves's procrastination, William Smith put it to Governor Tryon of New York: "Every hour is precious to Lord Cornwallis." One ship, the *Montague*, as noted by Captain MacKenzie, still lacked a mast and if all were ready to sail by October 10, it would take three days to get over the bar and seven before effective help could reach Cornwallis. Captain MacKenzie, in his journal, begins to doubt that the fleet will ever depart, and he wishes some other action could be undertaken elsewhere to "counterbalance our losses." He slips in an interesting admission when he wonders if such action might make "the enemy's thirst for peace be equal to our own." Graves now says they cannot sail until October 12, while the captains talk of not being ready for ten days. "If they cannot," notes MacKenzie, "they may as well stay for ten months." Clinton, reporting the Council meeting to Cornwallis, writes that barring an "unforeseen accident" we should pass the bar by October 12," but Yorktown is clearly not primary with him, for he comes back to a favorite project of his, if he could not come in time, "I will immediately make an attempt upon Philadelphia" to draw off "part of Washington's force from you." That was feeble comfort to a man under the daily pounding of 16-inch mortars. Another sailing date was missed when a storm broke on October 13, crushing one of Graves's ships against another and causing a smashed bowsprit. The paralysis had become pervasive.

At Yorktown during the night of October 6, workmen began digging the first Allied parallel facing the enemy. Stretching from the American quarters to the French, the Allied forces were supported by four redoubts, two in each camp, and a battery of guns aimed to "sweep with fire" enemy vessels coming up the river. The defenders' fire on the work party was desultory, causing two minor casualties.

On October 9, the first American guns at Yorktown opened fire on the British defense works. For the past three days, engineers had been directing artillerymen in the construction of the batteries while night workmen were employed in digging the parallels. Work continued during the day by men from Saint-Simon's troops, who constructed zigzag communicating trenches to the batteries and built *abatis* to fortify them. These were palisades of sharpened stakes pounded into the earth, with points up, to prevent attackers from climbing over the parapets. Casualties during the work were slight: one killed and seven wounded, but the toll increased, of officers as well as workmen, as the labor continued.

According to custom, the ceremonial opening of the first parallel of a siege called for troops to occupy the trench, flying flags with fife and drums. The honor was given to a detachment under Colonel Alexander Hamilton, whose appetite for public notice led him to order a useless and wanton display of his troop performing the *Manual of Arms* on the parapet. So astonished was the enemy by this act of bravado that they thought either it had some ulterior and menacing motive or that the Colonel was mad — and did not fire, sparing Hamilton a deserved lesson. Fifty guns from the Allied lines were now firing. Most were Saint-Simon's, which de Grasse's ships had brought down from Baltimore; the others were fieldpieces pulled by manpower down from White Plains under command of General Knox. When urged to wait until he could send them by ship, Washington, remembering how Knox's guns dragged overland from Ticonderoga had delivered Boston, insisted that they accompany the march. The difficulty of bringing them over rutted roads and unbridged streams slowed the pace, increasing the anxiety that Cornwallis might escape or so strengthen his defenses as to make them impassable. The guns were in place before he did either.

Europeans, from repeated practice, had developed a science and a formal ritual of siege warfare of which Americans on their wide-open continent and in their wooden cities were ignorant. They were soon instructed, in the guttural accents and cheerful profanity of their drillmaster and military teacher, Baron von Steuben, the authenticity of whose title — or lack of it — bore no relation to the affection in which he was held. All day convalescents and workers off duty from the regiments fashioned mysterious artifacts called *gabions* and *fascines* — earth-filled wicker baskets and bundles of dry sticks used to thicken the earthworks. Trees chopped down throughout the town to clear the field of fire supplied the material. By this time the response of British guns was diminishing, for Cornwallis, recognizing that he was under a real siege, had ordered the conserving of ammunition.

After Cornwallis sustained the opening barrage of gunfire from the Allied batteries in the first parallel, he informed Clinton on October 11 that "nothing but a direct move to York River which includes a successful naval action can save me." The cannonading that began on October 11 delivered by 16-inch mortars was so "horrendous," as described by Lieutenant Bartholomew James of the Royal Navy, another diarist, "that it seemed as though the heavens should split." The noise and thundering of the bombardment grew "almost unendurable." Lieutenant James saw "men lying nearly everywhere who were mortally wounded, whose heads, arms and legs had been shot off. The distressing cries of the wounded and the lamentable suffering of the inhabitants whose dwellings were chiefly in flames" intensified the carnage.

As the ring of siege drew closer, a last sharp thrust showing no sign of paralysis took place on October 3 on the Gloucester side, engaging the two bellicose cavalry leaders, Tarleton and the Duc de Lauzun. To blockade Gloucester as a possible land exit for Cornwallis, Washington had placed there a unit of 1,500 Virginia militia, who usually ran when confronted by the dragoons, plus Lauzun's legion of 600 as well as 800 armed marines. In

British command of the Gloucester camp, Tarleton had led his Cavalry Legion out for foraging and was returning with wagons loaded with Indian corn when he was met in a narrow lane by Lauzun's legion armed with lances. When a horse wounded by a lance thrust collided with Tarleton's, he was thrown; his dragoons scrambled to his rescue, enabling him to seize another horse to remount and escape under the protective rifle fire of his infantry. Outnumbered, they were ordered by Tarleton to retreat, while Lauzun's men charged in pursuit, protected in their turn by the steady fire of the Virginia militia. Tarleton's dragoons made good their retreat into Gloucester, which was thereafter invested by the French commander, the Marquis de Choisy. The clash of the two heroes terminated without changing the fortunes of the war except for a new respect for the firm stand of the Virginia militia.

During the night of October 11–12, the Allies moved closer to start work on a second parallel, 300 yards from the Hornwork, largest of the British redoubts and central piece of the defenses. The new parallel was within assault distance of the two most obstructive British redoubts, numbers Nine and Ten. Until these were eliminated, it was clear that, under the fire of their batteries, the parallels could make no further advance; a major assault upon the two redoubts was necessary. It was ordered for October 14, to be carried out by bayonet attack. In expectation of hand-to-hand combat, tremendous tension rose as the companies were selected and orders given. Tension was heightened when Washington addressed to the soldiers a brief speech of exhortation, which was not usual for him. He said that success depended on both redoubts being taken, for if the British recaptured either, they could add to it extra strength of men and guns, making impossible any further advance of the Allies' parallels and delaying the siege, with the attendant danger of giving time for British naval relief. Brought to a peak of fervor, French and Americans under the overall command of Lafayette plunged into battle. The French of the Royal Deux-Ponts had a fiercer fight in storming number Nine than the Americans of the Rhode Island Light Infantry, under Hamilton and Captain Stephen Olney, at number Ten, because the *abatis* at Nine had not been as thoroughly smashed by the siege guns as those at Ten. Bayonet thrusts and musket volleys at arm's length dealt death and wounds as the attackers were thrown back in their desperate climb over the stakes. So fierce was their assault that Lieutenant James thought the enemy had "stormed from right to left with 17,000 men." Under strong impressions, the veracity of eyewitness diaries is sometimes reduced. With losses of 15 French and 9 Americans killed, both the redoubts were taken by 10 p.m. To the surprise of the attackers, who expected a last-ditch defense, they found 73 prisoners in their hands, among them the commander of number Nine, a Major McPherson, who was said by his captors to have retreated from his post with thirty men when the firing began, virtually yielding the redoubt. Whether this was a sign of defeatism in Cornwallis' army or the tragic failing of one individual can never be known. As soon as the redoubts were taken, men of the Pennsylvania line who had been held in reserve dropped their guns to take up picks and shovels and go back to digging the second parallel further forward. Under a British battery still firing, the cost in the French sector was 136 wounded.

Capture of Redoubts Nine and Ten as posts for Allied artillery gave Washington command of the enemy's communication to Gloucester, the remaining possible point of exit. Cornwallis thought the same, for after this loss, in his own mind he gave up. He addressed to Clinton an extraordinary letter. Coming from a general commanding a vital position at a critical moment in a war of great import for his country and, whether or not he realized it, for history, it may be unique in military annals. Honest, and without evasion, taking no refuge in ambiguity, he wrote, "My situation now becomes very critical. We dare not shew a gun to their old batteries and I expect that their new ones will open to-morrow morning; experience has shewn that our fresh earthen works do not resist their powerful artillery, so that we shall soon be exposed to an assault, in ruined works, in a bad position and with weakened numbers. The safety of the place is therefore so precarious that I cannot recommend that the fleet and army should run great risque in endeavouring to save us." He looks finality in the eye, lays no blame, makes no excuses.

Yet he was too much of a soldier just to sit there and die. Custom in sieges required at least one effort to break out before yielding. Within 24 hours of the loss of Redoubts Nine and Ten, Cornwallis ordered 350 picked men to assault the Allies' second parallel, with the object of spiking their guns by jamming bayonets down their barrels. Just before dawn of October 16, in the quietest hour of the night, he launched an attack that succeeded in silencing seven cannon but in the process excited a sharp counterattack by the French grenadiers under the Vicomte de Noailles and the Allied engineers. In a parental fury to protect their cubs, they drove the enemy out and, while bullets whizzed over their heads, removed the spikes. By daybreak their batteries were again in action.

With Yorktown shaking under Allied fire, his casualties mounting and men falling sick with fever, Cornwallis decided upon a last effort to escape Yorktown. For the night of October 16, he planned to ferry his army in three trips across the York River to the Gloucester side, either to meet the relief ships at sea that Clinton had said were coming or, if he had to, somehow to make his way north by land. The night of the 16th was protectively black as the operation began. It was not Allied guns that aborted it. No spy or deserter or renegade Loyalist had alerted Washington. Nature, so often a careless arbiter of the addled affairs of men, did the job. A heavy storm at midnight and a cloudburst of pelting rain soaked the men in flight to a shivering chill and tossed their boats in confusion against the rocky shore, making a landing impossible. Before morning light, most returned to their starting point under the rifle fire of the now alerted Allies. A goodly number were blown by the storm out into the Bay.

At daylight on October 17, Allied batteries

on the captured redoubts opened a thunderous bombardment on British positions, knocking out British batteries still able to fire. With the hope of escape terminated, capitulation was the only course open to a Council of War convened by Cornwallis in the Hornwork.

At ten o'clock on the morning of October 17, a faint tattoo of drums, barely making itself heard over the pounding of the guns, was located coming from a small red-coated drummer boy standing on the parapet of the Hornwork. The taller figure of an officer waving a handkerchief in lieu of a white flag emerged from the Hornwork and walked toward the American lines with the drummer boy alongside, still furiously beating his drum. Upon this apparition, now both audible and visible, Allied guns ceased their fire. The silence that fell over the shattered town was a more eloquent sound than any heard in the last six and a half years. Its significance could hardly be believed. Still holding his white handkerchief, the British officer was escorted to American quarters, and the note he carried from Cornwallis was delivered at a run to Washington's tent. The note read:

Sir,
  I propose a cessation of hostilities for twenty four hours and that two officers

may be appointed by each side to meet at Mr. Moore's house to settle terms for the surrender of the posts at York and Gloucester.

I have the honour to be, &c:

Cornwallis

What were Washington's feelings when he read the word "surrender" and when he wrote his reply no diary tells. After years of privations and disappointments and bloodstained footprints in the snow of the men for whom he could not obtain decent footwear, to have now brought the war to this consummation and have the enemy give in could only have stirred profound emotion. Too deep for tears, or words, it was not confided to any person or page. In reply to the notice of surrender, he wrote, "An ardent desire to spare the further effusion of blood will readily incline me to listen to such terms for the surrender of your posts and garrisons of York and Gloucester as are admissible." He added that Cornwallis' proposed terms should be sent in writing to the American lines prior to the meeting of the Commissioners. The word "cessation" of hostilities during the time allowed was changed in the American reply to "suspension," at the suggestion of John Laurens, recently returned from France and acting as adviser to

Rochambeau and Washington. Still concerned about leaving too much time open for rescue by sea, Washington allowed a time limit of two hours instead of 24.

Cornwallis' feelings when he surrendered to rebels and contemptible foes, as he thought them, were equally unrecorded. The need to justify himself is uppermost in an interesting letter he wrote to Clinton on that day. Now that the fight was over, he began to find excuses and suggest blame. As might be expected, he laid the blame politely but unmistakably in Clinton's lap. At the same time, he seems conscious that his own passivity needed explanation.

> Sir,
> I have the mortification to inform Your Excellency that I have been forced to give up the posts of York and Gloucester and to surrender the troops under my command by capitulation on the 19th inst. as prisoners of war to the combined forces of America and France.

He goes on to say that he *"never saw this post in a favourable light,"* and when he found he was to be attacked in it by powerful forces — "nothing but the hopes of relief would have induced me to attempt its defence; for I would either have endeavored to escape to New York by rapid marches from the Gloucester side immediately on the arrival of General Washington's troops at Williamsburg [the opponent appears as "General" here for the first time] or I would have attacked them in the open field, but [here comes the knife] *being assured by Your Excellency's letters that every possible means would be tried by the navy and army to relieve us* I could not think myself at liberty to venture on either of those desperate attempts. . . ." Why not? Desperate attempts when the worst is in prospect is a general's business. Cornwallis was a man who could have thrust his hand in a flame if necessary, but not a man to organize the logistics and arrangements of a large campaign with a likely risk of failure. The smooth face in the Gainsborough portrait with no lines of thought or of frowns or of laughter — with no lines at all — tells as much. It is a face composed by a life of comfort and satisfaction without any need of desperate attempts.

As we know, Cornwallis took neither of the two courses he mentions to Clinton. He did nothing at the time of the Allied army's arrival at Williamsburg on September 26, except three days later to order withdrawal from his front lines to the inner defenses of Yorktown, nor did he make any effort to escape by way of

Gloucester until too late, and he certainly did not give any sign of contemplating an attack on them "in the open field."

The clue to Cornwallis, one might suppose, was his initial opinion that forceful coercion of the Americans was a mistake because it could not succeed. Other men of the army and navy who shared his opinion refused to fight for the mistake. Cornwallis did not refuse; on the contrary, he volunteered, supposedly from a sense of duty while holding the King's commission. It may be that his ambivalence about the war, from the beginning, lurked in his mind to become the reason for his halfhearted fight. His conduct during the last month is not easily understandable. Like Hamlet, he could say to us, the heart is not to be plucked from my mystery.

Perforce accepting the shortened truce, Cornwallis was able to deliver his proposals within the two hours allowed. His stipulations were more concerned with procedure and protocol than with military conditions, and, as such, they generated hours of controversy between the two parties when they met.

The parley Commissioners were John Laurens and the Vicomte de Noailles, Lafayette's brother-in-law, representing the Allies, and on the other side two aides, Lieutenant Colonel Thomas Dundas and Major Alexander Ross, for Cornwallis.

Cornwallis' conditions proved inadmissible. He asked for the honors of war to be granted to his garrison in the ceremony of surrender. Among these were the right to attend the ceremony with flags flying and the right to march to music of their choice. For some Byzantine reason of European custom, the right of the capitulators to play the national airs or anthems of the victor was considered to imply that they had put up a good fight. Washington did not think so. In his judgment, in a letter to Governor Sim Lee of Maryland, Cornwallis' conduct "has hitherto been passive beyond conception." In Washington's creed, danger was created to be overcome. Moreover, at the surrender of Charleston, eighteen months before, the British had allowed no honors of war to the defenders and required them to appear with flags cased — that is, furled. Laurens, who had taken part in that occasion, was adamant in refusing to allow the British the honor of marching to the music of their choice with regimental flags flying. When told by Major Ross that this was a "harsh article," Laurens reminded the Major that after a gallant defense of six weeks in open trenches at Charleston, the same had been refused by the British there. Ross replied that "Lord Cornwallis did not command at Charleston," and was firmly told by Laurens, "It is not the individual that is here considered. It is the nation. This remains an article or I cease to be a commissioner." Next, the British wanted honors for the garrison of Gloucester, while Laurens insisted it should be treated as one with the rest. A compromise was finally found, allowing the cavalry to ride with drawn swords and sounding trumpets while the infantry must keep its colors cased.

To plunge into passionate dispute over the trivialities of so-called honor is a queer but not uncommon gambit of men who have just come from putting their lives at stake in serious combat. These were men who had been fighting for empire in one case and for national independence in the other. Did they think they were altering the verdict of the battlefield?

A more substantive issue next arose in the British demand that British and German troops as prisoners be returned to their countries of origin under parole not to re-engage. The same provision granted at Burgoyne's surrender had permitted the prisoners to fill the places of other troops at home, who could then be sent to America. This time it was disallowed. The most obstinate issue concerned treatment of the Loyalists who had fought for

Britain and whose protection Laurens said he had no power to grant and which he was sure Washington would not permit. While the army waiting outside the parley stirred in restlessness at the delay, the arguments dragged on, until the terms were finally concluded at midnight.

When copied and delivered to Washington, he promised to reply to the modifications early in the morning, with another two hours granted for Cornwallis' signature, expected at 11 a.m., to be followed by surrender of the garrison at two o'clock, failing which, hostilities would resume. The signed papers were duly delivered in the given time. Promptly at 2 p.m. on October 19, 1781, the first steps took place in the ceremony so often described, inaugurating the existence of a new nation.

Lined up on one side of the road to Williamsburg were ten French regiments in their white uniforms, with white silk flags bearing the royal *fleur-de-lis* in gold. On the other side stood the Americans, with the Continentals drawn up in front and the less disciplined and shabbier militia, some with toes poking through broken boots, behind. The British, with polished black boots and gaiters whitened, and wearing fresh uniforms issued by their commissary so that they should not be included in the surrender of property, marched out between the lines with colors tightly cased, no flags flying to wave them along. As required, they marched to the music of their own nation — according to one of history's most memorable invented legends, a ballad, as everyone supposes, called "The World Turned Upside Down." In fact, no such song or melody by that name existed.*

In the surrender march, the Germans, stiff and correct, followed soberly in step, but the British, having emptied their last stores of rum and brandy, "appeared much in liquor" and exhibited *morgue* (bitterness) and insolence and, above everything else . . . "contempt for the Americans," as remarked by the French Quartermaster, Claude Blanchard. Contempt of the defeated for the victor, seemingly a perverse response, is a loser's sentiment — denying admission of its own fault or failure and believing itself robbed of victory by some malign mischance, as in sports when a gust of wind might divert the throw of a ball, giving victory to the opponent. The British kept their eyes on the French, refusing to look at their late subjects, until Lafayette called for the playing of "Yankee Doodle," which brought all British heads around in a

*See reference at the end of this chapter.

579

single turn toward the Americans.

The ceremony of surrender was too much for the soldierly heroism of Lord Cornwallis, who on the grounds of illness did not attend, sending his second in command, Brigadier General Charles O'Hara, to act for him. Admiral de Grasse, too, though an author of the victory, was kept absent by an attack of asthma and was represented by Admiral de Barras.

Washington, statuesque on horseback in his familiar buff and blue, was stationed at the head of the American line. When O'Hara approached as Cornwallis' deputy, he advanced toward Rochambeau, evidently intending to surrender his sword to the French rather than the Americans. Rochambeau with a smile shook his head and pointed to General Washington across the road. Washington, not willing as Commander-in-Chief to complete the ritual with the British second in command, pointed to his own deputy, General Lincoln, who had been the American commander at the surrender of Charleston. Whether Lincoln accepted the sword from O'Hara for Washington has been a disputed point. He did indicate to O'Hara the spot in the field called the Pigeon Quarter where the British should lay down their arms. Inebriated or not, the redcoats slammed the guns down with spiteful vigor in the hope of breaking the locks, until O'Hara, watching, ordered them to stop this petty revenge.

Taking place at a seaport of the Bay where a British Admiral had declared the French to be "absolute masters of its navigation," the surrender at Yorktown marked an overturn of naval sovereignty that added gall to the occasion. Within a year Rodney would prove the overturn ephemeral, but at Yorktown it had marked a further fall for the British.

On October 17, the day when Cornwallis, heralded by his little drummer boy, asked for terms, his would-be rescuers in New York, Graves and Clinton, setting a record for belated action in military history, finally fixed a time to leave on the mission that had been waiting ever since Clinton had acknowledged on September 2 that Cornwallis would have to be "saved." An army of 7,000 was boarded, sails were hoisted, Graves's fleet with Clinton on board moved slowly down the Hudson. They crossed the Hook on October 19, on the same day when, in Yorktown, Washington and Cornwallis signed and accepted the terms of surrender. Five days later, October 24, they were off Cape Charles without encountering the feared interference from de Grasse, who had no reason to risk battle for a cause already won. While small craft scuttled through the bay seeking news, a boat came out from the York to tell the tale. Time had not waited; the door was closed. All the expense and armed force exerted for nearly six years had gone for nothing. No victory, no glory, no restored rulership. As a war, it was the historic rebuke to complacency.

The two masters of lethargy, Admiral and General, with their 35 ships and 7,000 men turned around and sailed back uselessly to New York.

Officially the war was not over, nor American sovereignty recognized, nor would it be until the long-drawn-out process of negotiating a peace treaty, which was to last two years, was concluded in 1783. No shots heard round the world were fired to announce the surrender. The event spoke for itself, verifying the independent statehood of America saluted nearly six years before by the guns of St. Eustatius. At that time, American independence was not a fact but only a new-born Declaration. When de Graaff's guns spoke, hardly six months had passed since, as the second President, John Adams, was to say, "The greatest question was decided which ever was debated in America, and a greater never was or will be decided among men." The purport of those words hung over the capitulation at Yorktown, notifying the Old World that the hour of change to a democratic age had come.

*The words occur in one of many versions sung to the popular tune "Derry Down." Best known of these was the ballad "The King Enjoys His Own Again," an old Jacobite serenade to Bonnie Prince Charlie, anything but appropriate to this occasion. Another version, entitled "The Old Woman Taught Wisdom" or "When the World Turned Upside Down," contained these lines of notably uninspired poetry:

> If buttercups buzz'd after the bee
> If boats were on land, churches on sea
> If ponies rode men and if grass ate the cows
> And cats should be chased into holes by the mouse
> If the mamas sold their babies
> To the Gypsies for half a crown
> If summer were spring
> And the other way 'round
> Then all the world would be upside down!

That statement that "The World Turned Upside Down" was the tune played by the capitulators has been traced to John Laurens, who is supposed to have told it to William Jackson, his close associate during Laurens' trip to France and also the recorder of Laurens' conference on surrender terms with Cornwallis' aides. Jackson, later assistant to a Secretary of War, is said to have communicated what Laurens told him to Alexander Garden, author of *Anecdotes of the American Revolution*, published in Charleston in 1828. It has been suggested that what Laurens said was something to the effect that the capitulators marched in a slow and dispirited manner, as if they felt the "world had been turned upside down," and that Jackson presumed he was referring to the ballad containing those words. Variants as to date and origin of the ballad, as to whether it was or was not a marching tune — e.g., "The rhythm in 6/8 time is

583

not adapted to marching" (Frank Luther, *Americans and Their Songs*), and, alternatively, "The music makes an excellent march" (Kenneth Roberts, *Northwest Passage*) — have led students through a maze of contradictory references, leaving us with only one certainty: that the tune played by the capitulators at Yorktown, like what song the sirens sang, is historically obscure.

THE WORLD TURNED UPSIDE DOWN

TUNE: Another version of "Derry Down"

Library of Congress — Music Division

The tune "Derry Down," more plaintive than jaunty, is not particularly suitable for marching, but on the way to surrender jauntiness might not be wanted.

Epilogue

News of the great event was carried northward by Tench Tilghman, Washington's aide, who galloped from Yorktown to Philadelphia, spreading word of the surrender through village and farm like Paul Revere in reverse. The ride took four days, bringing him into Philadelphia at 2:30 in the morning of October 24. Pounding through the silent streets with clatter of hoofbeats that sounded to frightened residents like the noise of an invasion, he rode up to the house of Thomas McKean, President of the Congress, and banged loudly on the door. Seized by the night watch, he was saved from arrest by McKean, who, aroused from bed by the turmoil below, came down to vouch for his visitor. In the darkness Tilghman told his marvelous news to a gratifying response. McKean ordered bells to peal from the belfry of Independence Hall. The night watchman, a German-speaking veteran, carrying his lantern, started at once on his rounds, crying, "Basht dree o'glock und Gornvallis ist gedaken!" Windows flew open, excited residents thrust forth their heads to hear the words, then rushed into the streets to share the news and embrace each other; artillery salutes boomed; fireworks blazed, the city was illuminated; thanksgiving services were held in the churches; newspapers published extras; prominent citizens made speeches and gave balls; in distant Newburgh, New York, the populace enthusiastically burned Benedict Arnold in effigy.

The bells that pealed from Independence Hall spoke for more than military victory. They rang for the promise of a new world, for redemption from tyranny and oppression, for the hopes and dreams of America held not only by Americans who fought for the Revolution, but also by the French who had volunteered to share in the fight, by Dutch dissenters, by the Opposition Whigs in England, by spirits everywhere nurtured in the Age of Enlightenment and imbued by its optimism for the perfectibility of man. The triumph of the Revolution signaled the start of progress toward the guarantee of liberty offered by the American Declaration of Independence. It was for this, the "meliorating influence on all mankind," as Washington said in his Last Circular to the States of 1783, that bonfires burned and citizens embraced

— for the great hope that was America. It was for this that Lafayette carried home with him a quantity of American soil sufficient for a grave, and was buried in it when he died in 1834.

After disposal of the prisoners of Yorktown in guarded camps and garrisons, Washington wanted to carry the crest of victory forward to a combined attack on Wilmington and Charleston, but the departure of the French fleet made that impossible. Under orders to return to the West Indies by early November, de Grasse sailed for the Caribbean on November 4 with a mission to attack and take whatever British islands whose defense might be weakened after the hurricanes. On the general assumption that Jamaica, Britain's richest island, was his objective, the Admiralty called on Rodney, who, though barely out of surgery, could be counted on to make a determined fight for the defense of the island. Other candidates for naval command inspired no great confidence. One, Admiral Kempenfelt, who had been sent to intercept the French fleet, had avoided a fight on the ground that he had twelve ships of the line to the enemy's nineteen. The French grasp fell first on St. Eustatius, which Rodney thought he had left impregnable, but it was not proof against trickery. When the French landed an

English-speaking regiment of de Bouillé's troops wearing British red coats "exactly like the English with red jackets and yellow lapels," who were composed partly of native Englishmen and partly of Irishmen in French pay as soldiers of fortune, the defense was thrown into hopeless confusion. The golden rock was retaken in November, 1781, administering another wound to British pride so soon after the fall of Yorktown. In 1784 the French restored Dutch sovereignty, whose flag has flown over the rock of remembered renown until the present. Johannes de Graaff returned to the scene of his former governorship as a private citizen in 1779. St. Eustatius had not been razed to a "desert," as Rodney had wrathfully threatened, but was busily engaged in its normal occupation, the accumulation of wealth. De Graaff's property and influence enabled him to pursue the accumulation successfully. He lived on for thirty-five years and died a very rich man in 1813.

After the loss of St. Eustatius, two minor properties of the Leewards followed into the French bag while de Grasse, in partnership with the troops of the aggressive Marquis de Bouillé, moved on to capture St. Kitts and threaten Ste. Lucie, causing what was worse than hurt pride, a reduction of the sugar revenue on which England's budget depended.

With these blows, the wrath of the country fell on Sandwich for allowing Kempenfelt to sail like Byng with an inadequate force while "six of the line were lying in English ports." According to the Opposition leader, Lord Rockingham, "It is no secret that we have now ten ships of the line with scarce a man to put on them." A vote of censure upon Sandwich as responsible for this feeble maritime condition was defeated by the government with its majority of over twenty-one still intact, before the still feebler performance of Admiral Graves and the loss of America were yet known. Sandwich remained in office.

"May your Lordship never endure the pain and torture I have undergone," Rodney wrote to him. But, ill as he was, in recovery from his surgery, the navy while under attack could now not wait for his services to save Jamaica. In his new position as Vice-Admiral of Great Britain, an honorary rank outside the regular hierarchy, and with the massive *Formidable* as his flagship, he was, though exhausted by his ordeal, in hearty spirit and ready to serve. At age sixty-four he accepted active sea duty and in January, 1782, set out for Plymouth to take over the fleet that he would shortly bring to an unprecedented feat in the Battle of the Saints, the most significant sea combat prior to Nelson's victory at Trafalgar. Ending forever the tyranny of line ahead, he was to break the enemy's line in a historic and celebrated victory over the French. As visible token, the giant *Ville de Paris*, the largest ship afloat, would be taken by the British and de Grasse made a prisoner.

The feat was accomplished in April, 1782, when Rodney, reinforced by twelve ships of the line plus Hood's squadron from America, sighted de Grasse's fleet sailing northward, headed for Jamaica out of Fort Royal in Martinique, where de Grasse had taken up position on returning from America. With added ships, de Grasse had 33 of the line, and the joint British together had 36. Three days passed while the fleets maneuvered for the wind in the passage between Dominica and Guadeloupe called The Saints for the number of islets by that name located there. In passing, the fleets engaged and parted in sporadic gunfire coming within pistol shot at point-blank range, and in one case collision. Casualties were suffered, masts toppled and men killed on both sides. When the wind momentarily dropped as the French were trying to form a line, a gap appeared in their formation. Sir Charles Douglas, Fleet Captain on board the *Formidable*, perceived that windward gusts would let the *Formidable* sail through the gap. Hurrying to find Rodney, he cried,

"Only break the line, Sir George! The day is yours and I will ensure you victory." With no previously arranged plan and uncertain whether his captains would follow him, leaving him to be isolated in battle as once before, Rodney refused to order the helm to come about. It would mean defying the rules of *Fighting Instructions* and might bring him to court-martial or even, like Byng, to a firing squad. Douglas would not bear the responsibility; it must be the Admiral's alone. On Douglas' repeated urging, Rodney changed his mind. The great chance in which he had been frustrated once before was now offered again. The dare boiled in his blood. "Well, well, do as you like," he replied almost casually. He did not make the mistake of leaving his "line ahead" signal aloft but hauled it down, substituting the signal for "close action." As the bows of the *Formidable* slowly swung to starboard, midshipmen scurried to warn gunners to be ready to fire from the outer side. While Rodney watched in suspense to the stern, he saw the next five ships in his line follow him cleanly through the gap in the French line. The *Formidable*'s main topsail was in rags, an accompanying battleship, the *Prince George*, had lost its foremast, another was taking on water by three feet an hour, two others had spent their gunpowder, but French decks, equally mauled and crowded with troops, were piled with dead. In red turmoil in the water sharks lunged around the ship, viciously snatching at the bodies of dead sailors thrown overboard. With torn rigging and fallen masts, many of the French ships were motionless in the water, allowing other gaps to appear. English captains caught in the excitement of their Admiral's purpose, seized their chance. They luffed and, with sails flapping, made their way through gaps in three places. Now broken, the French line was rounded and brought under fire from both sides. Catching wisps of wind through the gathering dusk, the French pointed their heads southward to flee, hotly engaged by the English in pursuit. One by one the French struck their colors, abandoning the mighty *Ville de Paris*, on which de Grasse, throwing towlines to the disabled, was striving to rally his fleet. His giant figure was seen on deck standing alone. Too closely pursued by the English to take time for repairs, the French ships were overtaken. The *Ville de Paris*, deserted by her consorts, was raked by the British *Russell*, then hit broadside by a tremendous cannon blast from Hood's ship, the *Barfleur*, while the surrounding British concentrated their fire on the huge flagship. Her decks were ablaze; she had lost rigging, sail and rudder. After nine and a half hours of battle since the moment when Rodney had steered his prow to penetrate the line, de Grasse's flag fluttered down. Simultaneously, the flag of France came down from the ensign staff. English officers rowed over to accept the surrender.

On the *Formidable,* an armchair was brought to the quarterdeck, where Rodney sat in the moonlight contemplating his colossal prize and expressing from time to time murmurs of self-appreciation of his success in breaking the line. When day broke, de Grasse himself was accompanied aboard the *Formidable* to surrender in person and "is at this moment sitting in my stern galley," Rodney wrote in his reports of victory to Admiralty and family. "His Majesty's arms have proved victorious over the enemy's," he wrote to his son. "Jamaica will be saved by it. The French fleet have met with total defeat and I believe will not give us battle again in this war and are now so much shattered that it will be impossible for them to repair their losses."

So much was the fact, though it came too late to save the loss of America six months before. That had been, as Hood wrote in a letter reporting the news to a correspondent, "the most melancholy news Great Britain ever received." The shock of the event had caused political turmoil and would bring the fall of the government in England. London had learned the news of Yorktown from France on November 25, five weeks after the surrender. Rochambeau had dispatched two messengers — the Duc de Lauzun and Comte de Deux-Ponts, who had led the hard and bloodied French capture of Redoubt Nine — in two separate frigates to carry the announcement to the French King. It was received on the same day as another omen of joy, the birth of a dauphin to Marie Antoinette, assuring, as it seemed, the royal succession. But the baby boy was never to see his throne, and the King and Queen within ten years were to lose both their throne and their heads. For all the nearly 1.5 billion livres that Louis XVI had spent to support the American rebellion against the British Crown, success of the Revolution was not auspicious for his own crown, as, with better understanding of political consequences, he might have anticipated.

Agents quickly conveyed news of the Cornwallis catastrophe across the Channel, bringing it first to Lord George Germain, who in turn took it to Lord North in Downing Street. The First Minister flung open his arms "as [if] he would have taken a ball in the breast," crying in what may be the most quoted words of the war, "Oh, God, it is all over!" and repeating the words "wildly" as he strode up and down the room. Not he but Germain brought the news to King George, who, unshaken in his singleness of purpose, ordered Germain to make plans for the most feasible mode of continuing the war. Apart from diehards in the Cabinet surrounding Germain and Sandwich, few in Parliament and the country offered support. Most acknowledged that the war had been ineffectual, and that to continue it by defensive measures as proposed by Germain, with no hope of winning, but merely to hold out against independence and drive a stiff bargain with the Americans, would be no more effective. It would only mean unacceptable cost to raise new levies to replace the army lost by Cornwallis as well as to pay for the past costs of the war. General opinion concluded, in an excess of gloom equal to the previous apathy in the field, that to recognize the independence of America meant, in Germain's awful vision, the "ruin" of empire. Equally extreme, the King insisted that to recognize the independence of America would bring Britain to "inevitable destruction" and that he would abdicate rather than be a party to it. The real reason for his frantic resistance was his agony at the prospect of having to call in the detested Opposition men if North's government, as sponsor of the war, had to go. He could only return to his petulant thunder: "I would rather lose my crown than call in a set of men who would make me a slave." The inevitable, however, was approaching. North told Germain at this time that to recover America was impossible and he could not continue to finance a war for no purpose except to provide a platform for a stiff stand on peace terms. Since the Americans were adamant for independence, there seemed no way to bring them to peace short of anything less than that demand except by maintaining the pressure of a state of war.

Walpole curiously records in a letter to Horace Mann that "Cornwallis's disgrace does not make a vast impression, none in Parliament, but a drop will overset a vessel that is full to the brim. Our affairs are certainly dismal and will get worse." The war was nearing its end, he wrote to his friend, although its consequences were far from conclusion. "In some respects," he foresaw with a sense of history that went beyond gossip, "they are commencing a new date which will reach far beyond us." Parliament was already full to the brim. Following Yorktown, and the loss of St. Eustatius and expectation of further French offensives in the West Indies, with potential further loss of sugar islands and their revenue, a sense of military depression took hold. The will to win, never an overwhelming emotion in the nation, subsided to minor key. The City of London, sensitive to the prospect of prolonged and costly expenditure, petitioned the King to end the war. Country meetings echoed the sentiment. Motions in Parliament urging an end were resisted by the government with smaller and smaller majorities. On December 12, a motion by a private member, Sir James Lowther, that "all further attempts to reduce the revolted colonies are contrary to the true interests of this kingdom," was voted down by only forty-one, less than half the former majority. In February, Henry Seymour Conway, a former Secretary of State, moved that the war in America "be no longer pursued for the impracticable purpose of reducing the inhabitants by force," and this was put down by a majority of only one. A week later, a second motion by Conway to the same effect was carried. Implacably, a third time, on March 4, Conway moved to inform the King that "this House will consider as enemies to his Majesty and this country, all those who shall [advise] the farther prosecution of offensive war on the continent of North America." This rather startling proposition was carried without a vote. It put an end to the matter. To refuse Parliament's advice was unconstitutional. No lawless monarch, George III knew only that he must stay within the rules. To carry on as before would mean overt conflict with Parliament; he must either comply or step down. He actually drafted a statement of abdication which said that as the Legislature has "totally incapacitated him from either conducting the war with any effect or from obtaining any peace that would not be destructive to the commerce and essential rights of the British nation . . . His Majesty therefore with much sorrow finds he can be of no further Utility to his Native Country which drives him to the painful step of quitting it forever." In consequence, "His Majesty resigns the Crown of Great Britain and the Dominions appertaining thereto."

Rather than come to that point, he chose the lesser misery and agreed to drop North and treat for peace. On March 20, 1782, in "one of the fullest and most tense Houses . . . that had ever been seen," with the streets outside equally crowded, the First Minister, who for twelve years had placidly presided over the most turbulent times since the Gunpowder Plot, was relieved at last. Given his long-desired and perhaps now ambivalent wish, Lord North resigned. A government of the Opposition took over, with Rockingham, Shelburne, Fox and the young Pitt. On April 25, the

Cabinet agreed to negotiate peace terms with no allowance for a veto of independence.

In the interim, the Battle of the Saints had lifted British spirits even at the cost of disturbing Sir Horace Walpole's sleep. He complained, expressing the Whig view of Rodney, that his windows had been broken by a noisy demonstration "for that vain fool Rodney when he came out of his way to extend his triumph." The damage in the Battle of the Saints to French naval prestige ensured that the French would not return to America to lend further aid to Washington, which, together with restored British self-confidence won by Rodney, stiffened the British spine in the peace parleys. At the same time, the Americans were stiffened by formal Dutch recognition when the Dutch provinces cautiously, one at a time, voted to accept Adams' credentials as minister-envoy of the United States and the States General of the United Provinces confirmed the vote in 1782, becoming the first nation after France to register formal recognition of the United States. A British negotiator proposed by Shelburne — a liberal Scots merchant named Richard Oswald, not a figure of political eminence — had been chosen and accredited to the Congress. Issues to be settled were as many and as hard to handle as a barrel of fish. Boundaries of

Canada and the regions of the Northwest and of the Spanish territories in Florida and the South, and the perennial problem of treatment of the Loyalists, relations with the Indians, rights of trade and all the debris of military damage to lands and property required infinite discussion. After a preliminary treaty was reached on November 30, 1782, unfinished business was moved to Paris, where Franklin and John Jay negotiated for America. Differences and disputes between them, repeated by their respective partisans in Congress, prolonged the talks, which suffered further from interference of Vergennes in his effort to control the terms to French advantage. Difficulties stretched out the discussions for another ten months. The definitive peace treaty ending hostilities and acknowledging the independence of the United States was not signed until September 3, 1783.

Even then a new nation was not born from the labor pains. To create a national entity with agreed laws under a single sovereignty on a sound financial footing out of thirteen distinct colonies with interests and habits almost as separate as those of the Dutch was a path as rocky as the Revolution itself. Stumbling over the obstacles and amid the conflicts, the infant nation, at times nearly pulled apart by the strains, survived to become a federation that was to take its place among rulers of the world. While shortcomings and imperfections developed in the body as it grew, the body itself was so large and so rich in resources, and above all in the extra energies of newcomers who had had the grit to leave home for an untried land, that its future dominance as a great power was assured.

Long before the Treaty, in 1777, while hostilities were still alive and Britain was blockading ports of entry along the American coast, the *Andrew Doria*, bearer of the first greeting, was burned by her crew in the Delaware to prevent British seizure. Her former companions of the first squadron of the navy and of the first combat, the *Columbus* and the *Providence*, met the same fate, burned or blown up by their crews to prevent seizure by the enemy. The *Cabot*, and the *Alfred*, on which the flag of the Continental Congress was first raised in Philadelphia, were captured by the British. The *Providence*, last survivor of the originals, was destroyed in 1779 in the Penobscot in Maine. When commissioned in 1775, the squadron had been called "the maddest idea in the world." Now scattered in ruined timbers along the banks of the Delaware and on the shores of Narragansett and Chesapeake bays, the charred relics expressed the note of sadness that lies beneath human affairs.

A private sadness that haunted Washington to the end was in having no child of his own to be his continuance. He had not grasped the fact that an autonomous America was his child. Yet he was as proud and confident of its future as any father could be of a promising son. In an enraptured, if now heartbreaking, vision of America, he said in his Last Circular to the States, issued in June, 1783, that America "seemed to be peculiarly designated by Providence for the display of human greatness and felicity. Heaven has crowned its other blessings by giving the fairest opportunity for political happiness than any other nation has ever been favored with and the result must be a nation which would have a meliorating influence on all mankind."

Following his lead, historians of the 19th century, believers in progress, drew their nation's history as a steady advance of liberty, starting from the winning of the Revolution, which was considered the outstanding success in history of a popular military action, while the state it created was seen as having a mission assigned by God to build a model political nation of justice and equality and self-government. At the end of the 20th century we see in that proud design a more somber story, of injustice toward native Americans evicted from their lands, of inequality for those born of different colors and faiths, of government not by the best but by a collection of shoddy and peccant men, inept and corrupt yet always laced with workers and dreamers of a change for the better.

The two centuries of American history since the salute to the flag of the *Andrew Doria* can be celebrated for many things: for the opening of refuge for the wretched of other lands yearning to breathe free, for laws to establish the rules of decent working conditions, for measures to protect the poor and support the indigent, but the state of "human felicity" that Washington believed "must result from the sovereignty of America" has not been the outcome. Two thousand years of human aggression, greed and the madness of power reveal a record that blots the rejoicing of that happy night in Philadelphia, and reminds us how slow is the pace of "melioration" and how mediocre is the best we have made of what Washington and Greene and Morgan and their half-clad soldiers "without the shadow of a blanket" fought through bitter winters to achieve.

If Crèvecoeur came again to ask his famous question "What is this new man, this American?" what would he find? The free and equal new man in a new world that he envisaged would be realized only in spots, although conditions for the new man would come nearer to being realized in America than they would ever come in the other overturns of society. The new man would not be endowed with liberty, equality and fraternity in France; he would not be freed from oppression when the Russians overturned the Czars. A new man formed "to serve the people" instead of himself would not be created by the Communist Revolution in China in 1949. Revolutions produce other men, not new men. Halfway "between truth and endless error" the mold of the species is permanent. That is earth's burden.

Bibliography

The period covered in this book, leaving aside the Dutch excursion, is approximately six years, from 1776 to 1781.

On the several subjects that make up the body of the story, that is to say, the salute to the *Andrew Doria*, the affairs of the Dutch Republic, naval warfare of the period focusing on Admiral Rodney, the American land battles in the South, and finally the long march leading to the siege of Yorktown, the published and unpublished material is far more extensive than I realized when I began, and too much for a standard bibliography. I have offered a limited bibliography of the sources that I used, together with a selection of works that were most useful for my purposes or for anyone interested in further reading.

Sources will be found in the notes located by page number and an identifying phrase from the text. The book title in each case will be found under the author's name in the bibliography, with an indication of title in case he is responsible for more than one book.

The letter q. stands for material quoted from a secondary source.

Proceedings in the House of Parliament will be found under the given date of the statement in the relevant volume of *Great Britain, Parliament*.

On the *Andrew Doria* the most complete is J. Franklin Jameson's "St. Eustatius in the American Revolution" and on the beginnings of the American navy, William Bell Clark's *Naval Documents of the American Revolution* and Admiral Samuel Eliot Morison's *John Paul Jones: A Sailor's Biography*.

On the Dutch Republic, apart from the inevitable John Lathrop Motley, more modern and excellent works on the revolt of the Netherlands and the growth of the nation are Petrus Johannes Blok's *History of the People of the Netherlands;* C. M. Davies' *The History of Holland and the Dutch Nation* and Charles Boxer's *The Dutch Seaborne Empire*.

For my period, the most useful by far was Nordholt Schulte's *The Dutch Republic and American Independence,* which has something of everything.

For Admiral Rodney there are four biographies. The first and foundation work published in 1830, containing the most correspondence, is by Lieutenant-General George B. Mundy, Rodney's son-in-law, who is said by his editor, George Bilias, to have "taken liberties with the wording" of the letters (preface to vol. I, p. ix of 1972 edition). Mundy was followed, while Rodney was still living, by the biography of a naval writer, David Hannay, published in 1891. Two modern biographies have followed since then, by Captain Donald MacIntyre in 1963 and David Spinney in 1969.

On naval warfare in general, one must begin with Alfred Thayer Mahan's *The Influence of Sea Power upon History;* an essential study of shipboard life is

Tobias Smollett's novel *Roderick Random*, while the most informative work on management of sail and gunnery is Admiral Morison's *John Paul Jones*. The most useful histories of naval events in my period are Captain W. M. James's *The British Navy in Adversity* and Charles Lee Lewis' *Admiral de Grasse and American Independence*. A fine complement is A. B. C. Whipple's *Age of Fighting Sail*. Limited in subject matter but very readable is Harold A. Larrabee's *Decision at the Chesapeake* on the Battle of the Bay.

A military guide to American land battles of the time is *The Compact History of the Revolutionary War* by Colonel Ernest and Trevor Dupuy. For the general reader seeking a comprehensive and lively survey of the period, I recommend John C. Miller's *Triumph of Freedom 1775–1783* and Samuel B. Griffith's *In Defense of the Public Liberty*. The essential underpinnings lie in the seven volumes of Douglas Southall Freeman's *George Washington;* in the thirty-nine volumes of the *Writings* of Washington edited by John Fitzpatrick; in the life and correspondence of John Adams in three volumes by Page Smith; and in specialist studies like Samuel Flagg Bemis' *A Diplomatic History of the United States*.

For the Yorktown campaign itself two excellent books based on thorough research with well-chosen quotations by the participants, are Thomas J. Fleming's *Beat the Last Drum* and Burke Davis' *The Campaign That Won America*.

For the long march from the Hudson to Yorktown there are six eyewitness journals of particular interest: by Claude Blanchard, the Commissary or Quartermaster for the French army; by Baron Ludwig von

Closen, Aide to General Rochambeau; by Gaspard Gallatin of the French general staff; Rochambrau's own memoirs; and especially the indispensable journal of Karl Gustaf Tornquist, a Swedish Lieutenant serving under de Grasse, and an anonymous work of two French Officers entitled *Operations of the French Fleet Under the Count de Grasse.*

There is no English first-hand account of the American war overall, understandably in view of the outcome, except Sir Henry Clinton's sad post-war narrative. This lack is made up for by the thorough work concentrating on the American campaigns of Lord Cornwallis by Franklin and Mary Wickwire and by the psychological portrait of Sir Henry Clinton by the late Professor William Willcox. Of English diaries, the most interesting is that of Captain Frederick MacKenzie, a keen observer with a sharp pen, writing from General Headquarters.

English diaries of social life not directly connected to the war are ample and invaluable: they include Sir N. William Wraxall's *Memoirs;* the diaries of James Harris, First Earl of Malmesbury, who was British minister at The Hague and St. Petersburg; the memoirs of John Heneage Jesse; and above all the correspondence and *Last Journals* of Horace Walpole.

PRIMARY SOURCES

ADAMS, JOHN, *The Book of Abigail and John.* Butterfield, Lyman, ed. Harvard, 1963.

———, *Works,* 10 vols. Adams, Charles Francis, ed. New York, 1850–56.

ANONYMOUS, *Operations of the French Fleet Under the*

Count de Grasse Two Contemporaneous Journals in 1781–82. New York, 1864.

BIRON, ARMAND LOUIS — see Lauzun.

BLANCHARD, CLAUDE, *Journal of 1780–83.* Trans. Albany, 1867.

CLARK, WILLIAM BELL, ed., *Naval Documents of the American Revolution,* vol. 7. Washington, 1976. *Clinton Cornwallis Controversy,* 6 pamphlets, 2 vols. Stevens, Benjamin F., ed. London, 1888.

CLINTON, SIR HENRY, *The American Rebellion* (Sir Henry Clinton's narrative of his campaign). Willcox, William B., ed. New Haven, 1954.

CLOSEN, BARON LUDWIG VON, *The Revolutionary Journal of 1780–83.* Trans. Chapel Hill, 1958.

Continental Congress, Journals of (Index to papers of), 34 vols. Ford, Chancy, ed. National Archives, U. S. Government Printing Office, Washington, D.C., 1921–26.

CORNWALLIS, CHARLES, FIRST MARQUIS, *Correspondence,* 3 vols. Ross, Charles, ed. London, 1859.

CRÈVECOEUR, J. HECTOR ST. JOHN, *Letters from an American Farmer.* First published 1782; Modern edition, London, 1912.

DEUX-PONTS, COUNT WILLIAM DE, *My Campaigns in America.* Boston, 1868.

FITZPATRICK — see Washington.

FORTESCUE — see George III.

GALLATIN, GASPARD (Etat Major of the French army and Colonel of the Deux-Ponts regiment), *Journal of the Siege of Yorktown in 1781 of the Royal Deux-Ponts.* U. S. Government Printing Office, Washington, D.C., 1931.

GEORGE III, *Correspondence* from 1760 to December,

1783, 6 vols. Fortescue, John, ed. London, 1927–28.

GREAT BRITAIN, PARLIAMENT, *The History, Debates and Proceedings of the Houses of Parliament of Great Britain,* 1743–1774.

GREENE, NATHANAEL, *The Papers of General Nathanael Greene,* 4 vols. R.I. Historical Society, 1976 et seq.

HARRIS, JAMES — see Malmesbury.

JAMES, BARTHOLOMEW, REAR ADMIRAL, *Journal of 1752–1828.* London, 1896.

JESSE, JOHN HENEAGE, *Memoirs of the Life and Reign of George III,* 3 vols. London, 1867.

LAUZUN, ARMAND LOUIS DE GONTAUT, DUC DE, *Memoirs.* Trans. Scott Moncrieff, C. K. New York, 1928.

MACKENZIE, FREDERICK, *Diary of,* 1775–81, vol. II. Cambridge, Mass., 1930.

MALMESBURY, FIRST EARL OF (James Harris), *Diaries and Correspondence,* 4 vols. Ed. by his grandson, the third earl. London, 1844.

MARYLAND, ARCHIVES OF, vols. 11 and 12, in *Journal and Correspondence of the Maryland Council of Safety,* August 29, 1775, and July 6, 1776. Browne, William Hand, ed. Maryland Historical Society, Baltimore, 1892.

MCDEVITT, ROBERT, *Attacked: A British Viewpoint, Tryon's Raid on Danbury.* Chester, Conn., 1974.

ROCHAMBEAU, COUNT DE, *Memoirs of the Marshal Count de Rochambeau Relative to the War of Independence of the United States.* Trans. Paris, 1809 and 1838; New York, 1971.

——, *The American Campaign of Rochambeau's Army;*

vol. II, *Itineraries, Maps and Views*. Trans. Rice, Howard, and Brown, Anne S. K., eds. Princeton and Providence, 1972.

RODNEY, GEORGE, LORD (see Mundy), *Letter-Books and Order Book of George, Lord Rodney, 1780–1872*, 2 vols. New York, 1932.

Sandwich Papers, 4 vols. Barnes, G. R., and Owen, J. H., eds. London, 1932–38.

SCOTT — see Washington.

SPARKS — see Washington.

STEVENS, BENJAMIN F., Facsimiles of mss. in European archives relating to America, 25 vols. London, 1889–95.

TORNQUIST, KARL GUSTAF, *The Naval Campaigns of Count de Grasse*. Trans. Philadelphia, 1942.

TOWNSHEND, CHARLES HERVEY, *The British Invasion of New Haven, Connecticut*. New Haven, 1879. Contains contemporary material from the *Connecticut Journal* of July, 1779, about the raid.

WALPOLE, HORACE, *Correspondence*, 48 vols. Lewis, W. S., ed. New Haven, 1937–83.

——, *Last Journals (during the reign of George III, 1771–1783)*, 2 vols. Stewart, A. Francis, ed. London, 1910.

WASHINGTON, GEORGE, *The Correspondence of General Washington and Comte de Grasse*. Scott, James Brown, ed. Washington, D.C., 1931.

——, *Diaries*, 4 vols. Fitzpatrick, John C., ed. Boston, New York, 1975.

——, *Writings*, 39 vols. Fitzpatrick, John C., ed. Washington, D.C., 1931–44.

——, *Writings*, 12 vols. Sparks, Jared, ed. Boston, 1831–37.

WRAXALL, SIR N. WILLIAM, *Historical Memoirs of My Own Time*, 1772–1784. Philadelphia, 1837.

SECONDARY SOURCES

ALDRIDGE, ALFRED OWEN, *Benjamin Franklin*. Philadelphia and New York, 1965.

AUGUR, HELEN, *The Secret War of Independence*. New York, 1955.

BANCROFT, GEORGE, *History of the United States of America*, 6 vols. Boston, 1876.

BASS, ROBERT D., *The Green Dragoon* (life of Banastre Tarleton). New York, 1957.

BEMIS, SAMUEL FLAGG, *A Diplomatic History of the United States*. New Haven, 1936.

BLOK, PETRUS JOHANNES, *History of the People of the Netherlands*, 5 vols. (parts); Part III, *The War with Spain* 1568–1648. London and New York, 1912.

BOULTON, WILLIAM B., *Sir Joshua Reynolds*. New York, 1905.

BOXER, CHARLES, *The Dutch Seaborne Empire 1600–1800*. New York, 1965.

BROOKE, JOHN, *King George III*. New York, 1972.

BRUIN, FRED DE, *St. Eustatius "A Golden Link with the Independence of the United States," De Halve Maen*, Quarterly Journal of the Holland Society of New York, vol. 58, no. 2, New York, 1984.

BURCH, JR., LUCIUS E., "The Guns of Statia." Pamphlet, 1966.

CALLENDER, GEOFFREY, *Sea Kings of Britain: Keppel to Nelson*, vol. III. London and New York, 1911.

CARMER, CARL, *The Hudson*. New York, 1939.

CARTER, ALICE, "The Dutch as Neutrals in the Seven

Years War," *International & Comparative Law Quarterly*. July, 1963.

CLOWES, WILLIAM LAIRO, *The Royal Navy*, vol. IV. London, 1899.

CORWIN, EDWARD S., *French Policy and the American Alliance of 1778*. Princeton, 1916.

DAVIES, C. M., *The History of Holland and the Dutch Nation*. London, 1851.

DAVIS, BURKE, *The Campaign That Won America*. New York, 1970.

DONIOL, HENRI, *Histoire de la Participation de la France à L'Etablissement des Etats-Unis d'Amérique*, 5 vols. Paris, 1890.

DUPUY, R. ERNEST AND TREVOR N., *The Compact History of the Revolutionary War*. New York, 1963.

EDLER, FRIEDRICH, *The Dutch Republic and the American Revolution*. Baltimore, 1911.

FLEMING, THOMAS J., *Beat the Last Drum*. New York, 1963.

FREEMAN, DOUGLAS SOUTHALL, *George Washington; A Biography*, 7 vols. New York, 1952.

GARRATY, JOHN A., AND GAY, PETER, *Columbia History of the World*. New York, 1972.

GEYL, PIETER, *The Revolt of the Netherlands*, 2nd ed. London, 1958.

GOTTSCHALK, LOUIS, AND LACH, DONALD, *Toward the French Revolution; Europe and America in the 18th Century World*. New York, 1973.

GRIFFITH, SAMUEL B., *In Defense of the Public Liberty*. New York, 1976.

GRUBER, IRA D., *The Howe Brothers and the American Revolution*. Williamsburg, Va., 1972.

HALEY, K. H. D., *The Dutch in the 17th Century*. London, 1972.

HANNAY, DAVID, *Rodney*. Boston, 1972. First published London, 1891.

HARRIS, JAMES — see Malmesbury.

HART, FRANCIS RUSSELL, *Admirals of the Caribbean*. Boston and New York, 1922.

HARTOG, J., *History of St. Eustatius*. U.S. Bicentennial Committee of the Netherlands, 1976. Aruba, Netherlands, Antilles.

HASLIP, JOAN, *Catherine the Great*. New York, 1977.

HOOD, DOROTHY, *The Admirals Hood*. London, 1942.

HOUGH, R., *The Greatest Crusade*. New York, 1986.

JAMES, CAPTAIN W. M., *The British Navy in Adversity*. London, 1926.

JAMESON, J. FRANKLIN, "St. Eustatius in the American Revolution," *American Historical Review*, vol. 8, July, 1903.

JOHNSTON, HENRY P., *The Yorktown Campaign and the Surrender of Cornwallis*, 1781. New York, 1881.

KENNEDY, PAUL M., *The Rise and Fall of British Naval Mastery*. New York, 1976.

KING, LESTER S., *The Medical World of the 18th Century*. Chicago, Toronto and Cambridge, 1958.

LARRABEE, HAROLD A., *Decision at the Chesapeake*. New York, 1964.

LEWIS, CHARLES LEE, *Admiral de Grasse and American Independence*. Annapolis, 1945.

LEWIS, MICHAEL ARTHUR, *England's Sea Officers*. London, 1939.

——, *History of the British Navy*. London, 1957.

LORENZ, LINCOLN, *John Paul Jones*. Annapolis, 1943.

MACAULAY, T. B., *Critical and Historical Essays*, 2

vols. London, Toronto, New York, 1907.

MacIntyre, Captain Donald, RN, *Admiral Rodney*. New York, 1963.

Mackesy, Piers, *The War for America 1775–1783*. *Harvard, 1964*.

Maclay, Edgar S., *A History of American Privateers*. New York, 1899.

Madariaga, Isabel de, *Russia in the Age of Catherine the Great*. New Haven, 1981.

Mahan, Alfred Thayer, *The Influence of Sea Power upon History*. Boston, 1890; 12th ed., 1918.

——, *Types of Naval Officers*. Boston, 1901.

Malone, Dumas, *Jefferson and His Time*, 3 vols. Boston, 1962.

Manceron, Claude, *Twilight of the Old Order*. New York, 1977.

Martelli, George, *Jemmy Twitcher* [Sandwich]. London, 1962.

Mejean, Jacques, "Address to the Huguenot Society of America 13 April 1978," *Proceedings*, vol. XIII. New York, 1978.

Melville, Phillips, "Eleven Guns for the Grand Union." *American Heritage*, October, 1958.

Merlant, Joachim, *Soldiers and Sailors of France in the American War for Independence*. Trans. New York, 1920.

Miller, John C., *Triumph of Freedom 1775–1783*. Boston, 1948.

Mintz, Sidney, *Sweetness and Power; The Place of Sugar in Modern History*. New York, 1985.

Mitchell, Harold, *Europe in the Caribbean*. Edinburgh, Stanford, Calif., 1963.

Morison, Samuel Eliot, *History of the American*

People. New York, 1965.

——, *John Paul Jones: A Sailor's Biography.* Boston and New York, 1959.

MORRIS, RICHARD B., AND COMMAGER, HENRY S., *Encyclopedia of American History,* 6th ed. New York, 1953–82.

MOTLEY, JOHN LATHROP, *Rise of the Dutch Republic,* 3 vols. New York, 1875–78.

MUNDY, LIEUTENANT-GENERAL GEORGE B., *The Life and Correspondence of the Late Admiral Rodney,* 2 vols. London, 1830. New ed. 1836 (in 1 vol).

NAMIER, LEWIS, *The Structure of Politics.* London, 1957.

NORDHOLT, JAN WILLEM — see Schulte.

PALMER, R. R., AND COULTON, JOEL, *A History of the Modern World.* New York, 1962.

PARRY, J. H., *Trade and Dominion; European Overseas Empires in the 18th Century.* London and New York, 1971.

PRESCOTT, BENJAMIN F., "The Stars and Stripes. When, Where and by Whom was it First Saluted?" Republican Press Association, Concord, N.H., 1876.

SCHAMA, SIMON, *Patriots and Liberators; Revolution in the Netherlands 1790–1813.* New York, 1978.

SCHULTE, NORDHOLT, *The Dutch Republic and American Independence.* Chapel Hill and London, 1982.

SCOTT, JAMES BROWN, *de Grasse at Yorktown.* Baltimore, 1931.

SMITH, PAGE, *John Adams,* 3 vols. New York, 1962.

——, *A New Age Now Begins; A People's History of the American Revolution,* 3 vols. New York, 1976.

SPINNEY, DAVID, *Rodney.* Annapolis, 1969.

STEPHENSON, O. W., "The Supply of Gunpowder in 1776," *American Historical Review*, vol. 30, no. 2 January, 1925.

STEVENS, JOHN, A., ed., *Magazine of American History*. New York, 1877–1917.

STIRLING, A. M. W., *The Hothams*, 2 vols. London, 1918.

STONE, EDWIN MARTIN, *Our French Allies*. Providence, 1884.

VALENTINE, ALAN, *The British Establishment, 1760–1784; An 18th Century Biographical Dictionary*. Norman, Okla., 1970

——, *Lord North*, 2 vols. Norman, Okla., 1967.

VAN DOREN, CARL, *Benjamin Franklin*. New York, 1938.

VAN LOON, HENDRICK WILLEM, *The Fall of the Dutch Republic*. Boston and New York, 1913.

WARD, CHRISTOPHER, *The War of the Revolution*, vol. 11. New York, 1952.

WHIPPLE, A. B. C., *Age of Fighting Sail*. Alexandria, Va., 1978.

WHITRIDGE, ARNOLD, "Two Aristocrats in Rochambeau's Army" (Chastellux and Lauzun), *Virginia Quarterly Review*, vol. 40, winter 1969.

WICKWIRE, FRANKLIN AND MARY, *Cornwallis, the American Adventure*. Boston, 1970.

WILLCOX, WILLIAM B., "The British Road to Yorktown," *American Historical Review*, vol. 52, no. 1, October, 1946.

——, *Portrait of a General* [Sir Henry Clinton]. New York, 1964.

WINGFIELD-STRATFORD, ESME, *The History of Civilization*. New York, 1930.

WINSOR, JUSTIN, ed., *The American Revolution*. New York, 1972.

WOODWARD, WILLIAM, *Lafayette*. New York, 1938.

Reference Notes have been deleted. See original Alfred A. Knopf edition, page 309, for this information.

The Index has been deleted. See original Alfred A. Knopf edition, page 327, for this information.

We hope you have enjoyed this Large Print book. All our Large Print titles are designed for easy reading, and all our books are made to last. Other Thorndike Large or Magna Print books are available at your library, through selected bookstores, or directly from the publishers. For more information about current and upcoming titles, please call or mail your name and address to:

THORNDIKE PRESS
P.O. Box 159
Thorndike, Maine 04986
(800) 223-0121
(207) 948-2962 (in Maine and Canada, call collect)

or in the United Kingdom:

MAGNA PRINT BOOKS
Long Preston, Near Skipton,
North Yorkshire,
England BD23 4ND
(07294) 225

There is no obligation, of course.